Property Law and Human Rights

For Chris

Property Law
and Human Rights

Deborah Rook

Series Editor: John Wadham

 Blackstone Press

Published by
Blackstone Press Limited
Aldine Place
London
W12 8AA
United Kingdom

Sales enquiries and orders
Telephone +44-(0)-20-8740-2277
Facsimile +44-(0)-20-8743-2292
e-mail: sales@blackstone.demon.co.uk
website: www.blackstonepress.com

ISBN 1-84174-154-X
© Deborah Rook 2001
First published 2001

Royalties from the sale of this book go to support the work of
Amnesty International

British Library Cataloguing in Publication Data
A catalogue record for this book is available from the British Library

Typeset in 10/12pt Times by Montage Studios Limited, Tonbridge, Kent
Printed and bound in Great Britain by Antony Rowe Limited,
Chippenham and Reading

Contents

Preface

The Human Rights Act (HRA) 1998 incorporates the European Convention on Human Rights (the Convention) into our national law.[1] Under the HRA 1998, the Convention rights (which duplicate most of the Articles of the Convention) can be invoked in the English courts. This enables persons to enforce their human rights in the national courts instead of having to endure the inordinate time and expense of taking their case to the European Court of Human Rights in Strasbourg.

CONTENTS

The introduction briefly examines the extent to which property is, and should be, a human right. It is not intended as a comprehensive analysis of the nature of property ownership and the characteristics of a human right, which are complex jurisprudential problems, the intricacies of which could easily fill a book in their own right. Instead it is intended to introduce the reader to a few ideas in order to provoke thought as to the exactitude of conferring human rights status upon property rights.

Chapter 1 explains the provisions of the HRA 1998 as an English Act of Parliament. It examines the new interpretative obligations imposed upon the English courts to take into account the case law of the Strasbourg institutions and to interpret all legislation in such a way that ensures its compatibility with the Convention rights. Significantly, Parliamentary sovereignty is preserved and where it is impossible for the courts to reconcile the express words of the statute with the Convention rights, the statute prevails. In these circumstances, the higher courts may make a declaration of incompatibility thereby encouraging Parliamentary intervention to amend the offending legislation.

Since the case law of the Strasbourg institutions (the European Court of Human Rights and the European Commission of Human Rights) is likely to have

---

[1] The territorial extent of the Human Rights Act 1998 includes England, Wales and Northern Ireland.

considerable influence in the interpretation and application of the Convention rights under the HRA 1998, a basic appreciation of the Convention jurisprudence underlying those decisions is desirable. Consequently, chapter 2 explains some of the key Convention principles which regularly feature in the decisions from Strasbourg. For example, the margin of appreciation and the principle of proportionality are examined, both of which are especially prevalent and influential in property related cases.

The extent to which the HRA 1998 encroaches upon English property law will depend in part upon whether or not the HRA 1998 is found to have 'horizontal effect' meaning that it applies to relations between private parties. Whilst the Convention has 'vertical effect', meaning that it can only be enforced against a state, thereby requiring an element of state responsibility for an alleged violation of the Convention, the HRA 1998 is likely to apply to disputes between private individuals. The reason for this difference in application is the duty imposed on the English courts under s. 6 of the HRA 1998 to act compatibly with the Convention rights. The extent to which the HRA 1998 will apply in the private sphere is examined in chapter 3. Chapters 4, 5, 6 and 7 provide detailed analysis of those Articles of the Convention which are likely, under the HRA 1998, to have an impact on English property law. Article 1, Protocol 1 and Articles 8, 14 and 6 are examined in turn and in each chapter the relevant Strasbourg case law is explained. Given the importance of these cases to the interpretation and application of the Convention rights under the HRA 1998, Appendix 3 provides case summaries of those cases most relevant to property law. Although the case law of the Strasbourg institutions is very important, in some areas of law where ambiguity pervades, it is helpful to travel further afield and consider cases from the USA and the Commonwealth. The House of Lords has recognised that authorities from other jurisdictions can be relevant in interpreting human rights legislation (see *R* v *Khan* [1997] AC 558). In this respect, the decisions of the Privy Council in Commonwealth cases are particularly enticing. Although the decisions are inevitably confined to the particular Commonwealth Constitution at issue, at a more general level, the judgments provide an interesting insight into the intellectual workings of the Law Lords on human rights issues.

Finally, chapter 8 considers the implications of the HRA 1998 upon English property law, more specifically the impact upon land law. The author does not profess to provide an exhaustive account. The full impact of the HRA 1998 upon property law will not be known for many years. Instead, the chapter aims to provide examples of those particular areas where the Act is likely to have an impact leading to a possible change in the law. A good knowledge of the relevant Convention rights explained in chapters 4, 5, 6 and 7, together with an understanding from chapter 8 of how these can be applied to English law, will enable property lawyers to assess the impact of the HRA 1998 on other areas of property law not covered by chapter 8.

The law is stated as at 1 December 2000. However, chapter 8 contains more recent material. In particular, it includes an account of the following three property-related cases which have been decided by the English courts since the implementation of the HRA 1998: *R* v *Secretary of State for the Environment, Transport and Regions, ex parte Holding and Barnes plc* (9 May 2001, House of Lords); *R (on the application of Johns and McLellan)* v *Bracknell Forest District Council* (21 December 2000, Administrative Court) and *J A Pye (Oxford) Ltd* v *Graham* (6 February 2001, Court of Appeal).

ACKNOWLEDGEMENTS

I am indebted to my colleagues, Professor Phillip Kenny and Alan Davenport, who read draft chapters of this book and provided helpful feedback. Any mistakes are, of course, my own.

I would especially like to thank my husband, Chris and my sister, Karen for their constant support and encouragement. My particular thanks go to Jaffa and Mishka for being my inspiration.

Deborah Rook
May 2001

Table of Cases

Table of Primary Legislation

Table of Secondary Legislation

Table of International Instruments

Introduction

PROTECTING PROPERTY AS A HUMAN RIGHT

When the European Convention on Human Rights (the Convention) was being drafted, some of the contracting states were reluctant to include a human right to protect property and consequently it was difficult for the states to reach an agreement on the wording of the Article. An Article was proposed based upon the wording of Article 17 of the Universal Declaration which reads: '1. Everyone has the right to own property alone as well as in association with others. 2. No one shall be arbitrarily deprived of his property.'[1] However this proposed Article was rejected. Due to the failure of the states to reach any agreement on the wording, the human right to protect property was deferred until Protocol 1.

Article 1, Protocol 1, in its final form, protects the right to the peaceful enjoyment of possessions. Whilst this is drafted in wide terms to provide a broad guarantee to protect property, it is heavily qualified in order to allow the states to interfere with a person's property rights in pursuit of the public interest (see chapter 4). The substantial limitations on the human right to protect property were necessary to meet the concerns of a number of the contracting states that a right to property should not fetter a state's powers to nationalise industries or to adopt other policies involving a redistribution of wealth in the name of social justice. Davis comments upon how, in drafting the Convention, the debate of the Consultative Assembly 'illustrates vividly the argument between the idea of property as a right of personality basic to human flourishing and property as a relation of production which affects social inequality and a wide range of

---

[1] Article 17 of the Universal Declaration of Human Rights 1948.

collective goods and is, therefore, a legitimate matter for state action, including nationalisation'.[2]

As will be explained in chapter 4, the right to property contained in Article 1, Protocol 1 permits considerable state interference with a person's property rights. The absence of any express right to full compensation has resulted in instances of property owners suffering a financial loss for the benefit of the wider community (see *James v UK* in Appendix 3). Harris, O'Boyle and Warbrick observe that: 'The Court has made frequent reference to the drafting history of Article 1 of the First Protocol and its influence has been substantial in confirming the wide latitude states have in interfering with the right'.[3]

There is a general perception that the driving force behind conferring human rights protection upon certain rights is that those rights are so fundamental to all persons in a civilised society, that the rights are worthy of special protection. In this respect, it is interesting to observe that whilst this rings true for rights to protect, for example, a person from torture or to protect their family and private life, it does not sit comfortably with the protection of property as a human right. In some countries the stimulus to protect property as a human right has arisen from a wealthy minority who feared the risk of a redistribution of their wealth for the benefit of the wider community.[4] In the UK the idea of an entrenched Bill of Rights, which was on the whole fervently opposed by a majority of politicians, gained support in the mid 1970s. Why this sudden support for a written constitution to protect human rights? It has been observed that a number of Conservative politicians, 'concerned by industrial unrest and a Labour Employment Bill, believed that a Bill of Rights could work to protect private property and to challenge the unfettered power of the executive'.[5] This is illustrative of the fact that often the impetus to protect property as a human right is the desire of some to protect the status quo.

Therefore one consequence of affording property rights the protective mantle of human rights status is that social and economic policies, which seek to promote the redistribution of wealth and economic power in society, can become more difficult to implement. The Bill of Rights in the USA provides an interesting example of the difficulties that can arise as a result of conferring human rights

---

[2] Davis, H., *Collected Editions of the 'Travaux Préparatoires' of the European Convention on Human Rights:* The Hague, Martinus Nijhoff, vol. 2, 1976, p. 130.

[3] Harris, D. J., O'Boyle, M. and Warbrick, C., *Law of the European Convention on Human Rights*, London: Butterworths, 1995, p. 517.

[4] For example, see Allen, T., *The Right to Property in Commonwealth Constitutions*, Cambridge: Cambridge University Press, 2000, pp. 43–45, where he explains what happened in India. In 1934 the Parliamentary Joint Committee on Indian Constitutional Reform recommended the inclusion of a right to property in any Constitutional reform. The impetus of this recommendation came from the concern to protect the British interests as well as the Indian property-holding classes, such as the Zamindars, who provided a valuable source of revenue during the British rule.

[5] Wadham, J., and Mountfield, H., *Human Rights Act 1998*, London: Blackstone Press Ltd, 1999, p. 6.

protection upon a person's property rights. This is illustrated in the conflict between President Roosevelt's New Deal, which actively sought, by legislative reforms, to manage the economy and promote the economic interests of the disadvantaged, as against the conservatism of the courts in defending the liberalist conception of property and the laissez-faire philosophy. The liberalist conception of property, adopted by the courts at that time, originates from Locke's theory that ownership of property is a natural right and that the purpose of Government is to protect and preserve natural property rights, which Locke fuses with the idea of liberty.[6] Ely notes that: 'Strongly influenced by Locke, the eighteenth-century Whig political tradition stressed the rights of property owners as the bulwark of freedom from arbitrary government. Property ownership was identified with the preservation of political liberty'.[7] This was the predominant philosophy underlying the drafting of the Fifth Amendment and Fourteenth Amendment of the Bill of Rights in relation to the protection of property rights. In the 1930s, President Roosevelt's New Deal programme was grounded in the idea that the Government had a positive duty to promote social welfare, for example, to regulate prices of certain goods, to prescribe a minimum wage and to organise labour unions. The national courts, however, sought to block many of these welfare changes as unconstitutional.[8] Ely notes that: 'Never before had the Supreme Court struck down so many acts of Congress in such a short period of time. These judicial setbacks dealt a devastating blow to the New Deal program of economic revival and social reform'.[9] On the verge of a constitutional crisis, Roosevelt, who was strengthened by his re-election in 1936, proposed to enlarge the size of the Supreme Court which would thereby enable him to appoint new judges more sympathetic to his economic cause. Ely comments on the judicial retreat that ensued: 'The Supreme Court's stubborn defense of laissez-faire values precipitated a constitutional crisis. Ultimately, under great political pressure and President Roosevelt's threat to 'pack' the Court, several justices shifted their position and accommodated the New Deal's economic and social program'.[10]

This provides a fascinating illustration of the difficulties, in implementing social reform policies, that can arise from having conferred human rights status upon property rights. Similar difficulties arose in India. Articles 19 and 31 of the

---

[6] Locke, J., *Second treatise on Government*, 1689.

[7] Ely, J., *The Guardian of Every Other Right. A Constitutional History of Property Rights*, New York: Oxford University Press, 1998, p. 17.

[8] The case of *Lochner* v *New York* (1905) 198 US 45, 61, although from an earlier period, is a classic example of the court's adoption of laissez-faire constitutionalism. The Supreme Court held that legislation, which restricted work in bakeries to ten hours a day or sixty hours a week, was unconstitutional and thereby invalid.

[9] Ely (n. 7 above) p. 125.

[10] Ibid., p. 120.

Indian Constitution 1949[11] generated abundant case law and were eventually replaced, amidst great controversy, by Article 330A which simply provides that: 'No person shall be deprived of his property save by authority of law'.[12] Allen notes that: 'The conflict between the Indian Supreme Court and Parliament is attributable, in part, to the differences between the Supreme Court's liberal vision of property and Parliament's socialist vision'.[13] The fear of similar conflicts eventually resulted in a right to property being omitted from the Canadian Charter of Rights and Freedoms.[14]

To what extent has the inclusion in the Convention of a right to protect property caused difficulties in the implementation of national policies which interfere with the property rights of individuals for the benefit of the general public? Davis notes that:

> To uphold fundamental rights to property on the basis of a pre-legal, moral or naturally based conception of the person implies adopting into the 'public reason' of the state a neo-liberal agenda based on freedom of contract and the minimal state. It would open to constitutional challenge political schemes which use the law to redistribute property in order to advance collectively chosen purposes.[15]

However, the significant qualifications to the guarantee to the right of property under Article 1, Protocol 1, together with the principle of proportionality (see 2.3) and the margin of appreciation (see 2.2), provide the states with sufficient leeway to interfere with individual property rights without violating Article 1, Protocol 1 and thereby ensures the freedom of states to execute their economic and social policies. This is illustrated in the decision of the European Court of Human Rights (the European Court) in *James v UK* (see Appendix 3) where the leasehold enfranchisement legislation, which enables long leaseholders to compulsorily purchase the landlord's freehold reversion, was held not to infringe Article 1, Protocol 1 even though the applicant landlord did not receive full market value for the expropriation of his property.

---

[11] Article 19 of the Indian Constitution 1949 stated that: '(1) All persons shall have the right ... (f) to acquire, hold and dispose of property'. Article 31 provided that: '(1) No person shall be deprived of his property save by authority of law. (2) No property shall be compulsorily acquired or requisitioned save for a public purpose and save by authority of law which provides for acquisition or requisitioning of the property for an amount which may be fixed by such law or which may be determined in accordance with such principles and given in such manner as may be specified in such law; and no such law shall be called in question in any court on the ground that the amount so fixed or determined is not adequate or that the whole or any part of such amount is to be given otherwise than in cash'.

[12] See generally Seervai, H.M., *Constitutional Law of India*, 4th edn, N. M. Tripathi Ltd, 1991.

[13] Allen (n. 4 above) p. 145.

[14] Allen (n. 4 above) p. 145. More specifically, see Alvaro, A., 'Why Property Rights were Excluded from the Canadian Charter of Rights and Freedoms' (1991), 24 *Canadian Journal of Political Science* 309. See also *Re BC Motor Vehicle Act* [1985] 2 SCR 486, 504–505.

[15] Davis (n. 2 above) p. 127.

A fundamental concept in the application of Article 1, Protocol 1 is the principle of proportionality. The European Court assesses proportionality by means of a fair balance test in which it weighs various competing factors in the balance to ensure that there is a fair balance between the interests of the general community, for whose benefit the interference with property occurs, and the interests of the individual property owner to enjoy his or her property without interference. The problem is that the weighting to be allocated to the various competing factors will, in most cases, be left to the judges, which has raised concern, in some quarters, that this imbues an unelected and unaccountable judiciary with excessive political power.[16]

IS PROPERTY A HUMAN RIGHT?

Under the Convention the human right relating to property is not a right to have or acquire property but a right to the protection of a person's existing property (see 4.1). Therefore it does not guarantee that everyone should have a minimum quantity of individual property. In this respect, protecting property as a human right is on a very different level from other human rights such as protecting a person from torture or protecting family and private life. All natural persons have a body that needs protecting from torture and all have a private life but not everyone owns property.

There will be occasions where property owned by an individual may have to be interfered with in pursuit of the collective good of society. By protecting property rights as a human right, the Convention, and the HRA 1998, empower an individual to utilise the judicial arm to seek to prevent interferences with property which may be aimed at advancing the public interest. Inevitably this tension between individual rights and the collective good needs to be carefully contained. Can it be that the categorisation of a person's property rights as a human right, so that property acquires the protection of the HRA 1998, pushes the balance too far in favour of individual benefit in preference to the common good? Harris notes that:

> if maintenance of one's property-holdings, no matter how disproportionately great, is conceived of as a human right then this is a right which, by its very nature, arms its right-subject with power to dominate the lives of others. Ownership includes powers of control over access to that which is owned.[17]

For example, if the HRA 1998 could be invoked by landowners to completely deny the general public any right of access on foot to open countryside for

---

[16] Generally, see Griffith, J., *The Politics of the Judiciary*, 5th edn, London: Fontana Press, 1997.

[17] Harris, J. W., 'Is Property a Human Right?' in McLean, J. (ed), *Property and the Constitution*, Oxford: Hart Publishing, 1999, p. 78.

recreational purposes, it would be submitted, justifiably in the author's opinion, that the individual right of property had been elevated to an unreasonably high level of protection to the detriment of the public interest. In fact the latitude permitted to the Government, by virtue of the qualified nature of the protection under Article 1, Protocol 1 and the principle of proportionality, responds to this criticism and prevents the HRA 1998 from being invoked for this purpose (see 8.7.1). Nevertheless, in reference to Article 1, Protocol 1, Harris questions the exactitude of making property a human right:

> The peaceful enjoyment of his possessions' no doubt contributes to the well-being of an owner, but it may be the means of damaging the well-being of his fellows. Since 'possessions' covers anything from immense riches to the clothes someone stands up in, how could it be supposed that the well-being of all humans makes 'enjoyment' of all possessions a universal right?[18]

Schermers tackles the question of whether property is, and should be, a human right.[19] His starting point is to ascertain the particular characteristics of fundamental human rights that distinguish them from other rights and set them apart as rights which need special protection against amendments or abolition by the state (note, however, that the protection of human rights under the HRA 1998 does not provide any special protection, in terms of entrenchment, because the sovereignty of Parliament remains intact). He observes that there is no clear consensus on what constitutes a fundamental human right and therefore it can vary from one society to another. Some rights are universally accepted as fundamental human rights, such as the right not to be tortured, whereas other rights, such as freedom of expression, are not accepted by all societies as a fundamental human right. By this means he identifies a spectrum of fundamental human rights so that some rights are almost absolute rights and can only be set aside in extremely exceptional circumstances, whilst other fundamental human rights are little more than ordinary rights and are subject to a far greater number of qualifications and exceptions. It is likely that most societies would perceive the right to life at the opposite end of the spectrum to the right to the peaceful enjoyment of possessions. The qualified nature of the guarantee under Article 1, Protocol 1 means that there are many exceptions to the right to property whereby the right must give way to greater interests.

In assessing the nature of fundamental human rights Schermers distinguishes between what he calls 'strictly personal rights' and 'connected rights'. 'Strictly personal rights' are those rights that are vested in the human being and no other

---

[18] Ibid., p. 79.
[19] Schermers, H., 'The international protection of the right of property' in Matscher, F. and Petzold, H. (eds), *Protecting Human Rights: The European Dimension*, Köln: Carl Heymanns Verlag KG, 1988, p. 565–580.

person or goods are involved. The right to life and freedom from torture, for example, fall within this category. These rights cannot be transferred to another person nor inherited. 'Connected rights' are very different because these rights cannot exist independently of other people or goods. The right to form a family and the right to property are examples of connected rights. Property rights can be transferred and inherited and thus move from one person to another. In consequence of a transfer of property, the human right to protect the enjoyment of that property also transfers from one person to another. The English law of adverse possession provides an interesting illustration of this. After the expiration of a 12-year period the squatter acquires title to the property and enjoys the full protection of the human right to property whilst the original owner will lose that protection. Commenting upon a similar example, Schermers concludes that: 'in my opinion, a fundamental human right is of such a supreme nature that it cannot remain with one person up to a particular date and then be taken from him without his co-operation and even without his knowledge'.[20] In so far as the human right is dependent upon the ownership of the property it is inextricably connected with the ownership and therefore a total loss of ownership means a consequent loss of the human right protecting property.

Under the Convention, and the HRA 1998, those rights falling within Schermers' 'strictly personal rights' category, such as the right to the protection of life and freedom from torture, are examples of fundamental human rights which can claim universality and the need for permanent and unqualified protection. These Convention rights enjoy what Harris calls 'transparent universality' which the right to protect property lacks.[21] Therefore all persons have bodies that may be killed or tortured and all persons enjoy the same sense of well-being from not being tortured, but the right to property is different. Different persons possess differing proportions of property and for some people, e.g. the homeless, property rights may be virtually non-existent, being nothing more than the clothes on their back.

The question for consideration is to what extent Schermers' 'connected right' of property deserves protection as a fundamental human right. In seeking to answer this question, Schermers identifies four different kinds of property.

(a) Property necessary to facilitate private life. Schermers suggests that Governments should not be entitled to interfere with the private property that a person needs for developing their personal life. This is undoubtedly a subjective notion. Whilst a television or fridge are likely to be considered by the majority in the UK to be necessary to a normal domestic life, such items are considered as an unnecessary luxury in some parts of

---

[20] Ibid., p. 568.
[21] Harris (n. 17 above) p. 78.

Africa. A house, or at least some form of shelter, may also fall within this category.

(b)   Income and savings derived from work. People who save part of their income for future years need some guarantee that they will not be deprived of this income in the future.

(c)   Inheritance. As a human right, the right of inheritance can only be a right of the testator to dispose of his property as he so wishes. There can be no human right for children to inherit the property of their parents. Given that the only human right at stake is the right of the testator, Schermers asks whether a human right should continue after the person's death. He suggests that no matter how important inheritance may be for economic and other reasons, it is not necessary to make it a fundamental human right.

(d)   Income and savings derived from capital rather than being directly linked to work.

Inheritance and income (both from work and from capital) are usually taxed so that part of it is nationalised in order to finance the Government. National constitutions and international conventions permit the taxation of property. Thus Schermers concludes that:

> this means that either the right to property is only a minor kind of human right, subject to so many limitations that it is not really stronger than any normal right, or that the fundamental human right of property only concerns the property ... [necessary to facilitate private life] — which is normally not subject to taxation — and that all other property rights are normal rights which can be limited in the public interest.[22]

Schermers suggests that there may be an obligation on states that are parties to a treaty to intervene if a state violates the guaranteed rights. For the sake of this international protection he divides human rights into different categories, 'the most important category is the one containing human rights of such importance that their international protection includes the right, perhaps even the obligation, of international enforcement. Violations must be prevented or halted, if necessary by force'.[23] Property does not fall within this category except perhaps for certain goods necessary for private life. Schermers recognises that the: 'Systematic removal of all personal property, such as beds and clothes, may make any normal way of life impossible and could therefore justify strong international action', However most property rights come within a category of human rights, the violation of which would merit international attention, but would not justify strong international action. Schermers suggests that his 'conclusion that part of

---

[22] Schermers (n. 19 above) p. 575.
[23] Ibid., p. 579.

the right to property does not merit the status of a fundamental human right prevents a region such as Western Europe affording special protection to all property rights by means of a convention'.[24]

There is strong support for the view that the protection of existing property rights is not an appropriate right to enjoy human rights status, except perhaps for that limited class of personal property rights that are necessary for a normal way of life, e.g., clothes. Any attempt to define this limited class of property rights would undoubtedly lead to difficulties due to the subjectivity involved in defining what property is necessary for a 'normal life'. The Convention sidesteps this complex problem by classifying all 'possessions' (see 4.7) as worthy of protection. However, it may be useful, when interpreting and applying those Convention rights under the HRA 1998 that protect property rights, for the English courts to bear in mind the different kinds of property identified by Schermers and to have regard to the differing levels of human rights protection that ought to be accorded to them.

THE HUMAN RIGHT TO PROTECT PROPERTY BELONGING TO A COMPANY

The general perception is that human rights law empowers the small and weak individual against the might of the state. However the HRA 1998 can be invoked for a very different purpose. Article 1, Protocol 1 states that: 'Every natural or legal person is entitled to the peaceful enjoyment of his possessions'. The reference to 'legal person' means that it protects possessions belonging to a company. Therefore a company can invoke Article 1, Protocol 1 in the protection of its property (see 4.8). Is there a risk that the HRA 1998 will be used by large wealthy companies to protect their economic interests at the expense of the weaker and more vulnerable members of the general public? Smyth notes that:

> The notion that the United Kingdom's Human Rights Bill might, on coming into force, be relied upon by commerce as a legal tool continues, in some quarters, to offend. Rabinder Singh refers to: '... the irritation which many people feel at the prospect of the Incorporation Act being "hijacked" by the rich and powerful to protect their interests against progressive action by the State'. This is not, it is said, what the architects of the Convention had in mind.[25]

However, Smyth, as does Singh, suggests that such concerns are in fact misplaced. Smyth further suggests that for a significant number of companies which undertake a public function, e.g., Railtrack and British Telecom, the HRA

---

[24] Ibid., p. 580.
[25] Smyth, M., 'The United Kingdom's Incorporation of the European Convention and Its Implications for Business' [1998] EHRLR 273.

1998 appears more like a threat than an opportunity due to their public authority status bringing with it the consequent duty under s. 6 of the HRA 1998 to act in compliance with the Convention rights (see 1.7). Although this may be the case for some companies, it is, nevertheless, likely that for a large number of companies, Article 1, Protocol 1 will provide a valuable string to their bow.

Chapter One

The Human Rights Act 1998

1.1   THE AIM OF THE HUMAN RIGHTS ACT 1998

The Human Rights Act (HRA) 1998 incorporates provisions of the European Convention on Human Rights (the Convention) into UK law. In this way the HRA 1998 seeks to secure in national courts the rights that can be obtained by an applicant in Strasbourg and thereby prevent the unnecessary time and expense of taking a claim to the European Court of Human Rights. In its White Paper, *Rights Brought Home: The Human Rights Bill,* the Government calculated that it takes an average applicant five years at a cost of £30,000 to take a case to the European Court of Human Rights. The Government believes that allowing an applicant to argue for his or her human rights in the British courts will help to cut through this inordinate delay and cost. When highlighting the advantages of incorporating provisions of the Convention into domestic law, the Government stated that incorporation will 'mean that the rights will be brought much more fully into the jurisprudence of the courts throughout the United Kingdom and their interpretation will thus be far more subtly and powerfully woven into our law'.[1]

Therefore the aim of the HRA 1998 is to make the rights that people already enjoy under the Convention more directly accessible. The means of achieving this aim will be considered below through an examination of the key provisions of the HRA 1998.

1.2   THE CONVENTION RIGHTS RELATING TO PROPERTY

Section 1 together with Schedule 1 define the 'Convention rights'. The Convention rights mean the rights and fundamental freedoms set out in Articles 2

---

[1] The Government's White Paper, *Rights Brought Home: The Human Rights Bill* (1997; Cm 3782) para. 1.14.

to 12 and 14 of the Convention and Articles 1 to 3 of Protocol 1 and Articles 1 and 2 of Protocol 6 as read with Articles 16 to 18 of the Convention (see Appendix 1 which includes a copy of the HRA 1998. The Articles are listed in Schedule 1 to the HRA 1998). Section 1(4) empowers the Secretary of State with authority to amend the HRA 1998 to reflect any changes in the UK's obligations under the Convention as a result of an additional protocol to the Convention. This enables future protocols to be incorporated into UK law under the HRA 1998: for example, this could be used to incorporate Protocol 12 into UK law (see 6.6). The important Convention rights for a property lawyer are Articles 6, 8, 14 and Article 1 of Protocol 1.

Article 6 provides certain procedural guarantees such as the right to a fair hearing whilst the protection afforded under Article 1, Protocol 1 and Article 8 enshrine substantive rights protecting the peaceable enjoyment of possessions and the right to respect for the home respectively. The substantive rights under Article 1, Protocol 1 and Article 8 are framed in very wide terms, for example, Article 1, Protocol 1 provides a general guarantee for the right to property. These wide guarantees are then restricted by a number of limitations and qualifications. Interference with property rights by the state is therefore permissible in certain circumstances. It is essentially a matter of balancing the rights of individual property owners, whose property has been interfered with by the state, against other public interests, such as environmental protection. Although the interests of the general community may sometimes take precedence over individual property rights, the wishes of the majority must not be allowed to cause the minority to suffer a disproportionate burden.

Article 14 does not provide a substantive right in itself, but prohibits discrimination in respect of the substantive rights. It safeguards individuals who are placed in analogous situations against discriminatory differences of treatment in relation to the rights conferred on them by the other Articles. For example, if a property owner in an analogous situation to another enjoys preferential tax benefits on the grounds of his nationality, the disadvantaged property owner may be able to allege a violation of Article 14 in conjunction with Article 1, Protocol 1 unless the state can justify the differential treatment.

Article 1, Protocol 1 and Articles 8, 14 and 6 will be examined in detail in chapters 4, 5, 6 and 7 respectively.

1.3 THE STATUS OF THE CONVENTION PRIOR TO THE HUMAN RIGHTS ACT 1998

The decision of the High Court in the case of *The Parochial Church Council of the Parishes of Aston Cantlow and Wilmcote with Billesley, Warwickshire* v *Gail Wallbank and Andrew Wallbank* (2000) *The Times*, 30 March illustrates the status of the Convention in English law prior to the implementation of the HRA 1998.

The decision arose out of a preliminary hearing to an action by the Parochial Church Council (PCC) to require the defendants to repair the chancel of a parish church. The defendants owned a field, being part of a larger parcel of land (the rectorial property), which in 1743 had been allotted to the lay rector of the parish under an inclosure award. The purpose of the inclosure award was to enable the lay rector to use the rents and profits from the land to pay for repairs to the chancel of the church if required to do so. By 1994 the cost of the repairs to the chancel was estimated to be £95,000 and the PCC served notice on the defendants, as successors in title to part of the rectorial property, to repair the chancel. The defendants contended that an obligation to carry out the repairs would be an infringement of their human rights under Article 1, Protocol 1 taken alone and in conjunction with Article 14. However because the Convention was not at that time incorporated into English law under the HRA 1998, the defendants had first to establish the applicability of the Convention. The Convention only applied as an aid to the construction of legislation in cases of ambiguity (see *R* v *Secretary of State for the Home Department, ex parte Brind* [1991] 1 AC 696), and therefore, the defendants had to establish that the relevant law was uncertain. The defendants alleged that there was an ambiguity in the law due to the fact that it was unclear whether a lay rector, who had acquired only part of the rectorial property, was liable to repair the chancel. The defendants alleged that in the light of this uncertainty the court should interpret the law so that it was compatible with the Convention. The court held that it was settled law under the Chancel Repairs Act 1932 that a lay rector was liable for chancel repairs even though the lay rector owned only part of a larger parcel of land originally allotted under an inclosure award. It therefore concluded that there was no uncertainty in the law and the Convention was inapplicable. Therefore prior to the implementation of the HRA 1998 on 2 October 2000, the Convention could only be invoked in cases where the law was ambiguous.

1.4 THE INTERPRETATION OF CONVENTION RIGHTS — THE RELEVANCE OF THE STRASBOURG CASE LAW

Under s. 2 of the HRA 1998 a court or tribunal, when determining a question which has arisen in connection with a Convention right, must 'take into account' the Strasbourg case law in so far as, in the opinion of the court or tribunal, it is relevant to the proceedings before it. This includes any judgment, decision, declaration or opinion of the European Court of Human Rights. In addition, the decisions and opinions of the European Commission of Human Rights[2] as well as the decisions of the Committee of Ministers of the Council of Europe are to be

---

[2] The European Commission of Human Rights was abolished in 1998 by Protocol 11. The European Court of Human Rights has taken over the functions of the Commission, including decisions on admissibility.

taken into account where appropriate. Therefore in seeking to interpret the law in compliance with the Convention (see ss. 3 and 6) the court should not rely solely on domestic precedent, but must now take into account the Strasbourg case law. Consequently, the decisions and judgments of the Strasbourg institutions will be highly relevant to the English courts when they are interpreting the application and scope of the Convention rights. For this reason chapters 4, 5, 6 and 7, which explain the Convention rights relevant to property lawyers, will analyse the Strasbourg case law in depth. In addition, Appendix 3 includes case summaries of some of the principal Strasbourg decisions relating to property law. The fact that the English courts must take into account the Strasbourg cases inevitably requires them to consider the Convention jurisprudence underlying those decisions. These Convention principles, such as the principle of proportionality, will be discussed in chapter 2.

The cumulative effect of ss. 2 and 6, HRA 1998 and the application of the living instrument doctrine (see 2.6) is to remove the binding effect of previous decisions of the higher courts. The English courts will no longer be bound by an earlier precedent if that decision is incompatible with the Convention rights. It has been observed that the 'doctrine of precedent will be abrogated to the extent that is necessary to give effect to Convention rights'.[3]

The duty of the court or tribunal is to take the Strasbourg decisions into account but that does not necessarily mean that the court has to follow the decision. Section 2 leaves scope for the English courts to diverge legitimately from the decisions of the Strasbourg institutions. It is unlikely that the courts will adopt a more restrictive interpretation of the Convention rights than that taken by the Strasbourg institutions as this would thwart the aim of the HRA 1998 and would most likely result in an applicant taking the case to the European Court of Human Rights. However it may be that the English courts will, in some cases, adopt a more liberal interpretation. The House of Lords' decision in *Fitzpatrick* v *Sterling Housing Association Ltd* [1999] 4 All ER 705, which predates the implementation of the HRA 1998, illustrates this possibility. Their Lordships held that same-sex partners in a longstanding, homosexual relationship can constitute a member of the family of the original tenant within the meaning of the Rent Act 1977 and thereby enjoy the rights of succession afforded by that Act. The fact that the Strasbourg institutions have not been prepared to accept that same-sex couples have the right to respect for family life under Article 8 did not deter the House of Lords from reaching their decision. Lord Clyde observed:

> That the relationship in the present case may not as the law currently stands constitute 'family life' for the purposes of Article 8 of the Convention, does not require a restrictive meaning to be given to the reference to a tenant's family in the legislation before us.[4]

---

[3] Wadham, J. and Mountfield, H., *Human Rights Act 1998*, London: Blackstone Press, 1999, p. 31.
[4] *Fitzpatrick* v *Sterling Housing Association Ltd* [1999] 4 All ER 705, p. 730.

Therefore although the courts are obliged, under the HRA 1998, to take the Strasbourg cases into account, this does not require them to follow the decisions. There is ample room for the English courts to take a more liberal stance than that currently taken by the Strasbourg institutions.

1.5 THE INTERPRETATION OF LEGISLATION — ITS COMPATIBILITY WITH CONVENTION RIGHTS

Section 3 provides that 'so far as it is possible to do so', all primary and subordinate legislation must be read and given effect in a way which is compatible with the Convention rights. There is now an overriding presumption that in enacting legislation Parliament intended for it to comply with the Convention rights. This has retrospective application so that past legislation must also be read as being compliant with the Convention rights. If it is possible to interpret a statute in two ways, one that is compatible with the Convention rights and the other that is not, then the effect of s. 3 is that the courts must choose that interpretation which is compatible, even though a higher court may have previously adopted the other interpretation. Therefore the interpretation that the courts gave to a statute prior to the coming into force of the HRA 1998 can no longer be relied upon if that interpretation is incompatible with the Convention rights and a different, Convention compliant, interpretation is possible.

It is highly significant that this requirement is expressly qualified by the words 'so far as it is possible to do so'. Therefore s. 3 provides a scheme that attempts to maximise the protection afforded to individuals by the Convention rights whilst at the same time retaining the fundamental constitutional principle of Parliamentary sovereignty. This was emphasised by Mr Jack Straw, the Secretary of State for the Home Department, in the Parliamentary debates preceding the enactment of the HRA 1998, where he observed that:

> we want the courts to strive to find an interpretation of legislation that is consistent with Convention rights, so far as the plain words of the legislation allow, and only in the last resort to conclude that the legislation is simply incompatible with them ... there was a time when all the courts could do to divine the intention of Parliament was to apply themselves to the words on the face of any Act. Now, following *Pepper* v *Hart*, they are able to look behind that and, not least, to look at the words used by Ministers. I do not think the courts will need to apply themselves to the words that I am about to use, but, for the avoidance of doubt, I will say that it is not our intention that the courts, in applying [s. 3], should contort the meaning of words to produce implausible or incredible meanings. I am talking about plain words in what is actually a clear [Act] with plain language — with the intention of Parliament set out in Hansard, should the courts wish to refer to it.[5]

---

[5] House of Commons, 3 June 1998, Committee Stage, Hansard, HC, col. 421.

Therefore, s. 3 is only an interpretative tool and does not permit the courts to strike down Acts of Parliament. If the legislation cannot be interpreted in such a way as to be compatible with the Convention rights, s. 3(2) provides that the validity, continuing operation and enforcement of that incompatible provision will not be affected. In these instances the higher courts have power to make a declaration of incompatibility under s. 4 of the HRA 1998 (see 1.6)

The case of *R v DPP, ex parte Kebilene* [1999] 4 All ER 801 illustrates the potential scope of s. 3. The Divisional Court granted a declaration that the decision of the Director of Public Prosecutions (DPP) to consent to prosecutions under the Prevention of Terrorism Act 1989 was unlawful. The Divisional Court found the reverse onus provisions of that Act to be incompatible with Article 6(2) which provides that someone charged with a criminal offence is innocent until proven guilty. The House of Lords, in allowing the DPP's appeal, relied upon the common law presumption that a court will not judicially review a decision to prosecute unless there are exceptional circumstances, such as dishonesty. The basis of the House of Lords' decision was therefore the inappropriateness of judicial review as a mechanism for challenging the DPP's decision. However the case offers some insight into the likely effect of s. 3 of the HRA 1998. Lord Steyn described s. 3 as a 'strong interpretative obligation' and the power of this obligation was illustrated in the way that their Lordships were prepared to distort the ordinary meaning of the words of the offending Act in order to ensure its compatibility with Article 6(2). For example, Lord Cooke thought that the offending section, which imposed the reverse onus, could be interpreted as imposing only an evidential burden, as opposed to a legal burden, on the defendant. Although it was recognised that this was not the natural or ordinary meaning of the section it was a possible meaning and one that would be Convention compliant.

Hooper supports this creative approach to statutory interpretation and remarks:

> The authoritative view has been expressed in Parliament that the courts will be able, in almost all cases, to interpret legislation in a way that is compatible. This will only happen if the courts radically change their approach to statutory interpretation. One method may be to read into legislation which is incompatible but could be made compatible, the words: 'Subject to the Convention rights ...' or 'Provided that thereby the Convention rights are not abridged ...' or words to a similar effect.[6]

The example of creative statutory interpretation that the *Kebilene* case provides, anticipates that instances of declarations of incompatibility will be rare. In the majority of cases the courts are likely to be persuaded to adopt an interpretation that is compatible with the Convention rights. However, in the case of *Wilson* v *First County Trust* (2 May 2001) the Court of Appeal has decided to make a

---

[6] Hooper, Sir A., 'The Impact of the Human Rights Act on judicial decision-making' [1998] EHRLR 677, p. 683.

declaration of incompatibility, the precise wording of which will be settled after further submissions have been heard. The Court of Appeal held that the provisions of s. 127(3) of the Consumer Credit Act (CCA) 1974 are incompatible with the rights guaranteed by Article 1, Protocol 1 and Article 6(1) on the grounds that the absolute bar to the enforcement of a regulated agreement that does not contain all of the terms prescribed by s. 61 of the CCA 1974 constitutes a disproportionate restriction on the rights of a lender. The decision is illustrative of the Court of Appeal's evident willingness to raise the question of compatibility on its own initiative without either party to the proceedings having raised the argument.[7]

1.6 A DECLARATION OF INCOMPATIBILITY

1.6.1 When can a declaration of incompatibility be made?

The declaration of incompatibility is a novel device designed to maintain Parliamentary sovereignty whilst providing the higher courts with a mechanism for declaring their views as to whether particular legislation is compliant with the Convention rights. Section 4 empowers the higher courts (the High Court, the Court of Appeal and the House of Lords) to make declarations of incompatibility where the court is satisfied that the statutory provision in question is incompatible with a Convention right. A declaration can only be made in the course of proceedings in which the court has to decide whether legislation is compatible with the Convention rights. There is no right to commence court proceedings solely for the purpose of obtaining a declaration of incompatibility. It is highly significant that a declaration of incompatibility will not change the law itself. Section 4(6) provides that the offending statute or statutory provision will continue to apply despite its incompatibility with the Convention rights. Therefore it is clear that the courts cannot override primary legislation. However, they may quash subordinate legislation that is found to be non-compliant with the Convention rights, unless there is primary legislation that dictates the wording of that subordinate legislation. Although the declaration does not affect the validity, continuing operation or enforcement of the offending legislation, it is likely to lead to a remedial order being made under s. 10 of the HRA 1998. Whilst a declaration of incompatibility will not be binding on the parties to the proceedings in which it is made, and cannot therefore affect the outcome of their case, any remedial order made in response to the declaration can have retrospective effect.

---

[7] In compliance with its duty under s. 6, HRA 1998 — see 1.7.

The lower courts do not have the power to make a declaration of incompatibility. If a lower court, having complied with its duties under ss. 2, 3 and 6, cannot interpret the legislation before it in such a way that it is compatible with the Convention rights, the court must nevertheless apply the offending legislation. The opinion of the lower court as to the incompatibility of the legislation, which will inevitably be set out in its decision, will not be sufficient to trigger the s. 10 fast-track remedial procedure but it may put pressure on the Government for a change in the law. Once a decision reaches the higher courts a declaration of incompatibility can be made which acts as a clear signal to the Government and Parliament that a statutory provision does not comply with the standards of the Convention rights. It is expected that the Government and Parliament will respond with rapidity to any such declaration although there is no formal obligation on them to amend incompatible legislation.

1.6.2 The fast-track procedure

Section 10 provides a fast-track remedial procedure whereby the offending legislation can be amended by a 'remedial order'. The remedial order, made by statutory instrument, is available in two instances: first, where a declaration of incompatibility has been made by a higher court; secondly, where it appears to the Government, having regard to a decision of the European Court of Human Rights made after 2 October 2000, that UK legislation is incompatible with the Convention rights. Section 10(2) provides: 'If a Minister of the Crown considers that there are compelling reasons for proceeding under this section, he may by order make such amendments to the legislation as he considers necessary to remove the incompatibility'. Therefore the Minister must have 'compelling reasons' for making a s. 10 remedial order; however, the very fact of the incompatibility of the legislation with the Convention rights will be sufficient in itself.

There are procedural safeguards for the making of a remedial order and these are set out in Schedule 2 to the HRA 1998. No remedial order may be made unless a draft of it has been approved by a resolution of each House of Parliament made after the end of a 60-day period starting on the day that the draft was laid before Parliament. However, before the draft order can be laid before Parliament for its approval, a document containing a draft of the order and the 'required information' (see Schedule 2, para. 5) must be laid before Parliament and a 60-day period must have lapsed during which representations can be made and the order can be amended. The cumulative effect of these two stages in the procedure is that a minimum period of 120 days must lapse before the remedial order can be approved.

There is, however, an emergency procedure for use in urgent cases whereby the order can be made without the prior approval of a draft order. In this case the Minister making the order must make a declaration that it is necessary to make the order without a draft being approved because of the urgency of the matter.

After the original order has been made it must be laid before
accompanied by the 'required information' (see Schedule 2, para. 4).
opportunity for representations to be made within 60 days and for the
changed. In any event the order will lapse after 120 days from the day i
unless it is approved by both Houses of Parliament.

1.6.3   The limitations of a declaration of incompatibility

It is probable that declarations of incompatibility will be rare occurrences. One
reason for this is the effect of the 'strong interpretative obligation' imposed on the
courts by s. 3 which will induce the courts to reach a Convention compliant
interpretation (see 1.5). But it may also be that offending legislation will be slow
to reach the courts for a decision on its compatibility. The reason for this delay
may be the ineffectiveness of a declaration to influence the outcome of the
proceedings in which it is made together with the need for victim status to
commence an action (see 2.7). Feldman has observed that:

> The uncertainty of gaining any concrete advantage from a declaration of incompatibility
> will make it hard to obtain legal aid to apply for one, while the restrictive *locus standi*
> test under [section] 7 for litigation concerning Convention rights will make it difficult
> for public-interest and charitable bodies to take action on behalf of others.[8]

Therefore it is likely that there will be some areas of law that are incompatible
with the Convention rights but which remain unchallenged for some considerable
time (see 8.1.2).

1.7   THE COMPLIANCE OF PUBLIC AUTHORITIES WITH CONVENTION RIGHTS

1.7.1   The section 6 duty

Section 6(1) provides that public authorities cannot act in a way that is
incompatible with one or more of the Convention rights, unless they are required
to do so by statute. Therefore the overarching duty on all public authorities is to
act in ways that are Convention compliant. However s. 6(2) seeks to preserve
Parliamentary sovereignty by ensuring that the obligation imposed by s. 6(1) does
not apply in the following circumstances:

(a)   Where the public authority acts incompatibly with a Convention right
        because it could not have acted differently as a result of having to comply
        with primary legislation.

---

[8] Feldman, D., 'Remedies for Violations of Convention Rights under the Human Rights Act 1998'
[1998] EHRLR 691, p. 699.

(b)   Where the public authority was acting so as to give effect to or enforce primary legislation, or subordinate legislation which is mandated by primary legislation and which is incompatible with the Convention rights.

The boundaries of the s. 6(1) duty are further qualified by s. 6(6) which clarifies that although the term 'an act' does include a failure to act, it does not include a failure to introduce in Parliament any proposals for legislation nor to make any primary legislation or remedial order. Therefore it is not possible to commence action against the Government and Parliament for failing to introduce and pass legislation which is needed to protect a Convention right.

1.7.2   The meaning of a 'public authority'

The definition of 'public authority' under s. 6(3) has a wide ambit and its scope is likely to be the subject of considerable debate. It includes a court, a tribunal and 'any person certain of whose functions are functions of a public nature'. It specifically excludes the Houses of Parliament (except for the House of Lords in its judicial capacity), any person exercising functions in connection with proceedings in Parliament and organisations that have no public functions at all. The definition is designed to include organisations that are public bodies in certain respects but private in others (referred to as 'quasi-public' bodies hereafter). If the body has public functions it qualifies as a public authority for the purposes of the Act. However, in relation to these quasi-public bodies, s. 6(5) provides that if the nature of the particular act is private the body will not be regarded as a public authority in the context of that act. Therefore s. 6(1) only applies to the extent that the actions of the quasi-public body are of a public nature and will not affect its actions that are of a private nature. In the Parliamentary debates the Lord Chancellor illustrates this concept in the following terms:

> Railtrack, as a public utility, obviously qualifies as a public authority because some of its functions, for example its functions in relation to safety on the railway, qualify it as a public authority. However, acts carried out in its capacity as a private property developer would no doubt be held by the courts to be of a private nature and therefore not caught by the [Act].[9]

Thus a two stage process exists to ascertain whether the action complained of falls within s. 6(1):

(a)   Is the body a purely public authority, e.g., Government departments, local authorities, courts? In this case all of its acts are to be treated as being of a public nature even though the nature of the act in question may be

---

[9] HL, 24 November 1997, Hansard, col. 784.

private. For example, a local authority granting a lease to a tenant is a public authority within s. 6(1) even though granting a lease is an act within the realms of private law.

(b) Is the body a quasi-public body, e.g., the privatised utilities, regulatory bodies, charities which carry out a public role for the central Government or local authorities? If yes, the focus should turn to the nature of the action in question to determine whether or not in carrying out that act the body was exercising a public or private function. If the body was undertaking a public function the act can be challenged as unlawful under s. 6(1). But if the function of the body is private in nature, e.g., making employment contracts, the act falls outside the scope of s. 6(1). This raises the public/private law dichotomy (see chapter 3). Given that the new cause of action under s. 6 for acting in violation of Convention rights only applies to quasi-public bodies when they are undertaking public functions, the courts' interpretation of the concept of a public function will determine the reach of s. 6(1). There will inevitably be differences of opinion as to what constitutes a public function; for example, some commentators have queried the accuracy of the Lord Chancellor's illustration that Railtrack would be acting in a private capacity as a property developer and therefore its actions in this context would be outside s. 6(1). Wadham and Mountfield have observed that, for the purposes of planning legislation, Railtrack is treated as a statutory undertaker and is thereby afforded certain permitted development rights not given to ordinary private bodies.[10] This may be sufficient to transfer Railtrack's actions as a property developer from the private law domain into that of public law.

1.7.3 Housing associations as a public authority

If housing associations fall within the first category as purely public bodies then all of their actions, even those of a private law nature, will fall within the scope of s. 6(1). Housing associations are non-profit-making bodies that fulfil a public role in the provision of affordable housing. They are defined and regulated by statute (s. 1(1) of the Housing Associations Act 1985). They must register with the Housing Corporation in order to acquire eligibility for public grants, not only from the Housing Corporation itself (s. 18(1) of the Housing Act 1996) but also from local authorities (s. 22(3) of the Housing Act 1996). The vast majority of housing associations have become registered social landlords under s. 2 of the Housing Act 1996, thereby surrendering their independence. The Housing Corporation is a statutory body whose members are appointed by the Secretary of State for the Environment. Its general functions, which are prescribed by statute, include the duty to 'facilitate the proper performance of the functions of registered

---

[10] Wadham, J. and Mountfield, H. (n. 3 above) p. 37.

social landlords' and the obligation to 'maintain a register of social landlords and
to exercise supervision and control over such persons' (s. 75, Housing Association
Act 1985). The increasing intervention of statute in prescribing the actions of
housing associations together with the supervisory role of the Housing Corporation has led Langstaff to observe that housing associations are becoming 'hired
agents of central government, operating as branch offices of the Corporation'.[11]
There may, therefore, be a case for arguing that housing associations constitute
pure public authorities for the purposes of the HRA 1998.

It is more likely, however, that housing associations will constitute quasi-
public bodies. In this case only their public functions will be vulnerable to
challenge under s. 6(1) of the HRA 1998. It is arguable that, by analogy with the
judicial review cases, the housing associations will be able to circumvent the
effect of s. 6(1) in relation to their actions as a landlord. For example, a decision
by a housing association to evict a tenant was found to concern a matter of private
law because it related to its role as a landlord. Consequently its actions were not
subject to judicial review (*Peabody Housing Association Ltd* v *Green* (1978) 38 P
& CR 644).[12] By analogy, it may be argued that if the relationship that a housing
association has with its tenant is in private law, it is not a public authority in its
dealing with its tenants. Such an unduly formalistic approach is unlikely to find
favour with the courts. The counterargument that housing associations, by
providing social housing, are fulfilling a public function and carrying out a public
role that would otherwise be the responsibility of the local authorities, is far more
persuasive. Prior to the Housing Act 1988, housing associations formed a section
of the public housing sector complementing the social housing role of local
authorities. Both housing association tenants and local authority tenants enjoyed
the benefits of a secure tenancy under the Housing Act 1985. However the
Housing Act 1988 introduced a new regime for financing housing associations,
utilising private sector funding and in consequence all tenancies granted on or
after 15 January 1985 by housing associations are assured tenancies rather than
secure tenancies. Although the housing association tenant's position is now more
akin to the private rented sector, the tenant does still enjoy the additional
protection of the tenant's guarantee. This unique position and, in particular, the
fact that the housing associations are undertaking the role of social landlord on
behalf of the local authority, may be sufficient to move the relationship that a
housing association has with its tenant from outside the confines of private law

---

[11] Langstaff, M., 'Housing Associations: A Move to Centre Stage' in Birchall, J. (ed), *Housing Policy
in the 1990s*, London: Routledge, 1992, p. 42.

[12] See *R* v *Servite Homes and the London Borough of Wandsworth, ex parte Goldsmith and Chatting*
(12 May 2000), in which the Divisional Court reluctantly decided that the decision of a housing
association to close down a residential care home was not subject to judicial review. However, had
it not been bound by precedent, the Court may have been persuaded by the view that the decision to
close the residential home had such an impact on the local authority's public duties as to subject the
housing association's decision to public law scrutiny.

and into the ambit of its public functions and thereby bring it within the scope of the HRA 1998.[13] Alder suggests that the publicly funded activities of registered social landlords may fall within s. 6(1), as will activities carried out by housing associations under agreements with local authorities and other public bodies due to the fact that such activities are carried out under the control of, or on behalf of, the government. However, at the other end of the scale, the provisions of services for private landlords or owner occupiers, provided without the use of public funding, may not qualify as 'public functions'.[14]

1.7.4 Section 6 and the development of the common law

One interesting consequence of including the courts in the definition of public authorities for the purposes of s. 6 is to create a new interpretative obligation in respect of the common law. Although s. 3 of the HRA 1998 requires the courts to interpret legislation in a way that is compatible with the Convention rights, it has no direct application to the development of the common law. However, it seems likely that one consequence of s. 6 will be to expand the perimeters of this new interpretative obligation to include the common law. Feldman argues that: 'Since judges are public authorities, by virtue of [s. 6] they will act unlawfully if they fail to develop the common-law torts in ways which are compatible with Convention rights, even if the litigation is taking place between private parties'.[15] Therefore not only does s. 6 oblige courts to interpret the common law in compliance with Convention rights in cases where these rights have been specifically pleaded, but it is arguable that s. 6 requires the courts to undertake this interpretative obligation even in those cases where Convention rights have not been raised, for example in cases where the parties are private individuals (see *Wilson* v *First County Trust* at 1.5). This is discussed further at 3.3.2.

1.7.5 Relying on the unlawful act of the public authority in court

Section 7 creates new, directly enforceable rights against a public authority which has acted (or proposes to act) in a way that is contrary to its duty under s. 6. If a person believes himself or herself to be a victim of an act (or would be a victim of a proposed act) by a public authority which infringes his or her Convention rights, there are a number of ways that the victim can rely upon the unlawful act in court.

---

[13] Clayton and Tomlinson support this view stating that: 'It is likely that registered social landlords under the Housing Act 1996 (formerly housing associations) are functional public authorities'. Clayton, R. and Tomlinson, H., *The Law of Human Rights*, Oxford: Oxford University Press, 2000, vol. 1 at para. 12.193.

[14] Alder, J., 'Housing Law and the Human Rights Act 1998' (1999) 2 JHL 67 at p. 69.

[15] Feldman (n. 8 above) p. 702.

(a) The victim could commence private law proceedings against the public
     authority under s. 7(1)(a) in an appropriate court. This is a new cause of
     action introduced by s. 7 enabling a victim to bring a direct action against
     a public authority for a breach of its statutory duty under s. 6 due to its
     failure to act compatibly with Convention rights. For example, if a local
     authority landlord leases defective residential premises that cause the
     tenant to suffer excessive noise disturbance, the tenant may have grounds
     for complaining of a breach of the right to respect for his or her home
     under Article 8 (see 8.3.5). Therefore if the local authority is acting in a
     way that is incompatible with the tenant's Convention rights, the tenant
     can bring a direct claim against the local authority under s. 7. This cause
     of action is also available where a public authority proposes to act in a way
     that is incompatible with Convention rights even though it has not yet
     undertaken that action. The potential victim can bring an action to try to
     prevent the public authority from taking the alleged unlawful act.

(b) The victim could raise the unlawful act as a defence to a criminal or civil
     action instigated by a public authority against him or her. For example, if
     a local planning authority commences enforcement notice proceedings
     against a person for carrying out development without the requisite
     planning permission, the defendant may be able to raise, as a defence, the
     incompatibility with his Convention rights of the local planning author-
     ity's action in refusing the grant of planning permission.

(c) The victim could seek judicial review. Section 7 introduces a new ground
     of illegality into judicial review proceedings, namely, a failure to comply
     with Convention rights. This will be subject to a defence by the public
     authority of 'statutory obligation' reliant upon the provisions in s. 6(2).

1.7.6 The limitation periods

When applying the specified limitation period it is necessary to distinguish
between, on the one hand, proceedings brought by the victim against the public
authority under s. 7(1)(a) and, on the other hand, any civil or criminal proceedings
brought by a public authority against an individual and in which the individual
seeks to rely, under s. 7(1)(b), on the alleged unlawful act of the authority as a
defence.

1.7.6.1 *Proceedings brought against a public authority*

Section 7(1)(a) creates a new cause of action against a public authority for a
breach of its statutory duty under s. 6, but there are time limits on when a victim
can commence proceedings under this provision. Section 7(5) provides that
proceedings must be brought within one year from the date on which the act
complained of took place. There is scope for this one year limitation period to be

extended by the court to such longer period as the court considers equitable having regard to all the circumstances. This one year time period is considerably less generous than the existing six year limitation period for bringing claims concerning property. The one year limitation period is also subject to any rule imposing a stricter time limit in relation to the proceedings in question. For example, there is a three month time limit for bringing judicial review proceedings and this has precedence over the one year time limit in s. 7(5).

1.7.6.2 Proceedings brought by a public authority

Section 7(1)(b), which enables defendants to rely on their Convention rights in proceedings brought by or at the instigation of a public authority, is applicable whenever the alleged unlawful act in question took place (s. 22(4), HRA 1998). This means that where, for example, a local planning authority commences enforcement notice proceedings against an individual in a case concerning a breach of planning law, the defendant can raise as a defence to the action the fact that the public authority's refusal to grant him planning permission was in violation of his Convention rights even though the act of refusal took place prior to 2 October 2000. Therefore an individual, against whom a public authority is proceeding, can challenge the lawfulness of the public authority's actions whenever that action took place and to this limited extent the HRA 1998 has retrospective effect in relation to the acts of public authorities.

1.7.6.3 An example of the different limitation periods

Suppose that in 2001 a local planning authority (and the Secretary of State on appeal) acts in violation of a person's Convention rights in refusing planning permission. The victim may either commence judicial review proceedings within three months of the act or alternatively bring an action, under s. 7(1)(a) against the authority for breach of its statutory duty under s. 6, within one year of the alleged unlawful act. However, if the victim takes no legal action but simply proceeds with the development without any planning permission and after two years the local planning authority serves an enforcement notice on the victim, he or she can rely on the unlawful act of the public authority as a defence to the enforcement proceedings even though the alleged unlawful act of the public authority occurred two years earlier.

1.7.7 The need for victim status

Only a person who is a 'victim' is able to hold the public authority to account. Section 7(7) provides that a person is a 'victim' if he or she would be a victim under Article 34 of the Convention for the purposes of proceedings brought in the European Court of Human Rights (see 2.7). The Strasbourg institutions have taken a restrictive view of who can be a 'victim'. Only a person who is actually and directly affected by the offending act or omission can qualify as a victim. Therefore non-Government organisations (NGOs) that are not themselves a victim of the public authority's unlawful act cannot bring class actions. The meaning of 'victim' under the jurisprudence of the Convention is narrower than *locus standi* in English judicial review proceedings under the 'sufficient interest' test. However s. 7(3) provides that where the person seeks to challenge the alleged unlawful act of the public authority by judicial review proceedings, that person will only satisfy the 'sufficient interest' test if he or she is a victim as defined by s. 7(7) of the HRA 1998. This prevents NGOs, that are not victims and are therefore barred from commencing private law proceedings under s. 7, from circumventing the 'victim' rule by bringing judicial review proceedings instead. In recent years NGOs have been permitted to bring judicial review proceedings in appropriate cases involving matters of general public interest (see *R* v *Secretary of State for the Environment, ex parte Greenpeace* [1994] Env LR 76). Section 7(3) therefore amounts to a serious restriction on the current judicial thinking of what constitutes standing by requiring victim status in cases of judicial review arising from the HRA 1998. It is arguable that, where a human rights violation is the result of a public authority exceeding its powers, it is in the public interest for there to be a judicial check on this action which should not be barred by a victim's refusal to initiate proceedings. NGOs ought, in these circumstances, to be permitted to invoke court action in order to restrain alleged executive illegality in pursuit of the public interest of a limited and accountable Government.

However, since s. 11 of the HRA 1998 safeguards existing human rights and existing proceedings it is possible that an NGO, which is not a victim under s. 7(7) of the HRA 1998, can still commence judicial review proceedings and use arguments reliant upon the Convention in the same circumstances as it could have done before the enactment of the HRA 1998. For example, an NGO that satisfied the sufficient interest test in judicial review proceedings, could rely on *R* v *Secretary of State for the Home Department, ex parte Brind* [1991] 1 AC 696 to persuade the court to interpret ambiguities in the law in a way that is compatible with the Convention.

1.8   REMEDIES

Section 8 sets out the remedies available to a victim where a public authority acts (or proposes to act) in a way that is found by the court to be unlawful under s. 6. The court can grant whatever relief or remedy, or make such order, within its powers as it considers just and appropriate. Clearly the appropriate remedy will depend upon the facts of each case and different remedies will be befitting in different contexts. It is worth bearing in mind that in some cases the European Court of Human Rights has concluded that a finding of a violation of the Convention is a sufficient remedy in itself. For example, in *McLeod* v *UK* (see

Appendix 3), the state was found to have acted in violation of Article 8 due to the entry of police officers into the applicant's house to oversee her ex-husband removing furniture from the former matrimonial home (see 5.3.4.2). The European Court ruled that the state should pay the applicant £15,000 in respect of her costs and expenses, but that otherwise the finding of a violation of the Convention was sufficient just satisfaction for any non-pecuniary damage that she might have suffered.

Damages are likely to be particularly relevant to property related cases where there has been a violation of Article 1, Protocol 1 or Article 8. However, s. 9(3) states that where a person alleges that a court has acted unlawfully contrary to s. 6, damages cannot be awarded in respect of a judicial act done in good faith.

1.8.1 Damages

An award of damages for a violation of a Convention right is restricted in two ways. First, s. 8(2) states that damages can only be awarded by a court which has the power to award damages, or to order the payment of compensation, in civil proceedings. Secondly, s. 8(3) provides that damages can only be awarded if this is necessary to afford 'just satisfaction' for the applicant.[16]

1.8.1.1 Appropriate court or tribunal

Damages are restricted to civil proceedings because the criminal courts do not have the power to award damages. In addition, very few tribunals have the power to make an award for compensation. However, to remedy this position, s. 7(11) provides that a Minister, who may make rules for a particular tribunal, has authority to empower the tribunal to grant remedies 'to the extent he considers it necessary to ensure that the tribunal can provide an appropriate remedy in relation to an act (or proposed act) of a public authority which is (or would be) unlawful as a result of section 6(1)'. Therefore where a tribunal currently has no power to award damages, the appropriate Minister can use s. 7(11) to enable the tribunal to award compensation for violations of Convention rights.

1.8.1.2 Just satisfaction

In determining the issue of just satisfaction the court must take into account any other relief or remedy already granted in respect of the unlawful act of the public authority and also the consequences of any court decision in respect of the act. In this respect s. 8(4) provides that in determining the amount of damages, if any, to be awarded the court must take into account the principles applied by the European Court of Human Rights in relation to an award of compensation under Article 41, Protocol 11 of the Convention. As the levels of compensation awarded by the European Court of Human Rights under Article 41 are generally quite low

---

[16] Generally, see Amos, M., 'Damages for breach of the Human Rights Act 1998' [1999] EHRLR 178.

it may be that awards made under s. 8 by the English courts will also be of modest value. Feldman notes that s. 11(6) of the HRA 1998 safeguards existing procedures and he suggests that the restrictions on the quantification of damages imposed by s. 8 should be limited to damages awarded in respect of violations of Convention rights. He argues that s. 8(4) does not extend to damages awarded under an ordinary cause of action, e.g., trespass to land.[17] Therefore it may be necessary to distinguish between two types of action: first, an action against a public authority for a breach of its duty under s. 6(1), and secondly, an ordinary action in private law in those circumstances where the public authority's violation of a Convention right is held to constitute a tort such as trespass or nuisance. Suppose that a local authority landlord levies distress for rent to remedy a tenant's rent arrears and in the process seizes goods belonging to a third party. The owner of the goods may allege that the local authority has violated his or her Convention rights (see 8.3.6). In these circumstances, it may be necessary to distinguish between a claim under s. 7(1)(a) against the public authority for a breach of its duty under s. 6 on the one hand, and a claim in tort in relation to an interference with goods on the other. The reason for having to distinguish between the two types of claim is that any damages awarded reliant upon the claim under s. 7(1)(a) will be limited by the Strasbourg case law on Article 41, whereas an award of damages under a cause of action in tort will be assessed according to the traditional rules. The problem is that it will not always be easy to distinguish between an ordinary action for damages and an action against a public authority for a violation of Convention rights and this is therefore liable to cause difficulties in ascertaining which test to apply when quantifying damages.

1.8.2 The effect of a declaration of incompatibility on the claimant's remedy

There will be times when a person will allege that a public authority has breached its duty under s. 6 but in its defence the public authority will argue that it was acting to give effect to primary legislation. In these circumstances the s. 7 claim will fail but the higher courts may make a declaration of incompatibility under s. 4. Any such declaration will not have any direct effect on the failed claim because the offending legislation remains intact and valid (s. 4(6)). However, the claimant may not leave the court empty-handed. Feldman suggests that under s. 6 the court must act compatibly with Convention rights and therefore it may be called upon to exercise any discretion it may have to mitigate the effects of the offending legislation upon the claimant.[18]

---

[17] Feldman (n. 8 above) p. 703.
[18] Ibid., p. 691.

1.8.3   The influence of Article 13 on section 8

Article 13 of the Convention provides that:

> Everyone whose rights and freedoms as set forth in this Convention are violated shall have an effective remedy before a national authority notwithstanding that the violation has been committed by persons acting in an official capacity.

Article 13 was deliberately omitted from the HRA 1998. It was argued in Parliament that to include Article 13 would be superfluous as the remedial provisions in s. 8 are adequate to meet the obligations imposed by Article 13 on the state. However, Feldman suggests that Article 13 cannot be ignored because it is an essential component of Convention jurisprudence. He relies on the ministerial statements made during the Parliamentary debates that Article 13 is unnecessary due to the provisions of s. 8 and suggests that: 'In case of doubt, therefore, courts and tribunals should be able to refer to *Hansard* under the rule in *Pepper* v *Hart*, and interpret the remedial provisions in the [Act] in a way that meets the requirements of Article 13.'[19] Therefore it is arguable that s. 8 should be interpreted in accordance with the requirements of Article 13 to ensure that a victim always has an effective remedy.

1.9   DEROGATIONS AND RESERVATIONS

1.9.1   Derogations

Article 15 of the Convention permits a state to derogate from its obligations under the Convention in times of 'war or other public emergency threatening the life of the nation' provided that any derogation is proportional to the threat posed and is necessary in an emergency situation. The procedural requirements specify that the state must lodge a derogation with the Council of Europe in Strasbourg. Although Article 15 is omitted from the HRA 1998, the power of derogation is governed by s. 14 and Schedule 3 to the HRA 1998. Section 14 permits the Secretary of State to designate derogations from an Article or Protocol of the Convention. However, the Secretary of State cannot make a designated derogation for the purposes of domestic law unless it is in relation to a derogation already lodged with the Council of Europe. Section 14(1)(a) specifically retains the UK's only existing derogation which is a derogation from Article 5(3) in relation to the Prevention of Terrorism (Temporary Provisions) Act 1989 relating to the conflict in Northern Ireland. Under s. 16 designated derogations will last for five years with a power for the Secretary of State to grant an extension for a further five year period.

---

[19] Ibid., p. 692.

1.9.2 Reservations

Section 15 provides for 'designated reservations'. There is currently only one reservation to the Convention by the UK. This reservation concerns the right to education under Article 2, Protocol 1. The second sentence of Article 2 requires the state to respect the right of parents to ensure that their child's education conforms with their own religious and philosophical convictions. The UK's reservation to this Article states that the second sentence is 'accepted by the UK only so far as it is compatible with the provision of efficient instruction and training, and the avoidance of unreasonable public expenditure'. The use of reservations, therefore, is to exempt particular policies or law from challenge under the Convention. However, there is a significant restriction in that reservations can only be made at the time of ratification, although new Protocols which amend the Convention may allow a new reservation to be agreed.

1.10   STATEMENTS OF COMPATIBILITY

Section 19 of the HRA 1998 came into force on 24 November 1998. It provides that in respect of all new legislation passing through Parliament, the Minister introducing a Bill must make a written 'statement of compatibility' prior to the second reading in Parliament. The statement must be to the effect that in the Minister's view the provisions of the Bill are compatible with Convention rights. Alternatively, in the unlikely event that the Minister cannot make a statement of compatibility, a statement must be made that the Government nevertheless wishes Parliament to proceed with the Bill. It is anticipated that these Ministerial statements of compatibility, now a requisite element of the legislative process, will greatly assist the courts in exercising their duty under s. 3 to construe statutes in such a way that they are compliant with Convention rights.

1.11   A SUMMARY OF THE KEY PROVISIONS OF THE HUMAN RIGHTS ACT 1998

The key provisions of the HRA 1998 can be summarised as follows:

(a)   The courts must take decisions of the Strasbourg institutions into account when determining questions in connection with Convention rights (s. 2). This implicitly requires a consideration of Convention principles (see chapter 2).

(b)   The courts are required as far as it is possible to do so to interpret all legislation (past or future) in a way that is compatible with Convention rights (s. 3).

(c) Parliamentary sovereignty is preserved. Where legislation is clearly incompatible it continues to be valid in the courts. The higher courts can make a declaration of incompatibility, but this will not affect the outcome of the case in the court making the declaration (s. 4). It is likely, however, to trigger a fast-track procedure to create a remedial order to remedy the incompatibility (s. 10).

(d) Public authorities must not act in a way that is incompatible with Convention rights, unless statute prevents them from acting differently (s. 6).

(e) The definition of a public authority includes the courts and therefore the courts are under a duty to interpret all law, including the common law, in a way that is compliant with Convention rights (s. 6).

(f) Where a public authority has acted (or proposes to act) in a way that is incompatible with Convention rights, contrary to its duty under s. 6, any person who is a victim of that act may commence proceedings under s. 7 against the public authority (s. 7).

(g) The cumulative effect of ss. 2, 3 and 6 will have a profound impact upon the judicial approach to deciding cases, both in the interpretation of legislation and the common law and in the exercise of judicial discretion so as to ensure compliance with Convention rights wherever possible.

Chapter Two

The Convention Principles

2.1 THE CONVENTION JURISPRUDENCE

The Strasbourg institutions have their own Convention jurisprudence embodying a number of general principles that permeate their decisions. An understanding of these principles is therefore a prerequisite to an appreciation of the Strasbourg case law, which by virtue of s. 2 of the Human Rights Act (HRA) 1998, the English courts are now required to take into account when determining a question which has arisen in connection with Convention rights. This chapter will examine the key Convention principles and the extent to which these principles will apply to the HRA 1998.

2.2 THE MARGIN OF APPRECIATION

2.2.1 An element of discretion

The essence of the 'margin of appreciation' is that the contracting states are given an element of discretion and freedom in observing their obligations under the Convention. The European Court of Human Rights (the European Court) first developed the margin of appreciation doctrine in the case of *Handyside* v *UK* (see Appendix 3), which concerned, amongst other things, whether a conviction under the Obscene Publications Act 1959, which allegedly violated the right to freedom of expression under Article 10, could be justified as being necessary for the 'protection of morals' within the ambit of Article 10(2). The European Court stated (at para. 48) that:

> By reason of their direct and continuous contact with the vital forces of their countries, state authorities are in principle in a better position than the international judge to give

an opinion on the exact content of those requirements [of morals] as well as on the 'necessity' of a 'restriction' or 'penalty' intended to meet them.

This line of reasoning underpins the margin of appreciation doctrine and has been applied time and time again. For example, in *James* v *UK* (see Appendix 3), where the applicant alleged that his right to the enjoyment of his possessions under Article 1, Protocol 1 had been violated by the leasehold enfranchisement legislation which gives certain tenants a right to compulsorily purchase the freehold estate, the European Court observed (at para. 46) that:

> Because of their direct knowledge of their society and its needs, the national authorities are in principle better placed than the international judge to appreciate what is 'in the public interest' ... it is thus for the national authorities to make the initial assessment both of the existence of a problem of public concern warranting measures of deprivation of property and of the remedial action to be taken.

The European Court's statement makes it clear that the margin of appreciation evades both the identification of a problem of public concern and the remedial action taken by the state. These two issues will be examined separately below.

The European Court, in emphasising that the initial responsibility for securing the rights in the Convention rests with the state, has observed that:

> the machinery of protection established by the Convention is subsidiary to the national systems safeguarding human rights. The Convention leaves to each Contracting State, in the first place, the task of securing the rights and freedoms it enshrines (*Handyside* v *UK*, at para. 48).

However, the states do not enjoy unlimited discretion. The European Court has stressed that 'the domestic margin of appreciation thus goes hand in hand with a European supervision' (*Handyside* v *UK*, at para. 49). But where there are a number of options by which a state can comply with its obligations under the Convention, it is not for the Strasbourg institutions to substitute their own preferred option. In *Mellacher* v *Austria* (1989) 12 EHRR 391, the European Court stated (at para. 53) that:

> The possible existence of alternative solutions does not in itself render the contested legislation unjustified. Provided that the legislature remains within the bounds of its margin of appreciation, it is not for the Court to say whether the legislation represented the best solution for dealing with the problem or whether the legislative discretion should have been exercised in another way.

The role of the Strasbourg institutions is accordingly confined to ensuring that the states do not exceed the boundaries of permissible action, but within those boundaries a state has an element of discretion and freedom to act as it chooses.

2.2.2 The existence of a problem of public concern

James v *UK* illustrates the extent to which the margin of appreciation doctrine evades the question of whether the offending legislation pursues a legitimate aim (see 2.4). The European Court stated (at para. 47) that:

> The margin of appreciation is wide enough to cover legislation aimed at securing greater social justice in the sphere of people's homes, even where such legislation interferes with existing contractual relations between private parties and confers no direct benefit on the State or the community at large.

Although the European Court was satisfied that the margin of appreciation was wide enough to cover the leasehold reform legislation at issue, it did not attempt to identify the limits of the state's discretion. Since the offending legislation sought to eliminate social injustice in the housing sector, the European Court was satisfied that it pursued a legitimate aim which benefited the general community and justified the interference with the landlord's property rights. As to whether or not there was in fact any social injustice that needed rectifying was a question of debate for which there was room for legitimate conflicts of opinion. The applicant landlords contended that long leaseholders did not suffer from any unfairness so that the rights to enfranchise were not required to eliminate any social injustice. The Government felt, however, that the leaseholder had a 'moral entitlement' to ownership of the house which was inadequately protected by the previous legislation. The European Court stated that its role, in ascertaining to what extent a problem of public concern exists which justifies the state's interference, is to apply the test of whether the Government's belief in the existence of the social injustice is not 'manifestly unreasonable'. Such a test clearly gives the states considerable latitude in the identification of a problem of public concern.

2.2.3 The remedial action to be taken

The European Court has stated that it is 'for the national authorities to make the initial assessment both of the existence of a problem of public concern warranting measures of deprivation of property and of the remedial action to be taken' (*James* v *UK*, at para. 46). Whilst generally permitting the states considerable leeway in identifying an initial problem of public concern to justify the action taken, the European Court will generally exercise a more stringent power of review in respect of the remedial measures taken to rectify the problem. Therefore in *Sporrong and Lönnroth* v *Sweden* (see Appendix 3) the European Court stated (at para. 69) that:

> In an area as complex and difficult as that of the development of large cities, the Contracting States should enjoy a wide margin of appreciation in order to implement

their town-planning policy. Nevertheless, the Court cannot fail to exercise its power of review and must determine whether the requisite balance was maintained in a manner consonant with the applicants' right to the 'peaceful enjoyment of [their] possessions', within the meaning of the first sentence of Article 1.

In *Sporrong* the state's interference with the landowners' property rights was held to fall outside the ambit of its margin of appreciation and consequently there was found to be a violation of the Convention (see 4.5).

In contrast, in *Lithgow* v *UK* (see Appendix 3) the European Court noted that nationalisation legislation, by its very nature, involves the consideration of a large number of competing interests which the national authorities are, by reason of their direct knowledge of their society, better placed than an international judge to consider. In *Lithgow* the state was given a wide margin of appreciation in determining the levels of compensation to be paid to owners whose property had been nationalised. The European Court stated that: 'it will respect the legislature's judgment in this connection unless that judgment was manifestly without reasonable foundation'. The test of whether the decision was manifestly without reasonable foundation has overtones of the *Wednesbury* unreasonableness test in judicial review, i.e. is the decision one which no reasonable decision-maker could have reached in the circumstances, and it is a test which makes it very difficult to challenge administrative decisions. Therefore, the scope of the power of review varies with the action taken (see 2.2.4) and the application of the 'manifestly unreasonable' test in *Lithgow* indicates the wide ambit of discretion afforded to the states in the implementation of nationalisation policies.

2.2.4 A variable margin of discretion

The Strasbourg institutions have recognised the 'context dependent' nature of the doctrine which consequently inhibits consistency of approach. Their decisions include a wealth of statements confirming the dependency of the scope of the margin of appreciation upon the facts of the case. For example, the European Court has stated that: 'the scope of the margin of appreciation will vary according to the circumstances, the subject matter and its background' (*Rasmussen* v *Denmark* (1984) 7 EHRR 371 at para. 40) and 'the scope of the margin of appreciation is not identical in each case but will vary according to the context. Relevant factors include the nature of the Convention right in issue, its importance for the individual and the nature of the activities concerned' (*Buckley* v *UK*, at para. 74).

Commentators have remarked upon this variable degree of scrutiny which the European Court exercises under the doctrine, for example, Jones observes that:

The margin of appreciation is thus a doctrine of judicial self-restraint or deference: it governs the extent to which the Court will examine a practice which forms the subject matter of a complaint. If a wide version of the doctrine is applied, then there will be a presumption in favour of the defendant state (based on its assumed ability the better to assess the situation); if narrow, there can be no such presumption and a closer scrutiny will be made.[1]

Although there is no precise guidance on when the European Court will apply a wide as opposed to a narrow version of the margin of appreciation doctrine, a number of factors can be identified as influencing that decision. For example, the European Court has applied a variable standard of review dependent upon which of the Articles is under review. The margin of appreciation is often invoked in cases under Article 1, Protocol 1 but rarely mentioned in Article 6 cases. Similarly, although the margin of appreciation plays an important role in both Article 8 and Article 1, Protocol 1, the cases indicate a differing level of review dependent upon which Article is under consideration. The last paragraph of Article 1, Protocol 1 permits a state to interfere with a person's peaceful enjoyment of his or her possessions in order to 'enforce such laws as it deems necessary to control the use of property in accordance with the general interest'. The state's margin of appreciation is expressly recognised by the words 'such laws as it deems necessary'. Thus it is the state's perception of the necessity for the laws that is relevant. The wording of Article 8 is slightly different. Article 8 prohibits any interference with a person's family life and home 'except such as is in accordance with the law and is necessary in a democratic society'. It is possible that this test imposes greater objectivity, moving away from the idea that the state's perception of the necessity of the situation prevails (see *Handyside* v *UK*, at para. 62). To this end the European Commission of Human Rights (the European Commission) in *Gillow* v *UK* observed (at para. 152) that: 'the requirements of [Article 1, Protocol 1] permit the domestic legislature greater latitude in the choice of legislation which is appropriate for the control of the use of property than under Article 8 of the Convention'. Therefore the Strasbourg institutions have recognised that a more stringent level of review will be adopted under Article 8 compared to the greater latitude given to the states under the third rule of Article 1, Protocol 1 (see 5.5).

An important factor in the application of the doctrine is the presence of economic and social policy decisions. For example, in assessing whether leasehold enfranchisement legislation is Convention compliant, the European Court recognised that the state has a wide margin of appreciation in the housing policy arena. The European Court stated that:

> The decision to enact laws expropriating property will commonly involve consideration of political, economic and social issues on which opinions within a democratic society may reasonably differ widely. The Court, finding it natural that the margin of

---

[1] Jones, T., 'The Devaluation of Human Rights Under the European Convention' [1995] PL 430 at p. 431.

appreciation available to the legislature in implementing social and economic policies should be a wide one, will respect the legislature's judgment as to what is 'in the public interest' unless that judgment be manifestly without reasonable foundation (*James* v *UK*, at para. 46).

Therefore in matters concerning policy decisions, the state is given a wide margin of discretion, which recognises the sensitivity of the Strasbourg authorities to the political, economic and cultural traditions of each state. A similar level of deference is shown in matters concerning tax. In *Gasus Dosier-und Fordertechnik GmbH* v *Netherlands* (see Appendix 3) the European Court observed (at para. 60) that in passing laws that regulate the formalities of taxation:

the legislature must be allowed a wide margin of appreciation, especially with regard to the question whether — and if so, to what extent — the tax authorities should be put in a better position to enforce tax debts than ordinary creditors are in to enforce commercial debts. The Court will respect the legislature's assessment in such matters unless it is devoid of reasonable foundation.

The cases illustrate that there is a variable margin of discretion, so that for example, states generally enjoy a wide margin of appreciation in relation to interferences with property under Article 1, Protocol 1, especially where economic and social policy factors are concerned. The malleability of the concept permits flexibility but also engenders criticism. One commentator has observed that: 'The principal objection to the "margin of appreciation" is that it introduces an unwarranted subjective element into the interpretation of various provisions of the European Convention on Human Rights'.[2]

2.2.5 The application of the margin of appreciation doctrine to the Human Rights Act 1998

The margin of appreciation is an international concept to deal with the social, cultural and geographical barriers that face an international judge having to make decisions on matters of a local nature. The question is whether, and if so to what extent, the English courts will be willing to apply an analogous doctrine so that public authorities are given a similar margin of discretion in exercising their powers. There is considerable debate as to whether or not the international concept of the margin of appreciation can be transposed into the domestic arena. A large number of commentators suggest that the doctrine should not apply in the English courts because there is not the same political, cultural, geographical and historical gap between the local institutions, which make the disputed decisions,

---

[2] Lavender, N., 'The Problem of the Margin of Appreciation' [1997] EHRLR 380.

and the judges presiding in the domestic courts to justify the need for the doctrine. It has been argued that:

> If domestic courts translate the international law concept of the 'margin of appreciation' into domestic law, the judges are likely to fail in their statutory duty which is to decide for themselves whether a public body's decision constitutes a disproportionate infringement of human rights.[3]

Until the courts resolve this uncertainty, caution should be exercised when considering Strasbourg case law where the decision relied heavily upon the margin of appreciation. There may be questions in these cases which the Strasbourg institutions abstained from deciding on the basis that they fell within the state's margin of appreciation but which the English courts must now decide.

In judicial review proceedings, the courts are used to the fact that where policy considerations are concerned public authorities are given a certain amount of latitude in exercising their discretionary powers. A similar approach may be adopted where Convention rights are being considered. In the House of Lords' decision in *R* v *DPP, ex parte Kebilene* [1999] 4 All ER 801 (which predates the implementation of the HRA 1998), Lord Hope rejected the incorporation of the margin of appreciation into domestic law, but introduced the notion of 'the discretionary area of judgment' which his Lordship explained (at p. 884) in the following terms:

> questions of balance between competing interests and issues of proportionality ... [where] ... difficult choices may have to be made by the executive or the legislature between the rights of the individual and the needs of society. In some circumstances it will be appropriate for the courts to recognise that there is an area of judgment within which the judiciary will defer, on democratic grounds, to the considered opinion of the elected body or person whose act or decision is said to be incompatible with the Convention.

Therefore although it seems that the margin of appreciation, as applied by the Strasbourg institutions, will not apply to the English courts applying the HRA 1998, the courts will nevertheless apply an analogous doctrine which will accord a 'discretionary area of judgment' in relation to policy decisions made by the executive, legislature and public authorities, all of which may be better placed than the judiciary to decide matters in the social, economic or political spheres.

2.3 PROPORTIONALITY

The principle of proportionality requires that there be 'a reasonable relationship of proportionality between the means employed and the aim sought to be realised'

---

[3] Wadham, J. and Mountfield, H., *Human Rights Act 1998*, London: Blackstone Press, 1999, p. 18.

(*James* v *UK* at para. 50). In the words of Lord Irvine, 'Excessive means are not to be used to attain permissible objectives'.[4] Therefore in relation to an alleged breach of Article 8, the state's identification of a legitimate aim under Article 8(2), e.g., public safety or the protection of morals, is not sufficient to justify an interference with a person's right to respect for his or her private life and home. There is an additional requirement that the means adopted to secure that aim must not be excessive in the circumstances. No matter how worthy the legitimate aim being pursued, the state cannot interfere with a person's human rights disproportionately. Hart adopts the following metaphor to describe the concept of proportionality: 'a sledgehammer of interference with rights should not be used to crack a nut of social need'.[5] The measures taken by the state must be no more than are necessary to accomplish the legitimate aim to be achieved. In *Sporrong and Lönnroth* v *Sweden* (see Appendix 3), the European Court expressed the principle of proportionality in terms of a 'fair balance' test. It stated (at para. 69) that a fair balance 'must be struck between the demands of the general interest of the community and the requirements of the protection of the individual's fundamental rights'. This fair balance cannot exist where a person has had to bear an individual and excessive burden.

The principle of proportionality is a particularly vital concept for a property lawyer to grasp. The analysis of the Convention case law in chapters 4 and 5 demonstrates that the deciding factor in the majority of cases under Article 1, Protocol 1 and Article 8 is the principle of proportionality and the main cause of a violation of those Articles is a lack of proportionality. For example see the case summaries in Appendix 3 for *Sporrong and Lönnroth* v *Sweden*, *Gillow* v *UK*, *Holy Monasteries* v *Greece* and *Lopez Ostra* v *Spain*.

For the English courts the principle of proportionality may be a useful alternative to the margin of appreciation doctrine in the sense that if the margin of appreciation, being an international concept, is found to have no application to the HRA 1998, the courts can nevertheless rely on the principle of proportionality to enable them to give sufficient deference to the executive where policy choices have to be made. The notion of a 'fair balance' inevitably introduces an element of discretion as to the weighting to be given to the various factors to be weighed in the balance. In reference to the margin of appreciation doctrine, Hooper observes that:

> One may doubt whether the courts will give the measure of appreciation being referred to in [the Strasbourg] jurisprudence to public authorities, because English courts are in the position of being able to evaluate local needs, conditions and moral values. On the

---

[4] Irvine, Lord A., 'The Development of Human Rights in Britain under an Incorporated Convention on Human Rights' [1998] PL 221 at p. 231.
[5] Hart, D., 'The Impact of the European Convention on Human Rights on Planning and Environmental Law' [2000] JPL 117 at p. 120.

other hand, where the public authority has to reconcile competing interests, particularly in areas where the courts do not have the necessary expertise, courts will be more reluctant to interfere, at least if the court can see that the authority has itself properly applied the [proportionality] test.[6]

2.4   LEGITIMATE AIM

'Legitimate aim' is the terminology used to describe a state's justifications and reasons for interfering with a person's rights under the Convention. Article 8(2) provides a specific list of legitimate aims including the interests of national security, public safety, the economic well-being of the country and the protection of morals. In each case the legitimate aim provides a benefit for the general community which is in fact the essence of a legitimate aim. Benefit to others is what legitimises the aim or objective which the state pursues. For example, if a Government took measures which interfered with the property rights of a group of individuals for the purpose of benefiting a Government Minister, the aim of the state interference would not be seen to be a legitimate one. Consequently for an aim to be legitimate it must benefit the general public or a section of the public. This raises subjective considerations as to what constitutes a benefit and how large a section of the public has to benefit from the aim in order for it to be legitimate. In practice these questions have been unproblematic due to the fact that the Strasbourg institutions have generally shown considerable deference to the states in their identification of a legitimate aim. Therefore it is relatively easy for a state to satisfy this requirement and it is rarely the cause of a breach of the Convention (see 4.3.3, 5.3.3 and 6.3).

Article 1, Protocol 1 states that any state interference with a person's property rights must be in the 'public interest' or the 'general interest' (depending upon which rule is being applied, see chapter 4) and these tests incorporate a similar requirement for the state to establish the existence of a legitimate aim to justify the interference. The Commission has observed that any justification falling within the specific aims listed in Article 8(2) will satisfy the wider concept of 'general interest' under Article 1, Protocol 1 (see *Gillow* v *UK* in Appendix 3). Article 14 also incorporates the need for a legitimate aim in the requirement that any differential treatment of persons in an analogous situation must be reasonably and objectively justified (see 6.3).

2.5   THE BROAD, PURPOSIVE APPROACH TO INTERPRETATION

The Strasbourg institutions have adopted a broad, purposive approach to the interpretation of the law to give effect to the purposes of the Convention as set out

---

[6] Hooper, Sir A., 'The Impact of the Human Rights Act on judicial decision-making' [1998] EHRLR 677 at p. 684.

in its preamble. For example in *Golder* v *UK* (1975) 1 EHRR 524 the European Court had to ascertain whether the right of access to a court is an aspect of the rights guaranteed under Article 6(1) even though the Article does not make any express reference to it. In that case the applicant, a prisoner, had been refused permission to consult a solicitor with a view to instituting libel proceedings against one of the prison officers. He alleged that this refusal constituted a violation of Article 6(1). The European Court found in favour of the applicant stating (at para. 36) that:

> the right of access constitutes an element which is inherent in the right stated in Article 6(1). This is not an extensive interpretation forcing new obligations on the Contracting States: it is based on the very terms of the first sentence of Article 6(1) read in its context and having regard to the object and purpose of the Convention, a lawmaking treaty, and to general principles of law.

Therefore the 'object and purpose' of the Convention plays a vital role in the interpretation of its terms. Similarly, in interpreting the Convention rights under the HRA 1998, the English courts will need to adopt this purposive approach.

The court's judgment in the judicial review case of *Britton* v *Secretary of State for the Environment* [1997] JPL 617 illustrates how the purposive approach under the Convention differs from the traditional English law canons of construction. The applicants, who were community dwellers, purchased a site in a Special Landscape Area in order to establish an experimental, sustainable living system. Their application for planning permission was refused on a number of grounds including the policy against residential development in the open countryside. An enforcement notice was served on the applicants requiring the demolition of the dwellings and the restoration of the land to its original condition. The applicants' appeal to the Secretary of State was dismissed and consequently they appealed to the High Court. One issue for decision concerned the status of the Convention in planning law. Although it was acknowledged that generally the Convention could only be deployed for the purpose of resolving an ambiguity in the law (*R* v *Secretary of State for the Home Department, ex parte Brind* [1991] 1 AC 696), the Government had specifically undertaken to take the Convention into account in carrying out its planning functions (see PPG1). Judge Rich held that in order to take the Convention into account, in compliance with PPG1, the Secretary of State was under a duty to determine whether or not there had been a breach of the Convention. The significance of the case for the purposes of understanding the Convention Principles is Judge Rich's recognition of the different approach to interpretation under the Convention jurisprudence as compared to English law and the consequent differing outcomes. Judge Rich stated (at pp. 633–4) that:

> if the Secretary of State adopts as policy the obligation to take the Convention into account, he must apply his own policy in accordance with its meaning at least as

understood by him. This does not mean that the court could itself construe the Convention as if it were part of English law. If it were to do so in accordance with English canons of construction, it is by no means clear to me under which category of interest, set out in Article 8(2), the protection of the countryside would fall. The Strasbourg Court however construes the Article by what I believe is called a purposive construction which has, I understand, led it to weigh such environmental considerations against the rights set out in Article 8(1). That is the kind of construction which, contrary to the usual canons of English law, the Secretary of State would be entitled to apply in taking account of the Convention.

Therefore, whilst the protection of the countryside falls within Article 8(2) if the purposive approach is adopted, Judge Rich considered that this would not be the case if the traditional literal approach were to be used. This illustrates the importance of the English courts adopting a broad, purposive approach, which gives effect to the 'object and purpose' of Convention, in the interpretation of Convention rights under the HRA 1998.

The adoption of a purposive approach to statutory interpretation is not a novel concept to the English courts. Nevertheless, Lord Irvine, whilst recognising the increased use in recent years of the purposive approach to statutory interpretation by the English courts, welcomes the influence of the HRA 1998 in further encouraging the trend away from a literal towards a purposive approach and has predicted that:

as the courts, through familiarity with the Convention jurisprudence, become more exposed to methods of interpretation which pay more heed to the purpose, and less to whether the words were felicitously chosen to achieve that end, the balance is likely to swing more firmly yet in the direction of the purposive approach.[7]

2.6   THE LIVING INSTRUMENT DOCTRINE

The Strasbourg institutions have taken an evolutive and dynamic approach to the interpretation of the Convention. The European Court has stated that it must 'recall that the Convention is a living instrument which . . . must be interpreted in the light of present day conditions' (*Tyrer* v *UK* (1978) 2 EHRR 1 at para. 31). In *Tyrer* the European Court, influenced by the developments and commonly accepted standards in the contracting states, decided that birching, as a form of judicial punishment, was no longer an acceptable practice, and consequently it was found to violate Article 3 which prohibits torture and inhuman treatment.

The case of *Marckx* v *Belgium* (see Appendix 3) further illustrates this evolutive approach. The European Court decided that Belgian maternal affiliation laws that required a mother of an illegitimate child to undergo a procedure in

---

[7] Irvine (n. 4 above) p. 233.

order to be formally recognised as the mother of her child were in violation of Article 8 taken alone and in conjunction with Article 14. The European Court (at para. 41) observed that:

> It is true that, at the time when the Convention of 4 November 1950 was drafted, it was regarded as permissible and normal in many European Countries to draw a distinction in this area between illegitimate and legitimate family. However the Court recalls that this Convention must be interpreted in the light of present day conditions.

Therefore the Strasbourg institutions have recognised the need to 'ensure that the interpretation of the Convention reflects societal changes and remains in line with present day conditions' (*Cossey* v *UK* (1990) 13 EHRR 622). Recognising the rapidity with which society can change its values and composition, Hooper has remarked that: 'appellate decisions made one year may be open to attack only a few years later'.[8] Clearly this has significant implications as to the continuing role of the doctrine of precedent (see 1.5).

2.7 VICTIM STATUS

2.7.1 The meaning of 'victim'

Section 7(1) of the HRA 1998 restricts the persons who can bring proceedings against a public authority for acting unlawfully in contravention of s. 6(1) (see 1.7). Such a person can only commence an action if 'he is (or would be) a victim of the unlawful act'. Under s. 7(7) a person is defined as being a victim only if 'he would be a victim for the purposes of Article 34 of the Convention'. The meaning of 'victim' under Article 34 has been limited by the Strasbourg institutions to persons 'directly affected' by the act or omission of the State. *Tauira* v *France* (App. No. 28204/95) illustrates the boundaries of the term 'victim' within the jurisprudence of the Convention. The case concerned an application by a number of residents of Tahiti that their rights under the Convention would be violated by proposed nuclear tests to be carried out by France. The European Commission found their application to be inadmissible on the basis that they were not victims. They lived over 1,000 km from the proposed test site and had not been able to provide convincing evidence that any future nuclear tests would affect them personally and directly.

Given that s. 7 incorporates the same victim test into the HRA 1998, only persons who are 'directly affected' by an unlawful act of a public authority will have sufficient standing to challenge the act as being in breach of their human rights. In addition, if the proceedings are brought on an application for judicial

---

[8] Hooper (n. 6 above) p. 683.

review, s. 7(3) provides that: 'the applicant is to be taken to have sufficient interest in relation to the unlawful act only if he is, or would be, a victim of that act'. This displaces the English courts' existing interpretation of the 'sufficient interest' test in judicial review cases (see 2.7.2).

The inclusion of the wording, 'or would be a victim', in s. 7(1) of the HRA 1998, permits pre-emptive strikes by potential victims. In fact, persons who are potential victims of offending measures have sufficient victim status under the Convention in any event as illustrated by the case of *Marckx v Belgium* (see Appendix 3). The case concerned a challenge to inheritance laws which discriminated against illegitimate children. One of the applicants, who was an illegitimate child, was found by the European Court to be a victim even though her mother was living and therefore the child was not in a position to inherit property from her.

The Strasbourg institutions have also, on occasions, acknowledged the existence of an indirect victim. An indirect victim has been defined as:

> a person who can show that there was a special personal connection between himself and the direct victim and that the violation of the Convention has caused him harm, or that he had a justified personal interest that the violation should cease.[9]

Therefore a spouse or close relative or personal representative of the victim may, as an indirect victim, commence action if the victim is dead or is otherwise unable to initiate proceedings.

2.7.2 Victim status and non-governmental organisations

The current position under judicial review proceedings is that the 'sufficient interest' test is flexible enough to permit challenges to decisions to be brought by non-governmental organisations (NGOs) such as Greenpeace (see *R v Secretary of State for the Environment, ex parte Greenpeace* [1994] Env LR 76). This contrasts with *Greenpeace Schweiz v Switzerland and Others* (1997) 23 EHRR CD 116 in which the European Commission found that proceedings to licence the operation of a nuclear power plant did not involve the determination of the civil rights of Greenpeace. The applicants, which included individuals as well as environmental organisations, alleged a breach of Article 6(1) due to a lack of access to a court. The twelve individual applicants, who lived in the Emergency Zone 1 which surrounded the nuclear plant, were able to establish victim status and their complaints were held to be admissible. However, the European Commission stated that the environmental organisations, including Greenpeace 'have not shown that they were sufficiently affected in their "civil" rights so as to

---

[9] Delvaux, 'The notion of victim under Article 25 of the ECHR', *Fifth International Colloquy on the European Covention on Human Rights*, C. F. Müller, Juristischer Verlag, 1982.

imply a genuine and serious dispute in respect of their property rights'. Therefore Greenpeace was found to lack victim status and its complaint was consequently inadmissible.

The need to establish victim status under the HRA 1998, as a prerequisite to commencing an action under s. 7, means that NGOs will rarely have sufficient standing. An interest group, such as Greenpeace, may be a victim itself in which case it would have sufficient standing, for example if a public authority expropriated property belonging to Greenpeace. However, it will have no standing to bring representative actions. The existing interpretation of 'sufficient interest' in judicial review cases, which encompasses organisations such as Greenpeace, will continue to apply to cases falling outside the ambit of s. 7 (see s. 11 which safeguards existing proceedings).

The fact that there are different types of interest groups has greater relevancy under the HRA 1998. This is because some groups, such as HACAN/Clearskies (Heathrow Association for the Control of Aircraft Noise), which is an association of interested individuals, are likely to be able to identify persons within their membership who are victims. It is therefore possible for them to bring an action as a group of individual victims, for example, see *Hatton and others* v *UK* (App. No. 36022/97). Other types of groups, the purely 'representative' groups, for example Amnesty International, will have difficulty in satisfying the victim test unless they can find a victim who is able to front the action for them. There are undoubtedly cases where this distinction between these two types of groups is blurred and where it is therefore difficult to say with any certainty whether the group has sufficient standing as a victim. For example, it is arguable that an expert environmental group such as Greenpeace is not a representative group but is in fact an association of interested individuals because all of its members are affected by decisions concerning the environment. In which case it is arguable that its members ought to have sufficient standing as a victim to bring an action in cases involving environmental pollution.

2.7.3 Victim status and interference with company property

Where there has been an interference with property belonging to a company, the question arises whether the shareholders can claim to be an indirect victim of that interference. The cases indicate that this will be permissible only in very limited circumstances. The essence of the decision by the European Commission in *X* v *Austria* (App. No. 1706/62) was that where a shareholder owned a substantial proportion of the shares (in that case the applicant owned 91 per cent), he may be considered a victim having sufficient standing to complain of an interference with the company's property. The case of *Yarrow plc and three shareholders* v *UK* (1983) 5 EHRR 498 provided the criteria for establishing whether a shareholder owns a 'substantial proportion' of the shares. The case concerned the nationalisation of a subsidiary company, Yarrow Shipbuilders. Shareholders in the parent company claimed an infringement of their property rights as a result of the nationalisation. The European Commission decided that one of the applicants, Yarrow plc, could claim to be a victim because it held a majority interest in Yarrow Shipbuilders. However, the other applicants could not claim to have victim status because they did not hold a majority or controlling interest in the nationalised company.

More recently, however, the European Court, in *Agrotexim and others* v *Greece* (1996) 21 EHRR 250, rejected the approach of the European Commission which had found a majority shareholder to be a victim of measures affecting the company. The case concerned measures taken by the Athens Council with a view to expropriating land belonging to a brewery. The applicant companies were shareholders in the brewery, holding just over 50 per cent of its shares. The applicants alleged that the measures taken by the Council violated their rights under Article 1, Protocol 1. The question for the European Court was whether the applicants had sufficient status as victims to pursue their claim against the state. The applicants claimed to be victims, albeit indirectly, of the state's interference with the brewery's property rights because their own financial interests had been adversely affected as a result of a fall in the value of their shares. However, the European Court did not share the applicants' perception of the situation. It stated (at para. 66) that:

> the piercing of the 'corporate veil' or the disregarding of the company's separate legal personality will be justified only in exceptional circumstances, in particular where it is established that it is impossible for the company to apply to the Convention institutions through the organs set up under its articles of incorporation or — in the event of liquidation — through its liquidator.

As there were no exceptional circumstances, on the facts, justifying piercing the corporate veil, the applicants were found to lack victim status and in consequence were not entitled to apply to the Convention institutions. This case illustrates the European Court's general reluctance to allow shareholders to claim victim status in instances where the company's property has been the subject of state interference.

2.8   CONCLUSION

Given that the Strasbourg case law is important in the interpretation and application of the Convention rights under the HRA 1998, the English courts need to appreciate the Convention jurisprudence underlying those decisions. The margin of appreciation doctrine, which gives states an element of discretion, has proved especially influential in decisions concerning alleged violations of Article

1, Protocol 1. Whilst the margin of appreciation doctrine, as an international concept, has no direct application in the English courts, an analogous concept of a 'discretionary area of judgment' is likely to apply. The principle of proportionality is a vital concept which is likely, in most property-related cases, to be the deciding factor in determining whether or not there has been an infringement of the Convention rights under the HRA 1998. The courts must ensure that the means employed by the state to attain its specified objective are not disproportionate to that aim. In pursuit of ascertaining proportionality, the courts must undertake a process of weighing various competing factors in the balance, for example the interests of the general community in protecting its economy, its environment or the safety and welfare of its members as against the interests of those individual property owners subjected to state interference. Although the interests of individual property owners cannot be allowed to prevail to the detriment of the community as a whole, the individual property owner cannot be expected to suffer an excessive burden in the interests of others. Evidently the principle of proportionality will entail an element of subjectivity and the courts may face difficult choices as to the different weightings to be given to the various competing factors.

In the interpretation of Convention rights, the English courts will need to adopt the same broad and purposive approach used by the Strasbourg institutions to interpret the scope and meaning of the Convention. In addition, the English courts must utilise the living instrument doctrine to ensure that their decisions reflect the changing needs and attitudes of society.

Chapter Three

The Application of the Human Rights Act 1998 in the Private Sphere

3.1 HORIZONTAL AND VERTICAL EFFECT

An area of considerable debate concerns the extent to which, if at all, the Human Rights Act (HRA) 1998 governs relations between private individuals, the so-called 'horizontal effect' of the HRA 1998. Whilst one line of argument maintains that the HRA 1998 has horizontal effect and therefore applies to disputes between private individuals, the opposing view is that it is limited to having a 'vertical effect', meaning that it only applies to relations between the state and individuals so that an action can only be brought against the state.

In Ireland the Irish Constitution has direct horizontal effect which allows an individual to bring an action against another private individual by directly utilising his or her constitutional rights as the source of the claim (the case of *Lovett* v *Gogan* [1995] ILRM 12 illustrates this). This is in marked contrast to the constitutional law position of the USA which requires the existence of 'state action' as a prerequisite to invoking the protection of the Bill of Rights.[1]

3.2 THE EUROPEAN CONVENTION ON HUMAN RIGHTS

3.2.1 State responsibility

The European Convention on Human Rights (the Convention) was drafted to apply to acts of state authorities. For example, the European Court of Human

---

[1] For a comparison of the position in Ireland and the USA see Butler, A.S., 'Constitutional Rights in Private Litigation: A Critique and Comparative Analysis' (1993) 22 Anglo-American LR 1.

Rights (the European Court) has stated the object of Article 8 to be the protection of individuals against arbitrary interference by public authorities (*Marckx* v *Belgium*, at para. 31). The wording of Article 8(2), which justifies interferences with a person's right to respect for his or her home, in the interests of public safety and the economic well-being of the country, is inappropriate language in relation to interferences by private individuals. The wording of the Convention is geared to the fact that its application is limited to state action.

The decision of the European Commission of Human Rights (the European Commission) in *App. No. 11949/86* v *UK* (see Appendix 3) provides a clear example of the lack of direct horizontal effect of the Convention. This case concerned the forfeiture of a long lease by a landlord on the ground that the tenant had failed to pay the service charge by way of additional rent. The tenant alleged that by forfeiting the lease, the landlord had deprived her of her property and infringed Article 1, Protocol 1. The landlord's exercise of his remedy of forfeiture was a direct result of the presence of a forfeiture clause in the lease. Therefore the forfeiture of the lease, and hence the consequent deprivation of property, was occasioned by the contractual provisions of the lease as agreed between the landlord and the tenant. The forfeiture clause in the lease was neither directly prescribed nor amended by any legislation. On this basis the European Commission concluded that:

> In view of the exclusively private law relationship between the parties to the lease the Commission considers that the respondent Government cannot be responsible by the mere fact that the landlord by its agents, who were private individuals, brought the applicant's lease to an end in accordance with the terms of that lease, which set out the agreement between the applicant and the company.

Nor was the fact that the landlord had issued possession proceedings in the county court and obtained an order to forfeit the lease, sufficient to bring in the requisite element of state responsibility. The European Commission noted that:

> This fact alone is not however sufficient to engage State responsibility in respect of the applicant's rights to property, since the public authority in the shape of the County Court merely provided a forum for the determination of the civil right in dispute between the parties.

The lack of any state responsibility meant that the European Commission found the applicant's complaint to be manifestly ill-founded and rejected it as inadmissible.

Working on the premise that the content of the Convention rights in the HRA 1998 is the same as the content of the relevant Articles in the Convention, Buxton LJ concludes that the HRA 1998 will not be applicable in disputes between private individuals. His reasoning is based on the fact that the rights under the Convention are limited to rights against states, or emanations of the state (as illustrated by *App. No. 11949/86* v *UK*) and therefore these same restrictions will have been incorporated into the Convention rights under the HRA 1998. Buxton LJ argues that: 'Even, therefore, if the HRA 1998 did purport to create such rights against private citizens, it would simply beat the air: because the content of those rights does not impose obligations on private citizens'.[2]

3.2.2   The states' positive obligations

Although the Convention does not have direct horizontal effect between individuals, there are nevertheless ways in which it can affect relations between private individuals. One such area is where certain Articles have been found to impose positive obligations on the states. The Strasbourg institutions have recognised that Article 8 can impose positive obligations upon the state to take action to protect an individual's right to respect for family and private life and home against interferences by other private parties (see 5.2.1). The European Court has acknowledged that Article 8 imposes obligations on the states which involve: 'the adoption of measures designed to secure respect for private life *even in the sphere of the relations of individuals between themselves*' (*X and Y* v *Netherlands* (1985) 8 EHRR 235 at para. 23 (emphasis supplied)). This is not an example of direct horizontal effect because one individual cannot bring an action against another in respect of the state's failure to provide effective protection. In this context Buxton LJ has observed that: 'the ECHR invades the sphere of relations between two individuals, but it does so by requiring the state, as the object of Article 8, to conform its laws to the obligations imposed on it by that Article'.[3] Thus the state is held accountable for its failure to remedy private abuses and violations by taking positive steps to legislate or carry out other preventative action.

The position under the Convention contrasts with that under the US Bill of Rights. In *De Shaney* v *Winnebago County DSS* (1989) 109 Sup Ct 998, the Supreme Court stated that the Fourteenth Amendment (see 3.3.4) does not impose any positive obligations on the state to protect individuals from each other. In that case the DSS failed to intervene to protect a four-year-old boy from his violent father with whom he was living. The Supreme Court stated (at para. 2–5) that:

> But nothing in the language of the Due Process Clause itself requires the State to protect the life, liberty and property of its citizens against invasion by private actors. The Clause is phrased as a limitation on the State's power to act, not as a guarantee of certain minimal levels of safety and security.

---

[2] Buxton, Lord Justice R., 'The Human Rights Act and Private Law' (2000) 116 LQR 48 at p. 56.
[3] Ibid., p. 53.

This approach is somewhat different from that adopted by the Strasbourg institutions. Their interpretation of certain of the Articles, e.g., Article 8, has led to the imposition of positive obligations upon the contracting states which has thereby enabled the Convention to affect relations between private individuals indirectly.

3.3 THE HUMAN RIGHTS ACT 1998

The concept of state responsibility and the positive obligations of the state under the Convention will be incorporated into Convention rights under the HRA 1998. To this extent it is arguable that the horizontal effect of the HRA 1998 will be restricted in the private sphere in the same way that the Convention is. However, it is possible that the provisions of the HRA 1998, particularly ss. 3 and 6, take the scope of the Act further into the private sphere than that of the Convention. Reliance upon ss. 3 and 6, to determine the reach of the HRA 1998, necessitates drawing a distinction between statutory provisions and the common law.

3.3.1 Statutory provisions

There may be an element of indirect horizontal effect in private litigation where one party seeks to rely on statutory provisions to support his case but the other challenges the statute's compatibility with Convention rights under the HRA 1998. For example, if a private landlord levies distress for rent and seizes and impounds goods that belong to a third party and subsequently sells these goods relying on the power of sale granted to him by the Distress for Rent Act 1689, the third party owner may seek to claim that the landlord has acted in violation of Article 1, Protocol 1 and Article 6. Clearly this dispute falls within the private sphere involving two private parties, but because it involves reliance upon statutory powers given to a private individual by the state, Convention rights may be applicable. The English courts are required by s. 3 of the HRA 1998 to interpret legislation in a way that is compatible with Convention rights (see 1.5). By this means, relations between private individuals may be indirectly affected by the Convention rights due to the courts' interpretation of the statutory provisions which govern those relations.

3.3.2 The common law

The main area where the horizontal effect of the HRA 1998 raises considerable debate is in the context of a dispute between private individuals which requires the court to apply and interpret the common law. This raises two issues:

(a) Does the grant of a court order, in the determination of matters governed by the common law (e.g., a possession order to remove squatters trespassing upon land), satisfy the element of state responsibility? If the granting of a court order were held to be sufficient to satisfy the element of state intervention, all litigation between private individuals would become subject to the HRA 1998. It is extremely unlikely that the granting of court orders in private law disputes will be sufficient to invoke State responsibility (see *App. No. 11949/86* v *UK* in Appendix 3).

(b) Does the court, as a public authority, under s. 6 of the HRA 1998 have a duty to interpret the common law in such a way as to ensure its compatibility with Convention rights? There is certainly a very persuasive argument that the effect of s. 6, in expressly defining the courts as public authorities, imposes upon all courts a duty to decide private disputes, governed by the common law, in a way that is compatible with Convention rights. Therefore in exercising its duty under s. 6(1) to act compatibly with Convention rights a court may be required to modify or develop the common law (see the example at 3.3.3). The dissenting opinion of Lord Cooke in the House of Lords' decision in *Hunter* v *Canary Wharf* [1997] 2 All ER 426 illustrates how s. 6 could affect the development of the common law. Lord Cooke relied upon the protection afforded by Article 8 to support an extension of the common law to enable licensees, with no proprietary interest in property, to bring an action in private nuisance. The case predates the implementation of the HRA 1998 and consequently the Convention had little influence in the decision. However s. 6 of the HRA 1998 may impose a duty on the courts to follow Lord Cooke's example. This approach undoubtedly raises the question as to the extent of judicial activism in the development of the common law. It is not suggested that the HRA 1998 empowers judges to go beyond the boundaries of their existing function as a law-maker; however, as Hunt observes: 'Precisely where the line is drawn between legitimate judicial development of the common law and illegitimate judicial 'legislation' is a matter of degree and, ultimately, a matter of legal and political philosophy'.[4]

3.3.3   An example of the effect of s. 6 on the common law

Hunt provides a fictional scenario in which to analyse the possible approach of the English courts when faced with the question of the applicability of the Convention rights to the common law. The scenario is as follows: an all-male golf club excludes women from its facilities. A number of women enter the club house and are physically ejected. If the ejected women bring a claim against the club for assault, the club will raise a defence of lawful ejection relying upon the common law of trespass to land. In this scenario the HRA 1998 would not confer on the

---

[4] Hunt, M., 'The "Horizontal Effect" of the Human Rights Act' [1998] PL 423 at p. 441.

women a new cause of action against the club in respect of violations of Articles 11 (freedom of assembly and association) and 14 (prohibition of discrimination). However, it is suggested that the court would not be able to accede to the club's defence because to do so would infringe each woman's right to freedom of assembly without discrimination under Articles 11 and 14.[5] This example demonstrates that whilst Convention rights can be used by the women as a shield to resist a claim of trespass to land, the rights cannot be used as a sword enabling them to strike against the club by asserting a new claim reliant upon a breach of their Convention rights.

In contrast to Hunt's analysis, Buxton LJ maintains that s. 6 will have very little practical effect on the common law and he uses Hunt's example to illustrate his view. On those hypothetical facts he argues that it would not be enough for it to be 'merely arguable' that the golf club's reliance on its property rights, as a defence to the women's claim of assault, would involve a breach of Articles 11 and 14. Instead the court would have to be certain that the Convention jurisprudence prohibits the domestic court from granting the relief that it would otherwise provide under the domestic law. Buxton LJ suggests that:

> Bearing in mind the high level of conformity that already exists between the requirements of the Convention and the principles of the common law, it is likely to be only very rarely that a court will feel able to reach that conclusion in the absence of guidance from the Strasbourg Court on the specific facts of the case or on facts very close to it.[6]

3.3.4   A comparative analysis of the US Supreme Court's approach under the Bill of Rights

What approach would an English court adopt if it had to determine whether to permit a private party to enforce a restrictive covenant against another private party, in circumstances where to allow the enforcement would be incompatible with the Convention rights? Such a scenario raises the direct question as to whether the court is under an obligation under s. 6 of the HRA 1998 to deny the claimant a remedy if the grant of the remedy would infringe Convention rights. This was the very question that faced the US Supreme Court in a number of cases arising under the Fourteenth Amendment. The Fourteenth Amendment, which provides that no 'State shall deprive any person of life, liberty or property without due process of law; nor deny to any person within its jurisdiction the equal protection of the laws', can only be invoked in respect of state action. In the early 1900s a practice developed in a number of the Southern states of segregating neighbourhoods into racial groups by the use of restrictive covenants which

---

[5] Ibid., p. 442.
[6] Buxton (n. 2 above) p. 61.

prohibited a sale to, or occupancy by, any person who was not white. Loveland notes that this practice was initially accepted by the Supreme Court as being outside the scope of the Fourteenth Amendment due to the lack of state action.[7] He cites the case of *Corrigan* v *Buckley* (1926) 271 US 323 to illustrate this approach. In this case the court confirmed that the Fourteenth Amendment does not: 'in any manner prohibit or invalidate contracts entered into by private individuals in respect to the control and disposition of their own property'. Therefore the private nature of the restrictive covenant prohibiting a sale of property to non-whites, excluded the necessary element of state action needed to invoke the Fourteenth Amendment and the mere enforcement of that private right by the courts was not sufficient to constitute state action.

By 1948, however, the Supreme Court, in *Shelley* v *Kramer* (1948) 343 US 1, accepted that, in the application of the common law, the state courts constitute a part of the state. In that case, Shelley, who was black, purchased a house unaware that it was subject to a restrictive covenant forbidding the sale of the house to a black person. Kramer, a neighbour, sought to enforce the covenant in order to invalidate the sale of the house to Shelley. The Supreme Court recognised the role of the state in the exclusion of Shelley from his home. Although the restrictive covenant was not in itself found to be unconstitutional (it was too deeply embedded in the realm of private law for that to occur), the enforcement of the covenant was nevertheless seen by the Supreme Court to depend upon 'the active intervention of the state courts, supported by the full panoply of state power'. Therefore the court intervention in the enforcement of the covenant, supported by the availability of assistance by the state law enforcers such as the police, was found to be sufficient state action to invoke the Fourteenth Amendment. Since the enforcement of the covenant contravened the Fourteenth Amendment, the Supreme Court held the covenant to be unenforceable. Loveland suggests that:

> In broad analytical terms, Shelley offers a helpful guide to UK courts' response to s. 6, in so far as it offers compelling authority for the categorisation of all common law rules, irrespective of the identities of the parties contesting them, as part of the apparatus of government. Nonetheless, the case provides only a partial solution to the problem caused by private individuals'/organisations' infringement of covenant rights. The Shelley principle operates only as a negative restraint on court action by forcing it to withhold previously available remedies, not as a positive requirement to fashion new remedies.[8]

This analysis provides further support for Hunt's suggestion as to the effect of s. 6 upon the development of the common law, as well as indicating a possible approach for English courts faced with a similar problem.

---

[7] Loveland, I., 'The horizontal direct effect of the Human Rights Act' (2000) NLJ 1595.
[8] Ibid., p. 1596.

The enforcement of freehold covenants has been used in the UK to impede the use of ordinary housing for community care initiatives.[9] For example, in *C & G Homes Ltd* v *Secretary of State for Health* [1991] Ch 365 the Court of Appeal had to construe the meaning of a covenant which prohibited the use of the property other than as a 'private dwelling house', in order to ascertain whether the covenant could be used by a neighbouring landowner to prevent the local health authority from using two houses to provide supervised housing for a group of former residents of a mental hospital who were to be cared for in the community. Adopting the orthodox canons of construction, the Court of Appeal placed considerable weight upon the word 'private' and concluded that the freehold covenant prohibited the use of the houses as supervised housing. The continuing statutory responsibility of the Secretary of State for Health, towards supporting the former residents of the mental hospital, instilled the proposed use with a 'public' character which contravened the requirement that the use be of a 'private' nature. Nourse LJ conceded (at p. 385) that 'it might be possible to say that [the Secretary of State] is using the houses as dwelling houses. But I cannot agree that he is using them as "private" dwelling houses'. Consequently the inclusion of the single word 'private' was crucial to the Court of Appeal's decision.

In *C & G Homes Ltd* the enforcement of the covenant was against a public authority and therefore if an identical case were to come before the courts now, the HRA 1998 would be applicable regardless of any question of its horizontal effect. Nevertheless, this case is illustrative of this issue because a similar case could arise in which a private party seeks to enforce a freehold covenant against another private party. If, for example, there were four persons, with severe learning difficulties, residing in a group home and a neighbour sought to evict them by enforcing a freehold covenant, prohibiting use other than as a private dwelling house, against the private landowner, the occupants might be able to allege a violation of their right to respect for their home under Article 8. It is unlikely that the English courts would refuse to consider the Article 8 issues on the basis that the dispute is between private parties. Given that the enforcement of the covenant would lead to the occupants' eviction, which may be in breach of Article 8 (see 5.3), the court could take the view that, by virtue of its duty under s. 6, it cannot enforce the freehold covenant.

3.3.5   Conclusion

It is most probable that, unlike the Irish Constitution, the HRA 1998 is not directly horizontally effective. It does not confer on individuals any new private causes of action to be invoked against other individuals in respect of a breach of any of the

---

[9] See Edmunds, R. and Sutton, T., 'Who's afraid of the neighbours?' in Cooke, E. (ed), *Modern Studies in Property Law, Volume I: Property 2000*, Oxford: Hart Publishing, 2001.

Convention rights. However the Act will play a role in the development of existing causes of action between individuals to bring them in line with Convention rights. Hunt concludes that:

> Law which already exists and governs private relationships must be interpreted, applied and if necessary developed so as to achieve compatibility with the Convention. But where no cause of action exists, and there is therefore no law to apply, the courts cannot invent new causes of action, as that would be to embrace full horizontality which has clearly been precluded by Parliament.[10]

To conclude with an example, suppose that A complains of excessive noise or polluting fumes emanating from neighbouring land belonging to B, A cannot bring an action against B claiming a violation of his right to respect for his home and private life under Article 8. Instead A has two options: either he can commence proceedings in private nuisance and use his Convention rights to support his claim or he can bring an action, under s. 6, against the appropriate public authority for its failure to take positive action to prevent A's Convention rights from being violated by B's actions (see 8.8).

3.4   THE APPLICATION OF THE HUMAN RIGHTS ACT 1998 TO THE LANDLORD REMEDIES OF DISTRESS FOR RENT AND FORFEITURE

3.4.1   Where the landlord is a private landlord

If the English courts adopt the same approach as the European Commission in *App. No. 11949/86* v *UK*, it is possible that whilst the HRA 1998 will not apply to the forfeiture of a lease by a private landlord, it will apply where the same landlord uses the remedy of distress for rent in respect of rent arrears (see 8.3.6 and 8.3.7). The remedy of forfeiture is not automatically implied into all leases, instead the lease must expressly provide for it by the inclusion of an express re-entry clause. Therefore the landlord's right to forfeit a lease for a breach of covenant by the tenant is based in contract and arises out of the contractual relationship between the parties. This was the reason why in *App. No. 11949/86* v *UK* the applicant failed in her attempt to claim that her fundamental rights under the Convention had been violated by the landlord's forfeiture of her lease. The European Commission decided that the case fell purely within the realm of private relations between individuals. The fact that the landlord sought and obtained a court order to implement his right of forfeiture was not sufficient to invoke state responsibility.

---

[10] Hunt (n. 4 above), p. 442.

However, it is arguable that if the facts involve the remedy of distress for rent instead of forfeiture of the lease the invocation of state responsibility could be established. The crucial distinction between the two remedies, in this respect, is that whilst the availability of forfeiture lies in contract, the remedy of distress for rent arises automatically under the law by virtue of the fact that rent arrears have arisen. It is available to a landlord even though the lease makes no specific provision for it. The availability of the remedy, therefore, lies not in the contract between the parties but in common law and statute. This remedy does, therefore, attract state responsibility because it arises from the state's law even where the perpetrator of the disputed act is a private landlord.

It is, however, possible for the English courts to adopt a horizontalist approach which cuts through this distinction between forfeiture and distress for rent. The theoretical approach of the horizontalist identifies all legal rules as being the construct of the state and therefore those legal rules that govern and regulate private relations between individuals arise from the state, providing an inextricable link between the state and the private sphere. In analysing the theoretical underpinnings of the horizontal approach, Hunt explains that:

> The state is not only present in the enforcement of all law, it is present at the earlier stage of law's construction and evolution, even where that law is common law, and such law governs relations between individuals as well as relations between the individual and the state. Concentrations of private power are ultimately as dependent on the law, and therefore the state, for preserving that power in its 'private' relations with others, whether by enforcing its contracts, protecting its property, or imposing obligations on others not to cause harm to its interests.[11]

On this basis it is artificial to distinguish between, on the one hand, the tenant whose goods have been distrained upon and who can rely on human rights protection because the landlord's remedy of distress comes from statute and the common law, and on the other hand, the tenant who has no human rights protection because the forfeiture of his lease arises from the contractual relationship between two private parties. According to the horizontalist the relations between the landlord and tenant, although expressly provided for in the lease, are ultimately constituted by the state which constructed contract law in the first place.

At the other end of the spectrum the verticalist approach rests on the premise that a rigid distinction exists between the public and private sphere. The human rights protection preserves the sanctity of private relations between individuals from interference by the state. To permit any horizontal effect would be to undermine the personal autonomy of individuals by interfering with their freedom of choice. From this point of view it is important to preserve the landlord and

---

[11] Ibid., p. 425.

tenant's freedom of contract in providing for the availability of forfeiture and consequently a verticalist would argue that the use of this remedy should be outside the realm of human rights protection.

3.4.2   Where the landlord is a public authority

It may be that an anomaly will exist so that, in some circumstances, a tenant whose landlord is a public authority can assert the protection of Convention rights, whilst a tenant of a private landlord may be prevented from doing so. This anomaly springs from s. 6(1) of the HRA 1998 which provides that it is unlawful for a public authority to act in a way which is incompatible with a Convention right. Therefore any forfeiture proceedings involving a local authority landlord will be subject to s. 6 even though the right to forfeit arises in contract. If the English courts follow the decision in *App. No. 11949/86* v *UK*, so that the HRA 1998 does not apply to the forfeiture of a lease by a private landlord, the deciding factor governing the application of Convention rights to a case involving forfeiture will be the identity of the landlord, i.e. whether the landlord is a private or public body. In practice it may be very difficult to disentangle the private from the public sphere and to do so may leave a lacuna in the protection of human rights. If the landlord is found to be a pure public authority, it must not act in a way that violates the tenant's Convention rights; however a private landlord is not within the scope of s. 6(1). A quasi-public body will only be subject to s. 6(1) in carrying out its public functions. This may exclude its relations with a tenant because these are generally considered to be in the sphere of private law (see 1.7.2). The need to satisfy the court that the landlord is a public authority may lead to some difficult decisions as to the nature and functions of various organisations.

3.5   THE APPLICATION OF THE HUMAN RIGHTS ACT 1998 IN THE PRIVATE SPHERE

3.5.1   The problem of competing Convention rights

If Convention rights are held to have horizontal effect and to apply in proceedings between private individuals, there may be a problem of competing Convention rights. Each party to a dispute may seek to rely on their Convention rights as against the other party and this may raise complex questions as to which one prevails. For example, disgruntled mortgagors may claim that onerous mortgage conditions are a violation of their Convention rights but if the court seeks to amend them the mortgagee may argue that any alteration of the conditions would violate its Convention rights. Similarly, persons relying on their right to information under Article 10 may find that others are relying upon their right to respect for their private life and home under Article 8.

The Strasbourg institutions have some experience of weighing the competing rights of private individuals. For example, in one case a husband sought an injunction to prevent his wife from having an abortion. His claim under Article 8 that his right to respect for his family life had been violated was, however, found by the European Commission to be limited under Article 8(2) by his wife's right to respect for her private life (*App. No. 8416/79* v *UK*). This case illustrates the difficulties which could face the English courts and demonstrates how ultimately it may result in the courts having to make controversial policy decisions as to which of two competing Convention rights has a greater significance and is more deserving of protection.

3.5.2   The inapplicability of the Human Rights Act 1998 to private, domestic life

The HRA 1998 does not apply to private, domestic life. The Act respects the principle of freedom to order one's private life as one chooses. In domestic life one may treat one person less favourably than another however unreasonable or discriminatory that differential treatment may be. For example, if an elderly father orally agrees to give his daughter the farm where she lives alone with him but later decides to give it to his younger son on the basis that, in his opinion, a woman cannot run a farm, the father is not in violation of Article 1, Protocol 1 nor Article 8 either taken alone or in conjunction with Article 14. These facts fall solely within the realms of private, domestic life and therefore the daughter could not bring a direct action against her father for a violation of her Convention rights.

Chapter Four

Article 1, Protocol 1

Every natural or legal person is entitled to the peaceful enjoyment of his possessions. No one shall be deprived of his possessions except in the public interest and subject to the conditions provided for by law and by the general principles of international law.

The preceding provisions shall not, however, in any way impair the right of a State to enforce such laws as it deems necessary to control the use of property in accordance with the general interest or to secure the payment of taxes or other contributions or penalties.

4.1 A GUARANTEE FOR THE RIGHT OF PROPERTY

The essence of Article 1, Protocol 1 is that it provides a guarantee for the right of property.

The European Court of Human Rights (the European Court) has described this objective in the following terms:

> By recognising that everyone has the right to the peaceful enjoyment of his possessions, Article 1 is in substance guaranteeing the right of property. This is the clear impression left by the words 'possessions' and 'use of property' (in French: *biens, propriété, usage des biens*); the *travaux préparatoires*, for their part, confirm this unequivocally: the drafters continually spoke of 'right of property' or 'right to property' to describe the subject matter of the successive drafts which were the forerunners of the present Article 1 (*Marckx v Belgium*, at para. 63).

It provides both a positive guarantee to the peaceful enjoyment of possessions but also a negative guarantee that no one shall be deprived of their possessions by the state except in certain circumstances. These guarantees only protect existing property rights and do not give a person a right to property which he or she does not already own. Nor does the guarantee for the right of property require the state to take measures to ensure that privately owned property is protected from a reduction in its value, for example, Article 1, Protocol 1 does not safeguard savings accounts by protecting them from a loss of value due to market forces (*X* v *Federal Republic of Germany* (App. No. 8724/79)). However, the guarantee does protect the 'peaceful enjoyment' of possessions which embraces the right to own, possess, use, lend or dispose of the property as one so desires without interference by the state. This is clearly a valuable protection for all property owners. However, it will be apparent later that the broad terms of the guarantee are subject to a number of significant limitations and exceptions that dilute the strength of the guarantee.

4.2 THE THREE DISTINCT RULES

In *Sporrong and Lönnroth* v *Sweden* (see Appendix 3) the European Court analysed the meaning and scope of Article 1, Protocol 1 in detail and identified the existence of 'three distinct rules' within its ambit. The European Court explained (at para. 61) that:

> The first rule, which is of a general nature, enounces the principle of peaceful enjoyment of property; it is set out in the first sentence of the first paragraph. The second rule covers deprivation of possessions and subjects it to certain conditions; it appears in the second sentence of the same paragraph. The third rule recognises that the States are entitled, amongst other things, to control the use of property in accordance with the general interest, by enforcing such laws as they deem necessary for the purpose; it is contained in the second paragraph.

This analysis of Article 1, Protocol 1 as comprising three distinct rules has been consistently approved in subsequent cases and has become the established method of applying the Article. Although on some occasions the European Court has looked at Article 1 as a whole and has not identified which of the three rules is applicable, these instances are noticeably rare. Therefore Article 1, Protocol 1 will be examined as comprising the following three rules.

(a) The first rule — this general rule provides the guarantee to the right of property. It protects a person's right to the peaceful enjoyment of his or her possessions free from any state interference.

(b) The second rule — this is a limitation upon the wide scope of the first rule. It provides for circumstances in which a person may be deprived of his or her possessions by the state without invoking a breach of the first rule. The Strasbourg institutions have stated that there must be a narrow construction of the deprivation rule as it is a restriction on the general guarantee to the right of property contained in the first rule (*Lithgow* v *UK*).

(c) The third rule — this provides another qualification to the guarantee of property rights provided in the first rule. It defines when a state may interfere with a person's peaceful enjoyment of his or her possessions by means of controlling the use of the property.

Although in *Sporrong and Lönnroth* v *Sweden* the European Court referred to 'three distinct rules', it is clear that the three rules are not unconnected. In the case of *James* v *UK* (see Appendix 3) the European Court clarified the relationship between the three rules in the following terms (at para. 37):

> . . . before inquiring whether the first general rule has been complied with, [the Court] must determine whether the last two are applicable. The three rules are not, however, 'distinct' in the sense of being unconnected. The second and third rules are concerned with particular instances of interference with the right to peaceful enjoyment of property and should therefore be construed in the light of the general principle enunciated in the first rule.

Since the second and third rules must be interpreted in the light of the first rule the state must, when depriving a person of possessions under the second rule or controlling the use of his or her property under the third rule, take account of the general principle concerning every person's right to the peaceful enjoyment of his or her possessions. Therefore the concession granted to the states under the second and third rules to interfere with property rights is restricted by the guarantee provided by the first rule. Similarly, the wide scope of the general guarantee to the right of property within the first rule is qualified and limited by the second and third rules. Consequently the three distinct rules are inextricably linked to each other.

The common approach adopted by the European Court when analysing cases under Article 1, Protocol 1 is first to determine whether either the second or third rule is applicable. Only if neither is applicable will the European Court return to the first rule and inquire whether it has been complied with. The same method of analysis will be adopted here.

4.3   THE SECOND RULE: THE DEPRIVATION OF POSSESSIONS

(See the case summaries in Appendix 3 for the following cases: *James* v *UK*; *Lithgow* v *UK*; *Howard* v *UK*; *Papamichalopoulos* v *Greece*; *Hentrich* v *France*; *Holy Monasteries* v *Greece*).

4.3.1 The meaning of 'deprivation'

A deprivation of possessions comprises a dispossession of the subject of property. It normally involves the transfer of ownership in the property so that the rights of the owner are extinguished. Examples from the case law of the Strasbourg institutions include:

(a) the transfer of a landlord's freehold reversion to long leasehold tenants under the enfranchisement legislation (*James* v *UK*);

(b) the compulsory purchase of land by a local planning authority (*Howard* v *UK*);

(c) the nationalisation of industries (*Lithgow* v *UK*).

These examples, each comprising a transfer of ownership of the property, provide clear illustrations of a deprivation of possessions. However, there may be cases where there is no legal expropriation of the property and the owner thereby retains legal ownership of the property, but there is nevertheless a *de facto* expropriation. The European Court considered this possibility in the case of *Sporrong and Lönnroth* v *Sweden*. It recognised that the Convention is intended to guarantee property rights that are 'practical and effective' and therefore the European Court will look to the realities of the situation to determine whether or not there has been a *de facto* expropriation. In *Sporrong and Lönnroth* the European Court had to decide whether expropriation permits and prohibitions on construction in relation to the applicants' land imposed such limitations upon the applicants' right to property that they could be assimilated to a deprivation of property (see Appendix 3 for more details on the facts of this case). In the opinion of the European Court this was not the case. The European Court observed that the applicants were entitled to use, sell, donate or mortgage their properties. Although it was more difficult to sell the properties due to the imposed limitations, there was evidence that several sales had been completed in the area where the permits and prohibitions operated. On the facts the European Court found that there had been no deprivation within the ambit of the second rule.

Generally the European Court exercises considerable caution in accepting the existence of a *de facto* expropriation. *Papamichalopoulos* v *Greece* is a rare example of a case in which the European Court found that there had been a *de facto* expropriation. During the 1960s, in a time of a dictatorship in Greece, land owned by the applicants was occupied by the Navy Fund which subsequently constructed a naval base and holiday resort for officers on the land. Following the restoration of democracy in Greece, the authorities recognised the applicants' title to the disputed land but ordered that other land of equal value be given to the applicants in its place. However, the land chosen by the authorities for this exchange could not be used for that purpose and the applicants alleged a violation of Article 1, Protocol 1. The applicants' land had never been formally legally expropriated and therefore the state contended that the applicants had not suffered a deprivation of the land. However, the European Court sought to ascertain whether the situation amounted to a *de facto* expropriation. From the date of the occupation of the land by the Navy Fund, the applicants had been unable to use, sell, mortgage, bequeath or make a gift of their property. They were even refused access to the land. All attempts to exchange the land for other land of equal value had been unsuccessful and the applicants had not received any compensation for their loss. Taking these factors into account the European Court decided (at para. 45) that:

> the loss of all ability to dispose of the land in issue, taken together with the failure of the attempts made so far to remedy the situation complained of, entailed sufficiently serious consequences for the applicants *de facto* to have been expropriated in a manner incompatible with their rights to the peaceful enjoyment of their possessions.

A more recent example can be found in the case of *Vasilescu* v *Romania* (1998) 28 EHRR 241. This case concerned the seizure by the police of 327 gold coins belonging to the applicant. The coins were seized in 1966 during a police search of the applicant's house, without a warrant, in connection with an investigation relating to her husband. Although the police decided not to press charges against her husband, they kept the coins that had been seized. All attempts by the applicant to recover the coins through the national courts failed even though the courts and the Government had recognised the unlawfulness of the police action. It was accepted that the applicant remained the legal owner of the property, although she had been deprived of the use and enjoyment of the coins. The European Court concluded that, on the facts, there had been a *de facto* expropriation. It stated (at para. 53) that:

> the loss of all ability to dispose of the property in issue, taken together with the failure of the attempts made so far to have the situation remedied by the national authorities and courts, has entailed sufficiently serious consequences for it to be held that the applicant has been the victim of a *de facto* confiscation incompatible with her right to the peaceful enjoyment of her possessions.

Given the extreme factual scenarios involved, these two cases are unlikely to detract from the general reluctance of the European Court to find that a *de facto* expropriation has occurred.

4.3.2 Deprivation by the state

There must be a deprivation by the state for Article 1, Protocol 1 to be applicable. However, not every deprivation will come within the ambit of the second rule. A temporary deprivation of property does not infringe the second rule (*Handyside* v *UK*). Nor does the confiscation of property for the enforcement of criminal law or tax legislation, which has instead been held to fall within the third rule even though the owner's rights in the property are extinguished (see 4.4.1.8). The state is not obliged to act to prevent private interferences with property where parties have contractually agreed a provision permitting the deprivation of property in specified circumstances, for example, a landlord's right to forfeit a lease following a breach of covenant by the tenant (*App. No. 11949/86* v *UK*). However, it may be that the HRA 1998 will nevertheless be applicable in these instances (see 3.4)

It is also worth noting that in *Loizidou* v *Turkey* (see Appendix 3), the European Court held that state responsibility is not restricted by national territorial boundaries. Therefore Article 1, Protocol 1 can be invoked against a state which has deprived a person of his or her possessions even where the property is situated outside the national territory of that state.

4.3.3 The meaning of 'public interest'

What is understood by the phrase 'public interest' is not explicated in Article 1, Protocol 1. It is, however, apparent that the public interest requirement relates to the state's justifications and reasons for depriving persons of their property. The deprivation of possessions must be made in pursuance of a legitimate aim (see 2.4) that justifies the taking. Examples of where a 'public interest' has been found to exist in the case law of the Strasbourg institutions include the following:

(a) measures taken to eliminate social injustice in the housing sector (*James* v *UK*);

(b) nationalisation of certain specified industries (*Lithgow* v *UK*);

(c) measures taken in pursuance of the development plan for an area, as drawn up by the local planning authority (*Howard* v *UK*);

(d) the prevention of tax evasion (*Hentrich* v *France*).

In each case the state was found to be pursuing a legitimate aim that provided a benefit for the general community. The state has a wide margin of appreciation in determining the existence of a problem of public concern that warrants the particular measures leading to an interference with a person's property rights (see 2.2.2). The European Court has acknowledged that it has only a limited power of review in this respect (*Gillow* v *UK*, at para. 147) and thus it has shown a high degree of deference to the states' opinion when determining whether a legitimate aim exists that is in the public interest.

4.3.3.1   Is it necessary for the deprivation to be for the direct use of the Community?

In *James* v *UK* the European Court had to consider whether the deprivation could be regarded as being 'in the public interest' where there was a transfer of property between private individuals, the landlord and the tenant, and the general community as a whole enjoyed no direct benefit from the expropriated property. The European Court accepted that if the deprivation had been for no other reason than to confer a benefit on a private party then it could not be regarded as being in the public interest. However the European Court stated (at para. 45) that: 'a taking of property effected in pursuance of legitimate social, economic or other policies may be 'in the public interest', even if the community at large has no direct use or enjoyment of the property taken'. It was the fact that the deprivation was made in pursuance of a policy to enhance social justice within the community that enabled a transfer of property from one private party to another to be regarded as being 'in the public interest' for the purposes of the second rule.

The South African case of *Administrator, Transvaal* v *J. Van Streepen* (1990) 4 SA 644 (A) provides an example from the Commonwealth case law of a similar approach to the same wording. The South African Constitution permits the acquisition of property 'in the public interest'. The case concerned the expropriation of land for the construction of a new private rail link which involved the transfer of land from one private person to another. The landowner challenged the expropriation on the ground that it was not in the public interest because it involved a transfer of his land to another private individual. However, the court held that it was in the public interest because the new private rail link indirectly facilitated the construction of a public highway and this was undoubtedly in pursuance of the public interest. Although *James* v *UK* provides authority for this principle under the Convention, the *Van Streepen* case nevertheless provides interesting comparative analysis which supports the decision in *James* v *UK*.

4.3.3.2   Compensation is not relevant to the requirement of being 'in the public interest'

In *Lithgow* v *UK*, which concerned the nationalisation of certain industries, the applicants contended that taking property from the owner for a fraction of its value was unfair compensation which could not be regarded as being 'in the public interest'. The European Court rejected this contention observing (at para. 109) that: 'The obligation to pay compensation derives from an implicit condition in Article 1 of Protocol 1 read as a whole rather than from the 'public interest' requirement itself'. The European Court confirmed that the requirement of 'public interest' relates solely to the Government's reasons and justifications for depriving the applicants of their property. The question of compensation will be considered at 4.3.6 in relation to the principle of proportionality.

4.3.4 The meaning of 'subject to the conditions provided for by law'

The European Court has consistently held that the term 'law' in this context does, 'not merely refer back to domestic law but also relates to the quality of the law, requiring it to be compatible with the rule of law, which is expressly mentioned in the preamble to the Convention' (*Malone* v *UK* (1984) 7 EHRR 14 at para. 67). As the word 'law' has a wider scope than merely domestic law, the fundamental principles of law common to all of the contracting states become relevant. The case of *Malone* v *UK* related to the interpretation of Article 8 and relied heavily upon *Sunday Times* v *UK* (1979) 2 EHRR 245, a case on Article 10. Nevertheless the European Court has stated that the wording in Article 1, Protocol 1 should be interpreted in the light of the same general principles as were stated in *Malone* to apply to the comparable expression, 'in accordance with the law' under Article 8 (see 5.3.2).

In relation to the second rule the essence of the test is whether the deprivation is made in pursuance of domestic legislation that is sufficiently certain and accessible to the public and is not arbitrary. The applicants in *Lithgow* v *UK* argued that as the compensation, payable to the owners following the nationalisation of certain industries, was arbitrary and bore no reasonable relationship to the value of their property, the taking could not be regarded as being 'subject to the conditions provided for by law'. The European Court confirmed (at para. 110) that the relevant test requires, 'the existence of and compliance with adequately accessible and sufficiently precise domestic legal provisions'. All the parties accepted the existence of such domestic legal provisions in relation to the nationalisation and therefore the deprivation was subject to the conditions provided for by law. Similarly, in *James* v *UK* the European Court found no grounds for finding that the deprivation was arbitrary merely because the compensation was less than the full market value of the property. The leasehold enfranchisement legislation was sufficiently precise and adequately accessible and was consequently provided for by law.

There are very few cases where the European Court has found a violation of Article 1, Protocol 1 on the ground that the disputed measures failed to satisfy the requirement of being 'provided for by law'. However the case of *Hentrich* v *France* provides one such example. The applicant had purchased a plot of land which was subsequently expropriated by the Commissioner of Revenue. The Revenue exercised a right of pre-emption over the land because the purchase price had been too low with a consequent loss to the state of the appropriate transfer duty. In considering the lawfulness of the interference by the state, the European Court observed (at para. 42) that: 'In the instant case the pre-emption operated arbitrarily and selectively and was scarcely foreseeable, and it was not attended by the basic procedural safeguards'. The European Court observed that the right of pre-emption was not applied systemically to all cases where property was sold at an undervalue but was only exercised on rare occasions which were barely foreseeable. This meant that the relevant legislation, as applied to this particular person, failed to satisfy the requirements of precision and foreseeability that are implied by the concept of law within the meaning of the Convention.

4.3.5   The meaning of 'the general principles of international law'

In *Lithgow* v *UK* the European Court rejected the applicants' contention that the reference to 'the general principles of international law' in the second rule meant that the international law requirement of prompt, adequate and effective compensation for the deprivation of the property of foreigners also applied to nationals. The European Court reiterated its decision in *James* v *UK* that the reference to 'the general principles of international law' in the second rule is limited to non-nationals and has no application to nationals.

The European Court has provided the following reasons for limiting 'the general principles of international law' to non-nationals.

(a)   The principles of international law have been specifically developed for the benefit of non-nationals. The words of the Convention should be given their ordinary meaning and therefore the European Court should not extend the scope of the words 'the general principles of international law' beyond their normal sphere of applicability.

(b)   Article 1, Protocol 1 expressly states that any deprivation of property must be 'in the public interest'. If the general principles of international law applied to nationals, that express provision would be superfluous because the requirement that an expropriation of property be in the public interest has always been included amongst the general principles of international law.

(c)   A differentiation in treatment on the ground of nationality does not constitute discrimination in violation of Article 14 if there is an objective and reasonable justification for that differentiation (see 6.3). Where property is taken for the purpose of social reform or economic restructuring of the country there may be good reasons for distinguishing between nationals and non-nationals in respect of the compensation to be given. For example, it is arguable that in relation to a deprivation of property by the state, nationals should bear a greater burden in the public interest than non-nationals since non-nationals play no role in the election of the Government that carries out the deprivation.

(d)   The European Court has had recourse to the *travaux préparatoires* as a supplementary means of interpretation and this provides clear statements supporting the view that the reference to 'the general principles of international law' does not extend to nationals.

Having established these justifications for the limitation of the wording to non-nationals, the European Court has noted that the inclusion of the phrase serves at least two clear purposes:

> it enables non-nationals to resort directly to the machinery of the Convention to enforce their rights on the basis of the relevant principles of international law, whereas otherwise they would have to seek recourse to diplomatic channels or to other available means of dispute settlement to do so ... and the reference ensures that the position of non-nationals is safeguarded, in that it excludes any possible argument that the entry into force of Protocol No. 1 has led to a diminution of their rights' (*Lithgow* v *UK*, at para. 115).

4.3.6 The principle of proportionality

There is no specific reference in the wording of the second rule prescribing a need for proportionality. However, proportionality is a general principle of the Convention jurisprudence which permeates throughout the Articles and thereby applies to Article 1, Protocol 1 (see 2.3). The principle of proportionality requires that there be a reasonable relationship of proportionality between the means employed and the aim sought to be realised by any measures depriving a person of their possessions. This has been expressed as the 'fair balance' test in the case of *Sporrong and Lönnroth* v *Sweden* and embraces the notion of the fair balance that must be 'struck between the demands of the general interest of the community and the requirements of the protection of the individual's fundamental rights' (at para. 69). Even if a deprivation of property is undertaken in pursuance of a legitimate aim and consequently is 'in the public interest' and is undertaken 'subject to the conditions provided for by law', there will, nevertheless, be a violation of the second rule if the deprivation is disproportionate to the aim being pursued and thereby places an excessive burden upon the persons concerned.

Whereas it is relatively easy for the state to identify a legitimate aim to justify the measures it has adopted, it is much harder to demonstrate that these measures are proportionate to the stated aim. To this effect it is relevant that both the European Court and the European Commission have stated that they undertake differing levels of review in relation to the existence of a legitimate aim on the one hand and the existence of proportionality on the other. The European Commission has observed that: 'in assessing the necessity of a measure under [Article 1, Protocol 1] the Commission retains a limited review of the legitimacy of the aim of the legislation and a fuller review of the proportionality of the actual interference with the applicant's rights' (*Gillow* v *UK*, at para. 147). It is rare that the European Court will dispute the existence of a legitimate aim provided that one is identified by the state. Therefore the decisive factor is likely to be the issue of proportionality for which the European Court is willing to exercise a greater power of review. In most cases, past and future, the battleground for litigation has been and is likely to be the principle of proportionality.

The determination of the fair balance test will inevitably involve the European Court in having to weigh a number of competing factors in the balance and to assess the differing weights to be allocated to them. These factors will vary depending upon the facts of each individual case. Two factors that have been consistently recognised by the European Court as being particularly relevant to the assessment of proportionality under Article 1, Protocol 1 are:

(a) the availability of compensation (the compensation factor); and
(b) the availability of procedures to challenge the interference with property (the due process factor).

These two factors have been found to play a significant role in assessing whether a fair balance has been struck between the general interest of the community and the protection of the individual's fundamental rights. Although the two factors are relevant to each of the three distinct rules under Article 1, Protocol 1, it seems that the weighting of the two factors varies depending upon which rule is being applied. The compensation factor is particularly relevant to a deprivation under the second rule, whereas it has less weighting under the third rule where the due process factor is likely to be prevalent in assessing proportionality (see 4.4.3).

4.3.6.1   *Compensation and proportionality under the second rule*
Article 1, Protocol 1 is silent on the question of compensation. Although earlier drafts of the Article did include an express right to compensation, this was excluded at a later stage due to opposition by a number of states including the UK. In contrast most Commonwealth constitutions include an express guarantee for the payment of compensation following an acquisition of property by the State.[1] Not only is compensation explicitly guaranteed in these Commonwealth constitutions but also the owner of the property is certain to receive an amount of compensation that equates to the market value of the property. The position under Article 1, Protocol 1 is very different. In the absence of any express statement in the Article itself the European Court has been left to determine two questions:

(a) Must compensation always be available for a deprivation of property by the state to prevent the owner suffering a disproportionate burden?
(b) If so, must the quantification of the compensation relate to the market value of the property?

In answer to the first question, the European Court has stated that:

---

[1] See Allen, T., *The Right to Property in Commonwealth Constitutions*, Cambridge: Cambridge University Press, 2000.

the taking of property in the public interest without payment of compensation is treated as justifiable only in exceptional circumstances ... As far as Article 1 (P1–1) is concerned, the protection of the right of property it affords would be largely illusory and ineffective in the absence of any equivalent principle' (*James* v *UK*, at para. 54).

In *Holy Monasteries* v *Greece* the European Court held that the failure of the state to pay any compensation for a deprivation of property imposed a disproportionate burden on the property owners so that the deprivation constituted a violation of Article 1, Protocol 1. More recently in *The former King of Greece and others* v *Greece* (App. No. 25701/94, 23 November 2000) the European Court held that the offending legislation, which made the Greek state the owner of the applicants' property, was in violation of the second rule under Article 1, Protocol 1. The complete lack of any compensation for the deprivation of property upset the fair balance to the detriment of the applicants. As these cases illustrate, there is a clear principle that an owner should be compensated for a deprivation of property by the state. However the European Court qualifies this statement by acknowledging that no compensation need be payable where the deprivation occurs 'in exceptional circumstances'. Unfortunately the European Court provides no guidance as to what constitutes exceptional circumstances. Harris, O'Boyle and Warbrick suggest that it may include an uncompensated seizure of property during times of war.[2]

In relation to the second question, concerning the need for full compensation, the European Court has stated that:

Compensation terms under the relevant legislation are material to the assessment whether the contested measure respects the requisite fair balance and, notably, whether it does not impose a disproportionate burden on the applicants. In this connection, the taking of property without payment of an amount reasonably related to its value will normally constitute a disproportionate interference (*Holy Monasteries* v *Greece*, at para. 71).

Therefore in most cases the amount of the compensation must reasonably relate to the value of the property taken. But this does not mean that an owner can automatically expect to receive the full market value for his or her property. The European Court has stressed that:

Article 1 (P1–1) does not, however, guarantee a right to full compensation in all circumstances. Legitimate objectives of 'public interest', such as pursued in measures of economic reform or measures designed to achieve greater social justice, may call for less than reimbursement of the full market value (*James* v *UK*, at para. 54).

---

[2] Harris, D. J., O'Boyle, M. and Warbrick, C., *Law of the European Convention on Human Rights*, London: Butterworths, 1995, p. 532. For an example of a further possible 'exceptional circumstance' see 8.3.6.2 in relation to a deprivation of property by a local authority landlord exercising the remedy of distress for rent.

This statement indicates the existence of a proportional relationship between the public benefit and the individual burden. It appears that the greater the public gain to be achieved by the legitimate aim, the greater the financial burden the property owner can be expected to bear. To this extent the state enjoys a wide margin of appreciation in calculating compensation terms. It has been emphasised that: 'the Court's power of review is limited to ascertaining whether the choice of compensation terms falls outside the State's wide margin of appreciation in this domain' (*James* v *UK*, at para. 54). *Lithgow* v *UK* illustrates the European Court's general deference to the state's choice of compensation terms. The case arose out of the nationalisation of certain UK industries, under the Aircraft and Shipbuilding Industries Act 1977. The applicants did not contest the principle of nationalisation but maintained that the compensation which they had received was grossly inadequate and discriminatory. According to the applicants, the compensation formula, which calculated compensation on the basis of the value of the company shares at a point in time prior to the date of the announcement to nationalise the company rather than on the basis of the value of the company assets at the date of nationalisation, was unfair and imposed a disproportionate burden upon them. The fact that the property was taken for the purpose of nationalising an industry was found to be a particularly relevant factor to the outcome of the case. The European Court acknowledged that nationalisation legislation, by its very nature, involves the consideration of a large number of competing interests which the national authorities are, by reason of their direct knowledge of their society, better placed than an international judge to consider. Emphasising the state's wide margin of appreciation in deciding the terms for compensation, the European Court stated (at para. 122) that: 'it will respect the legislature's judgment in this connection unless that judgment was manifestly without reasonable foundation'. Having found sufficiently cogent reasons for the existence of the disputed compensation formula, the European Court concluded that the decision to adopt it was one which the UK Government was reasonably entitled to make in the exercise of its margin of appreciation. Commenting upon this decision, Harris, O'Boyle and Warbrick observe that:

> Because the disparities between the companies' own valuations and the amounts of compensation awarded under the Act and approved by the European Court were so great — for instance, one company received £1.8m in compensation when its cash assets alone totalled £2.2m — it is difficult to envisage the circumstances when the Court would find a breach of [the second rule] by reason of the level of compensation alone.[3]

This is further supported by the more recent case of *Papachelas* v *Greece* (App. No. 31423/96, 25 March 1999) in which the European Court upheld the

---

[3] Harris, O'Boyle and Warbrick (n. 2 above) p. 533.

Government's assessment of compensation terms payable to landowners whose land had been expropriated for the construction of a new major road. Although the owners did not receive full compensation the European Court concluded (at para. 49) that, on the facts, 'the price paid to the applicants bore a reasonable relation to the value of the expropriated land' and consequently, there was no violation of Article 1, Protocol 1 in respect of this part of the applicants' complaint (but see 4.3.6.2).

Therefore, once a deprivation under the second rule has been established the owner can be reassured that in all but exceptional circumstances compensation will be received. The area of contention is likely to be the amount of the compensation to be awarded. It is clear that the full market value of the property is not required in all circumstances. Allen has observed that: 'In this respect, the Protocol differs from the right to property under the written constitutions of the USA and most Commonwealth countries, where expropriation requires full compensation'.[4] What remains uncertain is the threshold of compensatability below which an infringement of Article 1, Protocol 1 will occur. Given that compensation is an integral part of the assessment of proportionality, it is probable that the threshold of compensatability will vary with the facts of each case (this will be considered further at 4.6.5.1).

4.3.6.2 Due process and proportionality under the second rule

The due process factor has not featured in many cases under the second rule presumably because, where a state deprivation of property occurs, the state is careful to ensure that adequate procedures are in place given the severity of the interference with property. However, it is clear that where such procedures are lacking the European Court will not hesitate to consider the due process factor as an aspect of proportionality. In *Hentrich* v *France*, the applicant received full compensation for her land which had been expropriated by means of the Revenue exercising a right of pre-emption over it: nevertheless, the European Court held that a breach of Article 1, Protocol 1 had occurred. One of the reasons for the breach was the absence of adequate procedural safeguards. The European Court stated (at para. 49) that the individual and excessive burden that the applicant bore, 'could have been rendered legitimate only if she had had the possibility — which was refused her — of effectively challenging the measure taken against her'. Thus the fair balance to be struck between the protection of the right of property and the requirements of the general interest has been upset by the absence of adequate procedures and the measure was consequently disproportionate.

The case of *Papachelas* v *Greece* (App. No. 31423/96, 25 March 1999) provides a further example of the role of the due process factor in assessing

---

[4] Allen, T., 'The Human Rights Act (UK) and Property Law' in McLean, J. (ed), *Property and the Constitution*, Oxford: Hart Publishing, 1999, p. 150.

proportionality. The applicants' land was expropriated by the state in order to build a new major road. The offending legislation created a presumption that the owners, whose land adjoined the new road, would derive an economic benefit from the building of the road and consequently their compensation was reduced to offset this presumed benefit. As a result of the application of this presumption as a blanket rule in all cases, the applicants were denied the opportunity to prove that they had suffered damage, or at least had not derived any benefit from the road, and thereby to assert their right to full compensation before the domestic courts. The European Court observed (at para. 54) that:

> They thus had to bear a burden that was individual and excessive and could have been rendered legitimate only if they had had the possibility of proving their alleged damage and, if successful, of receiving the relevant compensation.

Consequently, the lack of due process rendered the state in violation of Article 1, Protocol 1.

4.4   THE THIRD RULE: CONTROLLING THE USE OF PROPERTY

(See the case summaries in Appendix 2 for the following cases: *Handyside* v *UK*; *AGOSI* v *UK*; *Gillow* v *UK*; *Tre Traktörer Aktiebolag* v *Sweden*; *Pine Valley Developments Ltd and others* v *Ireland*; *Air Canada* v *UK*; *Gasus Dosier- und Fordertechnik GmbH* v *Netherlands*; *National and Provincial Building Society and others* v *UK*.)

4.4.1   The meaning of 'control the use of property'

The third rule deals with situations where the state interferes with a person's right of property by controlling the use of the property. For example, where the state imposes restrictions on the use of land due to planning controls or for environmental reasons, this is likely to involve a control of use within the scope of the third rule. The distinction between a deprivation and a control of use has at times drawn a fine line. It is advantageous to an applicant to be able to establish a deprivation rather than merely a control of use because it raises a presumption for the payment of compensation (see 4.6.5). One commentator has suggested that the distinction between deprivation and control in the Convention case law is 'an untidy and unsatisfactory one'.[5] Anderson observes that:

---

[5] Anderson, D., 'Compensation for Interference with Property', [1999] EHRLR 543 at p. 553.

In many of the cases ... the Court has bent over backwards to avoid classifying an interference with property as a deprivation. That is, no doubt, at least partly because of the presumption that compensation must be paid when a person is deprived of property.[6]

Therefore where the European Court considers that the facts do not give rise to a situation deserving of compensation, it may seek to classify an interference as a control rather than as a deprivation so that it retains the discretion to judge, on the merits of the case, whether the absence of compensation is acceptable or not.

The examples below, from the decisions of the Strasbourg institutions, illustrate instances where the interference was found to be a control of use and, in appropriate cases, examine the reasons given for applying the third rule instead of the second rule.

4.4.1.1   *Restricting the purposes for which the property can be used*

In *Pine Valley Developments Ltd v Ireland*, the applicants contended that there had been a deprivation of their possessions because the outline planning permission for the land they had purchased had subsequently been declared a nullity by the Irish Supreme Court. This meant that the applicants could not use their land for industrial purposes as they had intended and this resulted in a significant reduction in the value of their land. The European Court found no evidence of a formal expropriation nor of a *de facto* deprivation. The factors that were relevant to the European Court in reaching this decision included the following:

(a)   the applicants retained ownership of the land;
(b)   although the land could not be used for industrial development, it could be used for alternative means such as agricultural purposes;
(c)   although the value of the site was substantially reduced, it was not rendered worthless.

On this basis the European Court decided that the interference came within the ambit of the third rule and was a control of use of the property instead of a deprivation under the second rule.

Similarly, in *Sporrong and Lönnroth v Sweden* the European Court decided that the prohibitions on construction amounted to a control of use. However, the expropriation permits that had been issued by the Government to the Stockholm City Council, which permitted the Council to effect expropriation within a specified period should it wish to do so, did not control the use of the property. The permits placed no restrictions on the owners' use of their property prior to any expropriation and consequently the third rule was not applicable to them (see 4.5).

---

[6] Ibid.

4.4.1.2   Restricting the persons who can use the property
In *Gillow* v *UK* the property was used for residential purposes. The state restriction did not prevent use as a residence but did prevent the owners from being able to live in their property. They had been denied the requisite residence licence required to live in Guernsey. The legislation did not deprive them of their ownership of the house and they could still sell it or rent it to tenants so there was clearly no deprivation within the ambit of the second rule. Instead the European Court found there to be a control of use under the third rule because the owners were prevented from using the property as their own residence.

4.4.1.3   The imposition of positive obligations on the land owner
In *Denev* v *Sweden* (1989) 59 DR 127 the applicant, an owner of land which included a forest, was required by the state authorities to plant 2,500 Swedish pine trees per hectare evenly distributed over the forest on his land. He maintained that he intended to plant other types of trees as part of ongoing scientific experiments that he had been conducting over a seven-year period. The European Commission decided that the measures constituted a control of use of the property within the ambit of the third rule thereby making it clear that the imposition of positive obligations on the owner of property can amount to a control of use of property for the purposes of the third rule.

4.4.1.4   Inheritance law restrictions
Marckx v *Belgium* concerned discriminatory legislation relating to inheritance rights on intestacy. The European Court recognised (at para. 63) that: 'The right to dispose of one's property constitutes a traditional and fundamental aspect of the right to property'. Therefore restrictions on inheritance laws will be an interference with property rights by means of a control of use under the third rule.

4.4.1.5   Modifying or extinguishing freehold covenants
In *S* v *UK* (App. No. 10741/84) an order by the Lands Tribunal extinguishing two freehold covenants was found to amount to a control of use under the third rule (see 8.6 for a further explanation of this case).

4.4.1.6   The loss of certain exclusive rights over land
In *Banér* v *Sweden* (App. No. 11763/85) a landowner's loss of exclusive fishing rights on his estate, as a result of new legislation giving the general public a right to fish in privately owned waters, was held to constitute a control of use rather than a deprivation. Similarly, in *Chassagnou and others* v *France* (App. Nos. 25088/94, 28331/95 and 28443/95, 29 April 1999) the landowners were required by statute to transfer their right to hunt, which was one attribute of their right to property, to a municipal hunters association so that all of the members of the association could utilise the land for hunting purposes. The applicants had thus

lost their exclusive right to hunt on their land. In fact the applicants all objected to hunting and consequently the only thing they had lost was the right to prevent other persons from hunting on their land. The European Court stated (at para. 74) that:

> The compulsory transfer of the hunting rights over their land to [a municipal hunters association] prevents them from making use of their right to hunt, which is directly linked to the right of property, as they see fit. In the present case the applicants do not wish to hunt on their land and object to the fact that others may come onto their land to hunt. However, although opposed to hunting on ethical grounds, they are obliged to tolerate the presence of armed men and gun dogs on their land every year. This restriction on the free exercise of the right of use undoubtedly constitutes an interference with the applicants' enjoyment of their rights as the owners of property. Accordingly, the second paragraph of Article 1 is applicable in the case.

Therefore the landowners' loss of the exclusive right to hunt on their land constituted a control of use of property under the third rule.

4.4.1.7 The revocation of licences affecting business interests

Tre Traktörer Aktiebolag v *Sweden* concerned the state's revocation of the applicant company's licence to sell alcoholic beverages in its restaurant. The European Court examined the complaint under the third rule rather than the second. Although the applicant could not operate a restaurant business, it still kept some economic interests in the property represented by the leasing of the premises and the property assets contained within it. The European Court therefore concluded that the third rule was the applicable rule since the interference restricted the use of the property by preventing the sale of alcoholic beverages upon it. Similarly in *Fredin* v *Sweden* (1991) 13 EHRR 784, the applicant's licence to extract gravel, which had been revoked reliant upon a nature conservation law, was considered by the European Court to constitute a control of use rather than a deprivation. These decisions indicate that the revocation of a licence will be treated as a control of use rather than as a deprivation, the control being directed, not to the actual licence itself, but rather to the applicant's underlying business interests.[7]

4.4.1.8 Forfeiture and confiscation

In *Air Canada* v *UK*, customs officers found a consignment of cannabis resin on board an Air Canada airliner and seized the aircraft as liable to forfeiture. The applicant was required to pay the sum of £50,000 for its return. The applicant contended that it had been deprived of its possessions (a temporary deprivation of

---

[7] Also see the European Commission's decision in *Pinnacle Meat Processors* v *UK* (App. No. 33298/96).

the aircraft and a permanent deprivation of £50,000) within the ambit of the second rule. However the European Court decided that the interference amounted to a control of use under the third rule. The legislation in question, which prevented the aircraft from being used as a means of transporting illegal drugs, clearly sought to control the use of the aircraft. Since the forfeiture of the aircraft was a measure taken in furtherance of that policy, it amounted to a control of use and not a deprivation of property. A similar approach had been taken in the earlier case of *AGOSI* v *UK* in which customs and excise officers had seized illegally imported gold coins. The owner of the gold coins, being innocent of any wrongdoing in connection with the illegal activity, alleged that it had been deprived of its possessions by the state. The European Court noted that the prohibition on importing gold coins into the UK was a control of use of property and that the forfeiture of the gold coins was a measure taken to enforce that prohibition. It stated (at para. 51) that:

> The forfeiture of the coins did, of course, involve a deprivation of property, but in the circumstances the deprivation formed a constituent element of the procedure for the control of the use in the United Kingdom of gold coins.

Thus it concluded that the applicable rule was the third rule.

4.4.1.9   The seizure of property to satisfy tax debts
In *Gasus Dosier- und Fordertechnik GmbH* v *Netherlands*, the applicant, a German company, remained the owner of goods that it had sold to a Dutch company under a retention of title clause. The goods were seized by the tax bailiff to satisfy the Dutch company's tax debts. The applicant alleged that it had been deprived of its possessions in breach of Article 1, Protocol 1. However the European Court noted that the interference with the applicant's property arose as a direct result of the tax authorities' exercise of their powers of enforcement in respect of unpaid tax debts. The Dutch legislation permitted the seizure of all movable goods on the debtor's premises irrespective of who actually owned those goods. Therefore the European Court chose to deal with the applicant's complaint under the head of 'securing the payment of taxes' within the scope of the third rule.

4.4.2   The meaning of 'in accordance with the general interest'

The requirement that the interference with the use of property is 'in accordance with the general interest' has a similar purpose to the requirement under the second rule that any deprivation of property is made 'in the public interest'. In both cases the state needs to show that the interference is in pursuance of a legitimate aim that benefits the community at large (see 2.4). The examples given under the second rule (see 4.3.3) are equally applicable here. Further examples from the case law of the Strasbourg institutions include the following.

(a) The protection of the environment has been found to be a legitimate aim under the third rule (*Pine Valley Developments Ltd and others* v *Ireland*). In support of this the European Commission has observed that: 'the interest of preserving nature is commonly recognised in all the Contracting States as being of great importance in present-day society and this interest cannot be effectively protected without restricting the use of property' (*Fredin* v *Sweden* (1991) 13 EHRR 784 at para. 69).

(b) Measures taken to avoid unregulated hunting on land and to encourage the rational management of game stocks were found to be in the general interest (*Chassagnou and others* v *France*).

(c) Measures taken to combat international drug trafficking have been regarded as being in the general interest (*Air Canada* v *UK*).

(d) Measures to restrict the consumption and abuse of alcohol have been found to come within the general interest (*Tre Traktörer Aktiebolag* v *Sweden*).

(e) The protection of morality was held to fall within the concept of the general interest in a case involving the destruction of school books adjudged to be obscene due to the pornographic nature of the books (*Handyside* v *UK*).

The 'protection of morals' raises the question of what is a 'moral' and thereby opens the door to complex philosophical debates on morality. To this end it is notable that in *Handyside* v *UK* the European Court was careful to sidestep any such debate by leaving the issue of what constitutes a moral to the state's margin of appreciation. It stated (at para. 48) that:

> it is not possible to find in the domestic law of the various Contracting States a uniform European conception of morals. The view taken by their respective laws of the requirements of morals varies from time to time and from place to place, especially in our era which is characterised by a rapid and far-reaching evolution of opinions on the subject. By reason of their direct and continuous contact with the vital forces of their countries, State authorities are in principle in a better position than the international judge to give an opinion on the exact content of these requirements.

*4.4.2.1 Is there any difference between 'public interest' (the s
'general interest' (the third rule)?*
It is unclear whether there is any difference between these two phi
Any debate over the possible differing scope of these phrases is p
it is extremely unlikely that the Strasbourg institutions will disp

aim put forward by a state. As with the second rule, the deciding factor under the third rule is likely to be the principle of proportionality.

4.4.3   The principle of proportionality

This raises the same issues that have already been examined in respect of proportionality under the second rule (see 4.3.6). The European Court has confirmed the application of this principle within the context of the third rule and has stated that:

> an interference must achieve a 'fair balance' between the demands of the general interest of the community and the requirements of the protection of the individual's fundamental rights. The concern to achieve this balance is reflected in the structure of Article 1 as a whole, including the second paragraph: there must therefore be a reasonable relationship of proportionality between the means employed and the aim pursued (*Air Canada* v *UK*, at para. 36).

As always the states are permitted a margin of appreciation in implementing the fair balance test, but this is subject to the European Court's power of review.

In assessing proportionality the European Court takes into account different competing factors and weighs them in the balance to ensure that the property owner does not suffer an excessive burden. In this respect the European Court has consistently recognised the importance of the compensation factor and the due process factor which apply to both the second and third rule (see 4.3.6 and 4.4.3.2 respectively). Another factor, relevant to proportionality, but specific to the third rule, is the purpose for which the owner intends to use the property.

4.4.3.1   *The intended use of the property*

The European Commission has recognised the importance of the purpose for which the owner intends to use the property in the following terms: 'The principal criterion for establishing whether a fair balance has now been struck in the control of use of personal property is therefore the use for which that property was intended by the individual owner' (*Gillow* v *UK*, para. 147). In *Gillow* v *UK* the owners intended to use the property as their own residence but were prevented from doing so by the refusal of the relevant state authority to grant them a residence licence. The property could still be lived in by other people, but it was the fact that the owners intended to use the property for their own home that was the crucial factor in assessing proportionality. This factor had considerable weight in balancing, on the one hand, the benefit to the Guernsey community of a residence licence system to prevent a housing shortage for locals and, on the other hand, protecting the right of the owners to enjoy the use of their property without interference from the state. Therefore, when assessing proportionality under the third rule, the interference with the use of the property must be considered in the light of the purpose for which the owner intended to use the property and the ways in which the property can still be used.

In *Chassagnou and others* v *France* the European Court concluded that the compulsory transfer of the applicants' hunting rights over their land to a municipal hunters association upset the fair balance to be struck between the requirements of the general interest and the protection of the right of property. It was significant that the applicants were opposed to hunting on ethical grounds and therefore did not want their land used for hunting purposes. The European Court observed (at para. 85) that:

> Compelling small landowners to transfer hunting rights over their land so that others can make use of them in a way which is totally incompatible with their beliefs imposes a disproportionate burden which is not justified under the second paragraph of Article 1 of Protocol 1.

This is particularly interesting because the owners' anti-hunting beliefs were a relevant factor in ascertaining the intended use of the property (i.e. for something other than hunting) and thereby in assessing proportionality.

4.4.3.2   Compensation and proportionality under the third rule

Control of use is a less serious interference with property than a deprivation and therefore the need to provide compensation is not as great under the third rule. In *Banér* v *Sweden* (App. No. 11763/85) the European Commission referred to the principle that, where a deprivation of possessions has occurred, there is normally an inherent right to compensation. However, it went on to observe that:

> in the Commission's view such a right to compensation is not inherent in the second paragraph ... This does not exclude that the law may provide for compensation in cases where a regulation of use may have severe economic consequences to the detriment of the property owner.

As with the second rule there is no guarantee that an owner will receive full compensation for the state's interference. Under the second rule the owner can expect to receive some compensation in all but 'exceptional circumstances', but the position under the third rule is more precarious for the owner. The European Commission has stated that a control of use 'does not, as a rule, contain any right to compensation' (*Pinnacle Meat Processors* v *UK* (App. No. 33298/96)).

Nevertheless, the European Commission in *Banér* did acknowledge that compensation will be a relevant factor in assessing proportionality in some cases. There may be reasons to justify denying any payment of compensation on the facts. For example, in *Pine Valley Developments Ltd and others* v *Ireland* there was found to be no violation of Article 1, Protocol 1 under the third rule following the national court's declaration that the applicants' outline planning permission was a nullity, even though the applicants had not received any compensation. The European Court observed (at para. 59) that:

> The applicants were engaged on a commercial venture which, by its very nature, involved an element of risk and they were aware not only of the zoning plan but also of the opposition of the local authority . . . to any departure from it. This being so, the Court does not consider that the annulment of the permission without any remedial action being taken in their favour can be regarded as a disproportionate measure.

Similarly, in *Banér* v *Sweden* (App. No. 11763/85) the absence of any compensation in relation to the applicant's loss of his exclusive rights to fish in his lake, was not sufficient to contravene the principle of proportionality. The European Commission took into account the fact that he could not claim any direct loss of income as a result of the state interference, which was, in the opinion of the European Commission, a relatively minor interference with his property rights. For comparative purposes it is interesting to observe that a similar approach has been adopted by the Irish courts interpretating the Irish Constitution. Legislation which limited a landowner's use of his land in the interests of protecting national monuments was found to be constitutional (*O'Callaghan* v *Commissioner of Public Works* [1985] ILRM 364). In reaching its decision the Irish court took the view that the payment of compensation is not necessary when property rights are interfered with by controlling the use of the land.

There is a well-recognised category of cases which involve a control of use by the state but for which the owner will definitely not receive any compensation. This is where the state is exercising a type of 'police power' over the property (see 4.4.3.4). For example, where property is forfeited because it has been used in the commission of a criminal offence (*AGOSI* v *UK*; *Air Canada* v *UK*). In these types of cases, and in cases where the state seizes property to execute a civil judgment or satisfy a tax debt (*Gasus Dosier- und Fordertechnik GmbH* v *Netherlands*), the purpose of the interference with the property would be frustrated if compensation were payable. Therefore in these cases the emphasis in assessing proportionality rests on due process considerations (see 4.4.3.5).

4.4.3.3   Comparative analysis

The question of the payment of compensation under the third rule is likely to provoke fierce debate. Given the uncertainty, it may be helpful to consider briefly the position in the USA and Commonwealth countries for comparative purposes. Under the US Bill of Rights, the takings clause of the Fifth Amendment provides for the payment of full compensation in all cases where property is expropriated by the state. The due process clause of the Fourteenth Amendment deals with the regulatory control of land, similar to the third rule under Article 1, Protocol 1. Originally it was considered that a regulation of the use of property was not compensatable but was subject only to the procedural safeguards under the due process clause. The statement that 'Government hardly could go on if to some extent values incident to property could not be diminished without paying for every such change in the general law' is illustrative of the judicial attitude at that time.[8] However, in *Pennsylvannia Coal* v *Mahon* (1922) 260 US 393, the Supreme Court recognised that, in some circumstances, a statute which restricts or regulates the use of property can amount to a taking of land. Holmes J stated that: 'The general rule at least is that while property may be regulated to a certain extent if the regulation goes too far it will be recognised as a taking'. The decisions in *Mahon* and subsequent cases have thus blurred the edges of the initial distinction between a 'taking' and a 'control' by treating regulatory control as a compensatable taking under the Fifth Amendment in certain circumstances. Any attempt to delineate precisely between a compensatable regulation and one that is not compensatable has been unsuccessful to date and the area is consequently shrouded in considerable ambiguity.[9] For example, the controversial test proffered in *Lucas* v *South Carolina Coastal Council* (1992) 505 US 1003 has been the subject of extensive criticism.[10] In *Lucas* the court adopted an economic value approach to ascertain whether the regulation 'deprives land of all economically beneficial use' and, if it does, the regulation will be treated as a taking and compensation must be paid.

In a number of Commonwealth Privy Council decisions, British judges have approved the basic principle in *Mahon* that the regulation of property can be a compensatable acquisition, although some have suggested that to refer to a 'valueless shell', i.e. the loss of virtually all economic value in the property, is to overstate the situation needed for there to be a constructive deprivation (*La Compagnie Sucrière de Bel Ombre Ltee* v *The Government of Mauritius* [1995] 3 LRC 494 at 506 per Lord Woolf). The case of *La Compagnie Sucrière* concerned legislation in Mauritius that required landowners to renew leases with tenant farmers. The Privy Council rejected the landowners' claim that the legislation deprived them of their property without compensation contrary to the Mauritian Constitution. Analysing this decision, Allen observed that:

> the Privy Council refused to treat restrictions on a landlord's freedom to deal with land after the expiry of a lease as an acquisition of property. Instead, Lord Woolf said that the restrictions were analogous to a control on use, under Rule 3 of the Protocol. It seems

---

[8] *Pennsylvania Coal* v *Mahon* (1922) 260 US 393 per Holmes J.
[9] See Purdue, M., 'When a Regulation of Land becomes a Taking of Land — A Look at Two Recent Decisions of the United States Supreme Court' [1995] JPL 279.
[10] See Willmore, C., 'Of missiles and mice: property rights in the USA' in Cooke, E., (ed), *Modern Studies in Property Law, Volume I: Property 2000*, Oxford: Hart Publishing, 2001.

likely, therefore, that British Courts would treat regulation as a compensatable deprivation of property only in extreme cases.[11]

The protection of property rights under the US Bill of Rights and the constitutions of the Commonwealth countries is very different from Article 1, Protocol 1. Although Article 1, Protocol 1 does distinguish between a deprivation and a control of use, which is similar to the distinction in the US Bill of Rights between a taking under the takings clause and a regulatory control under the due process clause, it does not attach compensation guarantees to the second rule and due process guarantees to the third rule. Instead there are no express guarantees for compensation nor due process considerations but these factors are relevant to the principle of proportionality. By this means compensation and due process are relevant factors in all cases under Article 1, Protocol 1 whether the interference involves a deprivation or a control of use. However, as already suggested, it is likely that the relative weighting of these factors will vary depending upon the applicable rule (see 4.3.6).

4.4.3.4   *Compensation and police powers*

The concept of 'eminent domain' describes the right of a Government to take property for public purposes. In the United States the courts have distinguished between the sovereign power of eminent domain which necessitates the payment of compensation for a taking of property, and the sovereign 'police power' which permits the taking of property without compensation. Allen notes that many Commonwealth constitutions either expressly exclude the payment of compensation where the property acquired is injurious to the health of human beings, animals or plants; or if not expressly excluded, the courts, adopting the United States' doctrine of police power, impliedly exclude the payment of compensation in these circumstances.[12] Allen cites Lord Radcliffe's judgment in *Belfast Corporation* v *OD Cars* [1960] AC 490 as an illustration of the application of police powers. The case involved the refusal of a local authority to grant a company permission to erect factories and shops on land owned by the company. The refusal was due to the fact that the area in which the land was situated had been zoned for residential use. The company claimed compensation. The Irish Constitution at that time included a provision for the payment of compensation for the 'taking of property' which did not incorporate any express limitations upon that right to compensate. However, the House of Lords held that compensation was not payable on the facts because the right to use property in a particular way

---

[11] Allen (n. 4 above) p. 152. Also see Roberts, N., 'The Law Lords and Human Rights: The Experience of the Privy Council in Interpreting Bills of Rights' [2000] EHRLR 147 at pp. 173–176 which examines a number of the decisions of the Privy Council in respect of an alleged deprivation of property.

[12] Allen (n. 1 above) pp. 125–126.

does not in itself constitute property and therefore the planning law restrictions did not amount to a 'taking of property'. Lord Radcliffe, however, adopted a different approach which suggests that even if the land use restrictions had amounted to a taking, compensation would still not have been payable. Lord Radcliffe argued that the general constitutional law of property includes a principle that restrictions on the use of property in the interests of public health and amenity do not normally require compensation. Since the Irish Constitution did not exclude this principle, Lord Radcliffe assumed that it continued to apply, thereby negating the duty to compensate even in circumstances that amounted to a taking of property. This is a potentially wide-ranging doctrine and its future scope under the Human Rights Act 1998 will depend upon the English courts' reception of the doctrine. For example, the confiscation and destruction of contaminated food that is injurious to public health is justifiable, even in the absence of any compensation, on the basis that the danger to the public is caused by the property itself. In *Handyside* v *UK* copies of an obscene book, intended for distribution in schools, were forfeited and destroyed. The European Court stated (at para. 63) that:

> these measures were authorised by the second paragraph of Article 1, Protocol 1, interpreted in the light of the principle of law, common to the Contracting States, whereunder items whose use has been lawfully adjudged illicit and dangerous to the general interest are forfeited with a view to destruction.

4.4.3.5   Due process and proportionality under the third rule
It appears that the due process factor has greater relevance than the compensation factor when assessing proportionality under the third rule. This is particularly so in cases involving the forfeiture or confiscation of goods used in the commission of a criminal offence, where the compensation factor is excluded as irrelevant. *AGOSI* v *UK* illustrates the emphasis that the European Court will place on procedural matters when considering the presence of proportionality in such cases. In *AGOSI* v *UK* gold coins were illegally imported into the UK. The persons attempting to smuggle the coins into the country were duly arrested and the coins were seized and forfeited. The applicant company claimed that it owned the coins under a retention of title clause as the coins had not yet been paid for by the smugglers. The applicant contended that the forfeiture of the coins constituted a breach of Article 1, Protocol 1 since it was the legal owner of the coins and was innocent of any wrongdoing in connection with the criminal activity. The European Court examined the case under the third rule as a control of use and observed (at para. 55) that although there are no procedural requirements explicit within the wording of the third rule, nevertheless, the European Court must,

> consider whether the applicable procedures in the present case were such as to enable, amongst other things, reasonable account to be taken of the degree of fault or care of

the applicant company ... and also whether the procedures in question afforded the applicant company a reasonable opportunity of putting its case to the responsible authorities. In ascertaining whether these conditions were satisfied a comprehensive view must be taken of the applicable procedures.

The availability of judicial review of the decision of the customs and excise officers not to exercise their statutory discretion to return the forfeited coins to the applicant, was held by the European Court to be an adequate means of protecting the innocent owner and of complying with the procedural requirements under the third rule. Consequently there was found to be no violation of Article 1, Protocol 1. A similar approach was adopted by the European Court in the more recent case of *Air Canada* v *UK* which involved the forfeiture by customs and excise of an aircraft that contained a consignment of illegal drugs.

4.4.4   The meaning of 'to secure the payment of taxes or other contributions or penalties'

Article 1, Protocol 1 expressly recognises the power of the state to raise taxes or to impose penalties and fines. Although this concedes practically unlimited power on the states to interfere with property as a means of securing the payment of taxes, the protection of property is not entirely excluded from the field of taxes. The European Court still retains a power of review to ensure that the taxes or penalties are not abusive or disproportionate. The European Commission has stated that: 'a financial liability arising out of the raising of taxes or contributions may adversely affect the guarantee of ownership if it places an excessive burden on the person concerned or fundamentally interferes with his financial position' (*Svenska Mangementgruppen AB* v *Sweden* (App. No. 11039/84)). The power to secure the payment of taxes comes within the scope of the third rule as one aspect of the state's right to control the use of property. Consequently, it is subject to the same qualifications as any other control of use by the state. The two cases discussed below illustrate the difficulty facing an applicant seeking to challenge an interference with property that is linked to the payment of taxes, given the state's wide margin of appreciation in this area. In each case the applicant had attempted to bring the interference within the ambit of the second rule as a deprivation of property, hoping to increase the chances of a successful challenge. But in both of the cases the European Court rejected this approach and instead examined the complaints under the third rule as an aspect of the state's power to control the use of property to secure the payment of taxes. It is worthy of note that in *Hentrich* v *France* (see Appendix 3), the success of the applicant's challenge to the state's methods of enforcing its tax policies may have been partly attributable to the fact that the European Court decided the case under the second rule rather than the third.

In *Gasus Dosier- und Fordertechnik GmbH* v *Netherlands*, the applicant German company (G) sold a concrete-mixer to a Dutch company (A) subject to a retention of title clause. Shortly after installation, the mixer was seized by the tax bailiff to cover A's tax debts. At the time of the seizure the full purchase price had not been paid to G by A. The mixer was subsequently sold to another company. G retained its claim against A for the recovery of the purchase price but due to A's subsequent bankruptcy, G's claim was rendered worthless. The German company was clearly a non-national and therefore the facts provided an opportunity to consider the application of the 'general principles of international law' under the second rule following the deprivation of its property. However, the European Court identified the third rule as the applicable rule on the ground that the Dutch authorities had seized the goods in order to secure the payment of taxes. The European Court held that there was no infringement of Article 1, Protocol 1. The legislation which empowered the tax authorities with the authority to seize any moveable goods on the debtor's premises, irrespective of ownership by a third party, was in the general interest because it facilitated the enforcement of tax debts. In assessing the proportionality of the measure the European Court observed (at para. 60) that in passing laws that regulate the formalities of taxation (including the enforcement of tax debts):

> the legislature must be allowed a wide margin of appreciation, especially with regard to the question whether — and if so, to what extent — the tax authorities should be put in a better position to enforce tax debts than ordinary creditors are in to enforce commercial debts. The Court will respect the legislature's assessment in such matters unless it is devoid of reasonable foundation.

The European Court found reasonable foundation for the tax enforcement measure in dispute and consequently was satisfied that the requirement of proportionality had been met.

A further example of the latitude granted to the states in the area of taxes is the case of the *National and Provincial Building Society and others* v *UK*, which concerned changes to the system for taxation on interest paid to the investors of building societies. Transitional regulations, adopted by the state to cover a gap period, were subsequently successfully challenged in the House of Lords by the Woolwich Building Society and declared to be invalid due to a technical defect. The Inland Revenue was required to return to the Woolwich the sum of £57,000,000 with interest. This led to the enactment of legislation which retrospectively validated the invalid transitional regulations, except that the provisions were stated not to apply to any building society that had commenced proceedings prior to a specified date. Only the Woolwich satisfied this condition. The applicant building societies were thereby prevented from insisting on the repayment of sums similar to that paid to the Woolwich. The applicants alleged a breach of Article 1, Protocol 1 on the grounds that the retrospective legislation deprived them of their vested rights to restitution. The European Court examined the applicants' complaint under the third rule as a control of use to secure the payment of taxes rather than under the second rule as a deprivation of their restitutionary rights. The European Court concluded that the actions taken by the state did not upset the fair balance that must be struck between the protection of the applicants' rights to restitution and the public interest in securing the payment of taxes. The European Court reasoned that (at para. 81):

> There is in fact an obvious and compelling public interest to ensure that private entities do not enjoy the benefit of a windfall in a changeover to a new tax payment regime and do not deny the Exchequer revenue simply on account of inadvertent defects in the enabling tax legislation.

Although the retrospective legislation extinguished the applicants' claim for restitution, the European Court was satisfied that the measure was not without reasonable foundation having regard to the important public interest considerations involved. Therefore the European Court held that there had been no violation of Article 1, Protocol 1.

4.5   THE FIRST RULE: THE PEACEFUL ENJOYMENT OF POSSESSIONS

(See the case summaries in Appendix 3 for the following cases: *Sporrong and Lönnroth* v *Sweden*; *Loizidou* v *Turkey*; *Matos e Silva, Lda and others* v *Portugal*; *Iatridis* v *Greece*.)

If the interference with the right of property falls within the scope of the second or third rule, being a deprivation or a control of use, then the conditions specified in those rules must be satisfied to prevent a violation of Article 1, Protocol 1. If an act does not constitute a deprivation of possessions nor a control of their use but it does, nevertheless, interfere with the owner's peaceful enjoyment of possessions, it will be examined under the first rule. The first rule therefore provides a ground for complaint that is separate from, and additional to, those in the second and third rules. Sermet refers to it as 'a kind of catch-all category for any kind of interference which is hard to pin down'.[13]

In *Sporrong and Lönnroth* v *Sweden*, the applicants owned land in an area of the City of Stockholm that fell within the perimeters of a proposed redevelopment site. As a result of this redevelopment their properties were subject to expropriation permits issued by the Government on an application by the local authority and to a prohibition on any construction imposed by the local

---

[13] Sermet, L., *The European Convention on Human Rights and property rights*, Council of Europe Press, Human Rights files No. 11, 1992.

administration board. The properties were never expropriated and the prohibition notices eventually lapsed. The European Court decided that the expropriation permits did not constitute a deprivation of property within the ambit of the second rule because the land was never actually expropriated, nor were they intended to control the use of the property under the third rule. The European Court observed that (at para. 60): 'Although the expropriation permits left intact in law the owners' right to use and dispose of their possessions, they nevertheless in practice significantly reduced the possibility of its exercise'. The applicants' right to property was both precarious and defeasible given that the City of Stockholm could lawfully expropriate the land whenever it chose to. Therefore the European Court concluded that the permits came within the first rule as they interfered with the substance of the applicants' ownership of their land.

4.5.1 The lawfulness of the interference

The case of *Iatridis* v *Greece* arose from a complex set of facts which started with a land ownership dispute between the state and a certain person known as KN for the purposes of the case. KN had built an open-air cinema on part of his land. He commenced proceedings against the state to establish title to his land after part of it was designated by royal decree to be reafforested and another part was transferred by the state to a housing co-operative. On the death of KN his heirs continued the proceedings. In 1978 KN's heirs leased the open-air cinema to the applicant, who completely restored it. In 1988 the State Lands Authority assigned the cinema to the town council and the applicant was subsequently evicted by town council officials. An Athens court quashed the eviction order due to the fact that proceedings were pending in the land ownership dispute between KN's heirs and the state concerning the land on which the cinema had been built. The applicant made various attempts to have the cinema returned to him, but at the date of the European Court judgment in March 1999, the cinema was still being operated by the town council and the applicant had not set up a cinema elsewhere. The applicant complained of a breach of Article 1, Protocol 1 and the European Court sought to determine the applicable rule under that Article. The European Court stated that it was not for it to decide whether the lease was invalid or not, instead (at para. 54) it would:

> confine itself to observing that, before the applicant was evicted, he had operated the cinema for 11 years under a formally valid lease without any interference by the authorities, as a result of which he had built up a clientele that constituted an asset.

The European Court was satisfied that the eviction of the applicant from the cinema and the authorities' continued refusal to comply with the national judicial decision quashing the eviction order amounted to an interference with his property rights. It concluded that the interference was neither an expropriation nor an instance of controlling the use of property but instead came within the first rule.

Having established the applicable rule, the European Court observed (at para. 58) that: 'the first and most important requirement of Article 1, [Protocol] 1 is that any interference by a public authority with the peaceful enjoyment of possessions should be lawful'. Whilst the second and third rules make express reference to the requirement for the interference to be lawful, there is no such reference to this in the first rule. Nevertheless, the European Court stated (at para. 58) that:

> the rule of law, one of the fundamental principles of a democratic society, is inherent in all the Articles of the Convention and entails a duty on the part of the State or other public authority to comply with judicial orders or decisions against it.

The European Court noted that, once the Athens court had quashed the eviction order, the town council became an unlawful occupier of the cinema and should have returned it to the applicant. The European Court concluded (at para. 62) that: 'the interference in question is manifestly in breach of Greek law and accordingly incompatible with the applicant's right to peaceful enjoyment of his possessions'.

4.5.2   Proportionality

It was in *Sporrong and Lönnroth* v *Sweden*, that the European Court first devised the now well-established fair balance test as a means of assessing proportionality under Article 1, Protocol 1. The European Court has to determine whether a fair balance has been 'struck between the demands of the general interest of the community and the requirements of the protection of the individual's fundamental rights' (at para. 69). The applicants, whilst not disputing the lawfulness of the expropriation permits and prohibitions on construction, maintained that the length of the period that they were in force (23 and 8 years for the permits; 25 and 12 years for the prohibitions) amounted to an infringement of Article 1, Protocol 1. The European Court noted (at para. 69) that:

> In an area as complex and difficult as that of the development of large cities, the Contracting States should enjoy a wide margin of appreciation in order to implement their town-planning policy. Nevertheless, the Court cannot fail to exercise its power of review and must determine whether the requisite balance was maintained in a manner consonant with the applicants' right to the 'peaceful enjoyment of [their] possessions', within the meaning of the first sentence of Article 1.

The European Court found that the expropriation permits, whose consequences were aggravated by the prohibitions on construction, upset the fair balance between the demands of the general interest and the protection of the applicants' right of property. The applicants were found to bear an 'excessive burden w ⌐ could have been rendered legitimate only if they had had the possibility of seeking a reduction of the time-limits or of claiming compensation' (at para. 73). Therefore, as with the second and third rules, the compensation factor and the due process factor are relevant to assessing the fair balance test under the first rule. Since compensation and procedural safeguards were denied to the applicants, the expropriation permits gave rise to a breach of the first rule.

Similarly, in *Matos e Silva, Lda and others* v *Portugal*, the European Court found that the applicant had to bear an individual and excessive burden which had upset the fair balance to be struck between the public interest of protecting the environment and the protection of the applicant's right to the peaceful enjoyment of its possessions. The Portuguese Government decided to create a nature reserve on the Algarve coast which included part of the land owned by the applicant company. In pursuance of this scheme a number of public-interest declarations were made by the Government as a preliminary to expropriating the relevant land and other restrictions were put in place including a ban on building. The applicant commenced five sets of proceedings in the national courts challenging these declarations. The proceedings were still pending at the time of the European Court's judgment. In assessing proportionality, the European Court considered that the length of the proceedings, resulting in a period of more than 13 years during which the applicant neither knew what would become of its property nor whether any compensation would be paid, upset the balance to be struck between the protection of property and the requirements of the general interest, and consequently caused a breach of the first rule.

4.6 COMPARISONS BETWEEN THE THREE RULES

4.6.1 The relationship between the first and second rule

In *James* v *UK*, the European Court had to consider whether a deprivation that was justified under the second rule and was consequently not in violation of Article 1, Protocol 1, could nevertheless constitute a violation of the Article under the first rule. The applicants asserted a violation of their right to the peaceful enjoyment of their property as a result of the implementation of leasehold enfranchisement legislation which enabled certain tenants of long leases to compulsorily purchase the landlord's freehold reversion. The European Court held that the deprivation of the landlord's property was justifiable and not in breach of the second rule. Consequently the applicants submitted that, as a deprivation of property is the most radical kind of interference with the peaceful enjoyment of property, there could still be a violation within the wider scope of the first rule even though there was no violation of the second rule. The European Court rejected this submission concluding (at para 71) that:

supplements and qualifies the general principle enunciated in the
⌐eing so, it is inconceivable that application of that general principle
⌐ should lead to any conclusion different from that already arrived at
⌐pplication of the second sentence.

e any difference between 'public interest' and ⌐rest'?

In *Jame.. v UK* the applicants suggested that the use of the different phrases, 'public interest' in the second rule and 'general interest' in the third rule, indicates an intention to refer to different concepts. It was contended that in consequence of the different words used in the two rules the state is granted more latitude to control the use of property than it has to deprive an owner of it. Unfortunately the European Court chose not to decide this issue on the ground that any such distinction, if it did exist, was irrelevant to the particular facts at hand. Therefore it is unclear whether there is any difference between these two phrases, but it is suggested that any distinction is likely to have little practical significance because of the high degree of deference that the European Court has shown and is likely to show to a state seeking to establish the existence of a legitimate aim.

4.6.3 Distinguishing between a deprivation and a control of use

The conceptualisation of 'ownership' as a bundle of rights is a familiar one. Honore lists the incidents of ownership (which he treats as synonymous with property) and thereby conceives ownership as comprising a bundle of detachable rights.[14] Ackerman suggests that 'each resource user is conceived as holding a bundle of rights vis-à-vis other potential users'.[15] Visualising the ownership of property in this way is a useful starting point for distinguishing between a deprivation and a control of use of property. Where only one right in the bundle of rights is lost or restricted, so that the owner still retains the remainder of the bundle, a control of use will occur rather than a deprivation. The European Commission adopted this method of distinguishing between a deprivation and a control of use in *Banér v Sweden* (App. No. 11763/85). It noted that: 'Legislation of a general character affecting and redefining the rights of property owners cannot normally be assimilated to expropriation even if some aspect of the property right is thereby interfered with or even taken away'. Harris, O'Boyle and Warbrick explain this statement in the following terms: 'If ownership is seen as a bundle of rights, the fact that an owner has been deprived of one right will not usually be sufficient to say that he has been deprived of ownership: rather it is a control of the use of the property'.[16]

---

[14] Honore, A., 'Ownership' in A. G. Guest (ed), *Oxford Essays in Jurisprudence*, London: Oxford University Press, 1961.

[15] Ackerman, B., *Private Property and the Constitution*, New Haven: Yale University Press, 1977.

[16] Harris, O'Boyle and Warbrick (n. 2 above) p. 528.

In the House of Lords' decision in *Belfast Corporation* v *OD Cars* [1960] AC 490 (the facts of this case were discussed at 4.4.3.4), Viscount Simonds refused to accept that the right to erect buildings on land could in itself constitute property. He suggested (at p. 517) that a person defining property under the English language would agree that the word had an extensive meaning which included both tangible and intangible property:

> but he would surely deny that any one of those rights which in the aggregate constituted ownership of property could itself and by itself aptly be called 'property' and to come to the instant case, he would deny that the right to use property in a particular way was itself property.

The Act in Northern Ireland which, at that time, protected against state interference with property rights prohibited the taking of property without compensation. The landowner contended that the land use restrictions in question took away his right to build on his land and thereby deprived him of his property without the payment of compensation. The House of Lords rejected his submission. Viscount Simonds made it clear that he was not prepared to treat every right held by a property owner as property in its own right. In contrast the Strasbourg institutions have adopted a very broad interpretation of the word 'possessions' in Article 1, Protocol 1 (see 4.7). The European Court is less concerned to decide whether a particular incident of property ownership constitutes property in itself, but instead concentrates on whether the interference constitutes a deprivation or a control of the use of property. To this end Viscount Simonds' analysis may be a valuable tool in deciding whether the interference is a deprivation of property itself or is only a loss of one incident of property ownership which would thus constitute a control of use under the third rule and not a deprivation under the second rule.

The case of *Antoniades* v *UK* (App. No. 15434/89) provides an example of this approach. This case arose as a result of the House of Lords' decision in *Antoniades* v *Villiers* [1990] 1 AC 417. The House of Lords had held that two separate licence agreements, which the applicant had entered into with an unmarried couple, created a tenancy. The occupants therefore enjoyed the protection of the Rent Acts, in terms of security of tenure and rent protection, which would have been denied them had they occupied as licensees instead of tenants. As a consequence of the House of Lords' judgment, the occupants of the flat applied to the Rent Office for a 'fair rent' which turned out to be significantly less than their joint licence fee. The applicant alleged that this constituted a violation of his rights under Article 1, Protocol 1. In determining whether to examine the complaint as a deprivation under the second rule or as a control of use under the third rule, the European Commission observed that: 'It cannot be said that the rights of the applicant as stipulated in the agreements (principally to repossess the flat, but also to the licence fee) constituted individual rights enjoying, in their own right, the protection awarded to possessions'. Therefore the right to repossession of the flat was not held to be a possession in itself; however, it constituted one aspect of the applicant's ownership of the flat. Consequently, his inability to repossess the flat on giving notice was not a deprivation of property, but only a control of the use of the property.

4.6.4   Proportionality as applied to the second and third rules

A deprivation of property involves the loss of ownership whereas title is retained by the owner in instances where the state only interferes with the control of use of the property. On this basis the European Commission has noted that: 'the measure of proportionality clearly differs in the application of the two rules since ... a deprivation of property is inherently more serious than a control of its use' (*Gillow* v *UK*). This indicates that the measure of proportionality will vary from case to case depending upon the type of interference. For this reason, in this chapter, the principle of proportionality has been examined separately in relation to each of the rules. Similarly in *Gillow* v *UK*, it was also noted (at para. 154) that:

> Whereas the Commission has recognised a close parallel between the test of necessity in respect of deprivations of property and interferences with the right to respect for one's home under Art. 8 (e.g., *App. No. 9261/81* v *UK*), the test applicable in respect of measures for the control of property is less stringent and must depend principally upon the severity of the restrictions imposed.

4.6.5   Compensation and proportionality under the three rules

Since the principle of proportionality is likely to be the deciding issue in a large proportion of cases, the weighting that the European Court confers upon the compensation factor will hold considerable importance. Although of relevance to all three rules under Article 1, Protocol 1, the weighting to be given to compensation, when balancing the various factors in the fair balance test, differs depending upon which rule is under consideration. In particular, whereas a deprivation will require the payment of compensation in all but exceptional cases, it is arguable that a control of use is only likely to be compensatable in exceptional cases. Wolfgang Peukert (a former member of the Secretariat of the European Commission on Human Rights) provides support for this view. He refers to the two different types of state interference under Article 1, Protocol 1, namely deprivation and control of use, and suggests that:

> A distinction between the two types of interference can in fact only be justified if one assumes that in principle there is a duty to pay compensation on expropriation, for, in

other respects, the requirements prescribed by the Convention for both types of interference are substantially the same.[17]

On this analysis the justification for having two separate rules, and distinguishing between a deprivation and a control of use, is that whilst there is requirement to pay compensation for a deprivation, there is no duty to compensate for a control of use. The European Commission's decision in *Banér* v *Sweden* (App. No. 11763/85) lends support to this view (see 8.7.1.2). However, whilst recognising that there is no inherent right to compensation under the third rule, the European Commission did accept that: 'When assessing the proportionality of the regulation in question it will be of relevance whether compensation is available and to what extent a concrete economic loss was caused by the legislation'. Therefore, where the control of use of property has substantial economic consequences upon the landowner, the compensation factor will be relevant to assessing the proportionality of the interference.[18]

4.6.5.1 *Distinguishing between compensatable and non-compensatable interferences*

Allen has noted how some Commonwealth constitutions distinguish between an acquisition of property by the state on the one hand, and an owner's deprivation of property on the other. Where the state acquires property, meaning that ownership rights are transferred to it, the owner will be compensated. However, where an owner is deprived of his or her property but there is no consequent acquisition by the state, no compensation is payable. It seems that the initial reasoning behind this distinction was to prevent the need to pay compensation for the regulation of property. This distinction between acquisition and deprivation was initially endorsed and applied by the Privy Council in *Selangor Pilot Association* v *Government of Malaysia and another* [1978] AC 337. However, in the later case of *Société United Docks and others* v *Government of Mauritius* [1985] LRC (Conxt.) 801, Lord Templeman (at p. 841) dismissed the distinction as creating inconsistencies and argued that: 'loss caused by deprivation and destruction is the same in quality and effect as loss caused by compulsory acquisition'.

This distinction, however, has no relevance for Article 1, Protocol 1 which makes no reference to 'acquisition' but instead concentrates on the impact of an interference on the owner. If an owner is deprived of his property, compensation will be relevant, regardless of whether or not the deprivation is as a result of an acquisition by the state. This avoids a preoccupation with having to establish an

---

[17] Peukert, W., 'Protection of Ownership under Article 1 of the First Protocol to the ECHR' (1981) 2 HRLJ 37 at p. 54.

[18] See Anderson (n. 5 above) where he promotes the use of a legitimate expectation-based approach to assessing whether compensation should be paid for an interference to property rights.

acquisition by the state as a prerequisite to claiming compensation. The broad terms of Article 1, Protocol 1 make it relatively easy to cross the initial hurdle and establish an interference with possessions, this then leaves the court free to decide the issue of compensation by reference to the general principle of proportionality.

It is well established that an entitlement to receive compensation under Article 1, Protocol 1 will not guarantee the payment of full compensation to the owner (*Lithgow* v *UK*). The amount of compensation is just one of the factors to be weighed in the balance and it may be that other considerations justify a level of compensation at less than the full market value. It seems that the greater the public gain to be achieved by the legitimate objective, e.g. the pursuit of greater social justice by redistributing wealth (*James* v *UK*), the greater the economic burden that the individual can be expected to bear thereby negating the need for full compensation. Therefore if a fair balance can be achieved without the payment of the full market value for the property, there will be no infringement of Article 1, Protocol 1. This approach is in sharp contrast to the position in most of the Commonwealth countries where an owner will be generously compensated with the full market value of the property once it has been established that there has been an acquisition by the state. Thus the initial obstacle of having to establish a state acquisition will be the deciding factor because once that has been established full compensation is automatically guaranteed. Allen observes that:

> As Commonwealth constitutions are generally interpreted as guaranteeing full compensation, it is understandable that Commonwealth courts would wish to restrict the situations where a prima facie infringement of the right to property arises.[19]

In contrast, the Strasbourg institutions' interpretation of Article 1, Protocol 1 has been to shift the emphasis away from the linguistic interpretation of 'acquisition' and 'deprivation' towards a broad test of proportionality and a general consideration of whether a fair balance has been struck between the various factors.

4.7   THE MEANING OF 'POSSESSIONS'

No guidance is offered by the text of Article 1, Protocol 1 as to the meaning of 'possessions' and therefore the scope of this definition is left to the interpretation of the Strasbourg institutions. By determining the meaning of 'possessions' the English courts will decide the extent of the protection afforded by Article 1, Protocol 1 under the HRA 1998. However, since the Strasbourg institutions have adopted a very broad interpretation, it is unlikely that the threshold question of whether the thing interfered with is a 'possession', will be a difficult barrier to cross. One example where this was a problem is the case of *S* v *UK* (App. No.

---

[19] Allen (n. 1 above) p. 198.

11716/85) (see Appendix 3). The applicant lived with Mrs R in a lesbian relationship. Mrs R was a secure tenant of her council house and when she died the applicant claimed to be qualified to succeed Mrs R under a secure tenancy. The Court of Appeal held that the expression 'living together as husband and wife' in the relevant legislation did not include homosexual relationships and therefore the applicant could not succeed to the tenancy (see 8.3.2). Consequently, the applicant alleged a violation of her rights under Article 1, Protocol 1. However, the European Commission noted that there was no contractual nexus between the applicant and the landlord. The fact that the applicant had been living in the house for some time without legal title could not constitute a 'possession' within the meaning of the Article. Therefore the fact that the local authority had evicted her from the house did not invoke Article 1, Protocol 1.

4.7.1 The autonomous meaning of 'possessions'

The word 'possessions' has a wider meaning than the traditional concept of a proprietary right. In *Matos e Silva, Lda and others* v *Portugal*, the state submitted that because the applicants' alleged ownership of the land was debatable under domestic law, the applicants could not claim an infringement of a property right that had not yet been established. The European Court acknowledged that it was not its role to determine whether or not the right to property existed in domestic law; however it reiterated (at para. 75) that: 'the notion of 'possessions' in Article 1 of Protocol 1 has an autonomous meaning' and (also at para. 75) it was satisfied that, 'the applicants' unchallenged rights over the disputed land for almost a century and the revenue they derive from working it may qualify as "possessions" for the purposes of Article 1'.

4.7.2 Examples of 'possessions' from the case law

The cases suggest that the essential criterion in determining the existence of a 'possession' is the acquired economic value of the interest (although this is not determinative in all cases). Whilst the universal categories of real and personal property are included, there are also grey areas, such as social security benefits and licences, and these will need to be analysed in some detail (see 4.7.3 and 4.7.4). The fact that the national law of the contracting state does not recognise the right as property does not prevent it from being a possession for the purposes of Article 1, Protocol 1. Examples of 'possessions' from the decisions of the Strasbourg institutions include the following.

(a) Immovable property (*Wiggins* v *UK* (App. No. 7456/76)) as well as movable property.

(b) Company shares. The European Commission has observed that: 'a company share is a complex thing: certifying that the holder possesses . . .

rights (especially voting rights), it also constitutes an indirect claim on company assets. In the present case there is no doubt that the . . . shares had an economic value . . . therefore . . . the shares . . . were indeed possessions' (*Bramelid and Malmstrom* v *Sweden* (App. No. 8588/79)). This decision illustrates the European Commission's reliance on the economic value of an interest in determining whether or not it constitutes a possession.

(c)   Intellectual property rights such as patents (*Smith Kline and French Laboratories* v *Netherlands* (App. No. 12633/87)). However, in *British-American Tobacco Company Ltd* v *Netherlands* (1995) 21 EHRR 409 the European Commission distinguished between the protection of an existing patent and the right to apply for a patent. It recalled that Article 1, Protocol 1 applies only to existing possessions and does not guarantee any right to acquire property. On this basis it stated that: 'the applicant company did not succeed in obtaining an effective protection for its invention by means of a patent. Consequently, the company was denied a protected intellectual property right but was not deprived of its existing property'. However, the European Court declined to express any opinion on whether the patent application lodged by the applicant could constitute a possession.

(d)   The benefit of restrictive covenants in freehold land when combined with the receipt of an annual rent (*S.* v *UK* (App. No. 10741/84)).

(e)   A leasehold estate (*James* v *UK*).

(f)   Security rights under a retention of title clause (*Gasus Dosier- und Fordertechnik GmbH* v *Netherlands*).

(g)   The goodwill of a business (*Van Marle and others* v *Netherlands* (1986) 8 EHRR 491; *Fredin* v *Sweden* (1990) 13 EHRR 784). In *Iatridis* v *Greece* (see Appendix 3) the state maintained that since it owned the land on which the cinema was situated, the lease of the cinema to the applicant by a third party had never given him a sufficiently established property right that could be enforced against the state. In response, the European Court stated that it was not for it to determine whether the land in question did in fact belong to the state or to the third party, or whether the lease was invalid or not. Instead it stated (at para. 54) that it would 'confine itself to observing that, before the applicant was evicted, he had operated the cinema for 11 years under a formally valid lease without any interference by the authorities, as a result of which he had built up a clientele that constituted as asset'. On this basis the European Court concluded that the applicant's rights were sufficient to constitute a possession for the purposes of Article 1, Protocol 1.

(h)   Planning permission. In *Pine Valley Developments Ltd and others* v *Ireland*, the European Court held that the grant of outline planning permission could be regarded as a possession. When Pine Valley purchased the land, it did so in reliance on the outline planning permission which had been recorded in a public register and which it was entitled to assume was valid. On this basis the European Court noted (at para. 51) that: 'The applicants had at least a legitimate expectation of being able to carry out their proposed development and this has to be regarded, for the purposes of Article 1 of Protocol 1, as a component part of the property in question'. In *R* v *North Lincolnshire Council, ex parte Horticultural and Garden Products Sales* (Humberside) Ltd [1998] Env LR 295 at 304 Lightman J, citing the *Pine Valley* case, stated that: 'Planning permission is a property right which may fall to be protected by the first sentence of Article 1'.

(i) Rights of user. The case of *X* v *Federal Republic of Germany* (App. No. 8363/78) concerned a temporal limitation of a right to use a burial place. The European Commission assumed that Article 1, Protocol 1 did apply, thereby accepting that the rights of user constituted a possession.

4.7.3   Pecuniary claims

A distinction needs to be drawn between pecuniary claims arising from a relationship between two private individuals, e.g. a claim in tort (a private law claim), and those arising from a public law relationship, e.g., social security benefits (a public law claim).

4.7.3.1   A private law claim

The case of *Stran Greek Refineries and Stratis Andreadis* v *Greece* (1994) 19 EHRR 293 concerned the question of whether a pecuniary claim in private law could constitute a possession within the meaning of Article 1, Protocol 1. In 1972 the Greek state, which at that time was governed by a military dictatorship, entered into a contract with the applicants for the construction of a crude oil refinery. On the restoration of democracy, the Government relied upon legislation to enable it to terminate the contract as prejudicial to the national economy. Prior to the termination of the contract, the applicants had incurred expenditure in pursuit of their obligations under the contract. As a result of this expenditure, the applicants had commenced an action in the Athens Court of First Instance for a declaration that the state should pay compensation to them in respect of their losses. Although a court judgment was given in favour of the applicants, the court ordered that additional investigative measures be taken, including hearing witnesses, before ruling on the existence and extent of the alleged damage. Meanwhile the state had filed an arbitration petition requesting the arbitration court to declare that all of the applicants' claims for compensation against the Greek state were unfounded. However, the arbitration court found that the applicants' claims were well founded but, due to the fact that the applicants shared some of the responsibility for the losses, the arbitration court awarded an arbitration award for a lesser sum than the applicants had sought. Subsequently the arbitration award was declared void by the national courts on the ground that the effect of specified legislation was to make the arbitration award, which had been made after the termination of the applicants' contract, unenforceable. The applicants alleged that the enactment of the offending legislation deprived them of their possessions, namely the judgment debt recognised by the Athens Court of First Instance and the arbitration award, and thereby violated their rights under Article 1, Protocol 1. The European Court had to ascertain whether the judgment of the Athens Court of First Instance and the arbitration award 'had given rise to a debt in [the applicants'] favour that was sufficiently established to be enforceable' (para. 59) and thereby constituted a possession within the meaning of Article 1, Protocol 1. The European Court found (at para. 60) that whilst the judgment of the Athens court appeared to establish that the state owed the applicant a debt, the effect of the judgment was in fact 'merely to furnish the applicants with the hope that they would secure recognition of the claim put forward. Whether the resulting debt was enforceable would depend on any review by two superior courts'. Therefore the debt was not sufficiently established to amount to a possession on the grounds that the Athens court had ordered further investigative measures to be taken. However, the arbitration award was found to be 'final and binding: it did not require any further enforcement measure and no ordinary or special appeal lay against it' (para. 61). At the time of the enactment of the offending legislation, the arbitration award conferred on the applicants a right to the sums awarded and this constituted a 'possession' for the purposes of Article 1, Protocol 1.

Similarly, in *Pressos Compania Naviera SA v Belgium* (1995) 21 EHRR 301, the European Court held that the applicants' claim for damages in tort, which under Belgian law came into existence when the damage occurred, amounted to an asset and was therefore a possession within the ambit of Article 1, Protocol 1. The applicants' ships were involved in collisions which they attributed to the negligence of the Belgian pilots. However, retrospective legislation was enacted which deprived them of their claims for compensation in tort. The applicants alleged that the offending legislation infringed their rights under Article 1, Protocol 1. The Government contended that the applicants' claims for damages could not be regarded as 'possessions' as none of them had been recognised and determined by a judicial decision having final effect. The decision of the national court (the Court of Cassation) which had heard the claims was subject to review by the higher courts. Nevertheless, the European Court had regard to the fact that under the Belgian law of tort a claim for damages was generated when the damage occurred and the judicial decision merely confirmed its existence and quantified its amount. On this basis the European Court concluded (at para. 31) that: 'the applicants could argue that they had a 'legitimate expectation' that their claims deriving from the accidents in question would be determined in accordance with the general law of tort'. This was sufficient to ensure that their pecuniary claim in private law amounted to a possession.

4.7.3.2 A public law claim

Whilst private law claims generally come within the wide meaning of possessions, the extent to which public law claims can be protected as possessions is not definitively settled. The European Court has being willing on occasions to extend the protection of Article 1, Protocol 1 to public law claims. But the case law distinguishes between two types of public law claim; those based on the provision of consideration by the claimant and those based on state grants and concessions in relation to social or economic policy.

X v *Netherlands* (1971) 38 CD 9 concerned discriminatory payments of a state pension to married and unmarried persons. The European Commission stated that the Convention did not include a right to social security, but conceded that: 'The making of compulsory contributions to a pension fund may, in certain circumstances, create a property right in a portion of such fund and ... such right might be affected by the manner in which the fund is distributed'. Thus a contributory scheme may give the assured a claim to a share of the pension fund. Such a claim, being of a proprietary nature, can constitute a possession within the meaning of Article 1, Protocol 1.

In *Muller* v *Austria* (1975) 3 DR 25 the claimant, who did not receive his full entitlement to his state pension on his retirement, alleged an infringement of Article 1, Protocol 1. The European Commission accepted that his social security contributions might have given him a claim in the fund that was sufficient to amount to a possession, but stated that there could be no entitlement to a pension of a particular amount. It stated that:

> The operation of a social security system is essentially different from the management of a private insurance company. Because of its public importance, the social security system must take account of political considerations, in particular those of financial policy. It is conceivable, for instance, that a deflationary trend may oblige the state to reduce the nominal amount of pensions. Fluctuations of this kind have nothing to do with the guarantee of ownership as a human right.

However, it went on to observe that: 'a substantial reducing of the amount of the pension could be regarded as affecting the very substance of the right to retain the benefit of the age-old insurance system'. The outcome of this decision appears to be that while Article 1, Protocol 1 does not guarantee a claimant of a state pension a specific amount, it does protect the pension from being substantially reduced. Unfortunately there is no guidance as to what constitutes a substantial reduction for this purpose.

In *Gaygusuz* v *Austria* (1996) 23 EHRR 365 the European Court found that there had been a breach of Article 14 in conjunction with Article 1, Protocol 1.

This was due to a finding of discrimination on the grounds of nationality in circumstances where the claimant had been denied an advance on his pension in the form of emergency assistance. The right to emergency assistance was treated as a pecuniary right and a possession for the purposes of Article 1, Protocol 1 due to the contributions made by the claimant to the unemployment insurance fund. More recently, in *Szrabjer and Clarke* v *UK* [1998] EHRLR 230 the European Commission accepted that the state earnings related pension in the UK did constitute a possession. However, the suspension of state pension payments to prisoners was not found to be in breach of Article 1, Protocol 1 because it served the public interest to withhold the payments whilst the prisoner was being kept at state expense in prison.

In *Coke* v *UK* [1999] EHRLR 130 the European Commission found allegations of a violation of Article 1, Protocol 1, relating to the armed forces pension scheme, to be inadmissible. One of the main reasons for the inadmissibility of the application was that the applicants (who were all widows) had not made any contribution to the pension scheme and consequently they had no 'possessions' within the scope of Article 1, Protocol 1. In *Kleine Staarman* v *Netherlands* (App. No. 10503/83) the European Commission refused to treat a non-contributory scheme of disability benefits as possessions because the claimant had only a mere expectation of a benefit and not an identifiable and claimable share. Harris, O'Boyle and Warbrick summarise the position as follows: 'What is required is that the applicant demonstrate that he has a legal right to some benefit if he satisfies certain conditions, rather than that he seeks to ensure that a discretion is exercised in his favour'.[20]

4.7.4   Licences or authorisations required to run a business

In *Tre Traktörer Aktiebolag* v *Sweden*, a company which managed a restaurant had its licence to sell alcoholic beverages revoked. The European Court reasoned that as the economic interests connected with the restaurant business were possessions and, as the licence was a vital component in the continuation of that business, the revocation of the licence was an interference with the company's possessions. In its decision on the admissibility of the applicant's complaint, the European Commission had emphasised that generally licences do not, in themselves, constitute possessions. What is important is the existence of a strong link between the licence and the economic interests of the business, in particular, whether the revocation of the licence will result in a loss of the goodwill of the business.

This principle, however, is subject to an important proviso which arises from the conditional nature of licences. In *Gudmunsson* v *Iceland* (1996) 21 EHRR CD 89 the applicant complained of a breach of Article 1, Protocol 1 on the grounds that his taxi licence had been withdrawn. The European Commission noted that: 'a licence can be withdrawn if conditions attached to the licence are no longer

---

[20] Harris, O'Boyle and Warbrick (n. 2 above) p. 518.

fulfilled or if the licence is withdrawn in accordance with provisions of the law which were in force when the licence was issued'. Consequently, on the facts of the case, the withdrawal of the taxi licence did not constitute an interference with the applicant's possessions.

The Irish High Court in *Hempenstall* v *Minister for the Environment* [1993] ILRM 318 appears to have gone one step further in finding that a subsequent change in the law, which significantly reduces the value of an existing licence, is not unconstitutional. In this case, a moratorium on the granting of taxi and private hire vehicle licences was lifted with the inevitable effect of reducing the value of the licences held by existing licence holders. However, the existing licence holders were unsuccessful in their attempt to challenge the legislation as unconstitutional. Clayton and Tomlinson explain this decision in the following terms:

> The Court added that property rights arising in licences created by law are subject to the conditions created by law and to an implied condition that the law may change those conditions. An amendment of the law changing the conditions under which a licence is held and which has the effect of reducing the commercial value of the licence, cannot be regarded as an attack on the property right in the licence. It is the consequence of the implied condition which is an inherent part of the property right in the licence.[21]

Therefore, whilst interferences with licences or authorisations required to run a business can generally constitute an interference with possessions, the conditional nature of licences may prevent an alleged interference, in a particular case, from being one that does in fact constitute an interference with possessions for the purposes of Article 1, Protocol 1.

4.7.5   The exclusion of mere expectations

A person hoping to inherit property under the will of a friend or relative does not have a 'possession' for the purposes of Article 1, Protocol 1, but merely an expectation to acquire property at a future date (see *Marckx* v *Belgium*). The Privy Council decision in *Subramanien* v *Government of Mauritius* [1995] 4 LRC 320 further illustrates the principle that an expectation is not sufficient to constitute property. In consequence of a deal negotiated between the Government of Mauritius and the Roman Catholic Education Agency (RCEA), RCEA teachers would no longer be recognised as public officers. One effect of this was that the teachers were no longer entitled to certain benefits which other Government teachers enjoyed. The teachers alleged that the deal thereby infringed their right under the Constitution of Mauritius not to be deprived of property. However, the

---

[21] Clayton, R. and Tomlinson, H., *The Law of Human Rights*, Oxford: Oxford University Press, 2000, Volume 1, p. 1338 at para. 18.133.

Privy Council dismissed the teachers' appeal. Since the benefits enjoyed by the teachers were no more than lost opportunities or expectations, they did not acquire proprietary status and consequently the RCEA teachers had suffered no deprivation of their possessions.[22]

4.8 THE MEANING OF 'EVERY NATURAL AND LEGAL PERSON'

In comparing Article 1, Protocol 1 with the other rights enunciated in the Convention, an important difference can be identified. The right to property is the only Convention right that is expressly conferred on 'legal' as well as 'natural' persons. Therefore Article 1, Protocol 1 protects the property rights of companies. It may seem strange to include companies in the human rights arena, nevertheless the contracting states have chosen to confer on companies the protection of the human right which protects existing property rights. Presumably this relates to the fact that the property belonging to the company is ultimately owned by natural persons. This abstraction works to simplify the law by removing the need to identify which natural persons own the property concerned. However, to be able to invoke the protection of Article 1, Protocol 1, the company must be a 'victim' of the alleged violation. For a discussion of victim status and its application to companies see 2.7.3.

---

[22] Ibid., p. 1340 at para. 18.138.

Chapter Five

Article 8

1. Everyone has the right to respect for his private and family life, his home and his correspondence.

2. There shall be no interference by a public authority with the exercise of this right except such as is in accordance with the law and is necessary in a democratic society in the interests of national security, public safety or the economic well-being of the country, for the prevention of disorder or crime, for the protection of health or morals, or for the protection of the rights and freedoms of others.

5.1   THE SCOPE OF ARTICLE 8 FOR PROPERTY LAWYERS

The structure of Article 8 is a familiar one for the Convention Articles with the first paragraph broadly defining the rights to be protected and the second paragraph setting the boundaries for a legitimate interference with those rights by the state. For a property lawyer the relevant aspect of Article 8 is likely to be the right to respect for the home and this will be considered in detail in this chapter. The protection of the home will inevitably involve some overlap with family life and private life, but these aspects of Article 8 will only be considered in so far as they relate to the home.

The protection afforded to the home under Article 8 includes the following.

(a)   A right of access to the home.
(b)   A right of occupation of the home. This embraces the notion of a right to the peaceful enjoyment of occupation of the home and consequently raises issues concerning excessive noise and other environmental pollution that affects the home.

(c)   A right not to be expelled or evicted from the home.

(d)   Protection against an intrusion into the home by the state in order to arrest, search, seize or inspect.

5.2   ARTICLE 8(1): THE RIGHT TO RESPECT FOR THE HOME

(See the case summaries in Appendix 3 for the following cases: *Marckx* v *Belgium*; *S* v *UK*; *Gillow* v *UK*; *Buckley* v *UK*; *Loizidou* v *Turkey*; *Khatun and 180 others* v *UK*).

5.2.1   The meaning of 'respect' — the imposition of positive obligations on the state

The European Court of Human Rights (the European Court) in *Marckx* v *Belgium* sought to clarify the meaning and purport of the words 'respect for ... private and family life'. Although the European Court limited its consideration to private and family life, the meaning of 'respect' applies equally to respect for the home. The European Court relied upon its analysis of Article 8 in the *Belgian Linguistic Case (No. 2)* (1968) 1 EHRR 252 in which the European Court, whilst recognising the object of Article 8 to be that of protecting individuals against arbitrary interference by public authorities, stated (at para. 31) that: 'Nevertheless, it does not merely compel the State to abstain from such interference: in addition to this primarily negative undertaking, there may be positive obligations inherent in an effective 'respect' for family life'. Therefore, as early as 1968 the European Court had recognised the existence of positive obligations stemming from the word 'respect' in Article 8(1), in addition to the negative obligations imposed upon the states under Article 8(2) to abstain from certain action.

The question of the states' positive obligations under Article 8(1) arose more recently in the case of *X, Y and Z* v *UK* (1997) 24 EHRR 143. The question for determination by the European Court was whether Article 8 implies a positive obligation on a state to recognise formally, as the father of a child, a person who is not the child's biological father. The relevance to property lawyers is the consideration of the extent of a state's positive duty under Article 8. The European Court made the following statement (at para. 41):

> The court reiterates that, although the essential object of Article 8 is to protect the individual against arbitrary interferences by the public authorities, there may in addition be positive obligations inherent in an effective respect for private or family life. The boundaries between the State's positive and negative obligations under this provision do not always lend themselves to precise definition; nonetheless, the applicable principles are similar. In both contexts, regard must be had to the fair balance that has to be struck between the competing interests of the individual and of the community as a whole, and in both cases the State enjoys a certain margin of appreciation.

Consequently, there is a clear recognition that Article 8(1) does impose positive obligations upon the state to take steps, in certain instances, to protect an individual's right to respect for his or her home and private life.

Whilst the negative obligation under Article 8(2) is limited to non-interference by the state, the scope of the positive duty remains undefined. The case of *X and Y* v *Netherlands* (1985) 8 EHRR 235 made a significant inroad into defining the scope of this positive duty. The facts concerned the lack of criminal sanctions for the sexual abuse of a 16-year-old mentally handicapped girl. The European Court repeated the *Marckx* formula that the right to respect for family and private life under Article 8 may impose positive obligations upon the state. However, the European Court went one step further and stated (at para. 23) that: 'These obligations may involve the adoption of measures designed to secure respect for private life *even in the sphere of the relations of individuals between themselves*' (emphasis supplied). The full implication of this statement is not yet known. There is uncertainty as to the extent to which a state is obliged to take positive action to prevent violations of human rights between private individuals. This case confirms that the fact that a violator is a private individual does not necessarily mean that his or her actions fall outside the scope of Article 8. In *X and Y* v *The Netherlands* it was the state's failure to provide adequate protection, under domestic law, for a victim who had been abused by another private individual, that constituted the state's breach of Article 8. In response to that decision by the European Court, Clapham concludes that: 'Article 8 can now be said to have been interpreted so that the reference to 'public' in paragraph (2) does not prevent the application of paragraph (1) to both public and private actions'.[1]

In seeking to define the nature of these positive obligations imposed upon the states Harris, O'Boyle and Warbrick suggest that they could involve the following:

(a) the obligation of the authorities to take steps to make sure that the enjoyment of the right is effective;
(b) the obligation of the authorities to take steps to make sure that the enjoyment of the right is not interfered with by other private persons; and
(c) the obligation of the authorities to take steps to make sure that private persons take steps to ensure the effective enjoyment by other individuals of the right.[2]

Potentially the boundaries of the states' positive obligations could be very extensive were it not for the fact that these obligations are subject to a significant

---

[1] Clapham, A., *Human Rights in the Private Sphere*, Oxford: Clarendon Press, 1993 at p. 214.
[2] Harris, D. J., O'Boyle, M. and Warbrick, C., *Law of the European Convention on Human Rights*, London: Butterworths, 1995 at p. 284.

restriction. The concessions within Article 8(2), which define when a state can interfere with a person's respect for his or her home without being in breach of Article 8(1), limit the scope of the states' positive obligations under Article 8(1) (see 5.4).

The case of *Botta* v *Italy* (1998) 26 EHRR 241 illustrates the difficulties of establishing that a state has a duty to take positive action. The applicant went on holiday to a seaside resort. He discovered that the bathing establishments were not equipped with disabled facilities, as required by Italian legislation, and this prevented him from being able to access the beach and sea. He alleged that his private life had been impaired, in violation of Article 8, due to the state's failure to discharge its positive obligations to monitor compliance with domestic legislation in relation to the availability of disabled facilities at private beaches. The European Commission adopted the view that the right asserted by the applicant, involving the participation of disabled persons in leisure activities, was so broad in scope that it went beyond the concept of a legal obligation inherent in the idea of 'respect' for private life. The European Court reached the same conclusion. In its submission to the European Court, the Government had expressed its concern that to define the boundaries of the states' positive obligations to include the satisfactory development of each individual's recreational activities would open the floodgates. It argued (at para. 29) that:

> Once the door was open for a development of that type it would be extremely difficult to set limits. It would be necessary, for example, to take into consideration obstacles resulting from the insufficient means of those who wished to take part in such activities.

The European Court responded to this floodgates concern by devising an appropriate test to limit the scope of the states' positive obligations. It stated that for positive obligations to be imposed upon the state there must be 'a direct and immediate link between the measures sought by an applicant and the latter's private and/or family life' (para. 34). A direct and immediate link had been established in the cases of *Lopez Ostra* v *Spain* and *Guerra and others* v *Italy* (see Appendix 3), but in the instant case the European Court concluded (at para. 35) that:

> the right asserted by Botta, namely the right to gain access to the beach and the sea at a place distant from his normal place of residence during his holidays, concerns interpersonal relations of such broad and indeterminate scope that there can be no conceivable direct link between the measures the State was urged to take in order to make good the omissions of the private bathing establishments and the applicant's private life. Accordingly, Article 8 is not applicable.

The case illustrates that, although the scope of the states' positive obligations remains uncertain, the European Court will impose limitations and has devised the 'direct and immediate link' test for this purpose.

The extent to which the state is under a positive obligation to take steps to protect the right to respect for a person's home has been considered in relation to environmental pollution affecting the home. There have been a number of cases involving noise pollution from aircraft and motorways (*Powell and Rayner* v *UK*, *Arrondelle* v *UK* and *Hatton* v *UK*) and cases concerning pollution caused by hazardous emissions from privately owned factories (*Lopez Ostra* v *Spain* and *Guerra and others* v *Italy*). These cases will be examined at 5.3.1 and at 8.8. These positive obligations have also been found to arise in relation to acts of harassment and vandalism directed against the home and private life (see *Osman* v *UK* (1998) 29 EHRR 245).

5.2.2   The meaning of 'home'

In *Buckley* v *UK* the applicant, a gypsy, lived in caravans parked on land which she owned. She applied for retrospective planning permission to permit her to park her caravans on her land. Her application was refused by the local planning authority, which issued an enforcement notice requiring her to remove the caravans. She was later prosecuted for failing to comply with the enforcement notice. The European Court had to establish whether the land in question constituted her 'home' for the purposes of Article 8. The Government contended that since she had no planning permission for her caravans she had not established a legal 'home'. But the European Court rejected this submission. Despite the fact that she was in violation of national law by living in the caravans without planning permission, it was still her 'home'. She had purchased the land specifically to park her caravans there and she had lived there continuously for the preceding eight years without attempting to make a home elsewhere. The European Court, in applying the 'sufficient and continuous links' test expounded in *Gillow* v *UK* (see Appendix 3), was satisfied that the property was her home.

The 'sufficient and continuous links' test was also applied in the case of *Mabey* v *UK* (1996) 22 EHRR CD 123, which also concerned a local authority's refusal to grant planning permission for the applicant's caravan where he had lived for over 20 years. The European Commission stated (at p. 124):

> whether or not a particular habitation constitutes a 'home' for the purposes of Article 8(1) will depend on the factual circumstances, of the particular case, namely the existence of sufficient and continuous links. It is not limited necessarily to those homes which have been lawfully occupied or lawfully established.

Having regard to the length of his occupation in the caravan the European Commission was satisfied that it was his home.

The two cases, *Buckley* v *UK* and *Mabey* v *UK*, indicate that a caravan is capable of constituting a 'home' and therefore it may be expected that Article 8 will extend its protection to other forms of mobile shelter. In *Kanthak* v *Germany* (1988) 58 DR 94, the European Commission left open the question of whether a camper van parked on a public road could be a person's 'home' under Article 8. However, applying the test expounded in *Gillow* there appears to be no reason why a camper van could not constitute a home provided that 'sufficient and continuous links' exist.

In *Loizidou* v *Turkey* the applicant owned land in northern Cyprus, where she had grown up and where her family had lived for generations. She had not lived there since 1972 having moved away when she got married. However, in 1974 construction work began on a number of flats on the land. The applicant had intended to live in one of the flats but due to the Turkish occupation of Northern Cyprus in 1974 the construction works had not been completed. The Turkish forces, still occupying Northern Cyprus, prevented her from returning to her land. She alleged that this constituted an unjustified interference with her right to respect for her home in violation of Article 8. The European Court stated (at para. 66) that:

> In its opinion it would strain the meaning of the notion of 'home' in Article 8 to extend it to comprise property on which it is planned to build a house for residential purposes. Nor can that term be interpreted to cover an area of a state where one has grown up and where the family has its roots but where one no longer lives.

This was clearly distinguishable from *Gillow* v *UK* where the applicants had built a house on their land and had previously resided in it as their home before leaving Guernsey for a number of years to pursue employment abroad.

5.2.3 Is it necessary to have a proprietary interest in the home in order to qualify for protection under Article 8?

This question was considered in the case of *S* v *UK*, which concerned rights of succession on the death of a secure tenant. The Court of Appeal held that a lesbian partner of a secure tenant could not succeed to the tenancy of her deceased partner, under the provisions of the Housing Act 1980, because she was not a spouse or member of the deceased tenant's family. The applicant alleged that this was a violation of her rights under Article 8. The European Commission found the application to be inadmissible. In reaching this decision the European Commission observed that:

> the applicant was occupying the house, of which her partner had been the tenant, without any legal title whatsoever. Contractual relations were established between the local authority and the deceased partner and that contractual agreement may or may not have permitted long-term visitors. The fact remains, however, that on the death of the partner, under the ordinary law, the applicant was no longer entitled to remain in the house, and

the local authority was entitled to possession so that the house could no longer be regarded as 'home' for the applicant within the meaning of article 8.

This part of the European Commission's decision suggests that without some proprietary, or at least contractual, right to stay in the property, an applicant will not acquire any protection of his or her 'home' under Article 8. However, the European Commission was not entirely convinced of this point and therefore went on to discuss the position should the house constitute her home for the purposes of Article 8. It conceded that:

> Even if the applicant's right to respect for her home, as guaranteed by Article 8, could be regarded as having been interfered with by order of the county court for possession against her, the Commission considers that such interference was clearly in accordance with the law and was also necessary for the protection of the contractual rights of the landlord to have the property back at the end of the tenancy.

Therefore the European Commission was prepared to concede that where a person is unlawfully occupying property, that person may still be able to invoke Article 8.

This was the view of Lord Cooke in the House of Lords' case, *Hunter* v *Canary Wharf* [1997] 2 All ER 426. The case concerned an action in nuisance arising out of the construction of the Canary Wharf tower and the Limehouse link road in the London Docklands. Some of the claimants had no proprietary interest in their homes and it was contended by the defendant that the absence of an interest in the property excluded them from bringing an action in private nuisance. The House of Lords, reversing the decision of the Court of Appeal, held that a claim in nuisance can only be brought by a person with a proprietary interest in the property affected by the alleged nuisance. Lord Cooke, however, delivered a dissenting judgment which made reference to Article 8 to support this view. Lord Cooke, having cited Article 8, observed (at pp. 458–9) that:

> These provisions are aimed, in part, at protecting the home and are construed to give protection against nuisances: see *Arrondelle* v *UK* (aircraft noise) and *Lopez Ostra* v *Spain* (fumes and smells from a waste treatment plant). *The protection is regarded as going beyond possession or property rights*: see Harris, O'Boyle and Warbrick, Law of the ECHR (1995), p. 319 (emphasis supplied).

The citation that Lord Cooke relies upon states that:

> There is no right to a home, not even a family home, but the notion of 'home' *is not seen entirely as the protection of a particular category of established property right*. It includes a family home but it is not restricted to it. While its core idea is one of sanctuary against intrusion by public authorities, there are further connotations to the idea of

'home', in particular, that *the state will facilitate the right to live in one's home, rather than merely protect it as a possession or property right.*[3]

The recent case of *Khatun and 180 others* v *UK* seems to have settled the matter unequivocally by providing an affirmative statement that a person who has no proprietary interest in his or her home can nevertheless qualify for protection under Article 8. The application to the European Commission arose following the House of Lords' decision in *Hunter* v *Canary Wharf Ltd* [1997] 2 All ER 426. The complaint to the European Commission was limited to the effects of the severe dust contamination, emanating from the construction works for the Limehouse link road, upon the applicants' private lives and homes. Many of the applicants had no proprietary interest in their homes, being the spouse or relative of the owner or being only a lodger, and the House of Lords' decision in *Hunter* meant that those applicants could not bring an action in private nuisance. The European Commission stated that:

> in the domestic proceedings, a distinction was made between those applicants with a proprietary interest in the land and those without such an interest. For the purposes of Article 8 of the Convention, there is no such distinction. 'Home' is an autonomous concept which does not depend on classification under domestic law. Whether or not a particular habitation constitutes a 'home' which attracts the protection of Article 8(1) of the Convention will depend on the factual circumstances, namely the existence of sufficient and continuous links (see *Gillow* v *UK*). Even where occupation of the property is illegal, this will not necessarily prevent that occupation from being that person's 'home' within the meaning of Article 8 of the Convention (see *Buckley* v *UK*). The Commission considers that Article 8(1) applies to all the applicants in the present case whether they are the owners of the property or merely occupiers living on the property, for example the children of the owner of the property.

This raises the question of squatters and whether or not such persons can be considered to be occupying a 'home' for the purposes of Article 8. That squatters may be in unlawful occupation of a house is not fatal to their assertion that the property is their 'home' given the decision of the European Court in *Buckley* v *UK*. But surely a squatter, unlawfully occupying residential property belonging to another, cannot rely upon Article 8 to protect that home from repossession by the lawful owner? Although the squatter may be able to establish the applicability of Article 8, the landowner's interference with the squatter's 'home', by virtue of the acquisition of a court order to evict the squatter, will undoubtedly be justifiable under Article 8(2), being in accordance with the law and necessary in a democratic society in pursuit of the protection of the rights of others, i.e. landowners. Therefore assessing the threshold of what constitutes a 'home' for the

---

[3] Harris, O'Boyle and Warbrick (n. 2 above) p. 319 (emphasis supplied).

purposes of Article 8 may be a futile activity. A broad interpretation of 'h permits all occupiers, whether lawful or not, to jump the initial hurdle satisfying the criterion of 'home', but some, including squatters, will fall at the later hurdles of legitimate aim and necessity.

5.2.4 The extension of 'home' to include some business premises

The case of *Niemietz* v *Germany* (1992) 16 EHRR 97 concerned a police search of a lawyer's office. The state contended that Article 8 drew a distinction between home and business premises and there was no protection against state interference with a lawyer's office. The European Court stated (at para. 30) that:

> As regards the word 'home', appearing in the English text of Article 8, the European Court observes that in certain Contracting states, notably Germany, it has been accepted as extending to business premises. Such an interpretation is, moreover, fully consonant with the French text, since the word 'domicile' has a broader connotation than the word 'home' and may extend, for example, to a professional person's office.

The European Court recognised that some activities relating to a person's private life are carried on in an office or business premises, just as business activities may be conducted from a person's home. Therefore it is not always possible to draw a precise distinction between the two. Given that a state can still interfere with premises to the extent permitted by Article 8(2), the European Court felt that a state would not be unduly hampered by an extension of the term 'home' to include a professional person's offices. Moreover the European Court was prepared to recognise that the scope of permitted interferences may be more extensive where professional premises are involved. On this basis the European Court was satisfied that the search of the lawyer's office constituted an interference with his private life and home.

5.2.5 The meaning of 'private life'

Many of the cases involving an alleged interference with a person's right to respect for their home have examined, and in some cases been decided under, the broader concept of 'private life' (see *Lopez Ostra* v *Spain* and *Guerra and others* v *Italy* in Appendix 3). The notion of 'private life' includes the idea of an 'inner circle' in which individuals may live their personal lives as they so choose without interference from the state. However the European Court has held that:

> it would be too restrictive to limit the notion to an 'inner circle' ... and to exclude therefrom entirely the outside world not encompassed within that circle. Respect for private life must also comprise to a certain degree the right to establish and develop relationships with human beings (*Niemietz* v *Germany* (1992) 16 EHRR 97 at para. 29).

26 EHRR 241 the applicant complained of an impairment
~~the~~ development of his personality resulting from the state's
~~approp~~riate steps to remedy the lack of disabled facilities at
~~beach~~es. The European Court confirmed (at para. 32) that:

~~C~~ourt's view, includes a person's physical and psychological
~~~~ afforded by Article 8 of the Convention is primarily intended to
~~develop~~ment, without outside interference, of the personality of each
individual in his relations with other human beings.

However, on the facts, there was found to be no breach of Article 8 (see 5.2.1).
The case of *Lopez Ostra* v *Spain* illustrates the broad scope of the notion of
'private life' and its application to property law. In this case the European Court
was satisfied that severe environmental pollution could impact upon an individual's well-being in such a way as to affect his or her private life (see 8.8).

5.3   ARTICLE 8(2): INTERFERENCE BY A PUBLIC AUTHORITY

(See the case summaries in Appendix 3 for the following cases: *Howard* v *UK*;
Gillow v *UK*; *Powell and Rayner* v *UK*; *Lopez Ostra* v *Spain*; *Buckley* v *UK*;
Guerra and others v *Italy*; *Khatun and 180 others* v *UK*; *McLeod* v *UK*.)

5.3.1   Interference by a public authority

Article 8(2) provides that there can be no interference by a public authority with
the rights protected by Article 8(1), except such as is in accordance with the law
and is necessary in a democratic society. An applicant, alleging a violation of
Article 8, needs to show, first, that there has been an interference and, secondly,
that the interference was by a public authority.

5.3.1.1   Establishing an interference
An interference can be due to either an act of a public authority or its failure to act.
Establishing an interference will depend on the facts of each individual case, but
examples from the decisions of the Strasbourg institutions include the following.

(a)   A local authority issuing a compulsory purchase order in respect of the
      applicants' home (*Howard* v *UK*).
(b)   A refusal to grant retrospective planning permission for caravans in which
      the applicant lived and the issuance of an enforcement notice requiring the
      caravans to be removed (*Buckley* v *UK*).
(c)   A refusal to grant a residence licence to permit the applicants to stay in
      Guernsey to live in their home (*Gillow* v *UK*).

(d) Intense and persistent aircraft noise. The European Commission has stated that: 'Considerable noise nuisance can undoubtedly affect the physical well-being of a person and thus interfere with his private life. It may also deprive a person of the possibility of enjoying the amenities of his home' (*Powell and Rayner* v *UK*).

(e) Severe dust contamination to the home (*Khatun and 180 others* v *UK*).

(f) Severe environmental pollution (*Lopez Ostra* v *Spain*). The European Court has acknowledged that: 'severe environmental pollution may affect individuals' well-being and prevent them from enjoying their homes in such a way as to affect their private and family life adversely' (*Guerra and others* v *Italy*, at para. 60).

In most of the cases involving environmental pollution, the applicants were not complaining of an interference by an act of a public authority, but rather that the state had failed to act. Clearly a state can only be responsible for a failure to act where it has a corresponding duty to act. This is thus inextricably linked to the scope of the positive obligations imposed upon the states under the concept of 'respect'. In *Guerra and others* v *Italy*, the 40 applicants lived in a town one kilometre away from a chemical factory. The factory, which produced fertilisers and caprolactam, was classified as 'high risk'. In the course of its production cycle the factory released large quantities of inflammable gas and other toxic substances. Due to the geographical location of the factory, emissions into the atmosphere were often channelled towards the town where the applicants lived. The applicants alleged that there had been a violation of their rights under Article 8. The European Court rejected the state's argument that it was not responsible for the pollution. Emphasising the state's positive obligations under Article 8, the European Court stated (at para. 58) that:

> Italy cannot be said to have 'interfered' with the applicants' private or family life; they complained not of an act by the State but of its failure to act. However, although the object of Article 8 is essentially that of protecting the individual against arbitrary interference by the public authorities, it does not merely compel the State to abstain from such interference: in addition to this primarily negative undertaking, there may be positive obligations inherent in effective respect for private or family life.

On the facts the European Court found that there was an infringement of Article 8 due to the fact that the national authorities had failed to take the necessary steps to ensure the effective protection of the applicants' rights guaranteed by Article 8.

5.3.1.2 *By a public authority*
It is not necessary that the state or the public authority directly undertakes the act that is the cause of the interference. For example, in *Arrondelle* v *UK* (1982) 5

EHRR 118 the applicant alleged that excessive noise caused by air traffic at Gatwick Airport and road traffic on the M23 motorway violated her rights under Article 8. The state submitted that it could not be held responsible for the noise generated by vehicles on the M23 motorway. However, the European Commission found that the relevant factor was the geographical position of the motorway, which had been built and operated by public authorities, and since the state was responsible for the planning and construction of the motorway at that location it was responsible for any noise pollution. In an earlier case, concerning aircraft noise from Heathrow Airport, the European Commission had noted that Article 8:

> cannot be interpreted so as to apply only with regard to direct measures taken by the authorities against the privacy and/or home of an individual. It may also cover indirect intrusions which are unavoidable consequences of measures not at all directed against private individuals (*Baggs* v *UK* (App. No. 9310/81).

The location of the motorway and airport in *Arrondelle* amounted to an indirect intrusion for which the state was responsible.

In *Lopez Ostra* v *Spain*, where the apparent link between the source of the interference and the state was more tenuous, the European Court nevertheless held the state responsible. The applicant lived near a town with a heavy concentration of leather industries. A tannery waste treatment plant was built by a limited company with a state subsidy and on municipal land only 12 metres away from the applicant's home. The waste treatment plant began to operate without a licence from the municipal authorities. Owing to a malfunction the plant released gas fumes and smells into the atmosphere which immediately caused health problems and nuisance to local residents including the applicant. The Spanish authorities were not directly responsible for the fumes and smells because the waste treatment plant was built and owned by a private company; however, the plant was built on municipal land and the state had subsidised its construction. This in itself may have been sufficient to establish the necessary link between the interference and the state, but in any event the European Commission noted (at para. 55) that, regardless of the level of responsibility, direct or indirect, imputable to the state authorities, 'the Convention contains articles which not only protect the individual against the State but also oblige the State to protect the rights of the individual even against the actions of third parties'. The European Commission relied on the positive obligations under Article 8(1) to find that the Government had omitted to take the necessary measures to ensure the practical and effective protection of the rights under Article 8(1).

5.3.2   Is the interference in accordance with the law?

This relates to the lawfulness of the action by the public authority. There must be a specific, accessible legal rule (whether by statute, delegated legislation or part of the common law) which authorises the act that causes the interference and lets the individual know the basis for the interference with his property. For example, in *Buckley* v *UK*, the town and country planning regime authorised the local planning authority's refusal to grant the applicant planning permission. This legislation was accessible to the applicant and the local authority's action was consequently foreseeable. Similarly, in *Howard* v *UK*, the European Commission was satisfied that the interference with the applicant's home, as a result of a compulsory purchase order being issued by the local authority, was in accordance with the law as the order was made under statutory provisions that were both readily accessible and foreseeable.

In the case of *Sunday Times* v *UK* (1979) 2 EHRR 245, which concerned an alleged breach of the applicant's right to freedom of expression under Article 10, the European Court identified accessibility and foreseeability as the appropriate criteria for establishing the lawfulness of an interference. The European Court stressed the need for states to avoid arbitrariness in implementing their legal rules and stated (at para. 49) that:

> Firstly, the law must be adequately accessible: the citizen must be able to have an indication that is adequate in the circumstances of the legal rules applicable to a given case. Secondly, a norm cannot be regarded as a 'law' unless it is formulated with sufficient precision to enable the citizen to regulate his conduct'.

Therefore not only must a person have adequate access to the law in question, but that law must be sufficiently clear and precise to enable the person to foresee the circumstances in which the law will, or may, be applied.

5.3.2.1 Foreseeable

In *Gillow* v *UK*, the applicants' applications for residence licences to permit them to live in their home in Guernsey were refused by the housing authority. They complained that the relevant legislation gave the housing authority such wide discretionary powers that its decisions were unforeseeable and unpredictable. However, the European Court was satisfied that the interference was in accordance with the law. The European Court observed (at para. 51) that:

> A law which confers a discretion is not in itself inconsistent with the requirement of foreseeability, provided that the scope of the discretion and the manner of its exercise are indicated with sufficient clarity, having regard to the legitimate aim of the measure in question, to give the individual adequate protection against arbitrary interference.

The question of foreseeability also arose in the case of *McLeod* v *UK*, where the applicant maintained that the common law power of the police to enter private property without a warrant on the grounds of preventing an anticipated breach of the peace was not 'in accordance with the law'. The European Court stressed (at para. 41) the need for the measure to be formulated with sufficient precision to enable a person concerned:

> to foresee, to a degree that is reasonable in the circumstances, the consequences which a given action may entail. However, those consequences need not be foreseeable with absolute certainty, since such certainty might give rise to excessive rigidity, and the law must be able to keep pace with changing circumstances.

On this basis the European Court was satisfied that the common law power was in accordance with the law.

5.3.2.2   *Accessible*

To be accessible the rule must be available to an applicant either by access to the relevant text and/or through the availability of legal advice. In *Malone* v *UK* (1984) 7 EHRR 14, the police had tapped the applicant's telephone. The European Court found that the interference violated Article 8 because it was not prescribed by law. At the time the only regulation of telephone tapping was by means of an internal police code of practice that was not available to the public. The applicant could not therefore determine whether any surveillance might occur and why. A similar approach was taken by the European Court in the more recent decision of *Halford* v *UK* (1997) 24 EHRR 523 where the police interception of telephone calls made from the applicant's office violated Article 8 because it was not 'in accordance with the law'.

5.3.3   Is there a legitimate aim to justify the interference?

The need for a legitimate aim relates to the state's justification and reasons for the interference with the applicant's rights under Article 8(1) (see 2.4). Article 8(2) provides the following list of legitimate aims:

(a)   national security;
(b)   public safety;
(c)   economic well-being of the country;
(d)   prevention of disorder or crime;
(e)   protection of health or morals;
(f)   protection of rights and freedoms of others.

As the scope of these aims is extremely wide, it is relatively easy for the state to establish the existence of a legitimate aim to justify its actions. It is common for the state to raise more than one aim to justify the measure and the European Court need only be satisfied in respect of one of the cited aims. Examples from the case law of the Strasbourg institutions include the following.

(a) In *Buckley* v *UK* the refusal to grant the applicant retrospective planning permission for her caravans was based on a town and country planning policy aimed at furthering highway safety, the preservation of the environment and public health. Therefore the interference with the applicant's home was found to pursue the legitimate aims of public safety, the economic well-being of the country and the protection of the health and rights of others.

(b) In *Howard* v *UK* the European Commission concluded that the state interference with the applicants' home, as a result of the implementation of a compulsory purchase order against it, pursued the legitimate aim of 'the protection of the rights and freedoms of others' because the applicants' land, once compulsorily acquired, would be part of a redevelopment scheme of the deprived inner city area and would thereby benefit others.

(c) In *McLeod* v *UK*, the European Court acknowledged that the police power to enter into and remain on private premises without permission, in order to prevent the occurrence of a breach of the peace, was in pursuit of a legitimate aim, namely the prevention of disorder or crime.

5.3.3.1 *The economic well-being of the country*

The 'economic well-being of the country' has a wide scope and is regularly cited by the states as a justification for state interference. For example, in *Gillow* v *UK*, the European Commission accepted the state's assertion that the controlled market in houses and the residence licensing system, which prevented the applicants from being able to live in their home, was implemented to maintain a balance between the requirements of the existing population, horticultural and other economic interests, the interests of persons wanting to move to Guernsey to live and the interests of the tourist industry. This clearly pursued the legitimate aim of the economic well-being of the country and the European Court endorsed this view in its judgment. In *Lopez Ostra* v *Spain*, the construction of a tannery waste treatment plant, which subsequently caused severe environmental pollution, was justified because the town had a heavy concentration of leather industries and therefore the construction of the plant was found to be for the economic well-being of the town. Similarly, in *Khatun and 180 others* v *UK*, the construction of the Limehouse link road, which generated considerable dust affecting the applicants' homes, gave access to the Docklands from Central London and was seen as essential for the regeneration of the derelict urban areas in the Docklands. The European Commission was satisfied that the measures pursued the legitimate aim of the economic well-being of the country. Also in *Powell and Rayner* v *UK*, which concerned noise pollution caused by aircraft, the applicants themselves conceded that the operation of Heathrow Airport, occupying an important position in relation to international trade, communications and the economy of the UK, pursued a legitimate aim as being for the economic well-being of the country. Although there are plenty of examples of when an interference is found to be in pursuit of the economic well-being of the country, there is no clear guidance as to what kind of test the European Court is applying and what kind of evidence is required to demonstrate the economic advantages flowing, perhaps indirectly, from the interference.

5.3.4   Is the interference necessary in a democratic society?

Having established the existence of a legitimate aim, it must then be ascertained whether the measures employed to implement that aim are 'necessary in a democratic society'. As a starting point the European Court has recognised that:

> It is for the national authorities to make the initial assessment of the 'necessity' for an interference, as regards both the legislative framework and the particular measure of implementation. Although a margin of appreciation is thereby left to the national authorities, their decision remains subject to review by the Court for conformity with the requirements of the Convention (*Buckley* v *UK*, at para. 74).

The concept of necessity embraces two related issues. First, the existence of a 'pressing social need' and secondly, the principle of proportionality. The European Court has confirmed that this is its recognised approach to the question of necessity in Article 8(2). It has stated that: 'According to the Court's established case-law, the notion of necessity implies that an interference corresponds to a pressing social need and, in particular, that it is proportionate to the legitimate aim pursued' (*Olsson* v *Sweden* (1988) 11 EHRR 259 at para. 67).

5.3.4.1   *A pressing social need*
The European Commission has explained this requirement in the following terms:

> As the Convention organs have repeatedly recognised, to satisfy the requirement of necessity referred to in Art. 8(2) of the Convention, it must be established that the measure in question was not merely desirable or convenient, but responded to a real requirement (*Gillow* v *UK*, at para. 132).

This real requirement is often referred to as a 'pressing social need'. In making the initial assessment of the reality of a pressing social need the states enjoy a wide margin of appreciation. The European Court has recognised that national public authorities are in a better position to assess the necessity of a measure than an international judge. It is inevitable that the existence of a pressing social need will be closely linked to the legitimate aim, but it is not necessarily the case that establishing a legitimate aim will automatically lead to satisfying the requirement for a pressing social need. For example, in *Howard* v *UK*, the applicants, two brothers, were the owners and occupiers of Rose Cottage and the surrounding land where they had lived for over 50 years. The local authority issued a compulsory purchase order in respect of the applicants' land and it intended to demolish Rose Cottage, which was unsightly having a high corrugated iron fence and heaps of scrap, in order to make land available for the construction of new houses. This action was part of a scheme to redevelop the area which was a run-down, inner-city area in need of improvement. The European Commission accepted that there was a pressing social need for the compulsory purchase order which was necessary to pursue the legitimate aim of protecting the rights and freedoms of others. However, the position would have been different if Rose Cottage had been situated in a pleasant residential area that did not need to be redeveloped. In such a case the state could still try to contend that a legitimate aim existed; for example it could argue that the proposed redevelopment, by providing jobs, would be for the economic well-being of the town or that it protected the rights of neighbours whose property was adversely affected by the unsightly Rose Cottage (such arguments are somewhat tenuous and would be subject to debate). However, the state would have difficulty in showing that a pressing social need existed if there was no real requirement for the land to be redeveloped in the first place.

There is an inevitable link between the requirement of a pressing social need and the principle of proportionality. The European Commission drew attention to this nexus in its opinion in *Gillow* v *UK*. The reasons given to the applicants for the refusal of a residence licence relied principally upon the 'adverse housing situation' which the Government perceived as existing in Guernsey. The European Commission decided (at para. 137) that it must, 'examine the degree to which the refusal of the applicants' licence requests reflected a 'pressing social need' by reference to the question whether or not these refusals were proportionate to the aim which the licensing legislation pursued'.

5.3.4.2 *Proportionality*

In *Buckley* v *UK* the European Court had to assess whether the applicant suffered a disproportionate burden due to the refusal to grant her retrospective planning permission to allow her to continue living in the caravans parked on her land. In the sphere of town and country planning, the states are allowed a wide margin of appreciation. The European Court acknowledged (at para. 75) that:

> By reason of their direct and continuous contact with the vital forces of their countries, the national authorities are in principle better placed than an international court to evaluate local needs and conditions. In so far as the exercise of discretion involving a multitude of local factors is inherent in the choice and implementation of planning policies, the national authorities in principle enjoy a wide margin of appreciation.

Town and country planning schemes inevitably involve the exercise of discretionary powers by the public authorities acting in the interests of the whole
community. There may be scope for differences of judgment in the use of the
discretion, but the European Court stressed that it would not substitute its own
view of what would be the best policy in the planning sphere. In *Buckley*, the
European Court was satisfied that the public authorities had given due regard to
the interests of the applicant. They had taken her special needs as a gypsy,
following a traditional lifestyle, into account and had had regard to the shortage
of gypsy caravan sites in the area. However, they had concluded that the general
interest of the public in conforming to the planning policy, which was to promote
open countryside and to prevent all but essential development, outweighed the
applicant's needs. The European Court also had regard to the fact that she had
declined an invitation to apply for a pitch on an official caravan site because she
felt that it was unsuitable. The European Court observed (at para. 81) that: 'Article
8 does not necessarily go so far as to allow individuals' preferences as to their
place of residence to override the general interest'. Taking into account all of the
above considerations, the European Court concluded (at para. 84) that:

> proper regard was had to the applicant's predicament both under the terms of the
> regulatory framework, which contained adequate procedural safeguards protecting her
> interest under Article 8, and by the responsible planning authorities when exercising
> their discretion in relation to the particular circumstances of her case. The latter
> authorities arrived at the contested decision after weighing in the balance the various
> competing interests at issue.

There was consequently no violation of Article 8.

Howard v *UK* involved an interference with the applicants' right to respect for
their home by virtue of a compulsory purchase order. The European Commission
was satisfied that a fair balance had been struck between the applicants' interests
and the interests of the community as a whole. There were a number of relevant
factors in reaching this decision including the fact that if the applicants' land,
which was low lying and level land, were excluded from the redevelopment
scheme it would be impossible to include sheltered housing for the elderly. This
factor was weighed in the balance together with the fact that the applicants had
been offered alternative residential accommodation in the immediate vicinity of
their home and they were entitled to full compensation for the value of their land,
in addition to compensation for disturbance and removal expenses. The European
Commission concluded that the interference was justified as necessary in a
democratic society for the protection of the rights and freedoms of others who
would benefit from the proposed redevelopment.

In assessing the fair balance test in *Khatun and 180 others* v *UK*, the European
Commission noted that the construction of the Limehouse link road was essential

to the development of the London Docklands. Against this important public interest it weighed the considerable degree of inconvenience caused to the applicants by the dust produced during the construction of the road. The European Commission noted that, 'the inconvenience, whilst undoubtedly unpleasant, has not been claimed to have given rise to health problems for any of the applicants. Further, it was limited in time to the period of the works, some three-and-a-half years'. Taking these two factors into account and, bearing in mind the importance of the public interest, the European Commission concluded that a fair balance had been struck between the competing interests of the individual and of the community.

These cases illustrate the European Court's application of the fair balance test in weighing up the various competing interests to ascertain proportionality and thereby to ensure that the individual concerned does not suffer a disproportionate burden. In each case the Strasbourg institutions were satisfied that the interference was proportionate to the legitimate aim to be achieved.

However, *Gillow* v *UK* and *McLeod* v *UK* are examples of cases in which the state was found to be in breach of Article 8 due to a lack of proportionality between the legitimate aim pursued and the interference with the applicants' right to the respect of their home.

In *Gillow* v *UK* the applicants, who were husband and wife, moved to Guernsey in 1956 and having brought a plot of land, built a house called 'Whiteknights'. Due to work commitments they left Guernsey to work abroad and 'Whiteknights' was let to tenants. Under the legislation in force at that time the applicants had resident qualifications which enabled them to occupy 'Whiteknights' without a licence. However, in 1970 legislation was introduced which imposed a residency requirement with the effect that the applicants were no longer entitled to occupy 'Whiteknights' without a residence licence. They later returned to Guernsey to apply for a licence to occupy 'Whiteknights' as their retirement home, or for a period sufficient to put the property into repair for the purposes of sale or letting. The licences were refused in the light of the adverse housing situation in Guernsey and Mr Gillow was subsequently prosecuted for the unlawful occupation of his house and was fined. In assessing the pro-ortionality of the interference, the European Commission observed (at para. 141) that: 'In view of the protection given by Art. 8, the prohibition of the enjoyment of a property built and owned by an individual as his home can only be justified in the most exceptional circumstances'. The European Court took note of the fact that the applicants had initially built 'Whiteknights' and had let the house during their 18 years of absence from the Island. In this respect they had significantly contributed to the housing stock of Guernsey. It concluded (at para. 58) that:

the decisions by the Housing Authority to refuse the applicants permanent and temporary licences to occupy Whiteknights, as well as the conviction and fining of Mr.

Gillow, constituted interferences with the exercise of their right to respect for their home which were disproportionate to the legitimate aim pursued'.

Therefore the interference with the applicants' right to respect for their home was not necessary in a democratic society and was consequently in violation of Article 8.

In *McLeod* v *UK*, the applicant's ex-husband entered her home, during her absence, in order to remove furniture that belonged to him. His solicitors had arranged for two police officers to be present while the property was being removed on the grounds that a breach of the peace might occur. The European Court accepted that the police had the power to enter private property without the owner's permission in order to prevent a breach of the peace. However, on the particular facts, the European Court decided that the action of the police, though justified, had been disproportionate because it did not strike a fair balance between the applicant's right to respect for her home and the public interest in the prevention of disorder and crime. The European Court considered that the police should have taken steps to verify the terms of the court order to ensure that the ex-husband was entitled to enter the home. Had they done so they would have discovered that he was not so entitled. In addition, the fact that the applicant was not present at the time of the removal of the furniture was a relevant factor since her absence meant that there was little or no risk of a breach of the peace occurring and consequently the police should not have entered her house. Therefore the police measures were found to be disproportionate to the legitimate aim and a breach of Article 8 ensued.

It is interesting to observe that in the judicial review case, *R* v *North and East Devon Health Authority, ex parte Coughlan* [2000] 2 WLR 622, the Court of Appeal found the health authority to be in breach of Article 8. The applicant, who was severely disabled, was moved, with her consent, from a hospital to a National Health Service facility (Mardon House) for the long-term disabled. At the time, the health authority assured her that this would be her home for the rest of her life. Five years later the health authority decided to close down Mardon House. On an application for judicial review of the closure decision, the judge quashed the health authority's decision and the Court of Appeal dismissed the appeal by the health authority. Although the HRA 1998 was not in force at the time of the judgment, the Court of Appeal nevertheless had regard to the Article 8 considerations. It acknowledged that the public cost to be saved by the closure of Mardon House was not dramatic and it weighed this against the fact that the enforced move would be 'emotionally devastating and seriously anti-therapeutic' for the applicant. The Court of Appeal decided that the measure could not be justified by Article 8(2) without providing alternative accommodation which equally met the special needs of the applicant. On the facts, no such alternative accommodation had been offered and, consequently, the Court of Appeal found the health authority's conduct to be in breach of Article 8.

5.3.4.3   *Proportionality and due process*

In the assessment of proportionality under Article 8, a factor of particular significance is the procedural safeguards available to the individual. The European Court has stated that:

> Indeed it is settled case law that, whilst Article 8 contains no explicit procedural requirements, the decision-making process leading to measures of interference must be fair and such as to afford due respect to the interests safeguarded to the individual by Article 8 (*Buckley* v *UK*, at para. 76).

In *Buckley* the European Court was satisfied that the town and country planning regime contained adequate procedural safeguards to protect the applicant's interest. The appeal procedure to the Secretary of state involved an assessment by a qualified expert to whom the applicant could make representations and, in addition, the applicant could apply for judicial review by the High Court of the public authority's exercise of its discretionary powers.

The case of *Niemietz* v *Germany* (1992) 16 EHRR 97 further illustrates the importance of the due process considerations in assessing the fair balance test under Article 8. In this case the interference was held to constitute a breach of Article 8 because it was disproportionate to the aim to be achieved. One of the factors in reaching that conclusion was the absence of any special procedural safeguards, e.g. an independent observer, accompanying the police search of the lawyer's office.

5.3.4.4   *Proportionality and compensation*

The relevancy of compensation, as a factor to be weighed in the fair balance test, depends upon the nature of the interference complained of. In *Powell and Rayner* v *UK* the absence of compensation in respect of aircraft noise from Heathrow Airport did not prevent the European Commission from declaring the application under Article 8 to be inadmissible. However, compensation was a particularly relevant factor in assessing proportionality in *Howard* v *UK*, where the interference involved the expropriation of the applicants' home by means of a compulsory purchase order.

5.4   THE RELATIONSHIP BETWEEN THE IMPOSITION OF POSITIVE OBLIGATIONS UNDER ARTICLE 8(1) AND THE REQUIREMENTS OF ARTICLE 8(2)

In *Powell and Rayner* v *UK*, which concerned noise pollution caused by aircraft, the European Court avoided deciding whether the case involved positive obligations on the state under Article 8(1) or negative obligations under Article 8(2). The European Court said that in both cases the applicable principles are broadly similar as in both contexts regard must be had to the principle of proportionality and to the state's margin of appreciation. The European Court added (at para. 41) that: 'even in relation to the positive obligations flowing from the first paragraph of Article 8, in striking [the required] balance the aim mentioned in the second paragraph may be of a certain relevance'. This indicates the limits on the state's positive obligations to regulate relations between private individuals to prevent violations of the Convention. In *Powell and Rayner*, it was the legitimate aim of 'the economic well-being of the country' that provided a limitation to the positive obligations of the state.

In *Lopez Ostra* v *Spain*, the Spanish authorities were not directly responsible for the polluting fumes and smells emanating from the tannery waste treatment plant because it was owned by a private company. However, the plant was built on municipal land and the state had subsidised its construction. In its admissibility decision the European Commission noted that regardless of the level of responsibility, direct or indirect, imputable to the state authorities, 'the Convention contains articles which not only protect the individual against the state but also oblige the state to protect the rights of the individual even against the actions of third parties'. The European Court noted that there were two ways to analyse the case. Either it could determine whether the state had a positive obligation to take reasonable measures to secure the applicant's right to respect for her private life, family life and home (under Article 8(1)), or it could ascertain whether there had been a justifiable interference by a public authority (under Article 8(2)). The European Court observed that whichever approach it adopted, the applicable principles are broadly similar, being an application of proportionality within the context of the state's margin of appreciation. The European Court reiterated that the legitimate aims in Article 8(2) are relevant in determining the scope of the state's positive obligations under Article 8(1). Therefore the European Court in *Lopez Ostra* endorsed its earlier decision in *Powell and Rayner* v *UK* and thereby established a recognised approach to the question of state responsibility in cases involving environmental pollution.

5.5   THE RELATIONSHIP BETWEEN ARTICLE 8 AND ARTICLE 1, PROTOCOL 1

The applicants in *Howard* v *UK* alleged that the compulsory purchase of their home constituted a breach of both Article 8 and Article 1, Protocol 1. The European Commission was therefore required to consider the overlap between these two Articles. At a general level the European Commission recognised that: 'where, as here, administrative actions impinge on two separate but partially overlapping provisions of the Convention, the application of the relevant provisions must be reconciled'. Making a specific comparison of the second rule of Article 1, Protocol 1 (the rule governing the deprivation of possessions) and

Article 8, the European Commission observed that: 'the measure of necessity referred to in the second sentence of [Article 1, Protocol 1] closely resembles that which applies to the justification for an interference with the rights guaranteed by Art. 8(1)'. However, in *Gillow* v *UK* the European Commission observed (at para. 152) that: 'the requirements of [Article 1, Protocol 1] permit the domestic legislature greater latitude in the choice of legislation which is appropriate for the control of the use of property than under Art. 8 of the Convention'. Nevertheless, it is difficult to envisage a scenario in which the applicant's case would fail under Article 8 but succeed under Article 1, Protocol 1.

5.6 ARTICLE 8 AND COMPANIES

A corporate body has no family or home that can be protected under Article 8 nor, according to the European Commission, can it be capable of having a 'private life' (*Open Door and Dublin Well Woman* v *Ireland* (1991) 14 EHRR 131).

However, in the judicial review case, *R* v *Broadcasting Standards Commission, ex parte British Broadcasting Corporation* (6 April 2000), the Court of Appeal acknowledged that companies can have a right to privacy that can be protected under Article 8. The case concerned secret filming of company activities and Lord Woolf MR observed that:

> While the intrusions into privacy of an individual which are possible are no doubt more extensive than the infringements of privacy which are possible in the case of a company, a company does have activities which need protection from unwarranted intrusion. I consider that the BSC has jurisdiction to determine the application of Article 8 of the ECHR to companies.

This approach is in line with the position under the Canadian Charter of Rights. In Canada, the provision of the Charter which protects individuals from unjustified state intrusions upon their privacy, applies to corporations. In *Hunter* v *Southam* [1984] 2 SCR 145 which concerned an entry onto company premises for the purpose of searching and seizing evidence for an investigation, the Supreme Court of Canada held that the company had the same constitutionally protected expectation of privacy as a natural person.

Chapter Six

Article 14

The enjoyment of the rights and freedoms set forth in this Convention shall be secured without discrimination on any ground such as sex, race, colour, language, religion, political or other opinion, national or social origin, association with a national minority, property, birth or other status.

6.1 THE NATURE OF ARTICLE 14

(See the case summaries in Appendix 3 for the following cases: *Marckx* v *Belgium*; *Matos e Silva, Lda and others* v *Portugal.*)

There are two significant characteristics that define the nature of Article 14. First, its parasitic nature and secondly, its autonomous nature.

6.1.1 The parasitic nature of Article 14

Article 14 safeguards individuals who are placed in analogous situations against discriminatory differences of treatment. However, it does not create a general right not to be discriminated against. Instead Article 14 has a parasitic nature that is dependent upon the other Articles in the Convention. Article 14 states that: 'the enjoyment of the rights and freedoms set forth in this Convention shall be secured without discrimination'. Therefore the right to claim freedom from discrimination under Article 14 relates only to discrimination preventing enjoyment of the rights and freedoms conferred by the other Articles. The European Court of Human Rights (the European Court) has explained this in the following terms:

> Article 14 complements the other substantive provisions of the Convention and the Protocols. It has no independent existence since it has effect solely in relation to the

enjoyment of the rights and freedoms' safeguarded by those provisions (*Rasmussen* v *Denmark* (1984) 7 EHRR 371 at para. 29).

The case of *Botta* v *Italy* (1998) 26 EHRR 241 illustrates the parasitic nature of Article 14. The applicant went on holiday and discovered that the bathing establishments were not equipped with disabled facilities and this prevented him from accessing the beach and the sea. He alleged breaches of Article 8 and Article 14 in conjunction with Article 8. The European Court held that Article 8 was not applicable (see 5.2.1). Relying upon the fact that Article 14 does not have an independent existence, the European Court had no choice but to conclude that Article 14 was also inapplicable.

Given the parasitic nature of Article 14, the European Court will first consider whether or not there has been a breach of any of the substantive rights, e.g., Article 1, Protocol 1. In many cases, once the European Court has found an infringement of one of the substantive rights, it will consider it unnecessary to ascertain whether there has also been a violation of Article 14 in conjunction with that Article. *Matos e Silva, Lda and others* v *Portugal* provides an example of this. The Portuguese Government had taken a number of measures affecting the applicants' land with a view to creating a nature reserve. The applicants alleged a violation of Article 14 in conjunction with Article 1, Protocol 1 on the grounds that the measures had only affected their land and not their neighbour's land, and there was no difference in the two parcels of land. Having already established that the state action constituted a breach of Article 1, Protocol 1 taken alone, the European Court stated that it did not consider it necessary to examine the question separately under Article 14 of the Convention taken in conjunction with Article 1 of Protocol 1. In contrast, in *Marckx* v *Belgium* the European Court, having found there to be a breach of Article 8, proceeded to decide that there had also been a violation of Article 14 in conjunction with Article 8. The European Court has not adopted a uniform approach as to when it will go on to examine Article 14 having already found the state to be in breach of the Convention; however, it has stated that it will determine an Article 14 claim where 'a clear inequality of treatment in the enjoyment of the right in question is a fundamental aspect of the case' (*Airey* v *Ireland* (1979) 2 EHRR 305 at para. 30).

The restrictions on the use of Article 14, due to its parasitic nature, are qualified by the fact that discrimination issues have been held to apply in areas where the states are not obliged by the Convention to provide specific protection. Therefore if a state voluntarily guarantees the protection of rights, in excess of that required by the Convention, the state must nevertheless provide that additional protection in a non-discriminatory fashion. In the *Belgian Linguistics case (No. 2)* (1968) 1 EHRR 252 the European Court explained this principle by reference to an example in relation to Article 6. It stated (at para. 9) that:

Article 6 of the Convention does not compel states to institute a system of appeal courts. A state which does set up such courts consequently goes beyond its obligations under Article 6. However, it would violate that Article, read in conjunction with Article 14, were it to debar certain persons from these remedies without legitimate reason while making them available to others in respect of the same type of actions.

6.1.2   The autonomous nature of Article 14

Provided that the applicant's claim concerns the subject matter protected by one of the other Articles in the Convention, there does not need to be a breach of that other Article in order for Article 14 to apply. The European Court has qualified the parasitic nature of Article 14 by reference to its autonomous nature and stated that:

> Although the application of Article 14 does not necessarily presuppose a breach of those provisions — and to this extent it has an autonomous meaning — there can be no room for its application unless the facts at issue fall within the ambit of one or more of the latter (*Rasmussen* v *Denmark* (1984) 7 EHRR 371 at para. 29).

Therefore if a measure is found to be in conformity with the other Article, but is of a discriminatory nature incompatible with Article 14, the measure will be taken to violate both Articles taken in conjunction, e.g., Article 14 taken in conjunction with Article 8. The case of *Marckx* v *Belgium* illustrates this point. The applicants, a mother and her illegitimate daughter, complained that laws which imposed limits on a mother's capacity to bequeath property to her illegitimate child infringed Article 1, Protocol 1 taken alone and in conjunction with Article 14. The European Court accepted that the right of a mother freely to give or bequeath her property to her illegitimate child concerned a property right within the scope of Article 1, Protocol 1. However, the legislation was not in itself in conflict with Article 1 because the restrictions on the right to dispose of property *inter vivos* or by will were found to be justified as being necessary and in accordance with the general interest under the third rule of Article 1, Protocol 1 (see 4.4). Consequently, the European Court acknowledged that the restriction on the intestacy laws was not in itself in conflict with Article 1, Protocol 1 taken alone. Nevertheless, the European Court found a breach of Article 14 in conjunction with Article 1, Protocol 1 due to the fact that the disputed limitation applied only to unmarried and not to married mothers. The European Court stated (at para. 65) that:

> In view of Article 14 of the Convention, the European Court fails to see on what 'general interest', or on what objective and reasonable justification, a state could rely to limit an unmarried mother's right to make gifts or legacies in favour of her child when at the same time a married woman is not subject to any similar restriction.

Therefore the fact that there was no breach of Article 1, Protocol 1 did not prevent the applicability of Article 14. Once the complaint is found to come within the ambit of those rights protected by the Convention, Article 14 is applicable and having crossed this threshold of applicability, Article 14 enjoys an element of autonomy. A breach of Article 14 is not dependent upon a breach of the Article relied upon to invoke Article 14. However, in most cases the European Court will first ascertain whether a breach of the other Article exists and if it does the European Court may consider it unnecessary to examine whether there is also a breach of Article 14.

6.2   THE THREE COMPONENTS OF ARTICLE 14

(See the case summaries in Appendix 3 for the following cases: *Marckx* v *Belgium*; *James* v *UK*; *Lithgow* v *UK*; *S* v *UK*; *Gillow* v *UK*; *Pine Valley Developments Ltd and others* v *Ireland*; *Buckley* v *UK*; *National and Provincial Building Society and others* v *UK*; *Khatun and 180 others* v *UK*.)

There are in effect three components to Article 14. The first two concern the applicants who, in order to claim a violation of Article 14, will need to show first that they are persons placed in an 'analogous situation' to another and secondly that they have been treated differently from those other persons (however, also see 6.4.2). Once the applicants have crossed this threshold of applicability the third component of Article 14 is activated. This imposes an obligation on the state to show that the differential treatment, which has been identified by the applicants, can be reasonably and objectively justified. If it cannot be justified, a violation of Article 14 will ensue.

6.2.1   Persons in an analogous situation

The problem for the applicants in *Khatun* v *UK* was that they could not identify any other persons in a relatively similar position to themselves who were being treated more favourably. The applicants complained that they were been discriminated against on the grounds of poverty. The formula adopted by the state to calculate compensation to be paid to property owners, in respect of dust contamination caused by the construction of a highway, disadvantaged the applicants because the market value of their properties was very low. In determining the applicability of Article 14 the European Commission noted that:

> For a claim of violation of this Article to succeed, it has therefore to be established, *inter alia*, that the situation of the alleged victim can be considered similar to that of persons who have been better treated (see *Fredin* v *Sweden* (1991) 13 EHRR 784, para. 60). The applicants must show that they are persons in the same category as another, that they have been treated differently, that such treatment was not objectively and reasonably justified, and the treatment was carried out by the Contracting state against which the complaint is being made. There are no other persons in 'relevantly' similar situations to

the applicants. There is no evidence that there are persons in the same category as the applicants who have been treated more favourably.

All the properties located near the construction of the Limehouse link road were properties of a low value and therefore there were no property owners affected by the dust contamination whose property was of a high market value. The lack of evidence of persons in the same category as the applicants, who had enjoyed preferential treatment, meant that the application under Article 14 was inadmissible.

The case of *National and Provincial Building Society and others* v *UK* provides a further example of the importance of meeting this requirement. It concerned changes to the system for taxation on interest paid to the investors of building societies. Transitional regulations, adopted to cover a gap period, were subsequently successfully challenged in the House of Lords by the Woolwich Building Society (the Woolwich) and declared to be invalid with the result that the Inland Revenue was required to return to the Woolwich the sum of £57,000,000 with interest. Subsequently, legislation was passed which retrospectively validated the transitional regulations, with the significant exception that the provisions did not apply to any building society that had commenced legal proceedings prior to a specified date. Only the Woolwich satisfied this criterion and was therefore solely excluded from the effects of the retrospective legislation. The applicant building societies were thereby prevented from insisting on the repayment of sums similar to that which had been repaid to the Woolwich. The applicants alleged that this differential treatment amounted to discrimination contrary to Article 14 in conjunction with Article 1, Protocol 1. To establish the applicability of Article 14, the applicants maintained that they were in an analogous situation to the Woolwich in respect of the transitional regulations but that the Woolwich had enjoyed preferential treatment. The European Court took a different view of the situation. It decided that since the Woolwich had accepted the risks of litigation challenging the transitional regulations and borne the associated legal costs, the applicants were not in an analogous or relevantly similar position to the Woolwich. Therefore Article 14 was not applicable.

These two cases illustrate the importance for applicants to be able to show that they are placed in an analogous situation to others who enjoy preferential treatment. It is not sufficient to prove that hypothetical persons placed in a similar position to the applicants would be treated differently: there must be actual persons affected by the measures complained of, who have benefited from differential treatment.

6.2.2   Persons enjoying preferential treatment

The case of *Lithgow* v *UK* concerned the nationalisation of certain industries. One of the applicants, Sir William Lithgow, alleged that he had been the victim of discrimination. He maintained that whilst he was liable to pay capital gains tax on the disposal of the compensation stock which he received, former corporate owners of undertakings that had been nationalised were entitled to defer that liability under specified legislation. The European Court rejected this submission. It noted that the opportunity to defer liability would not have been available to a corporation holding the same proportion of shares in the company that was nationalised as Sir William Lithgow had held. Therefore the European Court concluded that he was not being treated any differently from any former owners placed in a situation analogous to his own.

6.3 REASONABLE AND OBJECTIVE JUSTIFICATION

Not every instance of differential treatment of persons in a similar situation will result in an infringement of Article 14. There may be grounds to justify the difference. In *James* v *UK* the European Court stated (at para. 75) that:

> For the purposes of Article 14, a difference of treatment is discriminatory if it has no objective and reasonable justification, that is, if it does not pursue a legitimate aim or if there is not a reasonable relationship of proportionality between the means employed and the aim sought to be realised ... the Contracting States enjoy a certain margin of appreciation in assessing whether and to what extent differences in otherwise similar situations permit a different treatment in law.

Therefore the need for an objective and reasonable justification for the differential treatment incorporates the familiar concepts of legitimate aim and proportionality (see 2.4 and 2.3 respectively).

The European Court has also acknowledged the states' margin of appreciation in this area (see 2.2), the scope of which will vary according to the circumstances, the subject matter and its background (*Lithgow* v *UK*, at para. 177). One relevant factor to the variable scope of the margin of appreciation is the ground relied upon for the difference in treatment, e.g., sex, nationality etc. Although Article 14 expressly includes a list of prohibited grounds of discrimination, the European Court has stated that this list is not exhaustive (*James* v *UK*, at para. 74). Cases suggest that there may be a scale of seriousness attached to the different grounds so that some grounds are more difficult to justify than others. The case of *Inze* v *Austria* (1987) 10 EHRR 394 concerned the hereditary rights of illegitimate children. The applicant alleged that a rule under Austrian law that made the legitimate child the principal heir of his or her parents' estate violated Article 14 in conjunction with Article 1, Protocol 1. In finding a breach of Article 14 the European Court observed (at para. 41) that: 'Very weighty reasons would ... have to be advanced before a difference of treatment on the ground of birth out of wedlock could be regarded as compatible with the Convention'. The arguments advanced by the Government for the differential treatment were not sufficiently 'weighty' to justify it. Similarly, 'very weighty reasons' have been found to be needed to justify a difference in treatment based exclusively on sex (*Schuler-Zgraggen* v *Switzerland* (1993) 16 EHRR 405 at para. 67) or on nationality (*Gaygusuz* v *Austria* (1996) 23 EHRR 365 at para. 42).

Therefore differential treatment and discrimination are not co-terminous. If the differential treatment can be justified, there will be no discrimination under Article 14. What is considered to be a reasonable and objective justification for the difference in treatment will vary with the facts of each individual case. Thus, a useful way in which to examine the concession of permissible differentiation that is granted to the states, is to consider examples from the case law of the Strasbourg institutions.

6.3.1   Article 14 in conjunction with Article 1, Protocol 1

6.3.1.1   Cases in which there was a reasonable and objective justification
In *James* v *UK* the applicants submitted that the leasehold enfranchisement legislation was discriminatory on the ground of 'property' because it only applied to the restricted class of property occupied by long leaseholders and, in addition, it disadvantageously treated landlords owning property of a lower value. The European Court found legitimate reasons to justify these differences of treatment. As to the applicants' first head of complaint, the European Court held that it was inevitable that, since the legislation was designed to remedy a perceived imbalance in the relations between landlords and long leasehold tenants, it would affect landlords falling within that restricted class of property owners rather than all other property owners. In respect of the second head of complaint, the European Court found that the provisions, which entailed progressively disadvantageous treatment for landlords the lower the value of their property, could also be justified. The introduction of rateable value limits and the use of two compensation schemes reflected Parliament's intention to exclude a small percentage of wealthy tenants from the benefits of enfranchisement and to provide more favourable terms of purchase for the vast majority of tenants who were in need of economic protection. Therefore having regard to the state's margin of appreciation, the European Court declared that the Government had not transgressed the principle of proportionality. There was no breach of Article 14 taken in conjunction with Article 1, Protocol 1.

It is interesting that Article 14 specifically prohibits discrimination on the grounds of 'property', which for these purposes encapsulates the wider concept of wealth. In capitalist societies there are large discrepancies in wealth between individuals. There are many examples of differential treatment of rich and poor whereby the poor are effectively excluded from activities or advantages, e.g. higher education, medical treatment or a home, due to their lack of economic resources. This would seem to be the inevitable consequence of capitalism. Yet it is curious that it is possible for a person to challenge some instances of differential treatment based on wealth as contrary to Article 14, whilst other instances are inherent within the nature of our society. Harris, O'Boyle and Warbrick, recognising this anomaly, have commented that:

> This is the most problematic of categories. On the one hand, it seems quite wrong that the enjoyment of fundamental rights should depend upon financial resources. On the other hand, in capitalist societies at least, the acceptance of even wide inequalities based on wealth is a central characteristic of a market system.[1]

It is likely that the national courts will tread with care when faced with questions of differential treatment based on wealth. *James* v *UK* is one example of the European Court's general reluctance to admit a violation of Article 14 on the ground of 'property' alone and the national courts may well imitate this cautious approach.

The facts of *National and Provincial Building Society and others* v *UK* are discussed at 6.2.1. The applicants maintained that they enjoyed the same restitutionary rights as the Woolwich Building Society to recover the monies they had paid to the Inland Revenue pursuant to an unlawful tax demand. The European Court held that there was no breach of Article 14 on the basis that the applicants were not in an analogous or relevantly similar position to the Woolwich. In the alternative, the European Court stated that even if the applicants were in a similar position to the Woolwich, a reasonable and objective justification for the differential treatment existed. The European Court recognised that the English Parliament, in enacting the retrospective legislation, would not have wanted to have interfered with the decision of the House of Lords in favour of the Woolwich. This justified the provisions which excluded the Woolwich from the effects of the retrospective legislation.

6.3.1.2 *Cases in which there was no reasonable and objective justification*
In *Pine Valley Developments Ltd and others* v *Ireland* the applicant company purchased land relying upon an existing outline planning permission. The Irish Supreme Court later declared the planning consent to be a nullity due to the fact that it was *ultra vires* the relevant legislation. Subsequently Parliament enacted legislation which gave compensation to all the holders of planning permissions affected by the Supreme Court's ruling, but it did not apply to the applicant's outline planning consent. The applicant thereby alleged a breach of Article 1, Protocol 1 taken alone and in conjunction with Article 14. The European Court held that the state's control of the use of the applicant's property was justified

---

[1] Harris, D. J., O'Boyle, M. and Warbrick, C., *Law of the European Convention on Human Rights* (London: Butterworths, 1995), at p. 473.

under the third rule and consequently there was no breach of Article 1, Protocol 1 (see 4.4.2 and 4.4.3.2). Nevertheless the European Court found that there was no justification for the differential treatment of the applicant compared to the other owners who benefited from the compensation provisions and thereby concluded that it had been discriminated against contrary to Article 14. This case illustrates that the states often enjoy a greater latitude in justifying their laws under Article 1, Protocol 1 than in establishing an objective and reasonable justification for differential treatment under Article 14.

In *Gaygusuz* v *Austria* (1996) 23 EHRR 365 the applicant, a Turkish national, was denied an advance on his pension in the form of emergency assistance. The right of emergency assistance was treated as a pecuniary right and a 'possession' for the purposes of Article 1, Protocol 1 due to the contributions that the applicant had made to the unemployment insurance fund and therefore the facts came within the ambit of Article 1, Protocol 1 (see 4.7.3.2). The refusal, by the relevant state authority, to grant the applicant emergency assistance was based exclusively on the fact that he did not possess Austrian nationality as required by the appropriate legislation. The European Court noted (at para. 42) that 'very weighty reasons would have to be put forward before the European Court could regard a difference of treatment based exclusively on the ground of nationality as compatible with the Convention'. The European Court was not persuaded by the arguments put forward by the Government and concluded that the difference in treatment was not based on any objective and reasonable justification.

The case of *Darby* v *Sweden* (1991) 13 EHRR 774 is another example of a breach of Article 14 due to discrimination based on a person's nationality. The applicant, a Finnish citizen, worked for some time in Sweden but returned home at weekends. He was not registered as resident in Sweden. He was obliged to pay full municipal taxes, part of which financed the Church of Sweden's religious activities. It was possible for non-nationals, who were registered as residents and who were not members of the Church, to apply for an exemption from the church tax, but this exemption was not available to non-residents. The applicant alleged a breach of Article 14 in conjunction with Article 1, Protocol 1. The Government failed to submit any justification for the differential treatment of residents and non-residents because administrative convenience, being the real reason for the difference, would not have been accepted by the European Court as a legitimate justification. Consequently the Government was found to be in violation of the Convention.

More recently in *Chassagnou and others* v *France* (App. Nos 25088/94, 28331/95 and 28443/95, 29 April 1999) the offending legislation required small landowners to transfer the hunting rights over their land to the municipal hunters' association in their area. However the measures did not apply to large landowners. The European Court held that since the Government had failed to provide any reasonable and objective justification for this differential treatment of landowners, it was discriminatory and infringed Article 14 in conjunction with Article 1, Protocol 1.

6.3.2 Article 14 in conjunction with Article 8

6.3.2.1 Cases in which there was a reasonable and objective justification
In *Gillow* v *UK* the applicants, who had been refused a residence licence to permit them to live in their house in Guernsey, relied upon two discriminatory measures which allegedly violated Article 14 in conjunction with Article 8. First, they contended that the existence of a category of open market houses constituted discrimination in favour of wealthy persons who were able to purchase and occupy open market houses without the need to apply for a residential licence. Secondly, the applicants maintained that the housing legislation discriminated in favour of Britons born in Guernsey as against Britons born elsewhere. As to the applicants' first head of complaint, the European Court accepted that the use of the rateable value limits reflected the Government's intention to exclude a small percentage of expensive houses from the control of the housing authority and the licensing system. It was felt that those persons who sought to buy these very expensive houses were not in need of protection. However, it was legitimate for the state to protect the poorer sections of the community by ensuring adequate housing for those with strong connections with Guernsey but with limited resources. The European Court concluded (at para. 66) that:

> In view of the legitimate objectives being pursued in the general interest and having regard to the State's margin of appreciation, that policy of different treatment cannot be considered as unreasonable or as imposing a disproportionate burden on owners of more modest houses like the applicants, taking into account the possibilities open to them under the licensing system.

In relation to the second head of complaint, the European Court found that the preferential treatment for persons with strong attachments to Guernsey pursued a legitimate aim and was justified on the facts.

The case of *S* v *UK* concerned the rights of succession for homosexual partners of a deceased tenant. The applicant's lesbian partner had been a secure tenant of her council house and when she died the applicant claimed to be qualified to succeed her partner under the succession provisions of the Housing Act 1980. The national courts held that the relevant succession provisions in the Act did not include homosexual relationships. The applicant alleged that she was being discriminated against because of her sexual orientation. The European Commission accepted that the aim of the legislation was to protect the family and that this was a legitimate aim, similar to the protection guaranteed to family life under Article 8. The issue was whether it was justifiable for the state to exclude homosexual relationships from the protection afforded to families. There was clear precedent from previous cases under the Convention that homosexual partners do not fall within the meaning of 'family' under Article 8. The European Commission concluded that the differential treatment of homosexual partners under the Housing Act 1980 could be objectively and reasonably justified. In this respect it is interesting to observe that the House of Lords' decision in *Fitzpatrick* v *Sterling Housing Association Ltd* [1999] 4 All ER 705 held that same-sex partners in a longstanding homosexual relationship can constitute a member of the family of the original tenant within the meaning of the Rent Act 1977 and thereby enjoy the rights of succession afforded by that Act. Given that a homosexual partner of a statutory tenant under the Rent Act 1977 can now enjoy rights of succession, it is difficult to envisage a valid justification for not extending this benefit to a homosexual partner of a tenant having a secure tenancy under the Housing Act 1985 (this is discussed further at 8.3.2).

6.3.2.2   *Cases in which there was no reasonable and objective justification*
The case of *Larkos* v *Cyprus* (App. No. 29515/95) provides an example of the European Court finding a breach of Article 14 in conjunction with Article 8 due to the lack of any valid justification for the differential treatment. In this case the applicant rented a house from the Government and lived there with his family for over 30-years. The Government sought to evict the applicant and as a Government tenant he was unable to invoke the protection from eviction, under the Rent Control Act, afforded to tenants renting from a private landlord. Consequently he alleged that as a Government tenant he had been unlawfully discriminated against in the enjoyment of his right to respect for his home. The Government maintained that, unlike a private landlord, it was not renting property primarily for profit but had to take account of the public interest in its transactions. Accordingly the state claimed that it was justified in not giving the applicant the protection from eviction afforded to private tenants because to give Government tenants security of tenure would fetter the authorities' duty to administer state-owned property in accordance with the requirements of the Constitution and the law. The European Court was not persuaded by these arguments. It noted that the terms of the tenancy agreement demonstrated that the Government had rented the house to the applicant in a private law capacity and that it was not acting in a public law capacity with the interests of the community in mind. The European Court stated (at para. 31) that:

> While [it] accepts that a measure which has the effect of treating differently persons in a relevantly similar situation may be justified on public interest grounds, it considers that in the instant case the respondent Government have not provided any convincing explanation of how the general interest will be served by evicting the applicant.

The European Court therefore concluded (at para. 31) that:

the legislation was intended as a measure of social protection for tenants ... A decision not to extend that protection to government tenants living side by side with tenants in privately-owned dwellings requires specific justification, more so since the Government are themselves protected by the legislation when renting property from private individuals. However, the Government have not adduced any reasonable and objective justification for the distinction which meets the requirements of Article 14 of the Convention, even having regard to their margin of appreciation in the area of the control of property.

Accordingly there was found to be a violation of Article 14 in conjunction with Article 8.

6.4 POSITIVE DISCRIMINATION

6.4.1 Positive discrimination as a reasonable and objective justification

The Strasbourg institutions have accepted that positive discrimination can be used as a reasonable and objective justification for the differential treatment of persons. In some instances inequalities in the law are needed to redress factual inequalities. For example, in *Lindsay* v *UK* (1986) 49 DR 181 married women, who were the sole breadwinners, enjoyed beneficial treatment under tax legislation compared to men in an analogous situation. The aim of the legislation was to encourage more married women to work with the consequential effect of promoting equality between men and women. The European Commission stated that: 'in the aim of providing positive discrimination in favour of married women who work', the Government had established the existence of a reasonable and objective justification for the differential treatment of the sexes.

6.4.2 The states' obligation to positively discriminate

In the recent case of *Thlimmenos* v *Greece* (App. No. 34369/97, 6 April 2000) the European Court accepted that the principle of positive discrimination may be extended to oblige the states to take positive steps to treat persons differently. The European Court acknowledged that where persons are different from others, e.g. due to their religious beliefs, those persons may need to be treated differently to accommodate their different beliefs and a failure to do so may constitute discrimination. In *Thlimmenos*, the applicant, who was a Jehovah's Witness, had been convicted in 1983 by an army tribunal for insubordination because he had refused, on religious grounds, to wear a military uniform at a time of general mobilisation. In June 1988 the applicant sat a public examination for the appointment of 12 chartered accountants. Despite having achieved the second highest results in the examination out of 60 candidates, the Greek Institute of Chartered Accountants refused to appoint him on the ground that he had been convicted of a felony five years earlier. The applicant alleged a violation of Article 14 in conjunction with Article 9.[2] He complained that the law which excluded persons convicted of a felony from appointment to a chartered accountant's post failed to distinguish between persons convicted as a result of their religious beliefs and persons convicted on other grounds. The European Court held that there had been a breach of Article 14 due to the discriminatory treatment of the applicant. It stated (at para. 44) that:

> The Court has so far considered the right under Article 14 not to be discriminated against in the enjoyment of the rights guaranteed under the Convention is violated when States treat differently persons in analogous situations without providing an objective and reasonable justification (see *Inze* v *Austria*). However, the Court considers that this is not the only facet of the prohibition of discrimination under Article 14. The right not to be discriminated against in the enjoyment of the rights guaranteed under the Convention is also violated when States without objective and reasonable justification fail to treat differently persons whose situations are significantly different.

The European Court concluded that the state had discriminated against the applicant in the enjoyment of his rights under Article 9 because the state had failed to introduce appropriate exceptions to the rule barring persons convicted of a felony from the profession of chartered accountants.

This is an interesting development in the scope of Article 14 and, in some circumstances, imposes a duty on the states to take positive discrimination measures to recognise that people are different and need to be treated differently.

6.5   THE STATES' POSITIVE OBLIGATIONS UNDER ARTICLE 14 TO PROTECT AGAINST PRIVATE ACTS OF DISCRIMINATION

It may be that the words 'shall be secured' in Article 14 impose a positive obligation upon the states to protect persons against private acts of discrimination in the enjoyment of their rights and freedoms in the Convention. Harris, O'Boyle and Warbrick have suggested that:

> The obligation of the state to take action to protect against private acts of discrimination which affect the enjoyment of Convention rights could embrace matters like . . . the right to be freed from privately imposed discriminatory fetters, like restrictive covenants on property rights.[3] (see 3.3.4)

---

[2] Article 9 of the Convention states that: 'Everyone has the right to freedom of thought, conscience and religion; this right includes freedom to change his religion or belief and freedom, either alone or in community with others and in public or private, to manifest his religion or belief, in worship, teaching, practice and observance'.

[3] Harris, O'Boyle and Warbrick (n. 1 above) p. 484.

However, the scope of any positive obligations imposed upon the states under Article 14 remains uncertain (see 5.2.1 for an explanation of the states' positive obligations under Article 8).

6.6 PROTOCOL 12

An additional Protocol to the European Convention on Human Rights was adopted by the Council of Europe on 26 June 2000 and was open for signature by the contracting states on 4 November 2000. Protocol 12 creates a free standing right to freedom from discrimination.[4] The parasitic nature of Article 14 (see 6.1.1) means that the Article has no independent existence from the other Articles under the Convention. As a result, certain forms of discrimination cannot be brought within the ambit of Article 14 (see *Botta* v *Italy* (1998) 26 EHRR 241). However, Protocol 12 seeks to remedy the inadequacies of Article 14, resultant upon its parasitic nature, by providing a right to equality and protection from unjustified discrimination which is not dependent upon the other Articles in the Convention.

Article 1, Protocol 12 provides a general prohibition of discrimination in the following terms:

1.   The enjoyment of any right set forth by law shall be secured without discrimination on any ground such as sex, race, colour, language, religion, political or other opinion, national or social origin, association with a national minority, property, birth or other status.

2.   No one shall be discriminated against by any public authority on any ground such as those mentioned in paragraph 1.

The explanatory report to Protocol 12 states that the meaning of the term 'discrimination' in Article 1, Protocol 12 is intended to be identical to that in Article 14 of the Convention.[5] Thus differential treatment is only discriminatory if it has no objective and reasonable justification, that is, if it does not pursue a legitimate aim or if there is not a reasonable relationship of proportionality between the means employed and the aim sought to be realised. Consequently, if an objective and reasonable justification exists for the differential treatment, it will not constitute discrimination under Article 1, Protocol 12. The explanatory report also notes that the list of non-discrimination grounds in Article 1 is identical to that included in Article 14 of the Convention.[6] It was considered to be

---

[4] Generally, see Moon, G., 'The Draft Discrimination Protocol to the European Convention on Human Rights: A Progress Report' [2000] EHRLR 49.

[5] Explanatory report to Protocol 12, Council of Europe, 2000 at para. 18. This report can be found at www.dhdirhr.coe.fr.

[6] Ibid., para. 19.

unnecessary to extend the list to include other categories, e.g., sexual orientation, because the list of protected classes is not exhaustive in any event and the Strasbourg institutions have frequently applied Article 14 to grounds not expressly included in Article 14. The second paragraph to Article 1 specifically relates to public authorities and provides that unjustified discrimination by public authorities will be prohibited in relation to any right within the law.

As to the additional scope of the protection against discrimination provided by Article 1, the explanatory report makes the following observations:

> Article 1 concerns cases where a person is discriminated against:
>
> i.   in the enjoyment of any right specifically granted to an individual under national law;
>
> ii.   in the enjoyment of a right which may be inferred from a clear obligation of a public authority under national law, that is, where a public authority is under an obligation under national law to behave in a particular manner;
>
> iii.   by a public authority in the exercise of discretionary power (for example, granting certain subsidies);
>
> iv.   by any other act or omission by a public authority (for example, the behaviour of law enforcement officers when controlling a riot)'.[7]

The report further states that:

> it was considered unnecessary to specify which of these four elements are covered by the first paragraph of Article 1 and which by the second. The two paragraphs are complementary and their combined effect is that all four elements are covered by Article 1.[8]

The extent to which the words 'shall be secured', in the text of Article 1, impose a positive obligation on the states to take measures to prevent discrimination in relations between private parties is unclear. In seeking to define the limits of Protocol 12, the explanatory report states that: 'While such positive obligations cannot be excluded altogether, the prime objective of Article 1 is to embody a negative obligation for the [states]: the obligation not to discriminate against individuals'.[9] However, the report further states that:

> any positive obligation in the area of relations between private persons would concern, at the most, relations in the public sphere normally regulated by law, for which the state has a certain responsibility (for example, arbitrary denial of access to work, access to restaurants, or to services which private persons may make available to the public such as medical care or utilities such as water and electricity, etc). The precise form of the response

---

[7] Ibid., para. 22.
[8] Ibid., para. 23.
[9] Ibid., para. 24.

which the state should take will vary according to the circumstances. It is understood that purely private matters would not be affected. Regulation of such matters would also be likely to interfere with the individual's right to respect for his private and family life, his home and his correspondence, as guaranteed by Article 8 of the Convention.[10]

The UK Government has indicated that it has no plans at present to sign or ratify Protocol 12 and consequently the freestanding right to freedom from discrimination is currently not incorporated into the Human Rights Act 1998.

---

[10] Ibid., para. 28.

Chapter Seven

Article 6

(1)   In the determination of his civil rights and obligations or of any criminal charge against him, everyone is entitled to a fair and public hearing within a reasonable time by an independent and impartial tribunal established by law. Judgment shall be pronounced publicly but the press and public may be excluded from all or part of the trial in the interests of morals, public order or national security in a democratic society, where the interests of juveniles or the protection of the private life of the parties so require, or to the extent strictly necessary in the opinion of the court in the special circumstances where publicity would prejudice the interests of justice.

7.1   ARTICLE 6(1)

Article 6 imposes certain procedural requirements upon the contracting states. Article 6(1) includes civil proceedings and is therefore directly relevant to property lawyers, whereas Article 6(2) and (3) relate solely to criminal proceedings. Article 6(2) and (3) will not be considered in this chapter and therefore any reference to Article 6 hereafter in this chapter is specifically to Article 6(1). Where an applicant alleges a breach of Article 6, there are two issues to be considered by the Strasbourg institutions. First the applicability of Article 6 and secondly, the compliance of the particular measures with the procedural requirements of Article 6.

7.2   THE APPLICABILITY OF ARTICLE 6

(See the case summaries in Appendix 3 for the following cases: *Sporrong and Lönnroth* v *Sweden*; *James* v *UK*; *Powell and Rayner* v *UK*.)

For Article 6 to apply the following conditions must be satisfied:

(a)   the proceedings must involve civil rights and obligations;
(b)   there must be a dispute (called a '*contestation*' in the French text);
(c)   the civil rights and obligations must be 'determined', meaning that the proceedings must be directly decisive for a person's private law rights.

Although Article 6 does not specifically include the word 'dispute', the word 'determination' in the phrase 'determination of his civil rights and obligations' has been interpreted to mean a dispute the outcome of which is directly decisive for the private rights of an individual.

7.3   THE MEANING OF 'CIVIL RIGHTS AND OBLIGATIONS'

7.3.1   The relevance of the private/public law distinction

In the English text of Article 6 'rights and obligations at a suit at law' was altered, at the very last stage of the drafting, into 'civil rights and obligations'.[1] This is interesting because although express mention of private law rights was removed from the text, the public/private law dichotomy has played a crucial role in ascertaining the meaning of 'civil rights and obligations'. From an early stage the Strasbourg institutions determined that the use of the word 'civil' incorporated the public/private law distinction, thereby restricting the scope of Article 6 to rights and obligations in private law. Consequently, purely public law claims (involving the exercise of a discretionary power by a state authority) were excluded from the ambit of Article 6. Although the European Court of Human Rights (the European Court) initially adopted this approach, it was never compelled to answer directly the question of whether civil rights were equated with private rights. In fact in *Konig* v *Federal Republic of Germany* (1978) 2 EHRR 170, the European Court explicitly left open this question stating (at para. 95) that it was not 'necessary in the present case to decide whether the concept of 'civil rights and obligations' within the meaning of [Article 6(1)] extends beyond those rights which have a private nature'. This early public/private law distinction, however, holds less significance in recent years as an expanding number of rights and obligations have been held by the European Commission of Human Rights (the European Commission) and European Court to come within the ambit of Article 6. Unfortunately the position is not clear-cut and this is likely to be an area of considerable debate. Harris, O'Boyle and Warbrick have commented upon the lack of a uniform test in the following terms:

> If the Commission and the Court have commendably acted to fill a gap by reading Article 6 as requiring that administrative decisions that determine an individual's right,

---

[1] Van Dijk, P., 'The interpretation of "civil rights and obligations" by the European Court of Human Rights — one more step to take', in Matscher, F. and Petzold, H., *Protecting Human Rights: The European Dimension*, Koln: Carl Heymanns Verlag KG, 1988 at p. 138.

for example ... to use his land, are subject to Article 6, they have yet to establish a coherent jurisprudence spelling out the nature of the resulting obligations for states'.[2]

Although the European Court has refrained from giving a precise definition of 'civil rights and obligations', it is nevertheless possible to distinguish between:

(a)   Relations between private persons. These will always be considered to involve civil rights and obligations, for example relations between a landlord and tenant (*Langborger* v *Sweden* (1989) 12 EHRR 416).

(b)   Relations between a private person and the state. This is an area of great complexity in determining the scope of Article 6. In recent cases, instead of excluding Article 6 on the basis that a public authority is involved or the character of the legislation concerns administrative law, the European Court has looked to the character of the right involved. Thus the character of the right (or obligation) is now the deciding factor. This was emphasised in the case of *H* v *France* (1989) 12 EHRR 74 where the European Court stated (at para. 47) that: 'Article 6(1) applies irrespective of the parties' status, be it public or private, and of the nature of the legislation which governs the manner in which the dispute is to be determined; it is sufficient that the outcome of the proceedings should be "decisive for private law rights and obligations"'. In *Sporrong and Lönnroth* v *Sweden* the European Commission took the view that the proceedings to issue and extend the expropriation permits, whilst concerning a civil right, were not within the ambit of Article 6 because they were administrative proceedings. However, the European Court did not share this view. Citing *Ringeisen* v *Austria (No. 1)* (1971) 1 EHRR 455 as authority, it stated (at para. 80) that: 'It is of little consequence that the *contestation* (dispute) concerned an administrative measure taken by the competent body in the exercise of public authority'. Therefore what mattered was the nature of the right interfered with and not the character of the authority interfering with that right. Similarly, in *Zander* v *Sweden* (1993) 18 EHRR 175, a public authority granted a company a licence to dump waste on a waste tip adjacent to the applicants' land. There was a risk that the waste would pollute the applicants' drinking water and therefore the applicants wanted to challenge the decision to grant the permit. However, the applicants' only right of appeal was to the Government and it had dismissed their appeal. They alleged a breach of Article 6 on the basis that they had been denied a hearing before an independent and impartial tribunal. The state emphasised the public law

---

[2] Harris, D. J., O'Boyle, M. and Warbrick, C., *Law of the European Convention on Human Rights* (London: Butterworths, 1995), at p. 165.

character of the decision to grant the licence and maintained that Article 6 was not applicable. The European Court rejected this argument. It relied upon the premise that the applicants' ability to use water on their land for drinking purposes was 'one facet of their right as owners of the land'. Since the right of property is a 'civil right', the European Court concluded that the applicants' claim concerned a civil right notwithstanding the public law aspects of the case.

7.3.2 An autonomous concept

The European Court has declared that 'civil rights and obligations' is an autonomous concept which is not interpreted solely by reference to the classification of rights in national law (*Konig* v *Federal Republic of Germany* (1978) 2 EHRR 170). The two examples below illustrate how the concept of a civil right, if treated as synonymous with private law, could produce differences between the law of the European Convention on Human Rights and English law.

7.3.2.1 An example of an area which under English law would be considered public law but which the European Court of Human Rights has held to fall within Article 6
The European Court has considered a number of cases where an essentially statutory claim, for example, a claim for social insurance or assistance, has been found to acquire the character of a civil right within the scope of Article 6. In *Schuler-Zgraggen* v *Switzerland* (1993) 16 EHRR 405 the European Court accepted that the applicant's statutory right to continue to receive a full state invalidity pension as a result of illness which incapacitated her for work, should be treated as a civil right under Article 6 and it rejected the Government's submission that it was a purely public law claim. The European Court emphasised the relevant factors that cumulatively made Article 6 applicable in its observation (at para. 46) that the applicant had 'suffered an interference with her means of subsistence; she was claiming an individual, economic right flowing from specific rules laid down in a federal statute'. Thus her claim arose not from the exercise of a discretionary power but from a positive statutory duty. The distinction that is being made is between:

(a) a mere expectation of receiving a state benefit, which is dependent upon a public authority exercising its discretion in favour of the claimant, and
(b) an entitlement to the receipt of a state benefit by virtue of the fact that the claimant satisfies the statutory criteria for the particular benefit and which is therefore independent of any administrative discretion.

A similar test is used by the Strasbourg institutions to ascertain whether a person having a pecuniary claim in public law has a 'possession' within the meaning of

Article 1, Protocol 1 (see 4.7.3.2). The European Court has increasingly relied upon this distinction between administrative discretion and legal entitlement to determine whether the right falls within the scope of Article 6 and has thereby cut across the private and public law distinction.

7.3.2.2   An example of an area which under English law would be considered private law but which the European Court of Human Rights has found to be outside the protection afforded by Article 6

According to the case law of the Strasbourg institutions, employment by a public body, e.g. as a policeman, does not give rise to 'civil rights' within the meaning of Article 6 on the basis that the policeman does 'not enter into contractual relationships of a private nature' (*X v UK* (1980) 21 DR 168). Therefore a policeman cannot claim the protection of Article 6 in employment related disputes. This distinction by the European Court can give rise to apparent anomalies so that, for example, whilst employment as a doctor with a private practice does involve 'civil rights', this is not the case where the doctor is employed by a public body (see *Konig* v *Federal Republic of Germany* (1978) 2 EHRR 170). If this approach is followed by the English courts, employees of local authorities and other public bodies will not enjoy the protection of Article 6 under the Human Rights Act (HRA) 1998. The exclusion of public service employment is not likely to be applied by analogy to other situations, for example, a local authority tenant would still be able to invoke Article 6 on the basis that he has a contractual lease with the local authority which gives rise to 'civil rights' in property law.

As these examples illustrate, the use of the private/public law dichotomy, when considering the nature of civil rights and obligations under Article 6, does not always provide a definitive answer as to whether or not Article 6 will apply. However, in the absence of any better classification it is a useful starting point.

7.3.3   The exclusion of Article 6 from purely public law claims

An examination of the decisions of the Strasbourg institutions reveals a number of property related cases in which Article 6 has been excluded due to the public law character of the claim. These include the following examples:

(a)   A decision determining a person's liability to pay tax. The European Court has stated that there are ' "pecuniary" obligations vis-à-vis the state or its subordinate authorities which, for the purpose of Article 6(1), are to be considered as belonging exclusively to the realm of public law and are accordingly not covered by the notion of "civil rights and obligations". Apart from fines imposed by way of ''criminal sanction'', this will be the case, in particular, where an obligation which is pecuniary in nature derives from tax legislation or is otherwise part of normal civic duties in a democratic society' (*Schouten and Meldrum* v *The Netherlands* (1994) 19 EHRR 432 at para. 50). However, merely because the dispute concerns tax legislation does not necessarily exclude it from the ambit of Article 6. In *National and Provincial Building Society and others* v *UK* (see Appendix 3) the applicants maintained that the subject matter of the restitution proceedings was pecuniary in nature and therefore the proceedings were decisive for their private rights. The Government disputed the applicability of Article 6 arguing that the matter concerned tax legislation which, being fiscal in nature, is outside the scope of Article 6. The European Court concluded (at para. 97) that the restitution proceedings 'were private law actions and were decisive for the determination of private law rights to quantifiable sums of money. This conclusion is not affected by the fact that the rights asserted in those proceedings had their background in tax legislation and the obligation of the applicant societies to account for tax under that legislation'.

(b) Patent applications are excluded from Article 6 (*X* v *Austria* (App. No. 7830/77)). However, it is only the initial creation of the right, i.e. the act of registration, that is considered to be a purely public law right. Any subsequent revocation of an existing patent would affect the civil right of property and would be subject to Article 6 (see 4.7.2).

In cases such as these, where the right is conferred by the relevant state authority through the exercise of a discretionary power or a statutory duty, the claim is likely to be of a purely public law character. In *Feldbrugge* v *The Netherlands* (1986) 8 EHRR 425 the European Court adopted a particular method of analysis for examining borderline cases which include aspects of both private and public law. The European Court examined the relative cogency of the various features of public and private law contained in the social security legislation and concluded, on balance, that the private law features were of greater significance than those of public law. Therefore, on the facts, there had been a determination of civil rights and obligations within the scope of Article 6. This method of weighing the various public law and private law features in the balance to decide which is prevalent has been adopted in subsequent cases to determine whether to apply Article 6 in the field of social security disputes (see *Schuler-Zgraggen* v *Switzerland* (1993) 16 EHRR 405 and *Schouten and Meldrum* v *The Netherlands* (1994) 19 EHRR 432). What remains unclear is how the European Court assigns the relative weighting to the various public and private law features and this may lead to uncertainty in predicting whether Article 6 will apply to such cases.

7.3.4   A substantive right

Another aspect of a 'civil right' is the need for the applicant to have a substantive right in the first place. The absence of a substantive right resulted in the inapplicability of Article 6 in *Powell and Rayner* v *UK*. The case concerned aircraft noise from Heathrow Airport and the applicants claimed that their access to the domestic courts to determine their 'civil rights' was denied by s. 76 of the Civil Aviation Act 1982. Section 76(1) provides that:

> No action shall lie in respect of trespass or in respect of nuisance, by reason only of the flight of an aircraft over any property at a height above the ground which, having regard to wind weather and all the circumstances of the case is reasonable, or the ordinary incidents of such flight, so long as the provisions of any Air Navigation Order ... have been duly complied with ...

The applicants maintained that since s. 76 acts as a procedural bar to bringing a claim in nuisance in respect of unreasonable aircraft noise, there was a breach of their right to a court guaranteed under Article 6. However, the European Court found that Article 6 was not applicable on the facts. The effect of s. 76 is to exclude liability in nuisance and consequently the applicants could not claim to have a substantive right under English law to obtain relief for exposure to aircraft noise. The European Court concluded (at para. 36) that: 'To this extent there is no 'civil right' recognised under domestic law to attract the application of Article 6(1)'. As the applicants had no 'civil right' under English law to compensation for nuisance, Article 6 was not applicable. This approach has been endorsed by the European Court in its admissibility decision in *Hatton and others* v *UK* (App. No. 36022/97, 16 May 2000).

At first sight the European Court's decision in *Osman* v *UK* (1998) 29 EHRR 245 seems to conflict with this approach. The case concerned an alleged breach of Article 6. The applicants, the family of a murder victim, complained of negligence by the police in their failure to prevent the murder of their relative, Mr Osman. However, due to the national court's interpretation of a rule in English law which gives the police immunity from a claim in negligence, the family were denied the opportunity to seek compensation in the national courts. One would surmise that the absence of the substantive right to pursue a negligence claim against the police would have excluded the application of Article 6; however, the European Court held that Article 6 was applicable. The significant feature of this case, which distinguished it from *Powell and Rayner*, was the fact that the exclusionary rule, preventing an action in negligence against the police, did not operate as a blanket ban. Instead the House of Lords' decision in *Hill* v *Chief Constable of West Yorkshire* [1989] AC 53 meant that the English courts were able to make an assessment, on a case by case basis, as to the applicability of the exclusionary rule. In reference to this, the European Court observed (at para. 138) that:

> the rule does not automatically doom to failure such a civil action from the outset but in principle allows a domestic court to make a considered assessment on the basis of arguments before it as to whether a particular case is or is not suitable for the application of the rule.

On this basis, the European Court concluded that the applicants had a right, derived from the law of negligence, to seek an adjudication on the admissibility and merits of an arguable claim against the police and since they had been denied access to a court in the determination of this civil right, a breach of Article 6 had ensued.

These cases illustrate that Article 6 only guarantees a right to a fair hearing, it does not control the content of the national law to provide a substantive civil right where one does not already exist. The European Court has stated that Article 6 'does not in itself guarantee any particular content for (civil) "rights and obligations" in the substantive law of the Contracting States' (*James* v *UK*, at para. 81). Therefore if a state were to enact a law that simply deprived a landowner of his property (as opposed to a public authority exercising discretionary expropriation powers granted to it by the state), Article 6 would be inapplicable. The landowner could not claim to have a substantive right to the expropriated property and consequently, the procedural guarantees under Article 6 could not apply. The landowner would, of course, be able to invoke Article 1, Protocol 1 in relation to the deprivation and procedural safeguards are a relevant factor in assessing proportionality under Article 1, Protocol 1 (see 4.3.6.2).

7.4 THE NEED FOR A DISPUTE IN DOMESTIC LAW

There must be a dispute in national law between two private parties or between a person and the state, the outcome of which is determinative of the applicant's civil rights and obligations. This embraces two interrelated elements: first, the proceedings must involve a dispute and secondly, the proceedings need to be directly decisive of civil rights and obligations.

7.4.1 A dispute (*contestation*)

The European Court has explained the need for a dispute in the following terms: 'Article 6(1) extends only to "*contestations*" (disputes) over (civil) "rights and obligations" which can be said, at least on arguable grounds, to be recognised under domestic law' (*James* v *UK*, at para. 81). Although the applicant must show that there is an arguable claim involving a matter under national law, it is not necessary to prove that the claim will be successful. In *Tre Traktörer Aktiebolag* v *Sweden* (see Appendix 3), the European Court gave a clear statement (at para. 37) as to what the need for a dispute entails:

> As to the existence of a dispute over a right within the meaning of Article 6(1), the Court refers to the principles enunciated in its case-law. In particular, the dispute must be genuine and of a serious nature; it may relate not only to the actual existence of a right but also to its scope and the manner of its exercise and, finally, the result of the proceedings concerning the dispute at issue must be directly decisive for such a right.

7.4.2   Determinative of civil rights and obligations

The fact that the proceedings must be in the determination of civil rights and obligations has been found by the European Court to mean that the outcome of the proceedings is 'directly decisive' for the applicant's civil rights and obligations. It is relatively easy to satisfy this requirement where the purpose of the proceedings is to determine the applicant's civil rights, for example in repossession proceedings between a landlord and a tenant. But it is more difficult to satisfy it where the purpose of the proceedings is something other than the determination of civil rights. The case of *Ringeisen* v *Austria (No. 1)* (1971) 1 EHRR 455 illustrates the approach that the European Court will adopt in these cases. An administrative law body, the Real Property Transactions Commission (RPTC), had to decide whether or not to approve a proposed sale of agricultural land to the applicant. Statute required the approval of the RPTC in all cases involving agricultural land and stated that the sale transaction had to correspond to the public interest in creating and maintaining agricultural and forest areas. The RPTC refused to give its approval for the sale to the applicant on the grounds that the land would be used for non-agricultural purposes. The purpose of the proceedings before the RPTC, being the granting of approval to sell the property by reference to the stated public interest, was a public law matter and was not specifically to determine the applicant's civil rights and obligations. Nevertheless the European Court held that Article 6 was applicable because the RPTC's decision was decisive of the civil law relations between two private parties, the buyer and the seller. The European Court stated (at para. 94) that:

> The character of the legislation which governs how the matter is to be determined (civil, commercial, administrative law, etc) and that of the authority which is invested with jurisdiction in the matter (ordinary court, administrative body, etc) are therefore of little consequence.

Article 6 is not, therefore, limited to proceedings between private persons. Its wording and scope is far wider, covering 'all proceedings the result of which is decisive for private rights and obligations' (para. 94).

A later case further qualified this test by emphasising the need for the outcome of the proceedings to be 'directly decisive', being something more than a mere 'tenuous connection' and not being too remote (*Le Compte* v *Belgium* (1981) 4 EHRR 1). This interpretation of the opening words of Article 6 has resulted in the extension of Article 6 to include the decisions of administrative tribunals in which the determination of civil rights is a consequence, although not the purpose, of the proceedings (see 7.7.4).

7.5   THE APPLICATION OF ARTICLE 6 TO MATTERS CONCERNING PROPERTY RIGHTS

The ownership, alienability and unfettered use and enjoyment of property is a 'civil right' and therefore any action by the state which is directly decisive of property rights will be subject to the right to a fair trial under Article 6. For example, the following interferences with property rights have been found to be subject to Article 6.

(a)   The expropriation of land (*Sporrong and Lönnroth* v *Sweden*). In *Holy Monasteries* v *Greece* the European Court observed (at para. 85) that: 'It is well-established in the Court's case law that as a matter of principle Article 6(1) guarantees a right of access to the courts for the determination of claims (*contestations*) under domestic law concerning compensation payable for expropriation of property'.

(b)   The Revenue's exercise of the right of pre-emption over property purchased at an undervalue (*Hentrich* v *France*).

(c)   The refusal of a residence licence to allow the applicants to live in their home in Guernsey (*Gillow* v *UK*).

(d)   The refusal by a public authority to grant approval for the proposed sale of agricultural land to the applicant (*Ringeisen* v *Austria (No. 1)* (1971) 1 EHRR 455).

(e)   The grant or refusal of planning permission and the implementation of the planning enforcement laws (*Bryan* v *UK*).

(f)   A building permit granted in accordance with the development plan for the area, which permitted building works on land adjoining that owned by the applicant as a result of which the applicant suffered a pecuniary detriment (*Ortenburg* v *Austria* (1994) 19 EHRR 524).

(g)   A licensing authority's decision to grant a permit to a company allowing it to dump waste on a waste tip which threatened to pollute the applicants' water supply (*Zander* v *Sweden* (1993) 18 EHRR 175).

(h)   The revocation of a licence to sell alcoholic beverages in a restaurant owned by the applicant (*Tre Traktörer Aktiebolag* v *Sweden*).

7.6   COMPLIANCE WITH ARTICLE 6

(See the case summaries in Appendix 3 for the following cases: *Sporrong and Lönnroth* v *Sweden*; *James* v *UK*; *App. No. 11949/86* v *UK*; *Tre Traktörer Aktiebolag* v *Sweden*; *Bryan* v *UK*; *National and Provincial Building Society and others* v *UK*.)

Once the Strasbourg institutions are satisfied that Article 6 applies to a given situation, their attention turns to an assessment of whether or not there has been compliance with the guarantees provided by Article 6.

7.7   THE GUARANTEES PROVIDED BY ARTICLE 6

In *Golder* v *UK* (1975) 1 EHRR 524 the European Court stated that Article 6 secures to all persons the right to have any claim relating to their civil rights and obligations brought before a court or tribunal. To this end the European Court observed (at para. 36) that: 'the Article embodies the "right to a court"'. This 'right to a court' embraces a number of issues including the question of access to a court and the reasonableness of the time involved in court proceedings, together with an examination of the characteristics of a fair hearing.

7.7.1   The right of access to a court

The European Court has stated that:

> Article 6(1) embodies the 'right to a court', of which the right of access, that is the right to institute proceedings before courts in civil matters, constitutes one aspect. Article 6(1) may [thus] be relied on by anyone who considers that an interference with the exercise of one of his (civil) rights is unlawful and complains that he has not had the possibility of submitting that claim to a tribunal meeting the requirements of Article 6(1) (*Holy Monasteries* v *Greece* (1994) 20 EHRR 1 at para. 80).

However, some restrictions on the right of access to a court may be permissible in certain circumstances if they are in pursuit of a legitimate aim and the measures are proportional to the aims to be achieved. The European Court has stated that:

> However, this right [of access] is not absolute, but may be subject to limitations; these are permitted by implication since the right of access by its very nature calls for regulation by the state. In this respect the Contracting States enjoy a certain margin of appreciation, although the final decision as to the observance of the Convention's requirements rests with the Court. It must be satisfied the limitations applied do not restrict or reduce the access left to the individual in such a way or to such an extent that the very essence of the right is impaired. Furthermore, a limitation will not be compatible with Article 6(1) if it does not pursue a legitimate aim and if there is not a

reasonable relationship of proportionality between the means employed and the aim sought to be achieved (*National and Provincial Building Society and others* v *UK*, at para. 105).

7.7.2 The characteristics of a fair hearing

The Strasbourg institutions have identified the following essential characteristics of a fair hearing.

(a) The hearing must be in public with a judgment given publicly (*Ringeisen* v *Austria (No. 1)* (1971) 1 EHRR 455 at para. 98). However, in certain cases the press and public may be excluded from the proceedings (see the grounds for exclusion that are expressly set out in Article 6(1)).

(b) The tribunal must be independent of the parties and of the executive. In *Bryan* v *UK* the European Court stated (at para. 37) that: 'In order to establish whether a body can be considered "independent", regard must be had, *inter alia*, to the manner of appointment of its members and to their term of office, to the existence of guarantees against outside pressures and to the question whether the body presents an appearance of independence'. *Langborger* v *Sweden* (1989) 12 EHRR 416 provides an example of a case in which the tribunal was held not to have the appearance of being independent. A landlords' union and a tenants' union agreed the wording of certain standard clauses to be incorporated in leases. The applicant wanted to remove the standard clause on rent review and applied to the appropriate housing tribunal who turned down his application. The European Court held that Article 6 had been breached by the membership of the housing tribunal, which included assessors appointed by the two unions, and which therefore had the 'appearance of lacking impartiality'. More recently, in *McGonnell* v *UK* (2000) 30 EHRR 289 the European Court held that in the determination of the applicant's planning appeal by the Royal Court of Guernsey, the Bailiff did not have the required 'appearance' of independence and impartiality and consequently there had been a violation of Article 6. The Bailiff, who acted as the sole judge in the applicant's planning appeal, had earlier presided over the States of Deliberation when Detailed Development Plan No. 6, at the heart of the applicant's case, had been adopted. The European Court observed (at para. 55) that: 'any direct involvement in the passage of legislation, or of executive rules, is likely to be sufficient to cast doubt on the judicial impartiality of a person subsequently called on to determine a dispute over whether reasons exist to permit a variation from the wording of the legislation or rules at issue'. Therefore the mere fact that he had presided over the relevant States of Deliberation cast doubt on his impartiality as a judge and this was sufficient to vitiate the impartiality of the Royal Court.

(c)   There must be 'equality of arms'. This means that the parties must be
       afforded a reasonable opportunity to present their case under conditions
       that do not place one party at a disadvantage. In *Hentrich* v *France* the
       applicant maintained that she had not been given a 'fair hearing'
       following the Revenue's exercise of a right of pre-emption over the land
       that she had recently purchased. The Revenue contended that the purchase
       price for the land had been too low with a loss to the state of the
       appropriate transfer duty on the sale. She had not been able to challenge
       effectively the Revenue's assessment of the situation by adducing
       evidence that she had acted in good faith and that the proper price had
       been paid. Consequently she complained that the principle of equality of
       arms had been contravened. The European Court noted (at para. 56) that:
       'one of the requirements of a "fair trial" is "equality of arms", which
       implies that each party must be afforded a reasonable opportunity to
       present his case under conditions that do not place him at a substantial
       disadvantage vis-à-vis his opponent. In the instant case, the proceedings
       on the merits did not afford the applicant such an opportunity'. Therefore
       there was found to be a breach of Article 6(1).

(d)   The state must provide access to any relevant information in its possession.
       In *McGinley and Egan* v *UK* (1998) 27 EHRR 1 (see 8.8.3.4) the applicants
       were stationed on Christmas Island in 1958 at the time of nuclear testing in
       the vicinity of the Island. They complained that their right to a fair hearing
       before the Pensions Appeal Tribunal (PAT) had been breached because the
       Government withheld documents, including the applicants' military
       medical records, which would have helped the applicants to ascertain
       whether there was a link between their leukaemia and their exposure to
       radiation during the 1958 nuclear tests. The European Court stated (at para.
       86) that: 'if it were the case that the respondent state had, without good
       cause, prevented the applicants from gaining access to, or falsely denied the
       existence of, documents in its possession which would have assisted them
       in establishing before the PAT that they had been exposed to dangerous
       levels of radiation, this would have been to deny them a fair hearing in
       violation of Article 6(1)'. On the facts there was found to be no violation of
       Article 6 because the national law provided an adequate procedure for the
       disclosure of the documents which the applicants had failed to utilise.

7.7.3   The right to trial within a reasonable time

Article 6 specifically states that a person is entitled to a fair hearing 'within a
reasonable time'. In *Katte Klitsche De La Grange* v *Italy* (1994) 19 EHRR 368
the European Court stated (at para. 51) that:

The reasonableness of the length of proceedings is to be determined in the light of the circumstances of the case and with reference to the criteria laid down in the Court's case law, in particular the complexity of the case and the conduct of the applicant and of the competent authorities.

On the facts the European Court held that the length of the proceedings, in which the applicant challenged the district council's development ban on his land, was reasonable and consequently there was no infringement of Article 6. The criteria to which the European Court made reference, namely the complexity of the case and the conduct of the parties, illustrate that the reasonableness of the length of the proceedings will depend upon the facts of each individual case. A similar approach was taken in *Papachelas* v *Greece* (App. No. 31423/96, 25 March 1999). The European Court found the length of the proceedings, being four years, to be reasonable having regard to the complexity of the case, owing to the large number of properties expropriated, and the conduct of the applicants, who had taken six months to lodge their appeal submissions before the Court of Cassation in Greece.

This need for a fair hearing to be 'within a reasonable time' is the most litigated requirement in Article 6 and there are many examples of cases in which the Strasbourg institutions have found a breach of Article 6 due to the unreasonable time periods involved. Examples relating to property law include the following.

(a) In *Hentrich* v *France*, the applicant appealed against the decision of the Revenue to exercise the right of pre-emption over the land that she had recently purchased. The appeal proceedings in the national courts continued over a four-year period. The European Court found this to be an unreasonable length of time on the facts.

(b) In *Matos e Silva, Lda and others* v *Portugal*, the five sets of proceedings in the national courts, challenging the measures taken by the state against the applicant's land in connection with the creation of a nature reserve, had taken between five and thirteen-years and were still pending at the time of the European Court's judgment. The Government had conceded that the length of the proceedings taken as a whole could not be considered reasonable.

(c) *Guillemin* v *France* (1998) 25 EHRR 435 concerned proceedings in the national courts in which the applicant successfully challenged the compulsory purchase of a plot of land that she owned. The public interest declaration, which authorised the compulsory purchase of her land for residential development, was made in 1982. Her appeal against the expropriation order in the ordinary courts failed and construction began on her expropriated land. However, her appeal in the administrative court against the public interest declaration succeeded and the declaration was set aside with the result that the expropriation order was subsequently declared to be unlawful. In 1990 the applicant commenced proceedings to obtain compensation but the proceedings were still pending at the date of the European Court's judgment in 1997. The European Court stated that 'reasonable time' for the purposes of Article 6 began to run when the applicant applied to the national courts. Therefore, time began to run from the time that the applicant applied to the administrative court in 1982 to have the public interest declaration set aside. As to the end of the proceedings the European Court noted (at para. 36) that: 'the period whose reasonableness falls to be reviewed takes in the entirety of the proceedings, right up to the decision which disposes of the dispute'. The European Court therefore found that the compensation proceedings, which were still pending, were relevant to assessing the length of the proceedings for the purposes of Article 6. On this basis the length of time had already exceeded 14 years. The European Court took the complexity of expropriation proceedings into account but nevertheless concluded that this length of time could not be regarded as 'reasonable' within the meaning of Article 6.

Harris, O'Boyle and Warbrick have commented that:

> the most striking feature of Article 6 cases has been the long line of decisions involving violations of the right to trial 'within a reasonable time'. If one feature of the administration of justice in European states has been highlighted by the working of the Convention, it is the delay with which justice can be delivered. Proceedings in some cases have lasted an astonishing number of years.[3]

This observation seems to bear particular relevance to cases relating to property rights, possibly due to the complexity of matters concerning the expropriation of property by the state.

7.7.4 Administrative decisions and the right to a court

Many decisions that are determinative of civil rights are taken by public authorities that are not a tribunal within the meaning of Article 6. However, the particular body deciding the issue does not have to function in accordance with Article 6 provided that there is an opportunity to appeal to a body that does comply with Article 6. The European Court has clearly stated this principle in the following terms:

> the Convention calls for at least one of the following systems: either the jurisdictional organs themselves comply with the requirements of Article 6(1), or they do not comply

---

[3] Ibid., p. 273.

but are subject to subsequent control by a judicial body that has full jurisdiction and does provide the guarantees of Article 6(1) (*Albert and Le Compte* v *Belgium* (1983) 5 EHRR 533 at para. 16).

Therefore where a decision is made by an administrative authority, there must be the opportunity of challenging its decision before a tribunal that complies with Article 6. This raises the question as to the level of subsequent control by the judicial body. Is the availability of judicial review sufficient to satisfy Article 6 given that the court does not review the merits of an administrative decision but only ensures that the public body did not act illegally, unreasonably or unfairly? Or is it necessary that the judicial body has 'full jurisdiction' to examine the merits of the decision by reference to the law and the facts? The answer depends upon the type of decision at issue and in particular whether or not policy considerations were applicable in reaching a decision. A right of appeal to a tribunal with 'full jurisdiction' was found to be necessary where the local authority decision concerned restricting parental access to their child in care (*W* v *UK* (1988) 10 EHRR 29), but not where the decision concerned the expropriation of land for the purpose of constructing a highway (*Zumtobel* v *Austria* (1993) 17 EHRR 116). The latter decision involved public policy considerations whilst the former did not. In *Zumtobel* it was held to be sufficient that the appeal court had jurisdiction to assess the legality of the administrative act even though it did not have full jurisdiction on all questions of law and fact. Similarly in *IKSCON* v *UK* (App. No. 20490/92), which concerned the enforcement notice appeal procedure in planning law, the European Commission held that the High Court's limited jurisdiction 'on a point of law' did not infringe Article 6. The applicant had argued that the High Court did not have 'full jurisdiction' and this constituted a breach of Article 6, even though the High Court had considered all the arguments that the applicant wished to make. Bearing in mind the fact that planning decisions inevitably involve public policy considerations, the European Commission stated that it is 'not the role of Article 6 to give access to a level of jurisdiction which can substitute [the court's] opinion for that of the administrative authorities on questions of expediency and where the courts do not refuse to examine any of the points raised'. Thus the fact that local authority decisions relating to compulsory purchase orders or planning decisions are subject to judicial review is likely to comply with Article 6 even though the national court does not have full jurisdiction to review the merits of the decision. The case of *Bryan* v *UK* supports this view. A local planning authority had served an enforcement notice on the applicant requiring him to demolish two buildings that had been unlawfully erected on his land. He appealed to the Secretary of State who appointed an inspector to conduct an inquiry and to reach a decision on the appeal. The inspector rejected the appeal and the enforcement notice was upheld. The applicant made a further appeal on a point of law to the High Court but this was also unsuccessful. The applicant then contended that the enforcement notice appeal proceedings did not comply with Article 6. The European Court examined the scope of the High Court's jurisdiction and concluded that it was sufficient to comply with Article 6 even though the appeal to the High Court was on a 'point of law' basis and did not permit the court to substitute its own decision on the merits for that of the inspector. On this basis the European Court concluded that the appeal proceedings as a whole complied with Article 6 even though the decision by the inspector was not of a satisfactory level of independence due to possible intervention by the Secretary of State under the power of recovery (see 8.10.1).

By way of comparison it is worth noting that in *Sporrong and Lönnroth* v *Sweden* the inability of the national court to undertake a 'full review of measures affecting a civil right' did not meet the requirements of Article 6. However, the distinguishing feature of this case was that the applicants were challenging only the time limits for the expropriation permits and not the administrative decision to build the roads for which the permits were required. The decision in issue did not involve any public policy considerations.

7.8 THE CONVENTION CASE LAW CONCERNING PROPERTY RIGHTS AND ARTICLE 6

In *James* v *UK* the applicants complained that the scheme set up under the leasehold enfranchisement legislation did not give the landlords the chance to challenge a tenant's entitlement to acquire the property compulsorily, once the criteria laid down in the legislation were satisfied. The applicants therefore submitted that the absence of any review by a court or tribunal of a tenant's hardship or individual merits infringed Article 6. The European Court noted that the Leasehold Reform Act 1967 gave the national courts jurisdiction over any disputes as to the tenant's entitlement to acquire the freehold under that Act. Thus any landlord who considered that there was a cause for alleging non-compliance with the legislation had unimpeded access to a national court. On this basis there was held to be no breach of Article 6. The fact that the landlord could challenge a tenant's compliance with the relevant criteria in the legislation was found to be sufficient to satisfy Article 6 and it was unnecessary for the landlord to be able to challenge other criteria such as the merits of the tenant's acquisition. The European Court emphasised that Article 6 is only a procedural guarantee to a fair hearing in the determination of the substantive legal rights that a state's national law provides. It does not guarantee the content of the national law. If the national law does not provide the applicant with a remedy to challenge the tenant's rights to acquire the freehold, where that tenant satisfies all the statutory criteria, Article 6 does not attempt to fill the gap and provide a remedy.

In *App. No. 11949/86* v *UK* the applicant claimed that she had been denied access to a court because neither the High Court nor the county court had jurisdiction to grant her relief from forfeiture of her lease. The European

Commission accepted that 'the dispute between the applicant and her landlord as to her obligations under the lease, and the question whether or not it should be ordered forfeit, involved the determination of her civil rights and obligations'. Therefore Article 6 was applicable and guaranteed her the right to a fair and public hearing by an independent and impartial tribunal. However, the European Commission noted that the applicant had had such a hearing before the county court in the initial possession proceedings. Thus the essence of the applicant's complaint was the lack of a superior review jurisdiction. The European Commission observed that: 'Art. 6(1) of the Convention cannot be interpreted so as to require the existence of a further jurisdiction to review or expand upon the jurisdiction provided by an inferior court, where that first court is capable of determining all questions of fact and law'. The European Commission found that there was no infringement of Article 6.

The cases of *Sporrong and Lönnroth* v *Sweden* and *Tre Traktörer Aktiebolag* v *Sweden* provide examples of a state being found in violation of Article 6. In considering the applicability of Article 6 in *Sporrong and Lönnroth* v *Sweden*, the European Court was satisfied that the expropriation permits affecting the applicants' land related to a 'civil' right. It also found that there was a dispute in national law the outcome of which was determinative of these civil rights. It acknowledged that the applicants had an arguable grievance that the Government had not complied with Swedish law due to the long time limits for which the permits had been granted. In determining the state's compliance with Article 6, the European Court had to consider whether Swedish law gave the applicants the opportunity to challenge the lawfulness of the decision to issue and extend the long-term expropriation permits. It was noted that the Government's decision to issue the permits was open to judicial review by the Supreme Administrative Court but this constitutes an extraordinary remedy that is rarely used because it is only exercisable on limited grounds. It did not enable the national court to assess the merits of the case nor undertake a 'full review of the measures affecting a civil right' and consequently there was found to be a violation of Article 6.

In *Tre Traktörer Aktiebolag* v *Sweden*, the applicant company managed a restaurant and its licence to serve alcoholic beverages was revoked by an administrative authority. The restaurant subsequently closed as a result of the withdrawal of the licence. The applicant alleged that there had been a violation of Article 6 due to the fact that there was no opportunity for the revocation of its licence to be reviewed by a national court. The Government contended that there was no right to retain such a licence and the licence could not in itself confer any right. However, the European Court did not share this view. It accepted that the licence conferred a 'right' on the applicant in the form of an authorisation to sell alcoholic beverages subject to the conditions in the licence. To this end the European Court recognised that the applicant had arguable grounds for maintaining that under Swedish law it was entitled to continue to retain the licence unless it contravened the conditions set out in the licence or any of the statutory grounds for revocation applied. Thus there was a dispute recognised under the domestic law. The European Court proceeded to ascertain whether the right at issue was a 'civil right'. The Government emphasised the public law features of the licensing system for the distribution of alcoholic beverages and argued that the licence could not be considered to confer a civil right. However, the European Court noted that the private individuals and companies entrusted to serve alcohol, carry on private commercial activities running restaurants and bars. These commercial activities have the object of earning profits and are based on a contractual relationship between the licence-holder and the customers. On this basis the European Court considered that the rights conferred on the applicant by virtue of the licence were of a civil character and that the public law aspects of the licensing system were not sufficient to outweigh this. Once the European Court had determined that Article 6 was applicable, it was inevitable that the state would be found to have failed to comply with Article 6 because of the absence of any right for the applicant to have the revocation of its licence brought before a court or a tribunal.

7.9   THE IMPACT OF THE HUMAN RIGHTS ACT 1998

The case of *R* v *Secretary of State for the Environment, Transport and the Regions, ex parte Slot* [1998] 4 PLR 1, decided prior to the implementation of the HRA 1998, illustrates the relationship between Article 6 and the rules of natural justice under English law. The applicant, who had applied for a diversion order under the Highways Act 1980, sought an order to entitle her to see all the written representations submitted against the order whilst the Secretary of State was deciding whether to confirm the order. The applicant raised Article 6 of the Convention to support her argument as well as relying upon the rules of natural justice under English law. The Court of Appeal allowed her appeal solely on the grounds of natural justice without finding the need to consider Article 6. Commenting upon this decision, Corner suggests that: 'By the rules of natural justice English law gives wide ranging protection to the right to be heard. It is therefore unlikely that the Convention will lead to major changes in approach to natural justice issues'.[4] However, there are some areas in which Article 6 is likely to have a sufficient impact upon English property law to prompt a change in the law, for example, in relation to the self-help remedies available to landlords and mortgagees (see 8.3.6.5 and 8.4.1.3).

---

r., 'Planning, Environment, and the European Convention on Human Rights' [1998] JPL at

Chapter Eight

The Implications of the Human Rights Act 1998 on Property Law

8.1 PRELIMINARY CONSIDERATIONS

8.1.1 Horizontal effect

The Human Rights Act (HRA) 1998 is clearly applicable in property related disputes concerning the actions of a public authority, for example, where a local authority makes a compulsory purchase order or refuses to grant planning permission. In other areas of property law, for example the law relating to leases, mortgages and adverse possession, the dispute may arise between private persons. The reach of the HRA 1998 into these areas of properly law depends upon the extent to which the HRA 1998 has horizontal effect (see 3.3).

8.1.2 Delays in challenging incompatible law

The cumulative effect of the inapplicability of a declaration of incompatibility to the proceedings in which it is made (s. 4(6), HRA 1998) and the need for victim status to commence an action (s. 7(7), HRA 1998) may mean that some areas of property law, which potentially violate the Convention rights, may be slow to reach the courts. Under s. 4 of the HRA 1998 the court is obliged to continue to apply offending legislation until a legislative change is implemented by Parliament. It is anticipated that a declaration of incompatibility will initiate legislative provisions to remedy the incompatibility, but there is no requirement that the new legislation will have retrospective effect for the benefit of the victim who commenced the action. It may be that a victim will have nothing personally to gain from raising violations of the Convention rights unless there is a possibility that the offending legislation can be interpreted, in accordance with s. 3 of the HRA 1998, in the victim's favour so as to be compatible with the Convention rights. If the offending law is common law the courts may be obliged to interpret the common law so that it is Convention compliant (s. 6, HRA 1998). However, blatant judicial activism is prohibited where legislation is indisputably incompatible with the Convention rights since Parliamentary sovereignty is preserved by the HRA 1998. Thus a victim may decide at the outset that it is not worth the time and expense of challenging law which is incompatible with the Convention rights if he or she is unlikely to benefit directly from the challenge. This would appear to be an ideal situation for an interest group to intervene and challenge the offending law. However, the requirement for victim status (s. 7(7), HRA 1998) means that interest groups will not have sufficient standing to bring an action where a victim does not wish to commence proceedings. An interest group usually has a wider purpose than the pursuit of individual advancement and therefore it will want to ensure the compliance of domestic law with human rights for the benefit of the general public as a whole. However, an interest group is prevented from challenging incompatible law unless it is directly affected by the offending law (see 1.7.7). The effect of these provisions may, therefore, result in delays in challenging some areas of property law that potentially violate the Convention rights.

8.2   THE IMPLICATIONS OF THE HUMAN RIGHTS ACT 1998 ON PROPERTY LAW

This chapter will examine the possible implications of the HRA 1998 on various aspects of property law as listed below. The list is not exhaustive and clearly the full impact of the HRA 1998 will not be appreciated for many years. A good understanding of the relevant Convention rights (see chapters 4, 5, 6 and 7), together with an appreciation from this chapter of how these rights can be applied to English law, will enable property lawyers to assess the impact of the HRA 1998 on other areas of property law not covered by this chapter.

The areas examined in this chapter are as follows.

(a) Landlord and tenant law: security of tenure and rights of succession, rent controls, Part II of the Commonhold and Leasehold Reform Bill, the positive obligations of a public authority landlord, distress for rent, forfeiture and introductory tenancies.

(b) Mortgages: the mortgagee's right to peaceable re-entry, s. 36 of the Administration of Justice Act 1970 and the bankruptcy of the mortgagor.

(c) Adverse possession.

(d) Freehold covenants: the modification or discharge of restrictive covenants by the Lands Tribunal.

(e) Land use: the Countryside and Rights of Way Act 2000 and the proposed legislation to prohibit hunting with dogs.
(f) Environmental pollution and a consideration of the tort of private nuisance.
(g) Compulsory purchase: compensation and the blight notice procedure.
(h) Planning law: the appeal procedures and the exercise of administrative discretion in planning decisions.

In order to avoid a repetition of the contents of chapters 4, 5, 6 and 7, the following analysis of the implications of the HRA 1998 upon the aspects of property law listed above, will not include a detailed explanation of the relevant Convention rights, but will assume a prior knowledge of these on the part of the reader.

8.3 LANDLORD AND TENANT LAW

Landlord and tenant law encapsulates a broad array of issues, the majority of which will remain unaffected by the HRA 1998. Some areas of the law, which aim to protect tenants by interfering with the property rights of landlords, for example legislative provisions concerning security of tenure and rent controls, have already been subject to challenge in Strasbourg as being incompatible with the Convention. The decisions of the Strasbourg institutions are considered below. It is unlikely, in the light of these decisions, that the HRA 1998 will have a significant impact on statutory provisions dealing with security of tenure and rent controls. Part II of the Commonhold and Leasehold Reform Bill, which introduces a tenants' 'right to manage' the premises and simplifies the existing rules for collective leasehold enfranchisement, may have human rights implications and these provisions will be examined in the light of the HRA 1998. The extent to which the HRA 1998 may impose positive obligations upon a public authority, in its capacity as a landlord, will also be considered.

The landlord remedies of forfeiture and distress for rent, which involve an interference with the tenant's property rights, may be affected by the HRA 1998. The European Commission of Human Rights (the European Commission) has considered one case involving the forfeiture of a lease by a private landlord but dismissed the tenant's application on the basis that there was no state responsibility for the landlord's actions. If the HRA 1998 has horizontal effect, it may be that the English courts will be faced with a tenant challenging the compatibility of forfeiture with the Convention rights. The remedy of distress for rent, which has not yet been challenged under the Convention, may provide one of the strongest cases in landlord and tenant law for a challenge under the HRA 1998, especially given that a landlord is permitted to distrain upon goods belonging to an innocent third party. The likely success of a challenge under the HRA 1998 to these landlord remedies will be considered. Finally the impact of the HRA 1998 upon the introductory tenancy scheme, which was a creation of the Housing Act 1996, will be examined.

8.3.1   Security of tenure

The Strasbourg institutions have considered a number of cases concerning security of tenure. In each case the legislative provisions that provided for security of tenure (or in some cases for suspending tenant eviction orders) were not found, in themselves, to be contrary to the Convention. However, the application of the legislation in individual cases has resulted in violations of Article 1, Protocol 1.

8.3.1.1   Article 1, Protocol 1 and security of tenure
The cases of *Spadea and Scalabrino* v *Italy* (1995) 21 EHRR 482 and *Scollo* v *Italy* (1996) 22 EHRR 514 were decided on the same day by the same judges. The cases concerned the emergency measures taken by the Italian Government to protect the interests of tenants on low incomes. These measures included rent freezes and statutory extensions of existing leases. In 1978 all current residential leases were statutorily extended until 1983. Due to the fact that a large number of leases were due to expire in 1983 the Government then adopted a policy of postponing, suspending or staggering the enforcement of eviction orders against residential tenants. The measures provided for a number of exceptions which included police assistance to enforce an eviction where the landlord urgently needed to obtain possession or where the tenant was in arrears with the rent.

In *Spadea* v *Italy*, the applicants had purchased two residential flats that were occupied by tenants. The applicants gave the tenants notice to quit when the leases expired in 1983 and they were subsequently granted eviction orders by the magistrate. However, in accordance with the above-mentioned Government policy, the eviction orders were suspended on four separate occasions over a course of several years. The applicants had to buy another property in which to live and did not recover possession of their flats until one of the tenants died and the other left of her own accord in 1989. The applicants alleged a violation of Article 1, Protocol 1 but the European Court of Human Rights (the European Court) rejected their claim. The European Court found that the restrictions on a landlord's ability to evict tenants amounted to a control of use of property under the third rule (see 4.4). It was satisfied that the impugned legislation pursued a legitimate aim. To have enforced all tenant evictions simultaneously would have led to large numbers of persons becoming homeless at the same time which could have resulted in social tension jeopardising public order. The Government policy of staggering the evictions of tenants eased this tension and was consequently held to be in the general interest. The deciding factor in this case was the principle of proportionality and whether there was a relationship of proportionality between the means employed, e.g., the suspension of eviction orders, and the aim pursued, so that the applicants did not suffer a disproportionate burden. The European Court concluded that, having regard to the legitimate aim being pursued and the state's wide margin of appreciation in the area of housing, the legislative measures adopted by the state could not be considered disproportionate. Consequently the restrictions on the applicants' use of their flats was not contrary to Article 1, Protocol 1.

In *Spadea* v *Italy* neither the legislation nor its application in the individual case caused a violation of Article 1, Protocol 1, but this was not the case in *Scollo* v *Italy* where the state was held to be in violation of the Convention. The applicant obtained a tenant eviction order in 1983 on the grounds that, being disabled and unemployed, he needed the flat for his own use; moreover the tenant had fallen into arrears with the rent. However, pursuant to the Government policy of postponing the enforcement of eviction orders, the eviction order was suspended on four separate occasions, and the applicant only obtained possession of the flat almost twelve years after he had first begun proceedings, and then only because the tenant left of his own accord. Although no reference was made to the decision in *Spadea*, the European Court inevitably reached the same decision as to the existence of a legitimate aim. However, in assessing proportionality, the European Court concluded that the applicant suffered a disproportionate burden. The applicant had made a 'declaration of necessity' which meant that he should have been given priority for the granting of police assistance to enforce the tenant's eviction. However the relevant state authority took no action in respect of his declaration of necessity and no police assistance was granted. The European Court concluded that although the legislation was not in violation of the Convention, the authorities' failure to apply the legislative provisions for exceptions to suspending eviction orders was contrary to Article 1, Protocol 1. What distinguishes *Scollo* from the facts in *Spadea* was that in the latter case the only reason for the evictions was the expiration of the leases since none of the exceptions applied to the applicants; however, in *Scollo*, some of the exceptions did apply to the applicant but the state failed to have sufficient regard to them. Thus in operational terms, an action of a public authority may not survive scrutiny, even though the legislation is justified under the Convention.

The more recent case of *G.L.* v *Italy* (App. No. 22671/93, 3 August 2000)[1] raises similar issues to the case of *Scollo* v *Italy*. Once again the European Court found that the legislative provisions suspending tenant eviction orders, whilst in themselves compliant with the Convention, had been applied in such a way as to constitute an infringement of Article 1, Protocol 1. The applicant served a notice to quit on the tenant upon the expiry of the lease in 1988. The applicant was granted an eviction order by the magistrate but the various attempts by the bailiff

---

[1] See also the decision in *Immobiliare Saffi* v *Italy* (1999) 7 BHRC 151.

to evict the tenant were unsuccessful due to the fact that the applicant was denied police assistance to enforce the possession order, even though he had made a declaration of necessity on the basis that he urgently required the property as accommodation for his son. The European Court noted that despite being entitled to priority in the grant of police assistance, he only recovered possession of his flat three and a half years after making the declaration of necessity and then only because the tenant vacated the property in 1997 of his own accord. The European Court stated (at para. 22) that:

> in principle, the Italian system of staggering the enforcement of court orders is not in itself open to criticism, having regard in particular to the margin of appreciation permitted under the second paragraph of Article 1. However, such a system carries with it the risk of imposing on landlords an excessive burden in terms of their ability to dispose of their property and must accordingly provide procedural safeguards so as to ensure that the operation of the system and its impact on a landlord's property rights are neither arbitrary nor unforeseeable.

The European Court took account of the fact that for over six years the applicant was left in a state of uncertainty as to when he would be able to recover possession of his flat and during this time he had no prospect of receiving any compensation.

Clearly these three cases are specific to the particular Italian legislation suspending tenant eviction orders. However, as well as indicating a possible approach to legislation that grants tenants security of tenure, the cases illustrate how the operation of the principle of proportionality can lead to different outcomes in respect of the same piece of legislation depending upon how the legislation is implemented in each individual case.

8.3.1.2 Article 8 and security of tenure

In *Velosa Barreto* v *Portugal* (App. No. 18072/91), a landlord argued that the national courts had infringed his rights under Article 8 by refusing to terminate the lease on the house that he owned. On inheriting the property from his parents in 1982 the applicant sought to obtain possession of the house by evicting the tenants who had resided there since 1964. The applicant, who was living with his parents-in-law in a large house rented by them, claimed that he and his family wished to occupy the house that he had inherited, as their family home. However, the national court declined to terminate the lease on the ground that the applicant had not proved that he had a real need to occupy the house as required by the Civil Code. The Civil Code did permit a landlord to evict a tenant in order to use the property as his own residence, but only where it was necessary, for weighty reasons, for the landlord to live in the property. The applicant did not dispute that the legislature was entitled to make the termination of a residential lease subject to a condition that the landlord must have a real need to live in the property, but he maintained that the court's application of the legislative provision to the particular facts of his case was in violation of the Convention. Thus he was not challenging the security of tenure provisions in themselves but rather whether the national court's assessment of what constituted 'need' within the meaning of the legislation had breached his rights under Article 8. He alleged that the national courts had failed to strike a fair balance between the general interest and his own interests. However the European Court, in rejecting his allegation, decided that the national courts had taken into account all the relevant issues. The European Court concluded (at para. 30) that: 'It has not been shown, and there is no evidence to suggest, that by ruling as they did the Portuguese courts acted arbitrarily or unreasonably or failed to discharge their obligation to strike a fair balance between the respective interests'. Accordingly there was held to be no violation of Article 8.

Although in *Velosa Barreto* the applicant was challenging the application of the security of tenure legislation based on the individual facts of his case rather than alleging that the legislation itself infringed the Convention, the European Court, nevertheless, examined the compatibility of the legislation with the Convention. It observed (at para. 24) that the positive obligations imposed upon the state by Article 8 do 'not go so far as to place the State under an obligation to give a landlord the right to recover possession of a rented house on request and in any circumstances'. The European Court, identifying the existence of a legitimate aim in terms of the social protection of tenants, found the legislation to promote the economic well-being of the country and to protect the rights of others within the scope of the justifications specified in Article 8(2). On this basis it seems improbable that the concept of security of tenure in English law will be found to be incompatible with Article 8, although the application of the legislation in individual cases could be found to cause a breach if, in operational terms, it contravenes the principle of proportionality.

8.3.2 Succession

One facet of the law governing security of tenure is the ability of a person to succeed to a deceased tenant's lease and thereby enjoy the benefits of an existing tenancy that is protected by the applicable housing legislation. These rights of succession, which are governed by statute, have diminished in practical significance since the introduction of assured tenancies under the Housing Act 1988. It is beneficial for a spouse or family member to succeed to a secure tenancy or a statutory tenancy due to the rent protection afforded to these tenancies. However, the assured tenant does not enjoy rent protection and has to pay a market rent, therefore on the death of the tenant there is less incentive for a spouse or family member to claim the benefit of rights of succession.

8.3.2.1   Spouse and family members

The rules governing rights of succession vary depending upon the type of tenancy in question. It is arguable that these differences may give rise to an allegation of discrimination contrary to Article 14 in conjunction with Article 8. Under the Rent Act 1977 (as amended by the Housing Act 1988) a spouse or a person who is a member of the tenant's family may qualify for succession. The Housing Act 1988 extends the meaning of a spouse to include those living together as husband and wife. Provided that the spouse has been residing in the dwelling-house immediately before the death of the tenant, he or she will succeed to a statutory tenancy. However, if the person claiming succession falls within the category of 'other family members', he or she will only succeed to an assured tenancy and not a statutory tenancy. This has significantly reduced the incentive for family members to claim succession rights under the Rent Act. What is understood by the term 'family member' is not explicated in the Rent Act, but there is a residence requirement specifying that the person must have been residing with the tenant at the time of the tenant's death and for the two immediately preceding years.

If the tenant had an assured periodic tenancy then only a spouse (or a heterosexual cohabitee living with the tenant as a husband or wife), who immediately before the tenant's death was occupying the dwelling-house as his or her only or principal home, qualifies for succession (s. 17, Housing Act 1988). Therefore a family member, living with the tenant at the time of his or her death, does not enjoy any rights of succession.

The Housing Act 1985 provides for rights of succession to periodic secure tenancies granted by local authority landlords. The successor must fulfil two conditions. First the dwelling-house must have been his or her only or principal home at the time of the tenant's death and secondly the successor must be either the tenant's spouse or another member of the tenant's family. In respect of the family member there is a residency requirement stating that that person must have resided with the tenant throughout the period of 12 months ending with the tenant's death (s. 87, Housing Act 1985). The 'member of the tenant's family' is defined by s. 113 of the Housing Act 1985. It includes spouses and those who 'live together as husband and wife' and proceeds to provide a list of relationships that fall within the scope of the definition, for example, parents, grandparents, children, brothers and sisters.

Having examined these different rules for succession under the various legislative provisions, it is possible to concoct scenarios in which a challenge under the HRA 1998 may arise. For example, the differential treatment of a member of the tenant's family under the Housing Act 1985 and the Housing Act 1988 provides a possible area for challenge. By way of illustration, consider the position of a daughter who, having lived for the last twenty years with her elderly father, claims a right to succeed to the tenancy on his death. She would be entitled to succeed to the tenancy if he had a secure tenancy under the Housing Act 1985.

However, a woman in a similar position whose father had an assured tenancy governed by the Housing Act 1988 would have no rights to succession and therefore could be evicted from her home. In these circumstances there may be a violation of Article 14 in conjunction with Article 8. The daughter who is denied any rights of succession under the Housing Act 1988 has clearly been treated differently from the daughter who qualifies for succession under the Housing Act 1985. The question is whether the former daughter can show that she is in an analogous situation to the latter. Would the courts be willing to treat these persons as being in a relatively similar position, or would the fact that one tenancy was granted in the private housing sector while the other was granted in the public housing sector be sufficient to differentiate them? Even if the courts accept that these two persons are in an analogous situation, a breach of Article 14 would only ensue if the Government failed to show that the differential treatment could be reasonably and objectively justified. Given the very different nature of the secure tenancy and the assured tenancy it may be relatively easy for the Government to justify the different treatment of the two daughters. However, if the landlord of both the assured tenancy and the secure tenancy is the same housing association, it may be more difficult to justify the difference. Prior to the Housing Act 1988, housing associations formed part of the public housing sector and granted their tenants a secure tenancy governed by the Housing Act 1985. It is only those tenancies granted on or after 15 January 1989 that are assured tenancies under the Housing Act 1988. Therefore it is possible for the same housing association landlord to have the daughter of one of its tenants succeed to the periodic secure tenancy while the daughter of another tenant is prevented from succeeding to her father's assured periodic tenancy.

8.3.2.2   Homosexual partners

Two cases have considered the question of homosexuality in relation to rights of succession under English law. One was decided by the European Commission in relation to discriminatory treatment contrary to Article 14 and interference with the home contrary to Article 8, whilst the other was recently decided by the House of Lords. An examination of these two cases makes interesting comparative analysis and indicates that the HRA 1998 is unlikely to have much effect on the law in an area where the House of Lords appears to be taking a more liberal stance than the Strasbourg institutions in protecting the succession rights of same-sex partners.

In *S v UK* (see Appendix 3) the European Commission rejected the applicant's complaints as inadmissible. The applicant lived in a lesbian relationship with her partner who was a secure tenant of a council house. Following the death of her partner the applicant claimed to be qualified to succeed to the secure tenancy under the Housing Act 1980 (now the Housing Act 1985). The relevant provisions of the Act stated that the rights of succession could be enjoyed only by the tenant's spouse or a member of the tenant's family which includes a couple living together as husband and wife. The Court of Appeal held that partners in a homosexual relationship could not qualify under the terms of the Act. The applicant alleged that this violated her rights under Article 8 taken alone and in conjunction with Article 14. However, the European Commission decided that any interference with the right of respect for her home under Article 8(1) could be justified under Article 8(2) as being in accordance with the law and necessary in a democratic society for the protection of the contractual rights of the landlord. This does not, however, explain why such interference is justified as being for the protection of the landlord's contractual rights where a homosexual partner is concerned but not where it is a heterosexual partner.

In determining whether there was discriminatory treatment in violation of Article 14 in conjunction with Article 8, the European Commission concluded that the legislative distinction between heterosexual and homosexual relationships could be objectively and reasonably justified. Its decision was based on the premise that the aim of the Housing Act 1980, in allowing certain categories of persons to enjoy rights of succession, was to protect family life. However, the European Commission observed that homosexual partners have been consistently excluded from the meaning of 'family' under Article 8 and consequently there was no infringement of Article 14 on this basis. This case can be compared to the recent decision of the House of Lords in *Fitzpatrick v Sterling Housing Association Ltd* [1999] 4 All ER 705 which involved the same issue of homosexuality and succession rights but under the Rent Act legislation instead of the Housing Act 1980. The term 'family' is left undefined in the Rent Acts but the meaning of 'spouse' has been statutorily extended to include a person who was living with the original tenant as his or her wife or husband. Mr Fitzpatrick, whose homosexual partner had a protected tenancy of the flat in which they both lived, sought a declaration that he succeeded to the statutory tenancy on the death of his partner. He claimed to qualify to the rights of succession either as a spouse because he had lived with the original tenant 'as his or her wife or husband' or alternatively that he was a member of his family. The House of Lords, reversing the decision of the Court of Appeal, held that same-sex partners in a longstanding, homosexual relationship can constitute a member of the family of the original tenant within the meaning of the Rent Act 1977 and thereby enjoy the rights of succession afforded by that Act. In allowing the appeal their Lordships went to considerable efforts to emphasise the limitations of the decision as relating purely to the meaning of 'family' within the confines of the Rent Act 1977. However, there are inevitably wider implications of this decision due to the incorporation of Article 14 into English law under the HRA 1998. In finding a homosexual relationship to constitute a family relationship and thereby allowing Mr Fitzpatrick to enjoy the rights of succession under the Rent Acts, the House of Lords' decision enables a homosexual partner, if excluded from the rights of succession under the Housing Act 1985, to raise an allegation of discrimination in contravention of Article 14.

8.3.3   Rent controls

There has already been a challenge to the UK legislation in this area of law in the form of a complaint to Strasbourg regarding the rent controls operated under the Rent Acts. The challenge in *Kilbourn* v *UK* (1986) 8 EHRR 81 was, however, unsuccessful. The case involved two properties let on controlled tenancies under the Rent Act legislation. The properties were inherited by the applicant in 1970 but she was unable to increase the rent on the properties due to the rent control legislation then in force. The European Commission examined the applicant's complaint under Article 1, Protocol 1 and was satisfied that the legislation imposed certain restrictions on the applicant's use of her property; in particular, it controlled her right to increase the rent payable by the tenants. This interference fell within the third rule as a control of the use of the property. However, the European Commission decided that the interference was justifiable. It pursued a legitimate aim of social policy by protecting the interests of tenants suffering from the effects of a shortage of inexpensive housing. The European Commission stated that: 'Although the restrictions are undeniably extensive, they may still be considered as necessary to control the use of property in accordance with the general interest'. In assessing proportionality, the European Commission con-cluded that the rent restrictions imposed on the applicant were not disproportion-ate. Reliance was placed on *X* v *Austria* (1979) 3 EHRR 285 in which similar rent control provisions were found not to transgress the state's margin of appreciation. In that case the European Commission had concluded that neither the legal regulations themselves, nor their application in the particular case before it, could be considered as excessive. In *Kilbourn* the European Commission decided, on similar grounds, that there was no violation of Article 1, Protocol 1.

However, the case of *Mellacher* v *Austria* (1989) 12 EHRR 391 reached the European Court after the European Commission found the application to be admissible. The applicants, who were landlords of a number of residential flats, alleged that statutory rent controls that caused a substantial reduction in the rent payable by their existing tenants violated Article 1, Protocol 1. The applicants alleged that the reductions in rent effectively constituted a deprivation of possessions. Whilst acknowledging that the legislation deprived the applicants of part of their income from the property, the European Court held that it amounted merely to a control of use within the ambit of the third rule and not to a deprivation of possessions within the scope of the second rule. The European Court found that the rent controls did constitute an interference with property but that the measures were justifiable as they were adopted in pursuance of a legitimate aim in the general interest and fell within the wide margin of appreciation granted to the states in the field of housing. In ascertaining a legitimate aim in the general interest the European Court reiterated (at para. 45) the approach taken in *James* v *UK* that in the implementation of social and economic policies:

> the legislature must have a wide margin of appreciation both with regard to the existence of a problem of public concern warranting measures of control and as to the choice of the detailed rules for the implementation of such measures. The European Court will respect the legislature's judgment as to what is in the general interest unless that judgment be manifestly without reasonable foundation.

The Government maintained that the aim of the legislation was to make more housing available to less affluent tenants, while also providing incentives for landlords to improve the condition of substandard properties. Although the applicants produced statistical evidence to support their submission that there was no underlying problem of social injustice to justify the rent controls, the European Court found (at para. 47) the legislation to be in the general interest because 'the explanations given for the legislation in question are not such as could be characterised as being manifestly unreasonable'. This test indicates that a high threshold of unreasonableness exists before the European Court will interfere with a state's justifications for its actions. Only where the explanations given are 'manifestly unreasonable' will the European Court intervene. Consequently, it is relatively easy for the state to discharge its burden of satisfying the requirement for a legitimate aim in the general interest. In assessing proportionality the European Court concluded that the applicants did not suffer a disproportionate burden even in those instances where the effect of the legislation had been to reduce the rent from 1,870 schillings a month to 330 schillings a month, a reduction of 82 per cent. The European Court's conclusion differed from that of the European Commission which had found such substantial reductions in the rent to be unjustified. The European Court laid considerable weight upon the state's margin of appreciation, finding that the measures complained of were not so disproportionate as to take them outside that discretion. The European Court observed (at para. 56) that:

> The fact that the original market rents were agreed upon and corresponded to the then prevailing market conditions does not mean that the legislature could not reasonably decide as a matter of policy that they were unacceptable from the point of view of social justice.

These decisions of the Strasbourg institutions indicate that the current measures on rent control in the UK are unlikely to be found to be incompatible with the Convention rights. However, it is worth noting that rent control legislation in Ireland, which was arbitrary in its operation, was held to be in breach of the Irish Constitution (see *Blake* v *A-G* [1982] IR 117).

8.3.4   The Commonhold and Leasehold Reform Bill

Part I of the Commonhold and Leasehold Reform Bill[2] (the Bill) introduces a new form of tenure for blocks of flats and other multi-unit properties, under which owners will own their individual units and, in addition, through a commonhold association (a private company limited by guarantee) will own and manage the common parts collectively. Conversion to commonhold status will only be permitted on a 100 per cent consent basis which means that all of the leaseholders in the building must agree to participate. The consultation paper, in acknowledging that this is likely to severely limit the rate of conversion to commonhold, states that: 'The Government recognises that this is a very high hurdle and that it may effectively make it impossible for the majority of long leasehold developments to convert to commonhold'.[3] Recognising the obstacles to converting existing leaseholds into commonhold, the Government has proposed a number of reforms to residential long leases which 'are intended to redress the uneven balance between landlords and leaseholders, and give leaseholders a greater degree of control over the management of their homes which reflects the substantial investment they have made'.[4] Part II of the Bill covers these residential leasehold reforms and the extent to which these reforms may raise human rights issues under the HRA 1998 will be considered.

8.3.4.1   The right to manage: a summary of the law

The Government has set out its aim behind the introduction of the 'right to manage' (RTM) in the following terms: 'The main objective is to grant residential long leaseholders of flats the right to take over the management of their building collectively without having either to prove fault on the part of the landlord or to pay any compensation'.[5] To this end clause 53 of the Bill confers the RTM on a qualifying company, the membership of which includes qualifying tenants of flats contained in the relevant premises. This new RTM is not intended to replace the existing right of collective enfranchisement but rather to provide an alternative option to those who cannot afford, or do not wish, to purchase the freehold. The RTM provisions seek to redress the problems which can arise from the fact that the management of the property normally remains in the hands of the landlord even though the financial value of the landlord's interest in the building will be very small compared to that of the long leaseholders. The leaseholders, who, therefore, have little control over the quality, cost effectiveness or promptness of any services rendered in relation to the management of the building are

---

[2] A joint publication from the DETR and the Lord Chancellor's Department, August 2000. A copy of the draft Bill and consultation paper is available at www.housing.detr.gov.uk.

[3] DETR, 'Commonhold and Leasehold Reform', draft Bill and consultation paper, August 2000, Part I, Section 2, 2.2 at para. 3.

[4] Ibid., Part II, Section 1, Introduction at para. 3.

[5] Ibid., Part II, Section 3, Chapter I at para. 10.

nevertheless often obliged under their leases to meet the full costs of these services. There are currently two systems for removing control of the management of flats from landlords. First the leaseholders can exercise a right of collective enfranchisement to buy the freehold. Secondly, where there is evidence of serious abuse by the landlord, the leaseholders can apply to the Leasehold Valuation Tribunal (LVT) for the appointment of a manager under the Landlord and Tenant Act 1987. The RTM provisions, however, will enable leaseholders to take over the management of the building without the need to prove fault or abuse by the landlord.

The eligibility criteria for RTM will accord with that under the Leasehold Reform, Housing and Urban Development Act (LRHUDA) 1993 (as amended by the Bill) for collective enfranchisement. Therefore only leaseholders that are qualifying tenants and eligible for collective enfranchisement will be eligible for RTM. The management body will be a company limited by guarantee with a prescribed Memorandum and Articles of Association suited for the purpose of managing a building. All qualifying tenants in a block of flats where RTM is exercised will be entitled to be a member of the RTM company. In addition, in recognition of the landlord's continued interest in the property, the landlord will also be entitled to membership of the RTM company. The Government proposes that:

> Membership of the company would allow the landlords to exercise some control over how the company carries out its management functions, and ensure access to relevant information. However, unlike under normal leasehold arrangements, this influence would be proportional to the actual interest in the property and would not arise from a monopoly management position.[6]

To exercise the RTM the company, set up by the leaseholders to manage the property, will have to serve a claim notice on all landlords with an interest in the property informing them of the intention to exercise the RTM (clause 61). Landlords will be entitled to serve a counternotice by a specified date which either indicates acceptance of the RTM or which disputes the company's entitlement to take over the management (clause 65). A landlord can only object on the grounds of non-compliance with one or more of the specific qualifying criteria. Other types of complaint, for example, that the company lacks the skills and resources to manage the block successfully, will not constitute a legitimate ground for objection. The LVT will have the authority to adjudicate any dispute between the parties over the company's entitlement to manage.

The RTM company will assume responsibility for managing the property on a specified date and will be entitled to receive from the landlord all the papers

---

[6] Ibid., Part II, Section 3, Chapter I at para. 34.

relating to the management, maintenance and insurance of the property and all reserves of money held on trust on behalf of the leaseholders. The RTM company will then be responsible for carrying out the 'management functions' of the landlord, which is defined in clause 71 of the Bill as 'functions relating to services, repairs, maintenance, improvements, insurance and management'. Both lease-holders and landlords will enjoy the right to take court action to ensure that the RTM company complies with its management obligations.

8.3.4.2   The right to manage: the implications of the Human Rights Act 1998
The RTM provisions need to be considered in the light of Article 1, Protocol 1 to determine whether they constitute an unjustifiable interference with the landlord's property. In ascertaining which of the three rules under Article 1, Protocol 1 is applicable, it is likely that any suggestion by the landlord that there has been a deprivation of possessions under the second rule will be unsuccessful. Although a landlord may allege that the RTM provisions deprive him of any profit element in the service charge that he currently enjoys under the lease, the English courts are likely to adopt the same approach as the Strasbourg institutions have taken to similar submissions. This approach is exemplified in the decision in *Antoniades* v *UK* (App. No. 15434/89) where a reduction in rent was treated as a control of use and not a deprivation (see 4.6.3). In *Antoniades* the licences that the applicant had entered into with two occupiers living in his flat were held, by the national court, to be leases which benefited from the rent protection and security of tenure provisions of the Rent Act 1977. In consequence the rent payable to the applicant was reduced and was less than the licence fee that the occupiers had been paying. The European Commission observed that: 'It cannot be said that the rights of the applicant as stipulated in the agreements (principally to repossess the flat, but also to the licence fee) constituted individual rights enjoying, in their own right, the protection awarded to possessions'. Therefore the reduction in the money paid to the applicants by the tenants was not a possession in itself, but merely constituted one aspect of the applicant's ownership of the freehold estate. On this basis the European Commission concluded that there had been a control of use within the scope of the third rule and not a deprivation of possessions. The effect of the RTM is to remove the day-to-day management of the building from the landlord's control but he still retains his freehold reversion in the property and the right to receive ground rent. Any loss of the profit element of the service charge is likely to be seen as a loss of one aspect of the landlord's ownership rights and therefore the applicable rule will be the third rule. It will be relatively easy for the Government to establish the existence of a legitimate aim relying upon the promotion of social justice, a justification which implements the objective of the RTM provisions. This is especially likely bearing in mind that in the implemen-tation of housing policies the states are afforded a wide margin of appreciation (*James* v *UK*). Therefore the deciding factor is likely to be the principle of

proportionality (see 4.4.3). It seems improbable that the RTM provisions will be found, in themselves, to infringe Article 1, Protocol 1. The removal of the landlord's overall control in the management of the building is unlikely to be perceived as imposing an excessive burden upon the landlord, especially as the landlord's continuing interest in the property is recognised and protected in a number of ways, for example the landlord enjoys membership of the RTM company and has a right to take the RTM company to court for non-compliance with its obligations. In consequence, a challenge to the RTM provisions under Article 1, Protocol 1, is unlikely to succeed.

8.3.4.3   Collective enfranchisement: a summary of the law

The Bill provides for a simplification of the existing rules for collective enfranchisement set out in the LRHUDA 1993. Collective enfranchisement is the right of long leaseholders of flats to compulsorily purchase the freehold of their block of flats. Working on the premise that the existing rules contain a number of unnecessary restrictions which have prevented leaseholders from enfranchising under the LRHUDA 1993, the Bill proposes a number of changes to the qualifying criteria including the following:

(a)   to abolish the 'residence' test which requires participating leaseholders to have lived in their flats as their main or only home for the last 12 months; and

(b)   to increase the proportion of the building that can be occupied for non-residential purposes from 10 per cent to 25 per cent.

In addition to a relaxation of the existing qualifying criteria, the Bill also introduces a requirement that the enfranchisement is carried out by a company limited by guarantee with prescribed Memorandum and Articles of Association which will thereafter be responsible for managing the building. These provisions replace the existing requirement for a 'nominee purchaser' whose constitution is unspecified.

The valuation basis for collective enfranchisement inevitably raises issues of concern for both landlords and tenants. The current rules provide that the price payable for the freehold is the aggregate of three components: the open market value of the freehold reversion; compensation for losses, e.g., development value; and the freeholder's share of the marriage value. The marriage value is the additional value created by the ability of the leaseholders to have new long leases, normally for 999 years, granted to them without the payment of a premium. The consultation paper states that:

> The Government has concluded that in a compulsory purchase situation, landlords are entitled to a fair market price for their interest in the building, including a share of the

marriage value which would normally occur in an open market sale between willing parties when leasehold and freehold interests are merged. However, the present arrangements for determining the enfranchisement price are complex and uncertain and can lead to costly arguments, often over matters which have a relatively small impact on the overall price.[7]

The current rules provide for the marriage value to be shared between the parties, and in the event of dispute over its apportionment, it is referred to the LVT for determination. To reduce the scope for costly dispute in this area, the Bill makes the following amendments to the current scheme:

(a)   to share the marriage value equally between landlords and leaseholders (clause 98);

(b)   to presume that there is no marriage value where all of the leases of the participating leaseholders have more than 90 years to run (clause 99);

(c)   to remove the unfettered right of appeal to the Lands Tribunal against the decisions of the LVT so that prior permission will need to be sought.

The introduction of the prescribed basis for apportioning 'marriage value' between the freeholder and leaseholders aims at preventing time-consuming and costly arguments between the parties which delay the completion process. It is noteworthy that under the existing scheme the LVT invariably apportions the marriage value on a 50/50 basis and therefore the proposed prescribed rule of sharing it equally between the landlord and leaseholders does not diverge from current practice.

In respect of the proposal to disregard the marriage value in cases of very long leases, the consultation paper explains that:

> Where the unexpired term of a lease is very long the marriage value is likely to be negligible, because the merging of the two interests will, in such cases, add to the individual values of the interests only marginally. We therefore propose that there should be a presumption that there is no marriage value where all of the leases held by members of the qualifying company have at least 90 years unexpired.[8]

8.3.4.4   Collective enfranchisement: the implications of the Human Rights Act 1998

The decision of the European Court in *James* v *UK* (see Appendix 3) makes any challenge under the HRA 1998 to leasehold enfranchisement legislation extremely improbable. The Bill amends the LRHUDA 1993 to simplify and relax the existing qualifying criteria for exercising the right of enfranchisement so that

---

[7] Ibid., Part II, Section 2, 2.1 at paras 9–10.
[8] Ibid., Part II, Section 3, Chapter II at para. 76.

more leaseholders will fall within the category of qualifying tenants. To this extent the Bill provides no more of a challenge under the HRA 1998 than the existing enfranchisement legislation which has already been accepted as Convention compliant by the European Court in *James* v *UK*. However there are some areas more open to challenge, principally the basis for calculating the purchase price to be paid to the landlord in respect of the compulsory purchase of the freehold reversion. The Government's objective in implementing changes to the marriage value is 'to reduce the likelihood of lengthy and costly disputes about the determination of the purchase price of the freehold interest'.[9] It is unlikely that any reduction in the marriage value received by landlords, due to the prescribed 50 per cent share or its disregard in applicable cases, will be sufficient to breach Article 1, Protocol 1 given that the Article does not guarantee a right to full compensation in all cases (see 4.3.6.1). The landlords in *James* v *UK* received a significantly reduced purchase price for some of the enfranchised flats but this did not constitute a violation of Article 1, Protocol 1. The European Court observed (at para. 54) that Article 1, Protocol 1:

> does not, however, guarantee a right to full compensation in all circumstances. Legitimate objectives of 'public interest', such as pursued in measures of economic reform or measures designed to achieve greater social justice, may call for less than reimbursement of the full market value.

Such considerations will be equally applicable to justify the proposed changes to the marriage value and indicate that there is unlikely to be any infringement of Article 1, Protocol 1.

8.3.5   The positive obligations of a public authority landlord

Public authorities have a duty under s. 6 of the HRA 1998 not to act in a way that is incompatible with Convention rights unless they are required to do so by statute (see 1.7). Consequently, a public authority which acts as a landlord, must ensure that it is not in violation of Article 8 in fulfilling its role as a landlord. In observing the tenants' rights to respect for their home and private life, a public authority landlord will be imbued with certain positive obligations. The form and scope of these positive obligations are explained at 5.2.1 and, in this context, include a duty to take steps to ensure that the tenants' enjoyment of their rights under Article 8 are effective and not interfered with by other tenants. Whether or not a positive obligation arises in a given situation will depend upon whether the interference falls within the scope of Article 8 (see 5.3.1.1) and, if so, whether it would constitute a breach of Article 8 (see 5.3.4). For example, severe noise pollution has been held, in a number of the decisions of the Strasbourg institutions, to

---

[9] Ibid., Part II, Section 3, Chapter II at para. 18.

constitute an interference with a person's rights under Article 8 (see 8.8.2). The European Commission has acknowledged that: 'Considerable noise nuisance can undoubtedly affect the physical well-being of a person and thus interfere with his private life. It may also deprive a person of the possibility of enjoying the amenities of his home' (*Powell and Rayner* v *UK*, see Appendix 3). This suggests that if a tenant of a public authority landlord suffers excessive noise levels due to the structural inadequacies of the building, or due to anti-social neighbours, the landlord may be obliged to take positive steps to reduce the noise to an acceptable level that does not interfere with the tenant's rights under Article 8. This may require a reconsideration of the House of Lords' decision in *Southwark London Borough Council* v *Mills* [1999] 3 WLR 939. The case raised the question of whether a local authority landlord is under an obligation to install sound insulation in premises which were built without sound insulation (but which complied with the building by-laws applicable at the time of their construction). The council tenants were plagued by the noise of their neighbours going about their normal domestic life, so that every light switched on, every door opened and closed and every pan placed on the cooker was audible. Due to the lack of sound insulation the tenants had to endure intolerable levels of noise and sought a remedy to require the landlord to install the necessary soundproofing. The House of Lords held that there had been no breach of the landlord's covenant for quiet enjoyment nor was the landlord liable under an action for private nuisance and consequently the tenants had no remedy against the landlord in respect of the excessive levels of noise.[10]

If the case of *Mills* had been decided after 2 October 2000, it seems likely that the considerable noise nuisance would have been sufficient to constitute an interference under Article 8. However, the principle of proportionality would, on the facts, be particularly relevant in determining whether or not the local authority had a positive obligation to protect the tenants' rights under Article 8. In assessing whether a fair balance had been struck between the general interest of the community and the rights of the tenants, the court would most likely weigh in the balance the fact that vast local authority financial resources would be swallowed up if it reached a decision favourable to the tenants. In 1998–99 the housing budget for Southwark LBC was less than £55 million and yet it would have cost in excess of £37 million to have installed sound insulation into its existing housing stock. Taking these figures into account, Lord Millett observed (at p. 961) that:

> These cases raise issues of priority in the allocation of resources. Such issues must be resolved by the democratic process, national and local. The judges are not equipped to

---

[10] See Rook, D., 'Excessive noise can be a breach of the landlord's covenant for quiet enjoyment' [2000] 64 Conv 161.

resolve them. All that we can do is to say that there is nothing in the relevant tenancy agreements or current legislation, or in the common law, which would enable the tenants to obtain redress through the courts.

In the light of Lord Millett's statement in *Mills* it is interesting to note that, in assessing proportionality under the HRA 1998, the courts will now be called upon to consider issues of priority in the allocation of limited financial resources. Bearing in mind the public interest in carefully allocating the limited resources of the local authority, it is arguable that the House of Lords would not have reached a different conclusion in *Mills* if the case had been decided after the implementation of the HRA 1998.

Excessive levels of noise is just one example of an area where a public authority landlord may be obliged to take positive steps to protect the tenants' rights under Article 8. Other potential areas include pollution, health and safety (for example, a cockroach infestation), serious disrepair and nuisance caused by neighbouring tenants. This may require a reconsideration of *Hussain* v *Lancaster City Council* [1999] 4 All ER 125, in which it was held that a landlord is not responsible for acts of nuisance committed by its tenants unless it has specifically authorised or adopted those acts.

This imposition of positive obligations upon public authority landlords may extend to private landlords undertaking a public function, for example, by providing housing for asylum seekers. It is arguable that private landlords, who are contracted by a local authority to provide accommodation for asylum seekers, act as a public authority in the provision of this housing because they are performing a function that the local authority would otherwise have to perform (see 1.7.2). Such landlords would then be obliged to take positive steps to protect the occupiers' rights under Article 8, for example, by preventing any excessive noise nuisance or remedying any serious disrepair.

A public authority's duty, under s. 6 of the HRA 1998, not to act incompatibly with Convention rights may also have an impact upon the now common use by local authority and housing association landlords of closed circuit television cameras to monitor the common parts of housing estates. The cameras are installed for security purposes in order to better protect the tenants' personal safety and the safety of their property by means of discouraging crime and anti-social behaviour on the estates. The cameras are likely to constitute an interference with the tenants' respect for their private life because they may record private events and, in these circumstances, the tenants will have a reasonable expectation of privacy (see *Halford* v *UK* (1997) 24 EHRR 523 in which the interception of private telephone calls was held to come within the scope of 'private life' under Article 8). However, it is most probable that the use of closed circuit television cameras, where they are used for the purpose of protecting the tenants' security and safety, are justifiable under Article 8(2) being in pursuit of a legitimate aim and necessary in a democratic society (see 5.3.3 and 5.3.4).

8.3.6   Distress for rent

An in-depth consideration of the implications of the HRA 1998 on distress for rent is warranted both because of the fact that the law governing the remedy is ripe for challenge under the HRA 1998 but also because it illustrates the possible approach of the courts to assessing HRA 1998 issues in other areas of property law.

8.3.6.1   A remedy provided for by common law and statute
The ancient remedy of distress for rent is available to a landlord where the tenant has fallen into arrears with the rent due under the terms of the lease. The remedy permits the landlord, or a bailiff employed by the landlord, to seize goods that are present on the demised premises and impound them until either the tenant pays the rent arrears or the landlord sells the seized goods in order to recoup the rent arrears from the sale proceeds. The origins of the remedy lie in the common law. The Statute of Marlborough 1267 sought only to restrict the scope of the existing remedy by limiting it to reasonable distraints that were not excessive. At common law the landlord could only retain the distrained goods until the tenant paid the rent arrears. Therefore the original purpose of distress for rent was to seize goods to act as a type of security for the payment of a debt, similar to a possessory lien. The effectiveness of the remedy depended upon causing the tenant inconvenience in the hope of inducing the tenant to pay the arrears. However the Distress for Rent Act 1689 introduced a power of sale enabling landlords to sell the seized goods in order to recoup the rent arrears. The new power of sale brought about a significant change in the purpose of the remedy. Instead of seizing goods to inconvenience the tenant and retaining them as security, the landlord can now use the goods directly to raise money to satisfy the debt. The effect of this significant change upon the distraint of goods belonging to a third party will be considered in the light of the HRA 1998.

In assessing the applicability of the HRA 1998, it is important to appreciate that the availability of the remedy of distress for rent is not dependent upon the terms of the lease to expressly provide for it. The remedy is available whenever there is a relationship of landlord and tenant between the parties and the rent has fallen into arrears. Therefore the remedy is provided for by common law and statute rather than by contract (see 3.4). It is arguable that therein lies the existence of sufficient state responsibility to invoke Convention rights even in a dispute between a private landlord and tenant.

8.3.6.2   *Article 1, Protocol 1 and distress for rent*

Distress for rent permits the landlord (or a certificated bailiff) to enter the tenant's premises and seize and impound any goods present (except for those goods subject to qualified or absolute privilege).[11] The fact that the goods belong to a third party does not prevent the landlord from distraining upon the goods. Goods belonging to a third party may, in certain instances, acquire absolute privilege; however, this is dependent upon the owner of the goods taking positive steps to acquire that protection. Under section 1 of the Law of Distress Amendment Act (LDAA) 1908, the owner of the goods must serve a declaration in writing on the landlord specifying that he owns the relevant goods and that the tenant has no property or beneficial interest in the goods. For the purposes of assessing the likely impact of the HRA 1998 on distress for rent it is necessary to distinguish between an interference with the goods of the tenant and an interference with goods belonging to a third party. Whereas it may be possible to justify levying distress against the goods of the tenant so that there is no breach of Article 1, Protocol 1, this is likely to be far more difficult in respect of goods belonging to an innocent third party.

(a)   The applicable rule   The Strasbourg institutions generally begin a consideration of an alleged breach of Article 1, Protocol 1 by identifying which of the three rules is applicable (see 4.2). The more obvious choice in respect of distress for rent is a deprivation of property under the second rule. Certainly a sale of the goods by the landlord will involve a transfer of ownership in the property so that the rights of the owner are extinguished. Where the goods belonged to a third party, a deprivation of property under the second rule seems the most appropriate rule to apply. However, a landlord may seek to argue that, as regards the tenant's property, the applicable rule is the third rule. Although this approach may not find favour with the courts, it will be considered on its merits. The argument relies upon the decisions of the Strasbourg institutions relating to the confiscation of property for the enforcement of the criminal law or under tax legislation which could be applied by analogy (see, for example, *Air Canada* v *UK* and *Hentrich* v *France*). These cases were held to fall within the third rule as a control of use, even though the owner's rights in the property were extinguished. In *Air Canada* v *UK* the aircraft was seized as liable to forfeiture because it had been used to transport illegal drugs and this activity was prohibited by statute. The relevant legislative provisions were clearly aimed at controlling the use of property. The European Court found that the forfeiture was merely a measure taken in pursuance of imposing that restriction on the use of the aircraft, hence the forfeiture of the property fell within the third rule. However, it may be difficult to satisfy the courts that the law governing distress for rent seeks to control

---

[11] For an explanation of privileged goods see Rook, D., *Distress for Rent*, London: Blackstone Press, 1999, chapter 2.

the tenant's use of the leasehold estate. The law aims to provide landlords with a remedy where the tenant has fallen into arrears with the rent. The law does not seek to control the use of the tenant's estate other than to discourage the tenant from using the premises without paying the rent. Nor can the European Court's approach in *Gasus Dosier- und Fordertechnik GmbH* v *Netherlands* (see Appendix 3) be relied upon. Although this case did concern the seizure of goods by the Tax Bailiff to satisfy a company's tax debts, the European Court held that the case came under the third rule because that rule specifically concerns the interference with property to secure the payment of taxes or other contributions or penalties. As the payment of rent by a tenant is unlikely to fall within this category, the case offers no support for the application of the third rule to distress for rent. It seems improbable that levying distress will fall within the ambit of the third rule.

(b)   A legitimate aim   Whether a challenge to distress for rent is assessed under the second or the third rule, the general considerations of legitimate aim and legality are unlikely to differ. It would be relatively easy to establish a legitimate aim for the landlord's use of distress for rent. The availability of a quick and effective remedy for rent arrears protects the property rights of private landlords and thereby encourages residential and commercial lettings in the private sector. In the residential public sector it serves a legitimate aim by providing local authority landlords with a cheap remedy for rent arrears thereby saving public expense which would otherwise have to be used in pursuing costly court action.

(c)   The principle of proportionality   The principle of proportionality requires there to be a reasonable relationship of proportionality between the means employed and the aim sought to be realised. It is in this respect that it may be possible to establish that in certain cases levying distress will constitute an infringement of Article 1, Protocol 1. The compensation factor is particularly relevant to a deprivation under the second rule, whereas it has less weighting under the third rule where the due process factor is prevalent in assessing proportionality (see 4.6.5). If a challenge to distress for rent comes within the ambit of the second rule then the compensation factor must be considered. The European Court has stated that:

> the taking of property in the public interest without the payment of compensation is treated as justifiable only in exceptional circumstances ... As far as Article 1 (P1–1) is concerned, the protection it affords would be largely illusory and ineffective in the absence of any equivalent principle (*James* v *UK*, at para. 54).

The deprivation of goods belonging to the tenant to satisfy rent arrears cannot be subject to the payment of compensation by the landlord as this would clearly defeat the purpose of the remedy. Therefore this would have to fall within the 'exceptional circumstances' category to which the European Court has referred. However, this is not necessarily the case in respect of goods belonging to a third party. It is arguable that a landlord should compensate any third party whose goods, being present on the demised premises, are seized by the landlord and later sold. Under the existing law the third party owner is not entitled to compensation from the landlord where the distraint is lawful and therefore it could be argued that innocent third parties suffer an excessive burden in contravention of Article 1, Protocol 1.

Similarly, in respect of the due process factor, an innocent third party owner may once again be found to suffer disproportionately. In *AGOSI* v *UK*, which concerned the confiscation of illegally imported goods belonging to an innocent third party, the European Court stated (at para. 55) that it had to:

> consider whether the applicable procedures in the present case were such as to enable, amongst other things, reasonable account to be taken of the degree of fault or care of the applicant company ... and also whether the procedures in question afforded the applicant company a reasonable opportunity of putting its case to the responsible authorities.

In that case the fact that the decision of the Customs and Excise Commissioners, of which the applicant complained, was open to judicial review was found to be an adequate means of protecting the innocent owner and of complying with the procedural requirements of the third rule. In applying these considerations to distress for rent, it raises the question of whether the current procedural safeguards to protect goods belonging to a third party are adequate. Although the LDAA 1908 enables an owner of goods to serve a written declaration upon the landlord in order for the goods to acquire absolute privilege from distraint, the declaration must be served prior to the sale of the goods which can be as little as five days after the levy took place. Significantly, there is no requirement on either the landlord or the tenant to give the owner of the goods notice of the distraint so that the owner may be unaware of the distress until after the goods have been sold by which time it is too late to claim any protection for the goods. Since the protection afforded to the innocent third party owner by the LDAA 1908 is 'largely illusory and ineffective' without an obligation on the parties to notify the owner about the distraint before the sale of the goods, these inadequate procedural safeguards may be found to upset the fair balance to be struck between the demands of the general interest of the community and the requirements of the protection of the individual's fundamental freedoms (see 8.3.6.5).

8.3.6.3   Article 8 and distress for rent
If a landlord of residential property enters the demised premises in order to levy distress it is safe to assume that in the majority of cases he will be entering the

tenant's 'home'. Clearly by entering the tenant's home in order to levy distress the landlord is taking intrusive measures which could amount to a violation of the tenant's right to respect for his home and private life under Article 8. As the term 'home' extends to include certain business premises (*Niemietz* v *Germany* (1992) 16 EHRR 97), there may even be a breach of Article 8 in respect of a business lease where the tenant is a professional person and the landlord enters the tenant's office in order to levy distress for rent (see 5.2.4). The question is whether the interference with the tenant's rights can be justified under Article 8(2). Article 8(2) provides that there must be no state interference with the rights protected by Article 8(1) except such as is in accordance with the law and necessary in a democratic society. Although the act of levying distress may be by a private individual, it is arguable that the state, as law-maker, is ultimately responsible for that interference.

(a) In accordance with the law The law governing distress for rent is accessible to the applicant (through the availability of legal advice) and the landlord's action is foreseeable (see 5.3.2). The act of intrusion into the tenant's home to levy distress is therefore 'in accordance with the law'.

(b) A legitimate aim Does distress for rent pursue a legitimate aim within the boundaries of Article 8(2)? The scope of the aims listed in Article 8(2) is extremely wide and therefore it is relatively easy for the state to establish the existence of a legitimate aim (see 5.3.3). In justifying distress for rent it would be possible to raise the protection of the property rights of a private landlord as a legitimate aim. Where the landlord is a local authority, the economic well-being of the country could also be relied upon as, without the availability of a quick, cheap and effective remedy to recover rent arrears, the local authorities may suffer financial loss which in turn would effect the general community due to reduced available local authority funding.

(c) The principle of proportionality The deciding factor is likely to be whether the interference with the tenant's home and private life is necessary in a democratic society. Is there a 'pressing social need' and is the interference proportionate to the legitimate aim being pursued? In respect of the requirement for a 'pressing social need' the European Commission has stated that:

> As the Convention organs have repeatedly recognised, to satisfy the requirement of necessity referred to in Art. 8(2) of the Convention, it must be established that the measure in question was not merely desirable or convenient, but responded to a real requirement (*Gillow* v *UK*, at para. 132).

It may be argued that there is no 'pressing social need' for landlords to levy distress to recover rent arrears, given the existence of alternative, less intrusive, methods of recovering rent arrears, e.g., a rent action in the courts. Is distress for rent merely a more desirable and convenient remedy that does not respond to a real requirement?

Due process considerations are of particular significance in the assessment of proportionality. The European Court has stated that:

> Indeed it is settled case law that, whilst Article 8 contains no explicit procedural requirements, the decision-making process leading to measures of interference must be fair and such as to afford due respect to the interests safeguarded to the individual by Article 8 (*Buckley* v *UK*, at para. 76).

In the public residential sector distress for rent can be levied by local authority landlords without the need for a prior court order. That a tenant's right to respect for his home and private life can be interfered with without any procedural safeguards preceding the interference lends considerable support to a finding of a lack of proportionality with a consequent breach of Article 8.

8.3.6.4   *The tenant's rights under Article 6(1)*

At common law distress for rent is a self-help remedy which can be carried out without legal process. Although the intervention of statute requires a landlord to obtain a court order prior to levying distress where the lease is a residential lease in the private sector (s. 19 of the Housing Act 1988 and s. 147 of the Rent Act 1977), these statutory provisions do not apply to business leases nor to public sector residential leases. Therefore a local authority landlord can levy distress without obtaining a prior court order. This lack of legal process in the use of the remedy may raise issues under Article 6(1). Article 6(1) guarantees the right to a fair hearing in the determination of a person's civil rights and obligations. For Article 6(1) to apply there must be a dispute (a *contestation*) the outcome of which is directly decisive for the private rights of an individual (see chapter 7). In *App. No. 11949/86* v *UK* the tenant was liable to make a service charge payment by way of additional rent in respect of her proportion of the insurance and any repair and maintenance costs. There was a disagreement between the landlord and the tenant as to the amount of the service charge payable and as a result of this the tenant withheld payment of the charge. The dispute escalated ending in the forfeiture of the lease by the landlord. The European Commission accepted that 'the dispute between the applicant and her landlord as to her obligations under the lease ... involved the determination of her civil rights and obligations'. Therefore a dispute concerning the payment of rent under a lease involves the determination of the tenant's civil rights and obligations and entitles the tenant, under Article 6(1), to a fair and public hearing by an independent and impartial tribunal.

The availability of the landlord's right to levy distress presupposes that the tenant has fallen into arrears with the rent. This raises the question as to whether the non-payment of rent by a tenant constitutes a dispute for the purposes of Article 6(1). In *Logan* v *UK* (1996) 22 EHRR CD 178, the applicant alleged a breach of Article 6(1) in relation to child maintenance imposed upon him by the Child Support Agency. The European Commission found the application to be inadmissible because the applicant did not deny that the maintenance assessment was calculated correctly under domestic legislation and therefore there was no 'dispute' of a genuine or serious nature. Similarly, it is arguable that where the tenant accepts that the stated amount of rent is due but fails to meet the obligations under the lease, there is no prior dispute and Article 6(1) is not applicable. However, there may be cases where a dispute exists as to the amount of rent, if any, payable by the tenant. For example, the tenant may claim that due to the effect of equitable set-off, any rent arrears accrued have been extinguished (for an explanation of the tenant's remedy of equitable set-off see *British Anzani (Felixstowe) Ltd* v *International Marine Management (UK) Ltd* [1980] 1 QB 137 and *Melville* v *Grapelodge Developments Ltd* (1979) 39 P & CR 179). Where a landlord brings court proceedings to recover rent arrears the tenant can raise equitable set-off as a type of counterclaim. In *Eller* v *Grovecrest Investments Ltd* [1994] EGCS 28 it was held that equitable set-off is equally applicable where a landlord levies distress for rent. The court recognised the injustice that would ensue if a landlord were able to levy distress against a tenant who had a justifiable cross-claim that would have defeated the landlord's action had the landlord gone to court. If, for example, a landlord fails to carry out repairs, the tenant may be able to show that he is entitled to recover compensatory damages for consequential loss, e.g., damage to furniture caused by a leaking roof. This claim can be set off against the landlord's claim for rent arrears and may extinguish the rent arrears altogether. In these circumstances there would appear to be a dispute between the parties which involves the determination of the tenant's civil rights and obligations. Accordingly Article 6(1) would be applicable and the absence of legal due process may be sufficient to invoke a violation of the tenant's Convention rights. To counteract this analysis it can be argued that if the rent arrears have been extinguished by equitable set-off, then the landlord's act of levying distress constitutes an illegal distress and in these circumstances the tenant does have access to a judicial forum because he is entitled to commence a court action for damages.[12] Therefore the opportunity for a tenant to institute court proceedings for damages in the event of the landlord committing a wrongful distress may be sufficient to satisfy Article 6(1). By way of comparative analysis, it is interesting to note that under the Bill of Rights in the USA, the due process clause has been invoked to challenge a similar practice. In *North Georgia Finishing* v *Di-Chem* (1975) 419 US 601 legislation which permitted creditors to

---

[12] For an explanation of the remedies available to a tenant in respect of an unlawful distress, see Rook (n. 11 above) chapter 4.

seize goods without giving the debtor prior notice, nor an opportunity of a hearing, was struck down as unconstitutional.

8.3.6.5   *A third party owner's rights under Article 6(1)*

Goods belonging to a third party can be distrained and sold by the landlord without any requirement for the landlord or tenant to notify that person that their goods are at risk. Under the LDAA 1908 the third party owner can take positive action to protect his or her goods by acquiring absolute privilege for them. To acquire this privilege the owner must serve a declaration in writing on the landlord at any time prior to the moment of actual sale of the goods (*Salford Van Hire (Contracts) Ltd* v *Bocholt Developments Ltd* [1995] 2 EGLR 50). However, the landlord's right to sell the goods arises five days after the levying of distress and, given that neither party is under any obligation to notify the third party owner of the distraint, the LDAA provides limited protection. If the third party does not know about the distraint until after the goods have been sold it is then too late to acquire any privilege for the goods. Therefore the third party is denied any right to a hearing to contest the distraint of his goods and loses any remedy he may have against the landlord. In *Perez de Rada Cavanilles* v *Spain* (1998) 29 EHRR 245 the applicant and a neighbour, who had been in dispute concerning a view over the applicant's property, entered into a settlement agreement. The neighbour failed to fulfil his obligations under the agreement, and the applicant sought to enforce the settlement agreement in the domestic courts. However, the applicant was out of time for lodging her application to the courts and consequently the agreement was declared void. The European Court stated that, on the facts, the strict application of a procedural rule that required a postal application to be filed within three days, was disproportionately restrictive and constituted a violation of Article 6(1) since it denied her a right of access to a court in the determination of her civil rights. The significance of this case is that the very short time period available to an aggrieved person in which to take action, after which access to the courts is denied, can be applied by analogy to the five-day period available to a third party owner in which to serve a written declaration claiming the protection of the LDAA 1908. Such a short period may be seen as disproportionately restrictive, especially in the light of the absence of any requirement to inform the third party of the distress having taken place. It is likely that the lack of adequate procedural safeguards to protect innocent third party owners will constitute a violation of Article 6(1).

Where the landlord is a public authority it is arguable that in order to comply with its duty under s. 6 of the HRA 1998, it ought to provide a third party owner with an opportunity for a fair hearing before it sells the goods. Under s. 6 of the HRA 1998 it is unlawful for a public authority to act in a way that is incompatible with a Convention right unless it is compelled to act in that way to give effect to, or to enforce provisions of, primary legislation (see 1.7). If the absence of procedural safeguards to protect goods belonging to a third party is in violation of Article 6(1), a local authority landlord will need to implement measures to attempt to ascertain who is the owner of the seized goods prior to any sale. This would effectively nullify the existing advantage to a landlord in levying distress rather than taking court action, namely that distress is a quick and cheap remedy. The risk that goods belonging to a third party could be sold with the consequence that action is commenced against the public authority under s. 7 of the HRA 1998 for a breach of Convention rights, may ultimately discourage local authority landlords from using distress for rent as a remedy for rent arrears.

8.3.6.6   A summary

Whether distress for rent is found to violate Convention rights will inevitably be dependent upon the facts of the case before the court. In particular, whether there is a local authority landlord, whether a court order was obtained prior to the levy, whether there is a dispute as to the existence of rent arrears and whether goods belonging to a third party have been sold. It is possible to envisage a factual scenario involving all, or some of, these factors which may succeed in establishing a violation of Convention rights. Whether this will result in a change in the law governing distress for rent or ignite further support for its abolition remains to be seen.

8.3.7   Forfeiture

8.3.7.1   Horizontal effect

A crucial factor in assessing the impact of the HRA 1998 on the law governing the forfeiture of a lease will be the approach of the courts to the horizontal effect of the HRA 1998 (see 3.4). It was noted in chapter 3 that a landlord's right to forfeit the lease for a breach of covenant by the tenant is dependent upon the presence of a forfeiture clause in the lease. Consequently it may be difficult to establish state responsibility since the deprivation of the tenant's property arises from contract and not from statute. This position contrasts to that in *James* v *UK* where the leasehold enfranchisement legislation gave the tenants the right to acquire the freehold estate. Therefore the deprivation of the landlord's property arose from a right given to tenants by statute and in those circumstances state responsibility could be readily established.

It was the absence of state responsibility for the forfeiture of a lease by a private landlord that led to the application in *App. No. 11949/86* v *UK* being declared inadmissible. This case was taken to the European Commission following the decision of the High Court in *Di Palma* v *Victoria Square Property* [1984] 2 All ER 92. The applicant purchased a long lease of a flat in 1975 for £6,000. Under the terms of the lease she was liable to make a service charge payment, by way of additional rent, to the landlord in respect of her proportion of the insurance and any repair and maintenance costs. There was a disagreement between the landlord and tenant as to the amount of service charge payable and as a result of this the tenant withheld payment of the charge. Eventually, having obtained a court order for possession, the landlord forfeited the lease. The applicant alleged that the forfeiture of the lease by the landlord constituted an infringement of her rights under Article 1, Protocol 1. In response the European Commission stated that:

> In view of the exclusively private law relationship between the parties to the lease the Commission considers that the respondent Government cannot be responsible by the mere fact that the landlord by its agents, who were private individuals, brought the applicant's lease to an end in accordance with the terms of that lease, which set out the agreement between the applicant and the company.

The fact that the landlord had issued possession proceedings and obtained a court order permitting forfeiture of the lease was not sufficient to bring in the requisite element of state responsibility. The European Commission observed that:

> This fact alone is not however sufficient to engage State responsibility in respect of the applicant's rights to property, since the public authority in the shape of the County Court merely provided a forum for the determination of the civil right in a dispute between the parties.

The European Commission therefore concluded that Article 1, Protocol 1 was not applicable on the facts. Although this case epitomises the probable outcome of any challenge to a forfeiture of a lease by a private landlord under the Convention, the outcome may be very different under the HRA 1998. As discussed in chapters 1 and 3, the cumulative effect of ss. 2, 3 and 6 of the HRA 1998 is that the national courts are under a duty wherever possible to ensure that all law, whether common law or statutory, complies with Convention rights and this may apply even in the resolution of disputes between private individuals. If Convention rights are held under the HRA 1998 to have horizontal effect, then a tenant of a private landlord will not fall at the first hurdle when alleging a violation of Convention rights as he would do in an application to Strasbourg.

8.3.7.2   *Peaceable re-entry and state responsibility*

The case of *App. No. 11949/86* v *UK* did not involve a forfeiture by peaceable re-entry. It is arguable that had it done so, the European Commission might have found sufficient state responsibility to invoke the Convention. Once a landlord has served a s. 146 notice on the tenant in compliance with s. 146 of the Law of Property Act (LPA) 1925 (for a breach of a covenant other than the covenant to pay rent), and the tenant has been allowed a reasonable time in which to remedy the breach, the landlord can proceed to forfeit the lease by effecting a re-entry of the premises. There are two methods of re-entry. First, peaceable re-entry by a physical re-entry on the premises and secondly, the acquisition of a court possession order. Section 2 of the Protection from Eviction Act (PEA) 1977 provides that where premises are let as a dwelling-house it is unlawful to effect a forfeiture of the lease otherwise than by court proceedings while any person is lawfully residing in the premises. However, a landlord will have a defence to an allegation of having committed an offence under s. 2 if it can be shown that 'he believed, and had reasonable cause to believe, that the residential occupier had ceased to occupy the premises' (s. 1(2), PEA 1977). Therefore a landlord can only peaceably re-enter where the demised premises are used for business purposes or where residential premises have been abandoned by the tenant. However, it is an offence for a landlord effecting a peaceable re-entry to use or threaten violence (against person or property) to secure entry to premises where, to the knowledge of the landlord, there is someone present on the premises who is opposed to the entry (s. 6, Criminal Law Act 1977). The effect of these statutory provisions is to enable a landlord to forfeit a lease of business premises by a physical, unannounced entry onto the premises outside working hours when the premises are likely to be unoccupied (as in *Billson* v *Residential Apartments Limited* [1992] 1 All ER 141). If a tenant alleges a breach of Article 6(1) on the grounds that the lease was forfeited by peaceable re-entry, it is arguable that it is not the contract that permits peaceable re-entry, but the law. The absence of statutory provisions to require a court possession order in all cases may be sufficient to invoke state responsibility because the state is ultimately responsible for the availability of peaceable re-entry. Whether or not peaceable re-entry is likely to constitute a violation of Article 6(1) is considered at 8.3.7.5.

8.3.7.3   Article 1, Protocol 1 and forfeiture

(a)   The applicable rule   The forfeiture of a lease clearly involves a deprivation of the tenant's property by the premature termination of the tenant's legal estate. However, it is arguable that a forfeiture of a lease could fall within the third rule as a control of use rather than as a deprivation of possessions under the second rule. An analogy can be drawn with *Air Canada* v *UK* (see Appendix 3) in which an aircraft was seized as liable to forfeiture. The legislation prevented the aircraft from being used to transport illegal drugs and that clearly amounted to a control of use of property. The forfeiture was merely a measure taken in pursuance of that policy. Similarly, the covenants in a lease specify the conditions under which the tenant can use the property, for example, the property can be used provided that the rent is paid and the repairs are carried out. These covenants thereby control the use of the property by prohibiting the tenant's continued use if the tenant fails to comply with the covenants. To this end the forfeiture of a lease is a constituent element of the measures for controlling the tenant's use of the demised premises

(see 8.3.6.2). To a certain extent, however, the question of which of the three rules is applicable is largely academic since it is probable that the interference is justifiable whichever rule applies.

(b)   A legitimate aim   A legitimate aim can be found to exist in the form of protecting landlords' property interests and thereby encouraging a buoyant market in private sector lettings. One commentator has suggested that:

> the deprivation of the tenant's property [is] for a legitimate purpose in that it ensures that commercial property [is] available for letting by providing assurance to landlords that should the tenant default and thereby infringe the landlord's [human] rights, a clearly set out and understood mechanism would operate to allow the landlord to recover possession of the premises.[13]

(c)   The principle of proportionality   The principle of proportionality is likely to be satisfied where the landlord has obtained a prior court order because the court will have taken the interests of the tenant into account when deciding whether to grant a possession order or grant the tenant relief from forfeiture in accordance with its discretionary powers under s. 146(2) of the LPA 1925. However, it is arguable that the forfeiture of a lease by peaceable re-entry is not proportionate to the aim to be achieved, on the basis that it is an unnecessary measure given that re-entry can be effected by a court order which provides better protection for the tenant's rights. It may be argued that the use of peaceable re-entry upsets the fair balance to be struck between the general interest of protecting the landlord's property and the protection of the fundamental rights and freedoms of the tenants. However, there are two significant factors providing a counterargument to this view. First, even where a landlord peaceably re-enters the property, the tenant still retains the right to apply to the court for relief from forfeiture under s. 146(2) of the LPA 1925 (*Billson* v *Residential Apartments Limited* [1992] 1 All ER 141). Secondly, the fact that a forfeiture clause must be expressly included in the lease means that the tenant has prior knowledge of, and agrees to, the remedy of forfeiture. On this basis it may be argued that forfeiture, even where it is implemented by peaceable re-entry, does not impose an excessive burden upon the tenant.

8.3.7.4   Article 8 and forfeiture

The concept of 'home' has been extended to include some types of business premises (see 5.2.4) so that it may be possible for a tenant to invoke Article 8 where the landlord forfeits a lease of business premises by peaceable re-entry. The landlord would need to show that the interference was justified under Article 8(2),

---

[13] Bruce, A., 'Barring Peaceable Re-entry', NLJ 31 March 2000, 462 at p. 463.

being in accordance with the law and necessary in a democratic society in the interests of a legitimate aim. The peaceable re-entry will be in accordance with the law provided that the lease contains an express forfeiture clause and the landlord does not offend any statutory provision in securing entry to the premises, for example a landlord must not use or threaten violence contrary to s. 6 of the Criminal Law Act 1977. The legitimate aim can readily be established as 'the protection of the rights and freedoms of others' because it protects the landlord's right to receive rent under the lease. The principle of proportionality is likely to be the crucial factor and to this end the same considerations as discussed at 8.3.7.3 in relation to Article 1, Protocol 1 apply, indicating that a challenge under Article 8 is unlikely to succeed.

8.3.7.5   Article 6(1) and forfeiture

The forfeiture of a lease involves a determination of the tenant's 'civil rights and obligations' (*Langborger* v *Sweden* (1989) 12 EHRR 416). Since Article 6(1) is applicable it may be possible for a tenant, whose lease has been forfeited by peaceable re-entry, to claim an infringement of this Article on the ground that he or she has been denied a fair hearing by an independent tribunal. After the expiry of the s. 146 notice the landlord can lawfully re-enter business premises without giving the tenant any further warning and without obtaining a prior court order. However, Bruce suggests that Article 6(1) will not always be applicable to forfeiture. He observes that:

> the right to effect a forfeiture pre-supposes that the tenant is in breach of term(s) of his lease and the landlord's contractual entitlement to re-enter is applicable. As such it is arguable that there is no 'contestation' or dispute at the national level, and given that for Art 6 to apply an individual must establish that he has a reasonable claim in domestic law to the civil right in question (see *H* v *Belgium* (1988) 10 EHRR 339 at para. 40), Art 6 is perhaps inapplicable to forfeiture situations.[14]

Although this may be the position in the majority of cases, involving a clear and undisputed breach of covenant by the tenant, there will undoubtedly be some cases where the parties are in dispute as to whether or not a breach of covenant has in fact occurred. For example, where a landlord seeks to forfeit a lease by peaceable re-entry reliant upon the tenant's alleged rent arrears, it is possible that no breach of covenant has occurred because the rent arrears have been extinguished by equitable set-off (see 8.3.6.4). Therefore a dispute may exist invoking the applicability of Article 6(1).

A more persuasive argument for disputing a breach of Article 6(1) is the tenant's continued access to the courts after the landlord has effected a peaceable

---

[14] Ibid., at p. 462.

re-entry. In *Billson* v *Residential Apartments Limited* [1992] 1 All ER 141, the House of Lords held that where a landlord lawfully forfeits by peaceable re-entry, the tenant is still entitled to apply to the courts for relief from forfeiture. The tenant therefore has access to the courts. In addition, if a landlord unlawfully forfeits a lease by peaceable re-entry the tenant can commence proceedings in court for damages (*South Tottenham Land Securities* v *R & A Millet (Shops)* [1983] 2 EGLR 122). Since English law already provides the tenant with a remedy which offers a judicial forum, it is likely that this will be found to satisfy the procedural guarantees under Article 6(1).

8.3.8　Introductory tenancies

The Housing Act (HA) 1996 introduced the concept of an introductory tenancy aimed at assisting local authorities with dealing with the problem of anti-social behaviour amongst local authority tenants. The basic framework is that local authorities and housing action trusts (but not housing associations) have the option of imposing introductory tenancies on new tenants. The introductory tenancy lasts for a probationary one-year period and, unless terminated by a court possession order, will thereafter become a secure tenancy. The tenancy agreement should specify the types of anti-social behaviour that may cause the landlord to terminate the tenancy. For example, the agreement may state that the tenant (or any one living with the tenant) must not cause a nuisance or annoyance to others by means of loud music, arguing and door slamming, offensive drunkenness, selling or abusing drugs or by the dumping of rubbish. If the tenant breaches one of these rules the local authority landlord can go to court for a possession order to evict the tenant. From a human rights perspective, it is arguable that the introductory tenancy scheme contravenes Article 6(1) because of the lack of any court discretion in the grant of a possession order and Article 14 in conjunction with Article 6(1) due to the optional nature of the scheme. According to ss. 127 and 128 of the HA 1996, the court 'shall' make an order for possession unless the landlord has failed to serve a requisite notice of proceedings on the tenant. In *Manchester City Council* v *Cochrane* [1999] 1 WLR 809 the Court of Appeal affirmed that the county court had no jurisdiction to entertain a defence by the tenants based on their denial of the landlord's allegation that a breach of the tenancy agreement had occurred. The Court of Appeal held that once the requirements of s. 128, HA 1996, regarding the notice of proceedings, had been complied with, the county court was obliged to grant the possession order sought by the local authority landlord. Commenting upon this limited jurisdiction, Sir John Knox referred to 'the remarkable constriction of the court's powers' (at p. 819). Under the introductory tenancy scheme a tenant who denies the landlord's allegations, can request only that the local authority itself review its decision to seek a possession order (s. 129, HA 1996). However, in conducting a review under s. 129, HA 1996, the local authority is subject to judicial review. Therefore if the county court is satisfied that there is a real chance of leave to apply for judicial review being granted to the tenant, it has jurisdiction to grant an adjournment of the possession proceedings, but this power of adjournment is available only in these very limited circumstances.

The fact that tenants can be evicted from their home without the opportunity to state their case before an independent and impartial tribunal arguably amounts to a contravention of their rights under Article 6(1) (see 7.7). The tenants' only forum for challenging the local authority landlord's allegations of a breach of the tenancy agreement, is the review carried out by the local authority itself. The availability of judicial review is limited to a review on a 'points of law' basis only so that the High Court is not able to review the merits of the local authority's decision to seek a possession order. However, in *R (on the application of Johns and McLellan)* v *Bracknell Forest District Council* (21 December 2000), the Administrative Court (Longmore J) held that the introductory tenancy scheme is compatible with Article 6(1). The facts concerned two introductory tenancies in which the council had served a notice of proceedings for possession upon the tenants on the grounds of their alleged anti-social behaviour and acts of nuisance. In each case the tenant first sought a review of the council's decision to seek possession and thereafter commenced judicial review of the review panel's decision. In both cases the council ultimately decided not to proceed with possession. Nevertheless, the Administrative Court was persuaded to hear the tenants' applications to determine the compatibility of the introductory tenancy scheme with the HRA 1998 even though the matter was academic on the particular facts. In assessing the applicability of Article 6(1), the Administrative Court had regard to the procedure for obtaining possession and specifically to the fact that, where the decision of the review panel confirms the council's original decision, the council can commence possession proceedings and the county court is then obliged to make an order for possession. In considering this procedure the Administrative Court felt satisfied that the decision of the review panel is 'directly decisive' of the tenant's civil rights. Longmore J stated (at para. 25) that:

> So where ... almost the only inhibition on the local authority obtaining a court order is that it must, if requested, have conducted a review in accordance with the terms of the statute, whereupon the court is bound to grant a possession order, it seems to me that the review conducted by the local authority is 'directly decisive' for the right of the local authority to obtain a possession order and the obligation of the tenant to yield up his or her tenancy. I therefore conclude that Article 6 is engaged.

Thereafter the Administrative Court had to consider the question of compliance with Article 6(1). It was accepted by all of the parties that the review by the council of its own decision to seek possession was not in itself a review by an independent and impartial tribunal. However, Strasbourg case law has long recognised that where there is an appeal to a court or tribunal with 'full jurisdiction' the procedure as a whole will comply with Article 6(1) (see 7. 7. 4). Thus the question was whether judicial review of the review panel's decision was sufficient to constitute 'full jurisdiction'. The Administrative Court considered the judgment of the European Court in *Bryan* v *UK* (see Appendix 3) and compared this to the decision of the Divisional Court in the *Alconbury Developments Ltd* case (*R* v *Secretary of State for the Environment, Transport and the Regions, ex parte Holding and Barnes plc* (13 December 2000)) which had been delivered a few days earlier (see 8. 10). Longmore J felt the present case to be closer to *Bryan* than to *Alconbury*. In *Alconbury*, the Divisional Court found a breach of Article 6(1) due to the fact that the Secretary of State, by calling-in a planning application, had acted both as policy maker and decision taker. However, Longmore J observed (at para. 32) that:

> In the present case there is no question of making or enforcing policy. The Council merely decides that there are reasons for seeking possession and if those reasons are challenged a different person decides whether those reasons are good reasons. The review officer (senior to the person deciding to serve the notice of possession proceedings in the first place) is analogous to an inspector in ordinary planning cases. Of course he is appointed by the Council, but it is his decision and not the later decision of some higher 'policy maker' that is the decision that counts, and is the decision which is amenable to judicial review.

On this basis the Administrative Court concluded that the High Court did have 'full jurisdiction' within the meaning of Article 6(1) and consequently the introductory tenancy regime was held to comply with that Article.

The applicants further alleged that the introductory tenancy scheme violated Article 8. The Administrative Court accepted that eviction from one's home engages Article 8 and reliance for this was placed upon *Buckley* v *UK* (see Appendix 3). The question was whether the interference with the tenants' rights to respect for their homes infringed Article 8. It was accepted by all of the parties that the introductory tenancy scheme is in accordance with the law as laid down in the Housing Act 1996. Thus the crucial issue was whether the interference was necessary in a democratic society for the protection of the rights and freedoms of others. The Administrative Court considered the reasons for which the council had chosen to adopt the introductory tenancy scheme. It noted that the scheme provided the council with an efficient, effective and relatively inexpensive means of dealing with the non-payment of rent and anti-social behaviour by tenants, thereby enabling the council to safeguard the well-being of all of its tenants. With this in mind, Longmore J concluded (at para. 40) that 'these considerations show that the interference with the respect for one's home, to which everyone is entitled, is indeed relevant, sufficient and corresponds to a pressing social need'. In examining the question of proportionality, the Administrative Court gave considerable weight to the fact that the interference with the tenant's right was of a limited nature. At each stage of the possession procedure, both at the issuance of a notice of proceedings and at the review (where requested by the tenant), the council must give reasons. Longmore J observed (at para. 42) that: 'The interference with the tenant's rights of respect for his home is thus little more than that the assessment of the grounds for possession is not made by the County Court'. Having reference to the alternative methods available to the council for dealing with tenants engaging in anti-social behaviour, e.g., injunction proceedings or police action, the Administrative Court concluded that the alternatives were liable to be more disproportionate than dispossession. Consequently, the Administrative Court held the introductory tenancy scheme to be compatible with Article 8.

Finally, one of the tenants challenged the introductory tenancy regime as being in violation of Article 14 in conjunction with Article 6 and Article 8 on the basis that, in some areas of the UK, council tenants are introductory tenants for their first year whereas in other areas, where the scheme has not been adopted, the council tenants enjoy the status of being secure tenants from the start of their tenancy. Whether this differential treatment of council tenants, based solely upon their geographical location in the country, can be reasonably and objectively justified depends upon the reasons for the introductory tenancy scheme being an optional one. Due to the lack of proper notice of the Article 14 complaint being submitted to the defendants, the Administrative Court ruled that it was too late for the point to be taken and thereby left it open for future debate.

Therefore, although the introductory tenancy scheme as a whole was held to be compatible with Article 6(1) and Article 8, it is still possible, under s. 6 of the HRA 1998, to challenge the council's implementation of the scheme in individual cases as being incompatible with these Convention rights. In addition, the question of the differential treatment of council tenants in different areas of the country, who are otherwise in an analogous situation to one another, will have to be considered under Article 14 in the light of the reasons for the scheme being optional as opposed to compulsory.

8.4 MORTGAGES

8.4.1 The mortgagee's right to peaceable re-entry and its exclusion of the court's discretionary powers under s. 36 of the Administration of Justice Act 1970

In *Ropaigealach* v *Barclays Bank plc* [1999] 3 WLR 17 the court was requested to determine whether a mortgagee was entitled to take possession of the mortgagor's house without first having obtained a court order. The Court of Appeal held that s. 36 of the Administration of Justice Act (AJA) 1970, which enables a court to stay or suspend an order for possession of the mortgagor's dwelling-house, only applies where the mortgagee brings an action for possession in the courts. It does not, however, prevent a mortgagee from exercising the common law right to take possession and thereby circumvent the protection afforded to mortgagors under the provisions of s. 36, AJA 1970. The facts related to a legal charge taken over residential property. The mortgagors fell into arrears with the mortgage repayments and the mortgagee made a valid demand for payment of the monies secured by the charge. After the lapse of a year the mortgagee wrote to the mortgagors notifying them that it was taking steps to realise its security by selling the property at an auction due to be held on a specified date. The mortgagors later denied having ever received this letter. At the time they were living elsewhere. It was their submission that the mortgaged house was empty due to the fact that it was undergoing substantial repairs. The house was subsequently sold at auction and in the meantime the mortgagors discovered from a neighbour that their house had been sold.

This set of facts raises a number of issues as to the compatibility of the common law right of a mortgagee to take possession of property, without any due legal process, with the Convention rights under the HRA 1998.

8.4.1.1   Article 8 and the mortgagee's right to peaceable re-entry

The applicability of Article 8 depends upon whether or not the property constitutes the mortgagor's 'home'. Since a mortgagee can only exercise the common law right to possession where the house is unoccupied, it is possible that the property will not be the mortgagor's home. If, for example, the mortgagors have set up their home elsewhere and are repairing the house with a view to selling or letting it, then it would be difficult to see how Article 8 would be applicable. However, if the mortgagors have only temporarily vacated the house for the purposes of repair or refurbishment and intend to return to the house as their permanent home once the works are completed, then the fact that the house is unoccupied at the date of repossession and sale by the mortgagee does not preclude the applicability of Article 8. It would then depend upon whether or not the evident interference with the mortgagors' home could be justified under Article 8(2). It will be relatively easy to establish a legitimate aim justifying the mortgagee's right to realise its security, relying upon the economic well-being of the country and the protection of the rights and freedoms of others. *Birmingham Midshires Mortgage Services Ltd* v *Sabherwal* (2000) 80 P & CR 256 illustrates the ease with which a legitimate aim could be ascertained in this area of law. The case concerned the question of priority as between a mortgagee and a person claiming an equitable interest in the family home, in this case the mother of the mortgagors. Counsel for the mother raised Article 8 of the Convention to support her claim for a stay of execution of the possession order granted to the mortgagee. The Court of Appeal found Article 8 to be inapplicable due to the fact that the HRA 1998 was not in force at the date of its judgment; however, Walker LJ observed (at p. 264) that the possession order, 'was necessary for the protection of [the mortgagee's] rights as a secured lender'. Similarly in *Wood* v *UK* (1997) 24 EHRR CD 69 the European Commission considered the effect of a repossession of the applicant's home by her mortgagee, and observed that:

> In so far as the repossession constituted an interference with the applicant's home, the Commission finds that this was in accordance with the terms of the loan and the domestic law and was necessary for the protection of the rights and freedoms of others, namely the lender.

Although it is possible to establish the existence of a legitimate aim under Article 8(2) to justify the interference with the person's rights under Article 8(1), it may nevertheless be difficult to satisfy the requirement of proportionality. It is arguable that the complete absence of any procedural safeguards to protect the mortgagor's rights is disproportionate to the legitimate aim being pursued with the result that the action could be held to infringe Article 8.

8.4.1.2 Article 1, Protocol 1 and the mortgagee's right to peaceable re-entry

Under the second rule of Article 1, Protocol 1 no one is to be deprived of their possessions except in the public interest and subject to the conditions provided for by law. The sale of the property by the mortgagee transfers the legal estate to the purchaser and thereby extinguishes the mortgagor's rights in the house. Such action clearly constitutes a deprivation of property within the second rule. The case of *Wood* v *UK* (1997) 24 EHRR CD 69 demonstrates the ease with which a legitimate aim could be established to justify the mortgagee's repossession. The European Commission noted that:

> To the extent that the applicant is deprived of her possessions by the repossession, the Commission considers that this deprivation is in the public interest, that is the public interest in ensuring payment of contractual debts, and is also in accordance with the rules provided for by law.

However, due process considerations, whilst not featured in many cases under the second rule, nevertheless have a role to play in assessing proportionality (see 4.3.6.2). In *Hentrich* v *France* (see Appendix 3) the Revenue exercised a right of pre-emption over the property that the applicant had recently purchased. The Revenue maintained that the purchase price paid by the applicant for the property had been too low with a consequent loss to the state of the appropriate transfer duty paid on the sale. One of the reasons relied on by the European Court when concluding that there had been a breach of Article 1, Protocol 1 was the absence of adequate procedural safeguards. The European Court stated (at para. 49) that the excessive burden placed upon the applicant, 'could have been rendered legitimate only if she had had the possibility — which was refused her — of effectively challenging the measure taken against her'. This suggests that where the deprivation of the mortgagor's property is occasioned without the mortgagee obtaining any prior court order, there may be an infringement of Article 1, Protocol 1.

8.4.1.3   *Article 6 and the mortgagee's right to peaceable re-entry*
The act of selling the mortgagor's house will be categorised as a determination of a civil right and will thus trigger Article 6(1) (see 7.5). Where, as in *Ropaigealach* v *Barclays Bank plc*, the mortgagor is denied any opportunity to a fair hearing prior to the sale of the house, there is ample scope for establishing a violation of the mortgagor's rights under Article 6(1).

8.4.1.4   *Article 14 and the mortgagee's right to peaceable re-entry*
There may be a case for alleging a violation of Article 14 in conjunction with either Article 1, Protocol 1 or Article 8. Article 14 safeguards individuals who are placed in analogous situations against discriminatory differences of treatment in the enjoyment of their Convention rights (see chapter 6). A mortgagor could argue that the current law discriminates between those mortgagors who are in occupation of their house and those who are not. Although this is not one of the grounds specified in Article 14, the list is not exhaustive and the Strasbourg institutions, in identifying an open-ended 'other status' category, have been willing to rely on grounds such as trade union membership, professional status and conscientious objection.

Where defaulting mortgagors are in occupation of their home the mortgagee must seek a court order for possession in order to avoid the risk of committing a criminal offence under s. 6 of the Criminal Law Act 1977. During the possession proceedings s. 36, AJA 1970 gives the court a discretion to adjourn proceedings, stay or suspend an order for possession or postpone the date for delivery of possession for such period as it thinks reasonable, where it appears to the court that 'the mortgagor is likely to be able within a reasonable period to pay any sums due under the mortgage or to remedy a default consisting of a breach of any other obligation arising under or by virtue of the mortgage'. This discretionary power gives mortgagors, who satisfy the criteria, a valuable source of protection against being evicted from their home. In *Ropaigealach* v *Barclays Bank plc* the court held that s. 36, AJA 1970 only applies where a mortgagee commences court proceedings for possession but does not apply where a mortgagee exercises its common law right to take possession. Therefore the protection afforded to a mortgagor's rights under Article 1, Protocol 1 and Article 8, by the operation of

s. 36, AJA 1970, is denied to mortgagors where the mortgagee takes possession without a court order. The outcome of the decision in *Ropaigealach* is that two mortgagors placed in an analogous situation, i.e. in arrears with their mortgage but likely to be able to pay the sums due within a reasonable period, may be subjected to differential treatment because one is in occupation of his or her home and the other is temporarily absent. The mortgagor who is in occupation will enjoy the advantage of being able to invoke s. 36, AJA 1970 whilst the other is denied this benefit. The existence of this differential treatment raises the question of whether it can be reasonably and objectively justified. Although it may be possible to argue that the lack of legal process saves time and expense where the property has been abandoned, this is certainly not the case where the property is merely temporarily unoccupied, for example, due to extensive repairs being carried out or due to the mortgagor temporarily working or travelling abroad. In fact it is likely to be very difficult to justify such differential treatment where such a serious interference as the expropriation of residential property is at issue. All mortgagors of residential property, whether in occupation or not, who satisfy the criteria under s. 36, AJA 1970, ought to be given the same opportunity to request more time to pay their mortgage arrears.

8.4.2   The bankruptcy of the mortgagor and Article 8

If the mortgagor is declared bankrupt his estate will vest in his trustee in bankruptcy. If the trustee in bankruptcy applies for a sale of the property after one year of the vesting of the estate in the trustee, there is a presumption that: 'unless the circumstances of the case are exceptional, the interests of the bankrupt's creditors outweigh all other considerations' (s. 335A(3) of the Insolvency Act 1986). It is arguable that, in some circumstances, this statutory provision may result in an infringement of Article 8. The mortgagor's partner and children have the right to respect for their home and family life under Article 8 even though they may have no proprietary interest in the house (*Khatun and 180 others* v *UK*). Therefore it is possible that the presumption of sale in s. 335A and the way that the courts have interpreted it, so that in the majority of cases an innocent partner and the children are evicted from their home, violates Convention rights. In *Re Citro (A Bankrupt)* [1991] Ch 142 Nourse LJ summarised the current position as follows (at para. 157):

> Where a spouse who has a beneficial interest in the matrimonial home has become bankrupt under debts which cannot be paid without the realisation of that interest, the voice of the creditors will usually prevail over the voice of the other spouse and a sale of the property ordered within a short period. The voice of the other spouse will only prevail in exceptional circumstances ... What then are exceptional circumstances? As the cases show, it is not uncommon for a wife with young children to be faced with eviction in circumstances where the realisation of her beneficial interest will not produce

enough to buy a comparable house. And, if she has to move elsewhere, there may be problems over schooling and so forth. Such circumstances, while engendering a natural sympathy in all who hear them, cannot be described as exceptional. They are the melancholy consequences of debt and improvidence with which every civilised society has been familiar.[15]

The eviction of the family from their home, an event that naturally ensues from the operation of the presumption of sale in s. 335A, could be considered to be an infringement of the right to respect of the home and family life under Article 8 if the presumption is given absolute priority without sufficient consideration being given to the Convention rights of the affected family. Allen observes that: 'As the law currently stands, the right to respect for family life and the home receives almost no consideration after the one-year period. Whether such a strict limitation is compatible with the Convention is doubtful'.[16]

It is interesting to observe that where the request for a sale is made by a secured creditor under s. 15 of the Trusts of Land and Appointment of Trustees Act 1996, the court has recently taken a more lenient approach towards the innocent spouse and children. In *The Mortgage Corporation* v *Marsha Shaire and others* (2000) EGCS 35, Neuberger J took the view that s. 15 had resulted in a change in the law and one that relieves the harshness of the previous law for families.[17] Neuberger J observed that:

> it does not seem to me unlikely that the legislature intended to relax the fetters on the way in which the court exercised its discretion in cases such as *Citro* and *Byrne*, and so as to tip the balance somewhat more in favour of families and against banks and other chargees.[18]

Similarly it may be that the courts, in applying s. 355A of the Insolvency Act 1986, will need to adopt a more sympathetic approach to defining what constitutes 'exceptional circumstances'. If an immediate sale of the property would violate the family's rights under Article 8, the court may be required, in compliance with its duty under s. 3 of the HRA 1998, to adopt a broad interpretation of 'exceptional

---

[15] In *Re Citro* the trustee in bankruptcy applied to the court, under s. 30, LPA 1925, for an order for the sale of the bankrupt's family home. Nowadays such an application by the trustee in bankruptcy would be determined under s. 335A of the Insolvency Act 1986.

[16] Allen, T., 'The Human Rights Act (UK) and Property Law' in Janet McLean (ed), *Property and the Constitution*, Oxford: Hart Publishing, 1999 at p. 163.

[17] See Pascoe, S., 'Section 15 of the Trusts of Land and Appointment of Trustees Act 1996 — A change in the law' [2000] Conv 315.

[18] Also see the Court of Appeal decision in *Bank of Ireland Home Mortgage Ltd* v *Bell* (4 December 2000). Although in this case the Court of Appeal granted the mortgagee an order for sale, it referred to *Mortgage Corporation Ltd* v *Shaire* and agreed that s. 15 of the Trusts of Land and Appointment of Trustees Act 1996 gave scope for some change to the principle that the creditor's interests should prevail save in exceptional circumstances. However, in this respect, the Court of Appeal observed that a powerful consideration in refusing an order for sale is whether a creditor is being recompensed for being kept out of its money.

circumstances' in s. 335A to ensure the compatibility of this legislation with Convention rights.

8.5 ADVERSE POSSESSION

Under s. 15 of the Limitation Act (LA) 1980 an owner of land is barred from commencing action for the recovery of land after a 12-year period has elapsed. For the purposes of calculating that 12-year period, time will begin to run against the owner where he has been dispossessed or has discontinued possession and another person has taken adverse possession of that land. There are three components to adverse possession.[19] First, the squatter must show that he has a degree of exclusive physical control over the land amounting to factual possession. Secondly, the squatter must establish that he has the requisite intention to possess the land to the exclusion of all others including the owner with paper title. Thirdly, the squatter must establish that the possession is 'adverse', i.e., without lawful authority. Section 15, LA 1980 has been justified in the following terms: 'It is more important that long and undisturbed possession of land should be protected, even if initially it was wrongful, than that the law should lend its aid to the enforcement of stale claims'.[20] The 12 years adverse possession does not actually extinguish the owner's title to the land. However, the effect of s. 15, LA 1980 is to prevent the owner from being able to bring a possession action on the expiration of the 12-year period. Thus, as it is the operation of statutory provisions that effectively deprive the owner of his or her property, there is sufficient state responsibility to invoke Convention rights even in disputes between private individuals. That an owner can be effectively deprived of his or her land without the payment of compensation and without due legal process raises questions as to the compatibility of s. 15, LA 1980 with Article 1, Protocol 1.

8.5.1 Article 1, Protocol 1 and adverse possession

The loss of property by adverse possession is likely to fall within the second rule of Article 1, Protocol 1, being a deprivation of possessions. Although there is no formal transfer of ownership from the owner to the squatter, the owner's rights are nevertheless extinguished. In determining whether such extreme interference with the owner's property rights can be justified, it would be possible to establish a legitimate aim, endorsing the principle of limitation on public policy grounds (*Stubbings* v *UK* (1996) 23 EHRR 213). However, in assessing proportionality, it is generally very difficult to justify a deprivation under the second rule without the payment of compensation. The European Court has stated that:

---

[19] *Buckinghamshire County Council* v *Moran* [1990] Ch 623.
[20] Megarry, R. and Thompson, M., *Megarry's Manual of the Law of Property*, 7th edn, London: Sweet and Maxwell, 1993, at p. 493.

the taking of property in the public interest without the payment of compensation is treated as justifiable only in exceptional circumstances ... As far as Article 1 (P1–1) is concerned, the protection of the right of property it affords would be largely illusory and ineffective in the absence of any equivalent principle (*James* v *UK*, at para. 54).

As the Strasbourg institutions give no examples of 'exceptional circumstances' it is difficult to say with any certainty whether public policy grounds will suffice. The due process factor is also a relevant consideration in assessing proportionality and given the severity of the interference, the absence of any adequate procedures to recover property after the limitation period has elapsed could upset the fair balance to be struck between the property rights of the individual and the interests of the general community in preventing the enforcement of stale claims.

However, in *J A Pye (Oxford) Ltd* v *Graham* (6 February 2001) the Court of Appeal decided, *obiter*, that s. 15, LA 1980 is not in breach of Article 1, Protocol 1. The High Court had upheld an adverse possession claim relating to 57 acres of prime development land in Berkshire worth millions of pounds with planning permission. The land had been transferred to the developer JA Pye (Oxford) Ltd for £250,000 and was earmarked by the company for development. In the meantime the company granted a farmer, Mr Graham, grazing licences. Although in 1984 the company refused to renew the licences, Mr Graham continued to use the land for grazing purposes. After 12 years had elapsed he claimed to have acquired the land by adverse possession. The High Court found that the Graham family had enjoyed factual possession and had the requisite intention to possess since 1984 and had consequently acquired adverse possession of the disputed land. The judge did not arrive at the decision with any enthusiasm as, in his opinion, it produced a result that did not accord with principles of justice. Neuberger J stated that:

I believe that the result is disproportionate, because, particularly in a climate of increasing awareness of human rights, including the right to enjoy one's own property, it does seem draconian to the owner, and a windfall for the squatter, that the owner should lose 57 acres of land to the squatter with no compensation whatsoever. (*J A Pye (Oxford) Ltd* v *Graham* [2000] Ch 676 at p. 710)

However, the Court of Appeal allowed the appeal. Although the grounds for its decision rest upon the fact that the Grahams lacked the required intention to possess the disputed land, the Court of Appeal also considered, *obiter*, the impact of the HRA 1998 upon s. 15, LA 1980. On the particular facts of the case the Court of Appeal was unable to find any clear evidence of the Graham family's intention to possess. It was particularly significant that they initially enjoyed a permissive use of the disputed land under a grazing licence. Mummery LJ observed that:

In my judgment, Mr Michael Graham's account of his state of mind, when considered in the context of the circumstances of an initial permissive use under licence and the continuation of the same use after the expiration of the licence, is not that of a person who is using the land with the intention of possessing it to the exclusion of Pye. It is that of a person who, having obtained the agreement of Pye to the limited use of the land in the past, continues to use it for the time being in exactly the same fashion in the hope that in the future Pye will again be willing to accede to his requests to enter an agreement authorising him to use it.

On this basis it was held that the Grahams did not have the necessary *animus possidendi* (intention to possess) in respect of the disputed land.

In considering the challenge under the HRA 1998, Mummery LJ took the view that Article 1, Protocol 1 does not impinge on the law of adverse possession because s. 15, LA 1980 does not deprive a person of his or her possessions or otherwise interfere with the peaceful enjoyment of them. Instead, where landowners have been dispossessed of their land by an adverse possessor for a period of at least 12 years, s. 15, LA 1980 deprives those landowners of their right of access to the courts for the purpose of recovering their property. Mummery LJ observed that: 'The extinction of the title of the claimant in those circumstances is not a deprivation of possessions or a confiscatory measure for which the payment of compensation would be appropriate: it is simply a logical and pragmatic consequence of the barring of his right to bring an action after the limitation periods'. Thus, by drawing a subtle distinction between the deprivation of property and the deprivation of the right to commence an action to recover property, Mummery LJ denies the applicability of Article 1, Protocol 1. A more persuasive approach may be to accept the applicability of Article 1, Protocol 1 but thereafter seek to justify the interference. The distinction Mummery LJ relies upon raises difficult questions as to what constitutes 'possessions' within the meaning of Article 1, Protocol 1. Is the ability to commence court proceedings to recover property from a trespasser a fundamental characteristic of property ownership? If it is, the loss of the right to commence court action impinges upon the very nature of property ownership and cannot be artificially dissected from it and treated as separate from it. Harris, who identifies the inextricable link between property and the right to commence court action to protect property from interference by trespassers, noted that 'trespassory protection is a necessary condition for it to be true that the mantle of property is thrown over any resource'.[21]

It is suggested that the preferred approach, and one consistently adopted by the Strasbourg institutions, is to adopt a broad interpretation of the meaning of possessions so that the threshold question of whether the thing interfered with constitutes a 'possession' is an easy criterion to satisfy (see 4.7). Thereafter the

---

[21] Harris, J. W., 'Is Property a Human Right?' in Janet McLean (ed), *Property and the Constitution*, Oxford: Hart Publishing, 1999 at p. 67.

question for the court is whether the interference with the possessions can be justified. This, in fact, was the alternative approach suggested by Mummery LJ, who went on to state that:

> Even if, contrary to my view, [Article 1, Protocol 1] potentially impinges on the relevant provisions of the 1980 Act, those provisions are conditions provided for by law and are 'in the public interest' within the meaning of Article 1. Such conditions are reasonably required to avoid the real risk of injustice in the adjudication of stale claims to ensure certainty of title; and to promote social stability by the protection of the established and peaceable possession of property from the resurrection of old claims. The conditions provided in the 1980 Act are not disproportionate; the period allowed for the bringing of proceedings is reasonable; the conditions are not discriminatory; and they are not impossible or excessively difficult to comply with as to render ineffective the exercise of the legal right of a person, who is entitled to the peaceful enjoyment of his possessions, to recover them from another person, who is alleged to have wrongfully deprived him of them.

By this means Mummery LJ sought to justify the interference with the property.

Keene LJ, in concurring with the judgment delivered by Mummery LJ, also took note of the fact that limitation periods, on bringing legal proceedings, are in principle not incompatible with the Convention and are expressly recognised by the Convention. For example, Article 35 of the Convention imposes a six-month limitation period for making an application to the European Court, with time starting to run from the date that the domestic remedies have been exhausted. Keene LJ referred to the case of *Stubbings* v *UK* (1996) 23 EHRR 213 in which the six-year limitation period in personal injury cases in the UK was held not to violate Article 6(1). The European Court in *Stubbings* observed (at para. 49) that:

> limitation periods in personal injury cases are a common feature of the domestic legal systems of the Contracting States. They serve several important purposes, namely to ensure legal certainty and finality, to protect potential defendants from stale claims which might be difficult to counter, and to prevent the injustice which might arise if courts were required to decide upon events which took place in the distant past on the basis of evidence which might have become unreliable and incomplete because of the passage of time.

Taking all these factors into account, the Court of Appeal concluded that s. 15, LA 1980 is not in violation of Article 1, Protocol 1.

8.6   FREEHOLD COVENANTS

It is arguable that the modification or discharge of a restrictive covenant by the Lands Tribunal under s. 84 of the LPA 1925 may constitute a violation of Article

1, Protocol 1. Section 84 gives the Lands Tribunal power to discharge or modify restrictive covenants on a number of specified grounds, for example on finding the covenant obsolete by reason of changes in the character of the neighbourhood or that the continued existence of the covenant impedes some reasonable user of the land. The admissibility decision of the European Commission in *S* v *UK* (App. No. 10741/84) is helpful in considering the possible impact of the HRA 1998 on the modification or discharge of restrictive covenants on freehold land.

8.6.1   The decision in *S* v *UK*

The case of *S* v *UK* (App. No. 10741/84) concerned an order by the Lands Tribunal for Northern Ireland extinguishing two covenants under a provision of the Property (NI) Order 1978 (which is equivalent to s. 84 of the LPA 1925). The covenants were contained in a fee farm grant, created in 1953, which under the Landlord and Tenant Amendment Act (Ireland) 1860 gave rise to a landlord and tenant relationship between the grantor of the fee farm grant and grantee. The grantee acquired the freehold estate subject to a perpetual rent of £100 per annum. In acquiring the fee farm grant, the grantee covenanted not to build on the land without the written consent of the grantor and to use the land only for the purposes of sport or recreational activities. The applicant acquired the interest of the original grantor of the fee farm grant and the Belfast Education Board acquired that of the original grantee. Having obtained planning permission, the Board built a nursery school on its land without the consent of the applicant. Four years after the completion of the building, the Board discovered the existence of the restrictive covenants and requested a waiver of the covenants from the applicant. As the parties failed to reach any agreement, the Board applied to the Lands Tribunal for an order extinguishing the two covenants. The Lands Tribunal granted the Board the order it sought and extinguished the covenants on the ground that the restrictions had, in the opinion of the Tribunal, become obsolete. No compensation award was made under the provision equivalent to s. 84(1)(i) of the LPA 1925, in respect of any loss or disadvantage suffered by the applicant in consequence of the discharge, because the Tribunal concluded that she had not suffered any loss. However, under the provision equivalent to s. 84(1)(ii) of the LPA 1925, the sum of £350 was awarded to compensate for any effect which the restrictions had, at the time when they were imposed, in reducing the consideration then received for the land affected by the covenants. The applicant alleged that the action of the Lands Tribunal in extinguishing the two covenants violated her rights under Article 1, Protocol 1. She claimed that it amounted to a deprivation of her possessions within the ambit of the second rule. However, the European Commission disagreed with this approach. It concluded that there had been no deprivation of possessions but that the interference constituted a control of use under the third rule. In deciding that there was no deprivation of possessions, the European Commission did not consider that the benefit of a restrictive covenant constitutes a possession in itself, even though under UK law it does enjoy proprietary status. In the opinion of the European Commission, the applicant's possession was 'an interest in the land in question which is limited to the benefit of the restrictive covenants contained in the fee farm grant and an entitlement to collect the annual rent charge from the Board as grantee'. Therefore her 'possession' consisted of an accumulation of the two covenants at issue, other covenants contained in the grant and the annual rent charge of £100. Since the decision to extinguish the two covenants only affected a small part of her 'possession' as defined by the European Commission, it was not sufficient to amount to a deprivation of possessions (see 4.6.3).

Having established that the decision of the Lands Tribunal amounted to an interference with the control of use of the applicant's property under the third rule, the European Commission had to consider whether or not it was justifiable as being in the general interest and proportionate to the aim being pursued. The European Commission found that the legislation gave the Lands Tribunal the power to 'free land in certain circumstances from unreasonable impediments and thus enable it to be used constructively where this is desirable. Such a power is accordingly "in the general interest"'. On the facts the European Commission was satisfied that the measures taken were proportionate to the aim to be achieved. It noted that the extinction of the covenants 'upon payment of compensation was not disproportionate to the legitimate aim of ensuring the most efficient use of the land for the benefit of the community'.

8.6.2   The application of *S* v *UK to English law*

The decision in *S* v *UK* was particular to its facts and to the specific Northern Ireland legislation under consideration. However, a number of general points concerning the application of Article 1, Protocol 1 to this area of property law can be deduced for wider application.

In *S* v *UK*, defining the scope of the word 'possession' was crucial to ascertaining the applicable rule under Article 1, Protocol 1. The applicant's possession was held to be the accumulation of the discharged covenants, other covenants in the grant and the annual rent. Therefore losing the benefit of two restrictive covenants out of a bundle of rights was not sufficient to constitute a deprivation of possessions. This approach, for distinguishing between a deprivation and a control of use, was adopted by the European Commission in *Banér* v *Sweden* (App. No. 11763/85) (see 4.6.3) and, commenting upon that decision, Harris, O'Boyle and Warbrick observe that:

> If ownership is seen as a bundle of rights, the fact that an owner has been deprived of one right will not usually be sufficient to say that he has been deprived of ownership: rather it is a control of the use of the property.[22]

---

[22] Harris, D. J., O'Boyle, M. and Warbrick, C., *Law of the European Convention on Human Rights*, London: Butterworths, 1995, p. 528.

Therefore, on the particular facts in *S* v *UK*, the question of deprivation was dismissed. However, what would the position be if a person's property in the land consisted solely of the benefit of two restrictive covenants which were subsequently extinguished by the Lands Tribunal? In this case the act of extinguishing the restrictive covenants may be seen to be a deprivation of property. This scenario is clearly distinguishable from the facts in *S* v *UK* where the decision of the Lands Tribunal left the majority of the applicant's ownership rights intact. In any event, even if extinguishing freehold covenants under s. 84 of the LPA 1925 is not found to constitute a deprivation of property, it is likely, as in *S* v *UK*, to amount to a control of use under the third rule.

Whichever rule is relied upon, in ascertaining whether the interference can be justified, it will be relatively easy for the Lands Tribunal to establish the existence of a legitimate aim. In *S* v *UK* the European Commission found that the ability of the Lands Tribunal to free land from 'unreasonable impediments' and thereby facilitate the constructive use of land was a legitimate aim in the general interest. Therefore the success of any challenge under the HRA 1998 to the use of s. 84 of the LPA 1925 will rest upon the principle of proportionality. This will depend upon the facts of the case and, in particular, the application of the compensation factor and the due process factor (see chapter 4). Section 84 of the LPA 1925 includes a provision for the payment of compensation. For example, if the Tribunal proposes to discharge or modify a restriction relying upon the ground that it impedes the reasonable user of the land, s. 84(1A), LPA 1925 specifically states that the Tribunal can only do so provided that the restrictive covenant

> does not secure to persons entitled to the benefit of it any practical benefits of substantial value or advantage to them . . . and that money will be an adequate compensation for the loss or disadvantage (if any) which any such person will suffer from the discharge or modification.

As regards the application of the due process factor, the existence of a right of appeal to the courts against the decision of the Lands Tribunal is likely to be a relevant factor in satisfying the need for proportionality. Consequently, s. 84, LPA 1925 is likely to be found to be proportionate to the aim being pursued. However, its application in an individual case could be challenged under the HRA 1998 as being in breach of Article 1, Protocol 1 if, for example, the Lands Tribunal failed to compensate an owner for his or her loss.

8.7   LAND USE

8.7.1   The Countryside and Rights of Way Act 2000

The Countryside and Rights of Way Act 2000 received the Royal Assent on 30 November 2000. A brief explanation of the main provisions of the Countryside and Rights of Way Act (CRWA) 2000 will follow. These will then be analysed in the light of the HRA 1998 to ascertain whether there is any scope for a challenge to the CRWA 2000.

8.7.1.1   A summary of the main provisions of the Act
Part I of the CRWA 2000 introduces a new statutory right of access on foot to open countryside for the purpose of open-air recreation. By this means the Act creates a new right for the general public, being a right not to be excluded from 'access land'.

(a)   The definition of 'access land'   Land which is predominantly mountain, moor, heath or down is defined as 'open country' and will qualify as 'access land' if it is shown on a map issued by the countryside bodies (the Countryside Agency, the Countryside Council for Wales and the National Park authorities). The countryside bodies are responsible for deciding whether land falling within the category of open countryside qualifies as 'access land'. There is also provision in the Act for the definition of 'access land' to be extended to include coastal land. Two categories of land are identified as automatically qualifying as access land. These categories are land over 600 metres above sea level and land registered as common land under the Commons Registration Act 1965.

The Act specifically identifies certain land which is expressly excluded from the definition of access land so that the new statutory right of access is inapplicable to that land. This exclusion relates to the following land: first, to land where there is an existing statutory right of access, for example, under Part V of the National Parks and Access to the Countryside Act 1949 or under s. 193 of the LPA 1925; secondly, to land which qualifies as 'excepted land' (as described in Part 1, Schedule 1 to the CRWA 2000). This is land which falls within the statutory definition of open country but which is specifically excluded, as 'excepted land', from the provisions of the CRWA 2000. Land falling within this 'excepted land' category includes cultivated land, developed land which has buildings on it, land used as a park, a garden, a racecourse, a golf course or an aerodrome or for the purpose of a railway or a tramway and land used for extracting minerals by surface workings. Any planning consents must have already been obtained before the land can qualify as 'excepted land'.

(b)   The discretionary powers of the countryside bodies   There are two areas under the CRWA 2000 which involve the exercise of a discretionary power by the countryside bodies. These areas are as follows:

   (i)   drafting the maps of access land; and
   (ii)   deciding whether or not to agree to a landowner's application for an exclusion or restriction of the public right of access.

In producing the maps of access land, the countryside body must initially publish draft and provisional maps which will enable landowners to identify which parts of their land have been designated as access land. There are procedural safeguards to enable any person with an interest in the land to appeal against the decision of the countryside body to designate his or her land as access land. If the relevant countryside body qualifies as a public authority under s. 6 of the HRA 1998, it will be under a duty to exercise its discretionary powers in a way that is not incompatible with the Convention rights.

(c)   Restrictions on the landlord's duty to allow public access   The CRWA 2000 provides for landowners to exclude or restrict public access to their land subject to the following qualifications.

(i)   The landowner can exclude or restrict access, for any reason, up to 28 days a year without seeking any permission from the countryside bodies. The landowner can choose which days to exclude or restrict access to his land but generally he cannot do so at a weekend nor on a public holiday.

(ii)   In all other cases the landowner must seek the permission of the relevant countryside body in order to exclude or restrict access. The countryside body may grant permission reliant upon one of the following specified grounds: land management, nature and heritage conservation, fire prevention, avoiding danger to the public, defence and national security.

If the land in question is subject to a restrictive covenant which is incompatible with the right of public access, the Act states that the covenant will be overruled by the existence of the statutory right of access (see 8.6 for an account of the human rights implications of modifying or extinguishing freehold covenants).

The CRWA 2000 does not increase the liabilities of landowners towards persons accessing their land. The duty under the Occupiers' Liability Acts remains the same as that owed to a trespasser (with the exception that the landowner is not liable in respect of the natural features on the land).

(d)   Compensation   The CRWA 2000 does not include any provision for the payment of compensation to affected landowners for the loss of their rights of exclusive possession over their land.

8.7.1.2   *Article 1, Protocol 1 and the Countryside and Rights of Way Act 2000*

(a)   The applicable rule   The state's interference with the landowner's property does not amount to a formal deprivation under the second rule because there is no

transfer of ownership of the land to the state. The land can still be used, sold, mortgaged or bequeathed subject to the public right of access. On this basis there is unlikely to be a *de facto* deprivation given the narrow scope of this concept under the Convention (see *Papamichalopoulos* v *Greece* (Appendix 3) and *Vasilescu* v *Romania* (1998) 28 EHRR 241).

Giving the public a right of access over land belonging to another person is undoubtedly a control of the use of property within the ambit of the third rule. In *Banér* v *Sweden* (App. No. 11763/85) the applicant owned a large estate which included part of a lake. New legislation was enacted, in pursuance of the Government's public recreation policy, which made fishing with hand-held tackle licence-free for all persons. Therefore the applicant's exclusive right to fish in his waters was transformed into a right that the general public could enjoy at leisure. The applicant alleged that the introduction of the legislation, and its effects, constituted a breach of Article 1, Protocol 1 because he had been deprived of his possessions without the payment of any compensation. The European Commission observed that the applicant had not been deprived of his right to fish. The effect of the legislation was to deprive him of his exclusive right to fish with hand-held tackle, although he retained the exclusive right to fish by other methods, e.g., with a net. Therefore the essence of his loss was his right to exclude others from fishing in his lake with hand-held tackle. With this in mind the European Commission stated that: 'Legislation of a general character affecting and redefining the rights of property owners cannot normally be assimilated to expropriation even if some aspect of the property right is thereby interfered with or even taken away'. On this basis the European Commission concluded that the restrictions on the applicant's property amounted to a control of use and not a deprivation of possessions. The European Court confirmed this approach in *Chassagnou and others* v *France* (App. Nos 25088/94, 28331/95 and 28443/95; judgment delivered on 29 April 1999) which concerned the compulsory transfer of landowners' hunting rights to a municipal hunters association. The landowners' loss of their exclusive rights to hunt were treated by the European Court as a control of use (see 4.4.1.6). On the basis of these cases, it would appear that a landowner's loss of ability to exclude the general public from walking across access land owned by him will come within the scope of the third rule.

However, it is arguable that there is something more than a mere control of the use. Given that the effect of the legislation will be to prevent a landowner, whose land is designated as access land, from being able to exclude other persons from his land, the landowner will lose exclusive possession of that land. The ability of landowners to protect their ownership by excluding trespassers from their land is seen by many commentators as a necessary incident of property ownership. For example, Harris suggests that: 'trespassory protection is a necessary condition for it to be true that the mantle of property is thrown over any resource'.[23] Therefore

---

[23] Harris, J. W. (n. 21 above) at p. 67.

it is arguable that compulsorily taking away the landowner's exclusive possession of his land impinges upon the nature of property ownership itself and is not merely a restriction on the use of the land. However, the removal of exclusive possession under the CRWA 2000 is not absolute. The landowner retains the right to exclude or restrict access by others for up to 28 days a year or for a longer period with the consent of the relevant countryside body. In addition, the landowner can exclude any person who fails to comply with the restrictions imposed in Schedule 2 to the CRWA 2000, for example any person who intentionally or recklessly takes, kills, injures or disturbs any animal, bird or fish. It may, in any event, be arguable that exclusive possession is no longer an essential criterion for the ownership of property. It has been suggested that transferability, a characteristic which remains unaffected by the Act, has greater significance. Allen observes that: 'Indeed many courts ignore the question of possession, and treat transferability itself as sufficient to establish property'.[24]

It may be that the interference, being less than a formal deprivation but arguably more than a control of use, will fall within the scope of the first rule as in *Matos e Silva, Lda and others* v *Portugal* (see Appendix 3). The Portuguese Government decided to create a nature reserve for animals on the Algarve coast which included part of the land owned by the applicants. In pursuance of this scheme a number of public-interest declarations were made as a preliminary to expropriating the relevant land and other restrictions were put in place including a ban on building. The applicants submitted that the measures had resulted in a *de facto* expropriation of their land. The European Court disputed this, observing that all of the methods of exploiting the land had not disappeared, which was evidenced by the fact that the applicants did in fact continue to work their land. Therefore the European Court concluded that the second rule was not applicable. Whilst the European Commission, having reached the same conclusion in respect of the second rule, applied the first and third rule, the European Court only applied the first rule. The same approach could be adopted in respect of the restrictions imposed on landowners under the CRWA 2000.

(b) A legitimate aim   The Government's consultation paper, *Access to the Open Countryside in England and Wales*,[25] referred to the improvement in public health accruing from the increased opportunities for recreation and also to the consequent reduction in social divisions. Similar arguments based on the improvement of public recreational facilities were advanced by the state, and accepted by the European Commission, in *Banér* v *Sweden*. Thus the Government will have little difficulty in satisfying the need for a legitimate aim to justify the new right of public access to open countryside for recreational purposes.

---

[24] Allen (n. 16 above) at p. 134.
[25] DETR, 'Access to the Open Countryside in England and Wales', February 1998. A copy of the consultation paper is available at www.wildlife-countryside.detr.gov.uk.

(c)   The principle of proportionality   The question remains whether the measures to be adopted are proportionate to the aim to be achieved so that the individual landowner does not suffer an excessive burden. In assessing proportionality the compensation factor is likely to be a controversial issue. Compensation is a relevant factor in assessing proportionality under both the first rule and the third rule (see 4.6.5). In respect of the first rule, the European Court in *Sporrong and Lönnroth* v *Sweden* (see Appendix 3) held that the expropriation permits upset the fair balance test and imposed an excessive burden on the applicants. The fact that the applicants were denied the possibility of claiming any compensation in respect of the interference was a relevant factor in establishing that a breach of Article 1, Protocol 1 had occurred. Similarly it is arguable that the absence of compensation in the CRWA 2000 may be sufficient to tip the scales of the fair balance test in favour of the landowner with a resultant infringement of Article 1, Protocol 1.

However, the case of *Banér* v *Sweden* is particularly illuminating given that it also concerned a landowner's loss of ability to exclude the general public from using his estate for recreational purposes. The applicant maintained that the absence of any compensation in respect of this interference with his property rights constituted a violation of Article 1, Protocol 1. The European Commission, whilst recognising that the payment of compensation is not inherent in the third rule, noted that:

> This does not exclude that the law may provide for compensation in cases where a regulation of use may have severe economic consequences to the detriment of the property owner ... When assessing the proportionality of the regulation in question it will be of relevance whether compensation is available and to what extent a concrete economic loss was caused by the legislation.

In *Banér* it was relevant that the applicant could not claim any direct loss of income as a result of the new legislation since he had not sold fishing licences prior to the legislative reform. Significantly, the European Commission did not accept that any reduction in the value of his property, as a result of general legislation affecting many fishing properties all over Sweden, was a type of loss that must necessarily be compensated under Article 1, Protocol 1. On the facts, it concluded that there was no infringement of Article 1, Protocol 1.

It is arguable that the lack of any provisions for the payment of compensation may raise concerns that a fair balance has not been struck and that individual landowners are suffering disproportionate losses that should be more evenly shared among the general public. The sufficiency of any such concern will depend upon whether there are any grounds to justify the non-payment of compensation to affected landowners. There is inevitably a difference of opinion between the Government and the landowners in this respect. The Government consultation paper states that the measures to be adopted would 'not have major financial implications' for the majority of landowners affected.[26] This appears to be a relevant factor, in the Government's view, for dispensing with the need for compensation payments. The CRWA 2000 does not, however, provide any exceptions allowing for the payment of compensation to the minority of landowners who do suffer a financial burden. By way of contrast, research commissioned by the Country Landowners Association contradicts the Government's view of the financial effects of the Act. The research suggests that there will in fact be significant cost implications which could have an effect upon the value of access land.[27] Ultimately the question of compensation will depend upon a court's assessment of evidence submitted as to the financial loss, if any, suffered by landowners together with an assessment of the extent to which the proportionate relationship between public benefit and individual burden may require landowners to shoulder some financial burden for the greater good (see 4.3.6.1). To this end the courts may also take into account the fact that existing statutes, which permit public access over private land, provide for the payment of compensation in proportion to the value by which the land has depreciated by reason of the public access (see Part V of the National Parks and Access to Countryside Act 1949 and ss. 25 to 28 of the Highways Act 1980).

8.7.1.3   Article 14 and the Countryside and Rights of Way Act 2000

It may be that the provisions of the CRWA 2000 can be challenged due to the discriminatory treatment of different property owners contrary to Article 14 in conjunction with Article 1, Protocol 1. Given the cumulative effect of the parasitic nature and autonomous nature of Article 14 (see 6.1), it is not necessary to show that there has been a breach of Article 1, Protocol 1 provided that the facts at issue fall within the ambit of that Article. The right of landowners to use their land for their own purposes and to exclude others from their land concerns a property right within the scope of Article 1, Protocol 1. Therefore Article 14 may be considered in conjunction with Article 1, Protocol 1 even though there may be no violation of Article 1, Protocol 1 if the interference is found to be justifiable.

The CRWA 2000 provides that where there is an existing statutory right of public access for recreational purposes, that existing right of access will endure and the new statutory right of access under the Act will not apply. Therefore land that is subject to an access agreement or an access order made under Part V of the National Parks and Access to the Countryside Act (NPACA) 1949 will not be regarded as access land. A local planning authority may make an access agreement with any person having an interest in land defined in the NPACA 1949 as 'open country' which includes, for example, mountain, moor and heath. For the

---

[26] Ibid., para. 3.48.

[27] Russell, N., 'An analysis of the potential costs to landowners under a statutory right of "Open Access" over mountain, moorland and common land', University of Manchester, December 1997.

purposes of Article 14 it is significant that under s. 64(2) of the NPACA 1949 the landowner can expect to receive consideration for having entered into the agreement and/or payments by way of contribution towards any expenditure incurred by him as a result of making his land accessible to the public for recreational purposes. Where there is no access agreement in force, and it is impracticable to secure the making of such an agreement, the local planning authority has power to make an access order. Where this occurs, s. 70 of the NPACA 1949 provides for the payment of compensation to the landowner. It states that:

> Where the value of the interest of any person in land is depreciated in consequence of the coming into operation of an access order ... the local planning authority in whose area the land comprised in the order is situated shall pay to that person compensation equal to the amount of the depreciation.

Therefore a landowner of moorland who provides a right of access to the public for the purpose of recreation, by means of an access agreement or access order under the NPACA 1949, is entitled to receive compensation, or a contribution to any costs incurred, whereas a landowner of moorland who has to provide a similar right of access to the public under the CRWA 2000 will not be entitled to any compensation. The question is whether this differential treatment of persons placed in an analogous situation can be reasonably and objectively justified. As it is difficult to envisage a reasonable justification for this differential treatment, the success of this argument may depend upon whether the courts accept that the landowners are placed in an analogous situation and this in turn may raise questions as to the financial loss, if any, suffered by the respective landowners.

8.7.1.4   Article 8 and the Countryside and Rights of Way Act 2000

If the public are given a right of access to land where the landowner lives, there may be an infringement of Article 8. In its consultation paper the Government recognised the need to protect landowners' privacy in their homes. The paper states that:

> In general the Government considers that people should have a right of access only to land which is not developed. This will protect people's privacy in their homes, gardens, and places where they go to work, other than on agricultural and forestry land.[28]

Schedule 1, Part 1 of the CRWA 2000 defines the scope of 'excepted land', which is land that is excluded from the statutory right of public access. 'Excepted land' includes 'Land covered by buildings or the curtilage of such land' and 'building'

---

[28] DETR (n. 25 above) para. 3.16.

is further defined to include any structure or erection including temporary or movable structures such as a tent or a caravan. It therefore seems unlikely that a challenge under the HRA 1998 for an infringement of the landowner's rights under Article 8 will arise provided that the word 'buildings' in Schedule 1, Part 1 is given a wide meaning so that it does not conflict with the broad conception of the 'home' taken by the Strasbourg institutions under Article 8. Given that the definition of 'buildings' in the Act expressly includes temporary structures such as tents and caravans it seems improbable that anything but a broad interpretation will be taken.

8.7.2   Hunting with dogs

The Government Hunting Bill contains three legislative options on which Members of Parliament were given a free vote. On 17 January 2001 the majority of the House of Commons voted to adopt the option which provides for a prohibition on hunting with dogs. The other two options (self-regulation through an independent supervisory body and the creation of a statutory licensing authority) were rejected by the House of Commons. On 26 March 2001 the House of Lords voted for the option to allow hunting to continue under a system of self-regulation. If legislation is enacted imposing a ban on hunting with dogs it will amount to an interference with the property rights of landowners and could therefore potentially trigger a challenge under the HRA 1998.

8.7.2.1   Article 1, Protocol 1 and hunting with dogs

(a)   The applicable rule   The interference, being a restriction on the way that landowners can use their land, will fall within the scope of the third rule as a control of use of the property by the state (see 4.4.1).

(b)   A legitimate aim   The Government would need to show that the interference is in pursuance of a legitimate aim that benefits the general community. It may be possible to argue that animal welfare is in itself a legitimate aim but, in any event, it is likely that the Government could rely upon the recognised legitimate aim of the 'protection of morals'. The 'protection of morality' was accepted as a legitimate reason for the destruction of schoolbooks containing pornographic material in *Handyside* v *UK* (see Appendix 3). In *Handyside* the European Court accepted the flexibility of the concept of 'morality' and observed (at para. 48) that:

> it is not possible to find in the domestic law of the various Contracting States a uniform European conception of morals. The view taken by their respective laws of the requirements of morals varies from time to time and from place to place, especially in

our era which is characterised by a rapid and far-reaching evolution of opinions on the subject. By reason of their direct and continuous contact with the vital forces of their countries, State authorities are in principle in a better position than the international judge to give an opinion on the exact content of these requirements.

It is arguable that morality is protected by legislation which bans a sport in which animals suffer unnecessarily. This raises the controversial question of whether or not the hunted animals do in fact suffer unnecessarily and the Final Report of the Committee of Inquiry into Hunting with Dogs in England and Wales, June 2000 (the Burns report) fails to reach any conclusion on this matter. However, it does state that the 'death [of a fox] is not always effected by a single bite to the neck ... in a proportion of cases it results from massive injuries to the chest and vital organs'.[29] This is a strong indication of the existence of unnecessary suffering. In this respect it is interesting to compare the attempts to ban hunting with dogs in the twenty-first century to the attempts to ban bull-baiting in the nineteenth century. Bull-baiting was, at that time, a widespread recreational activity mainly amongst the working classes. Two attempts to pass a Bill to prohibit bull-baiting failed in 1800 and 1802, principally on the grounds that the Bill was anti-working class. It has been noted that:

> In some ways the choice of bull-baiting as the first attempt at wholesale legislative change [in animal welfare] was a strange one. At the time, the suffering of many other animals, such as horses used for transport purposes, was recognised as being of much greater magnitude in terms of the number of animals involved. But the bull-baiting issue took on significance because of the distaste shown towards it as an exercise undertaken purely for human 'enjoyment and pleasure' at fairs and wakes.[30]

The distaste for bull-baiting, which was eventually declared illegal in 1835, therefore rested mainly upon the fact that animals suffered unnecessarily purely for the purpose of human entertainment and this was felt to be barbaric in a civilised society. Similar considerations for the protection of morality applied to cockfighting which was made illegal in the UK in 1911. Although hunting with dogs is not solely for recreational purposes because it also serves the collateral purpose of pest control and culling, nevertheless, the fact that the human participants in the hunt take pleasure from a sport in which a wild mammal is pursued at length by a pack of dogs and eventually killed is particularly relevant to the morality debate. This lends further support to the argument that a ban on

---

[29] The Burns report, chapter 6, 'Animal Welfare' at para. 6.49. In making this statement, the Committee relied upon two post mortem reports from the Department of Clinical Veterinary Science at the University of Bristol which showed very few injuries to the head and neck of some of the foxes but indicated that death was caused by massive injuries to other vital organs. The Burns report is available at www.huntinginquiry.gov.uk.

[30] Brooman, S. and Legge, D., *Law Relating to Animals*, London: Cavendish Publishing, 1997, at p. 40.

hunting with dogs protects morals and thereby pursues a legitimate aim in the general interest.

(c) The principle of proportionality In assessing proportionality the courts will need to ascertain whether the state's interference with the use of the land achieves a fair balance between the demands of the general interest of the community and the requirement for the protection of the landowners' fundamental rights. The question of whether compensation should be payable under the third rule for a control of use by the state is a controversial one and is considered in detail at 4.4.3 and 4.6.5. Whatever the outcome of the debate as to whether a regulatory control should be compensated, it is suggested that compensation is not necessary where the state's control is by means of the criminalisation of certain activities on land. A person can never have total ownership of property in the sense of using it for whatever he or she wants regardless of domestic laws restricting the use of that property. Harris refers to the concept of 'totality ownership' as an 'Aunt Sally' concept, being an invention of sceptics, put up to be knocked down.[31] No owner is at liberty to use his or her property for absolutely everything; a hammer cannot be used to hit another person or to smash windows. Many writers have identified this limitation as an important aspect of property. Honore, in identifying the standard incidents of ownership recognised that ownership of property is subject to a limitation on harmful use, for example, land cannot be used in such a way as to cause a nuisance to a neighbour.[32]

The use to which property is put can also be limited by the criminal law. Land, in the UK, cannot be used for bull-baiting or cock fighting as both constitute illegal acts under the criminal law. However if a state extends the list of activities that constitute a criminal offence, in order to keep pace with a changing and developing society, it surely cannot be suggested that landowners, who are thereby restricted from using their land in a way in which they previously could, can insist upon the payment of compensation. For example, the Computer Misuse Act 1990 created a new offence of unauthorised access to computer programs which prevents an owner of a personal computer from using it for the purpose of computer hacking (s. 1, Computer Misuse Act 1990). It would, however, be unusual to suggest that had the criminalisation of this activity occurred after 2 October 2000, all the owners of computers should be entitled to compensation for the control of their property by the state. Thus the criminal law must be allowed to develop without the need for the state to compensate owners for not being able to use their property for these new criminal activities. Similarly, it is suggested that to ban hunting with dogs and to make it illegal for a landowner to use, or permit others to use, his land for that purpose does not require compensation to be

---

[31] Harris (n. 21 above) at p. 66.
[32] Honore, A., 'Ownership' in A. G. Guest (ed), *Oxford Essays in Jurisprudence*, London: Oxford University Press, 1961 at p. 123.

paid to the landowner for the restriction in the use of his property by the state.[33] In assessing proportionality under the third rule, it is very unlikely that the Government's control of use of land will necessitate the payment of compensation to landowners based purely on their loss of the rights to hunt with dogs on their land. However, there may be exceptional cases in which a landowner alleges he has suffered a financial loss as a direct result of the legislative ban on hunting with dogs. For example, the Burns report acknowledged that some farmers may suffer a financial loss due to the loss of a free 'pest control' service and the consequent increase in predation of lambs, poultry and game birds. The counterargument to this submission is that the farmers' ability to use other methods of 'pest control', for example shooting and the use of humane traps, remains unaffected by the ban. Ultimately, it will depend upon the court's assessment of whether or not a landowner has suffered a financial burden which, in the absence of compensation, is so excessive that it outweighs the benefit to the general community in banning hunting with dogs.

An important factor in assessing proportionality is likely to be whether or not the state can show that it has sufficiently considered the interests of the affected landowners in making the decision to interfere with their property rights. The careful consideration of all the relevant concerns of the landowners by the Committee of Inquiry into Hunting with Dogs in England and Wales, is likely to go a long way to satisfying the principle of proportionality under the third rule. Consequently, legislation to ban hunting with dogs is likely to comply with Article 1, Protocol 1 because it pursues a legitimate aim and is proportionate to the attainment of that aim.

8.7.2.2   *Article 8 and hunting with dogs*

It may be that the recreational activity of hunting with dogs will come within the concept of 'respect for private life' under Article 8(1). The Burns report recognised that hunting with dogs plays a critical role in the social and cultural life of rural communities. Some landowners argue that to implement a ban on hunting will 'mark the end of an important, living cultural tradition'.[34] The concept of 'private life' does embrace the wider notion of social interaction with others and is not limited to 'an "inner circle" in which an individual may choose to live his personal life as he chooses and to exclude entirely the outside world not encompassed within that circle'. (*Niemietz* v *Germany* (1992) 16 EHRR 97 at para. 29; see 5.2.5). Therefore it is arguable that the interference will fall within the ambit of Article 8(1). Whether or not that interference can be justified under Article 8(2) will involve a similar consideration of legitimate aim and proportionality as discussed in relation to Article 1, Protocol 1 (see 8.7.2.1). In respect

---

[33] Rook, D., 'A Ban on Hunting with Dogs' NLJ 16 March 2001, p. 372.
[34] The Burns report, 'Summary and Conclusions' at para. 27.

of the overlap between Article 8 and Article 1, Protocol 1 (see 5.5), it is worth remembering that where legislation impinges on both of these Articles, the European Commission has stated that 'the application of the relevant provisions must be reconciled' (*Howard* v *UK*, see Appendix 3). If the legislative ban on hunting with dogs is found to be justifiable under Article 8, it is likely to be equally justifiable under Article 1, Protocol 1 and vice versa (see *Gillow* v *UK* in Appendix 3).

8.8 ENVIRONMENTAL POLLUTION AND THE TORT OF PRIVATE NUISANCE

8.8.1 State responsibility for environmental pollution

Subject to the question of the horizontal effect of the HRA 1998, Convention rights can only be invoked where it can be shown that the environmental pollution is attributable to the state. This does not necessarily mean that the state itself must be the polluter. A failure by the state to prevent private individuals from polluting may be sufficient to engage state responsibility, for example if there is a lack of appropriate legislation to regulate the sources of environmental pollution (see 5.3.1). In addition, the effect of s. 6 of the HRA 1998 is likely to mean that the courts have a duty to develop the common law to ensure that a person's human right to enjoy his or her home is not infringed by pollution caused by a privately owned factory or an individual neighbour.

8.8.2 Noise pollution

There have been a number of cases taken to Strasbourg against the UK in respect of noise pollution, principally concerning aircraft noise. In particular, the case of *Hatton and others* v *UK* (App. No. 36022/97) concerning noise caused by night flights at Heathrow Airport, was declared admissible on 16 May 2000 and the applicants are awaiting the final verdict of the European Court.

8.8.2.1 *Article 8 and noise pollution*
Two cases, both involving noise from airports, were declared admissible by the European Commission but were resolved by means of a friendly settlement in which the applicant received an *ex gratia* payment. In *Arrondelle* v *UK* (1982) 5 EHRR 118 the applicant alleged that her rights under Article 8 and Article 1, Protocol 1 were infringed due to noise from Gatwick Airport and the M23 motorway. A similar claim was made in the case of *Baggs* v *UK* (1987) 9 EHRR 235 which involved noise from Heathrow airport. In both cases the European Commission found the application to be admissible due to the complexity of the facts involved, and so the cases do not offer any specific guidance on the

possibility of establishing a violation of Convention rights on the basis of noise pollution. However, in *Powell and Rayner* v *UK* (see Appendix 3), which concerned noise pollution caused by aircraft arriving and departing from Heathrow Airport, the European Commission examined the question of whether the aircraft noise caused a breach of Article 8 or Article 1, Protocol 1 but, on the facts, decided that there was no violation of these Articles. The case is important in that it provides a clear statement that excessive noise is capable of causing a violation of Article 8. The European Commission acknowledged that: 'Considerable noise nuisance can undoubtedly affect the physical well-being of a person and thus interfere with his private life. It may also deprive a person of the possibility of enjoying the amenities of his home'. However, the level and frequency of the noise must be such as to be intolerable. In *Vearncombe* v *UK and the Federal Republic of Germany* (App. No. 12816/87) the European Commission found that the noise from a military shooting range was not so excessive as to be intolerable. The application was consequently found to be inadmissible. Therefore, provided that the noise level is found to be intolerable, an interference with a person's rights under Article 8(1) may arise even where the acts complained of are not due to direct measures directed against the applicant's home. The European Commission has stated that Article 8 covers: 'indirect intrusions which are unavoidable consequences of measures not at all directed against private individuals' (*Powell and Rayner* v *UK*). However, in *Powell and Rayner*, the European Commission concluded that the interference caused by the excessive noise was justified under Article 8(2), being necessary in a democratic society for the economic well-being of the country. The applicants conceded that the operation of Heathrow Airport, occupying an important position in relation to international trade, communications and the economy of the UK, pursued a legitimate aim. In assessing proportionality the European Commission found that the applicants did not suffer an unreasonable burden. In reaching this decision considerable importance was attached to the fact that the applicants had 'the possibility of moving elsewhere without substantial difficulties and losses'. This suggests that it is within the ambit of the fair balance test, and therefore permissible, for the applicant to suffer a difficulty or loss that is less than substantial.

The applicants also alleged a violation of Article 13 and the European Commission found this to be admissible and referred it to the European Court. Article 13, which is excluded from the provisions of the HRA 1998, gives a right to a national remedy for anyone whose rights under the Convention are infringed (see 1.8.3). The applicants argued that there was no remedy in the UK courts for the breach of their rights under Article 8. Therefore the European Court had to first consider whether or not the applicants had an arguable case that their rights under Article 8 had been breached, even though the European Commission had found their application under Article 8 inadmissible. The European Court decided that there was no breach of Article 8 on the facts. It was satisfied that a fair balance had been struck between the competing interests of the affected individuals and the community as a whole and concluded that the state could not be said to have exceeded the wide margin of appreciation afforded to it in such a difficult social and technical sphere.

In *Hatton and others* v *UK* (App. No. 36022/97) the applicants alleged that the increase in the level of noise caused by aircraft using Heathrow airport at night regularly disturbed their sleep and constituted an interference with their right to respect for their private and family lives and their homes, contrary to Article 8. The applicants also complained of a violation of Article 13 relying upon their submission that judicial review does not provide an adequate remedy because it fails to examine the merits of decisions by public authorities and is prohibitively expensive to individuals. On 16 May 2000 the European Court found that 'the complaints under Articles 8 and 13 of the Convention raise serious issues of fact and law under the Convention' and consequently declared the applicants' complaints to be admissible. Whether the applicants' case succeeds under Article 8 will depend upon whether or not the European Court will accept the UK Government's justifications for the retention of night flights at Heathrow airport and, in assessing proportionality, consider those reasons to outweigh the interests of the applicants.

8.8.2.2 Article 1, Protocol 1 and noise pollution

The applicants in *Powell and Rayner* v *UK* also sought to rely on a violation of their rights under Article 1, Protocol 1. The European Commission rejected their application as inadmissible observing that Article 1, Protocol 1 was 'mainly concerned with the arbitrary confiscation of property and does not, in principle, guarantee a right to the peaceful enjoyment of possessions in a pleasant environment'. However the European Commission was prepared to accept that in some cases excessive noise could amount to a 'confiscation' of property if it so substantially reduced the value of the property. In *Powell* v *UK* (App. No. 9310/81), it observed that: 'It is true that aircraft noise nuisance of considerable importance both as to level and frequency may seriously affect the value of real property or even render it unsaleable and thus amount to a partial taking of property'. However the European Commission decided that on the facts of the case this had not occurred and therefore there was no breach of Article 1, Protocol 1. Nevertheless, the European Commission's recognition that serious noise nuisance can constitute a deprivation of possessions is in line with the position taken by the courts in the USA in interpreting the Bill of Rights. In the case of *US* v *Causby* (1946) 66 Sup Ct 1062 a poultry farmer's business was ruined by the excessive noise caused by military aircraft frequently flying at low altitude over his property. The Supreme Court was satisfied that the loss to his business constituted a 'partial taking' of his property within the scope of the Fifth Amendment and consequently awarded him compensation for that expropriation.

8.8.3   Other types of environmental pollution

8.8.3.1   General principles

In *S* v *France* (App. No. 13728/88) a nuclear power station was built 300 metres from the applicant's home, an eighteenth-century French chateau. As a direct consequence of this the applicant complained of noise pollution, a disturbance to the microclimate, visual intrusion caused by high cooling towers and the fact that there was considerable artificial light during the night. The European Commission found the applicant's claim that there was a violation of Article 8 and Article 1, Protocol 1 to be inadmissible. The European Commission accepted that the various forms of pollution did amount to an interference with her rights under Article 8(1) but decided that they could be justified by reference to Article 8(2). It was found that the existence of the nuclear power station pursued a legitimate aim because it was for the economic well-being of the country. The European Commission was satisfied that a fair balance had been struck between the applicant and the general community. She had not suffered an excessive burden because she had received compensation from the state in respect of the reduction in the value of the property due to the noise pollution. However she was not entitled to compensation for her other causes of complaint because they did not cause her 'abnormal or special prejudice' as required by the national legislation. The European Commission categorically rejected her application under Article 1, Protocol 1 on the ground that she had received adequate compensation for the depreciation in the value of her property. Since the interference with the economic value of her property had been compensated she had no grounds for complaint under Article 1, Protocol 1 given that this Article does not protect the aesthetic qualities of property.

A number of general principles can be extrapolated from *S* v *France* and other decisions of the Strasbourg institutions on issues concerning environmental pollution. First, Article 1, Protocol 1 'does not in principle guarantee a right to the peaceful enjoyment of possessions in a pleasant environment' (*Powell and Rayner* v *UK*). This Article protects against interference with the economic value of property, but it does not extend to purely aesthetic qualities relating to the greater peace, comfort or enjoyment of the property. Although the protection of the aesthetic qualities of property may be possible under Article 8, this will only apply where the relevant property constitutes a person's home. Otherwise, interference with property caused by excessive noise, fumes or other environmental pollution will not be in violation of Convention rights. Secondly, it is clear that environmental pollution can be sufficient to constitute an interference with the rights protected by Article 8(1); however, in many cases the interference will be justifiable under Article 8(2). Since the states enjoy considerable latitude in establishing the existence of a legitimate aim, it is relatively easy for a state to justify the operation of a power station or chemical factory as necessary for the economic well-being of the country. In the majority of cases the crucial issue will be the principle of proportionality and whether a fair balance has been struck between the interests of the general community and the property rights of the individual affected by the pollution. In this respect the payment of compensation is likely to be a relevant factor (*S* v *France*).

8.8.3.2   The implications of Lopez Ostra for English law

The case of *Lopez Ostra* v *Spain* (see Appendix 3) provides a landmark ruling because it was the first time that the Strasbourg institutions found a breach of the Convention due to environmental pollution. The applicant lived near a town with a heavy concentration of leather industries. A tannery waste treatment plant was built by a private limited company, with a state subsidy, on municipal land only 12 metres away from the applicant's home. The waste treatment plant, in breach of state regulations, began to operate without a licence from the municipal authorities. Owing to a malfunction the plant released gas fumes and smells into the atmosphere which immediately caused health problems and nuisance to local residents including the applicant. The European Court awarded the applicant substantial compensation (four million pesetas) in respect of the state's breach of Article 8. In its judgment the European Court endorsed the view that environmental pollution, if sufficiently serious, can constitute an interference under Article 8(1). It stated (at para. 51) that: 'severe environmental pollution may affect individuals' well-being and prevent them from enjoying their homes in such a way as to affect their private and family life adversely, without, however, seriously endangering their health'. On the facts, the interference could not be justified under Article 8(2). The European Court found that the state authorities had not only failed to take the necessary steps to protect the applicant's right to respect for her home, but had contributed to prolonging the interference by appealing against a domestic court decision to close the plant temporarily. It held that the state had not succeeded in striking a fair balance between the interests of the town's economic well-being (that of having a waste treatment plant to solve the serious pollution problem caused by the concentration of tanneries) and the applicant's enjoyment of her right to respect for her home and family life. Accordingly there was a violation of Article 8.

Under English law local authorities have a duty to serve abatement notices in relation to any statutory nuisances that they discover following an inspection of their area (ss. 79 and 80, Environmental Protection Act 1990). If facts similar to *Lopez Ostra* occurred in England, the victim of the pollution could notify the local authority and if it refused to serve an abatement notice, the victim could seek judicial review of the local authority's decision. However, under existing English law the victim would not be entitled to claim damages from the local authority for its failure to act (*Lam* v *Brennan and Torbay Council* [1997] PIQR 488). It is arguable that this position could change under the HRA 1998. Corner remarks that: 'The *Lopez Ostra* case suggests the possibility of a new cause of action for what would effectively be damages for breach of Convention rights, where a local authority failed to take action to require the abatement of a nuisance'.[35] He suggests that this is in fact unlikely to occur in practice due to the fact that a person affected by a nuisance can commence court proceedings in private nuisance directly against the perpetrator of the nuisance and the courts may expect a person to exhaust this option before seeking to claim damages against the local authority. Although this is the position as regards an owner of property, the new cause of action may, nevertheless, be a valuable option to those persons who cannot currently invoke the law of private nuisance, for example, licensees. A licensee, whose home is affected by a nuisance, cannot currently bring an action in private nuisance due to the absence of the requisite proprietary interest in the land (*Hunter* v *Canary Wharf* [1997] 2 All ER 426) (but see 8.8.4). However, such a person may be able to commence action against the local authority under s. 7 of the HRA 1998 for its failure to serve an abatement notice provided that that person qualifies as a victim (see 1.7).

8.8.3.3   Is injury to health necessary?

Khatun and 180 others v *UK* (see Appendix 3) concerned the contamination of residential properties due to large quantities of dust emanating from the construction works of the Limehouse link road in the London Docklands. The applicants did not allege that the dust contamination directly endangered their health; however, they were unable to use their gardens or open their windows without being covered in dust and they relied upon this to constitute a violation of their rights under Article 8. The European Commission, relying upon a statement by the European Court in *Lopez Ostra* v *Spain* that it is not essential to establish the existence of health problems in order to raise an infringement of Article 8, stated that: 'Naturally, severe environmental pollution may affect an individual's well-being and prevent them from enjoying their homes in such a way as to affect their private and family life adversely, without, however, seriously endangering their health'. The European Commission, therefore, found that: 'although none of the applicants has alleged any ill health as a result of dust contamination ... the fact that they could not open windows or dry their laundry outside for a period of three years severely impaired their right to enjoy their homes and private or family lives'. Although the absence of any health problems does not prevent the finding of an interference under Article 8(1), it will be a relevant factor in assessing any justification for the interference under Article 8(2). In particular, it is likely be an important factor to weigh in the balance when assessing proportionality and the fair balance test.

---

[35] Corner, T., 'Planning, Environment, and the European Convention on Human Rights' [1998] JPL 301 at p. 313.

8.8.3.4   *Article 8 and procedural issues: access to information*

The notable feature of the European Court's judgment in *Guerra and others* v *Italy* (see Appendix 3) is the emphasis it places upon the public authorities' positive duty under Article 8 to keep local residents informed about any possible health risks from potential causes of environmental pollution. The applicants lived in a town 1km away from a chemical factory. The factory, which produced fertilisers, was classified as 'high risk' pursuant to criteria set out in a Presidential Decree. In the course of its production cycle the factory released large quantities of inflammable gas and other toxic substances, including arsenic trioxide. Due to the geographical location of the factory, emissions into the atmosphere were often channelled towards the town where the applicants lived. The European Court had to ascertain whether the national authorities had taken the necessary steps to ensure the effective protection of the applicants' rights as guaranteed by Article 8. It concluded that the state had persistently failed to provide the applicants with essential information of an emergency plan in the event of an accident occurring at the chemical factory. The state authority had information in its possession that would have enabled the applicants to assess the risk that they were exposed to and to take appropriate steps to avert the risk. Consequently, there was a breach of Article 8. The scope of this decision is uncertain. It will undoubtedly be argued by public authorities that this positive duty to provide such information must be seen in the context of the specific facts of the *Guerra* case which had involved maladministration by the local authority. In addition, in *Guerra* it was not disputed that the inhabitants of the town were at risk from the factory. It may be that the positive duty on the state to provide information will be limited to factual scenarios similar to *Guerra*.

There was a similar emphasis on access to information in the case of *McGinley and Egan* v *UK* (1998) 27 EHRR 1. This case concerned nuclear testing carried out at Christmas Island in 1958. The applicants were stationed on the island during the tests and later alleged that a failure by the state to allow them access to the records of the nuclear tests violated their rights under Article 8. The European Court observed (at para. 5) that:

> Where a Government engages in hazardous activities ... which might have hidden consequences for the health of those involved in such activities, respect for private and family life under Article 8 requires that an effective and accessible procedure be established which enables such persons to seek all relevant and appropriate information.

The European Court found that the applicants needed access to information concerning radiation levels during the nuclear tests, either to allay their fears of possible adverse effects on their health or to enable them to assess the risk of their suffering from ill health due to their exposure to the radiation. This was sufficiently closely linked to the private and family life of the applicants to make

Article 8 applicable. However on the facts there was no infringement of Article 8 because the applicants had not availed themselves of a procedure under domestic law which would have enabled them to request the relevant documents. The very fact that this procedure existed under domestic law meant that the state had discharged its positive duty under Article 8 in relation to these applicants. As the applicants were merely working on the island and did not have their homes there, the facts do not involve any interference with property; nevertheless, the decision can be applied to cases in which environmental pollution affects a person's home. Therefore the existence, or absence, of a procedure to enable persons whose homes are affected by hazardous activities to acquire relevant information is likely to be a crucial factor in determining whether a violation of Article 8 has occurred.

8.8.3.5   *Article 6(1) and environmental pollution*

The only time that Article 6 has been successfully invoked in a case concerning environmental issues is *Zander* v *Sweden* (1993) 18 EHRR 175. A state authority granted a company a licence to dump waste on a waste tip adjacent to the applicants' land. There was a risk that the waste could pollute the applicants' drinking water and they wanted to challenge the decision of the licensing authority to grant the permit; however, their only right of appeal was to the Government. The European Court found that there was a violation of Article 6(1) because the applicants were unable to challenge, in legal proceedings, the licensing authority's decision to grant the permit. This decision is unlikely to have any impact on English law due to the availability of judicial review proceedings to challenge the decisions of public bodies (see 7.7.4).

8.8.4   Article 8 and the tort of private nuisance

In some circumstances it may be possible for persons to invoke Article 8 in respect of an interference with their home, where a claim in private nuisance under English law would not be possible. There are two ways in which the scope of Article 8 exceeds the law of private nuisance. First, Article 8 applies independently of proprietary rights and therefore a mere occupant can invoke Article 8 to protect his or her home. By contrast an occupant having no proprietary interest in land cannot bring a claim in private nuisance even though the interference affects their home and family life (*Hunter* v *Canary Wharf* [1997] 2 All ER 426). Secondly, Article 8 applies to types of interference that fall outside the scope of the law of nuisance. For example, interference with the view from a person's house, or with light entering through the windows, caused by the presence of a building on neighbouring land cannot constitute a nuisance under English law; but it is arguable that it could, if sufficiently obtrusive, be in breach of Article 8(1) (see 8.8.3.1). It is likely that the courts will be under a duty under

s. 6 of the HRA 1998 to develop the common law governing private nuisance claims so that the common law complies with the wider scope of Article 8.

To illustrate these discrepancies between Article 8 and the law of private nuisance, and to assess the possible impact of the HRA 1998 upon this tort, it is helpful to consider the facts of *Hunter* v *Canary Wharf* [1997] 2 All ER 426. This case arose out of the construction of the Canary Wharf tower and the Limehouse link road in the London Docklands area. In order to undertake a programme of regeneration, the Secretary of state designated the London Docklands as an enterprise zone which meant that the area was deemed to be granted automatic planning permission for development without the need to comply with the usual procedures for obtaining planning permission. The claimants commenced an action in private nuisance against the developers in respect of the development and the courts had to consider whether an interference with television reception could constitute a nuisance and whether a claimant must have a proprietary interest as a prerequisite to commencing an action in nuisance.

8.8.4.1 Visual intrusion

The applicants claimed damages for nuisance due to an interference with their television reception caused by the presence of the Canary Wharf tower. The Court of Appeal decided that the interference with the television reception was not capable of constituting an action in private nuisance because it was purely as a result of the presence of a building on the defendant's land. Pill LJ reasoned that:

> the erection or presence of a building in the line of sight between a television transmitter and other properties is not actionable as an interference with the use and enjoyment of land. The analogy with loss of prospect is compelling. The loss of a view, which may be of the greatest importance to many householders, is not actionable and neither is the mere presence of a building in the sight line to the television transmitter. ([1996] 2 WLR 348 at 357)

On appeal the House of Lords endorsed this decision.

The decision of the appeal courts in *Hunter* v *Canary Wharf* can be compared with the decision of the European Commission in *S* v *France* in which it was prepared to accept that visual intrusion affecting the applicant's home, caused by high cooling towers at a nuclear power station, interfered with the applicant's rights under Article 8(1) (see 8.8.3.1). However, on the facts, the visual intrusion was just one of a number of complaints attributable to the operation of the nuclear power plant. Other complaints included noise pollution, artificial light pollution at night and a disturbance to the microclimate. It is questionable whether the loss of the view on its own would have been sufficient to invoke Article 8. *S* v *France* does, however, leave the door open to allegations of interference under Article 8 which includes severe visual intrusion, whilst the existing interpretation of the law of private nuisance slams the door firmly shut. It is arguable that the English law will have to develop in this respect to comply with the wider application of Article 8.

8.8.4.2   *The need for a proprietary interest*

Hunter v *Canary Wharf* raised the important question of whether it is necessary for a person to have an interest in land in order to bring an action in private nuisance. The Court of Appeal decided in the negative but the House of Lords reversed that decision reaffirming the traditional view that an action in nuisance can only be commenced by a person with an interest in the land affected. When the case reached the European Commission (*Khatun and 180 others* v *UK*, see Appendix 3), the applicants alleged a breach of Article 8 on the basis of the severe dust contamination caused by the construction of the Limehouse link road. The European Commission found the application to be inadmissible but it did provide valuable clarification on the question of standing. It stated that: 'Article 8(1) applies to all the applicants in the present case whether they are the owners of the property or merely occupiers living on the property, for example, the children of the owner of the property'. Consequently, there is a clear discrepancy between Article 8 and the existing interpretation of the law of private nuisance. It seems likely that the law of nuisance will need to be developed by the courts in order to enable licensees to protect their rights under Article 8 by giving them sufficient standing to bring an action in nuisance. This was the opinion of Lord Cooke, who delivered a dissenting judgment in the House of Lords' decision in *Hunter* v *Canary Wharf*. His Lordship relied upon Article 8 to support the view that an occupant, with no interest in the land, can bring a claim in private nuisance (see 5.2.3).

The more recent Court of Appeal decision in *Pemberton* v *Southwark LBC* [2000] 1 WLR 1672 lends support to the submission that the courts must develop the law of nuisance in line with Article 8. In this case a secure tenant had become a tolerated trespasser because she had failed to pay instalments of rent arrears in breach of a suspended possession order. Nevertheless, the Court of Appeal held that she had sufficient standing to sustain an action in nuisance against her local authority landlord. Whilst accepting that her tenancy had ended due to her failure to comply with the conditions of the suspended order for possession, the Court of Appeal concluded that her exclusive right to occupation of the premises as a tolerated trespasser gave her a sufficient interest in the property to bring an action in nuisance in respect of an infestation of cockroaches from the common parts of the building. In reaching this decision the Court of Appeal considered arguments based on Article 8 of the Convention. Clarke LJ gave the example of excessive noise from one flat causing a nuisance to the person occupying the adjoining flat. Whether that person is a tenant or a tolerated trespasser, Clarke LJ observed (at p. 1684) that:

there would, as I see it, be an infringement of the right to respect for private and family life, which is protected by Article 8 of the European Convention of Human Rights, which I regard as a relevant factor in determining whether a tolerated trespasser has a sufficient right to sue the council in trespass or nuisance.

Therefore Article 8 was a relevant factor in persuading the Court of Appeal to expand the category of persons who are qualified under the common law to bring a claim in nuisance. This case was decided prior to the implementation of the HRA 1998. Arguments based on Article 8 will now have considerably greater influence.

8.8.4.3 The use of Article 8 as a defence to state interference

Although Article 8 has a wider scope and application, its justifications for state interferences also have a wider scope and application than under the English law of private nuisance. Therefore the HRA 1998 may be a double-edged sword. Although it entitles a victim to invoke Convention rights in respect of violations of his or her human rights, it also entitles a public authority to justify its interferences on a much broader footing. For example, the defendant in *Hunter* v *Canary Wharf* raised the defence of statutory authority on the ground that the interference with the television reception caused by the presence of the Canary Wharf tower was an inevitable consequence of a statutory duty conferred on the defendant. The Court of Appeal rejected this submission and the defence of statutory authority was rejected as inapplicable. However in *Khatun and 180 others* v *UK*, the defendant's argument that the dust contamination was justified under Article 8(2) was accepted by the European Commission (and these justifications could have equally applied to the interference with the television reception). The regeneration and development of the Docklands area was in pursuit of a legitimate aim under Article 8(2), being for the economic well-being of the country and the measures taken were found to be proportionate to that aim. Consequently there was no breach of Article 8.

8.9 COMPULSORY PURCHASE

8.9.1 Compulsory purchase procedures and Article 6(1)

A local authority can acquire land compulsorily where it has statutory authority to do so and the acquisition is ancillary to its primary functions. Certain specified non-state owned bodies, for example airport operators and water undertakers, also enjoy these same powers subject to the same provisos. Having resolved to make a compulsory purchase order (CPO) the local authority must advertise it and notify any interested parties of their right to object. If there are unresolved objections a public inquiry is held and the inspector reports to the Secretary of

State who decides whether to confirm the CPO or reject it (see the Acquisition of Land Act 1981). If the Secretary of State authorises the CPO, the local authority may proceed to implement the purchase of the land by one of two methods. Either a notice to treat is served followed by a notice of entry whereupon the local authority can take possession of the land, but it will not complete the purchase and transfer ownership until the compensation has been assessed. Alternatively, the local authority may make a general vesting declaration which vests ownership in itself with immediate effect leaving the compensation to be assessed in due course. Whichever procedure is adopted a landowner whose land is compulsorily acquired has an absolute right to compensation. The calculation and quantification of the compensation payment is governed by the Land Compensation Act 1961.

The HRA 1998 will not prevent the compulsory purchase of land where it is in the public interest. In *S* v *UK* (App. No. 13135/87) the European Commission held that the compulsory purchase of part of a Highland estate, for the purposes of constructing a public road, was not in violation of Article 1, Protocol 1. However, it is possible that some of the procedures for effecting a compulsory purchase will be found not to accord with Convention rights. Following the decision of the European Court in *Bryan* v *UK* (see Appendix 3), the availability of the judicial review procedure to challenge a CPO on a point of law should generally be sufficient to satisfy Article 6(1). However, there may be exceptional cases which do not comply with Article 6(1). For example, if the Secretary of State decided not to follow the inspector's recommendations and denied the parties an opportunity to make further representations, it is arguable that an objector has not been given a fair hearing by an independent and impartial tribunal even though he or she could appeal on a point of law to the High Court.[36]

8.9.2   Compensation and Convention rights

8.9.2.1   Owners of low value houses subject to compulsory purchase
In the DETR final report 'Fundamental review of the laws and procedure relating to compulsory purchase and compensation', the advisory group recognised that calculating compensation on the basis of the open market value of the property can be harsh on some owner-occupiers displaced from low value homes. Home owners compelled to move out of an area in which the property market has collapsed, leaving them in a position of negative equity, face specific problems due to the funding gap between the compensation received for the property compulsorily acquired and the finance needed to purchase a reasonably similar home in another location. The advisory group accepted that: 'there is a need, in human rights terms, to ensure that such displaced owner-occupiers are not made

---

[36] Redman, M., 'Compulsory Purchase, Compensation and Human Rights' [1999] JPL 315 at p. 318.

to bear a disproportionate burden as a result of the compulsory purchase of their homes'.[37] If a local authority compulsorily purchases a family's home and the compensation payable is not sufficient to enable that family to buy a reasonably similar home elsewhere, it is arguable that there has been a violation of their rights for the respect of their private life, family life and home under Article 8(1). Although the interference is likely to pursue a legitimate aim there will, nevertheless, be a lack of proportionality if the displaced persons have to bear a disproportionate burden. On this basis the advisory group recommended that:

> further consideration should be given to the extent to which acquiring authorities should be given additional powers to help them to ensure that no displaced owner-occupier has to bear a disproportionate financial burden because the amount of compensation payable to him on an open market value basis for the compulsory acquisition of his property is insufficient to enable him to buy a reasonably similar property elsewhere'.[38]

The Government will need to take heed of this recommendation in order to avoid any future challenge to this area of law under the HRA 1998.

8.9.2.2   An adjacent landowner who suffers injurious affection
Section 10 of the Compulsory Purchase Act (CPA) 1965 enables a person to claim compensation for the 'injurious affection' of his or her land where it has been affected by the compulsory acquisition of adjoining land for public works. One of the four rules (referred to as the McCarthy Rules; *Metropolitan Board of Works* v *McCarthy* (1874) LR 7 HL 243) governing the courts' current interpretation of s. 10, CPA 1965 is that the damage or loss must be an injury to land and not a personal injury or an injury to trade. The Court of Appeal decision in *Wildtree Hotels Ltd* v *Harrow LBC* [1998] 3 WLR 1318 illustrates the application of this rule. In this case land adjacent to an hotel was compulsorily acquired by the local authority for use in a road improvement scheme. The owners of the hotel, whose land was not subject to compulsory purchase, nevertheless claimed substantial compensation under s. 10, CPA 1965 in respect of noise, dust and vibration from the road works which interfered with the use of their land. The Court of Appeal held that the hotel owners were not entitled to any compensation under s. 10, CPA 1965. It interpreted 'injurious affection' in s. 10 to mean direct physical damage to the land or a permanent devaluation of the land. Given that there had been no physical interference with the hotel and, the disturbances caused by the noise, dust and vibration were of a temporary nature during the works, the Court of Appeal held that no compensation was required.

---

[37] Department of the Environment, Transport and the Regions, 'Fundamental review of the laws and procedures relating to compulsory purchase and compensation', final report, London: DETR, July 2000 at para. 163.

[38] Ibid., at para. 174.

In the DETR final report 'Fundamental review of the laws and procedure relating to compulsory purchase and compensation', the advisory group recommended that, as a result of the decision of the Court of Appeal in *Wildtree Hotels Ltd* v *Harrow LBC*:

> the legislation should be amended to provide that compensation entitlement [under s. 10] should be extended to include interference with land from non-physical factors, and any entitlement to compensation, should include temporary losses sustained by the landowner.[39]

The case went on appeal to the House of Lords, and its decision has, in part, addressed the recommendation of the advisory group. The House of Lords in *Wildtree Hotels Ltd* v *Harrow LBC* (22 June 2000), accepted that the claimant could recover compensation under s. 10, CPA 1965 in relation to temporary damage. However, their Lordships recognised that it would be extremely rare for damage caused by noise, dust or vibration arising out of construction works authorised by statute, to give rise to a valid claim for compensation under s. 10.

It is arguable that a narrow interpretation of 'injurious affection' in s. 10 is incompatible with Convention rights where a landowner's rights under Article 1, Protocol 1 or Article 8 are affected. In assessing compliance with Article 1, Protocol 1 and Article 8 the deciding factor will undoubtedly be the principle of proportionality and whether the affected landowner suffers an excessive burden. If a narrow interpretation of s. 10 would result in a violation of Convention rights, then the courts would be obliged, under s. 3 of the HRA 1998, to interpret s. 10 in such a way that ensures its compliance with Convention rights (see 1.5).

8.9.3   Blight notices and Article 1, Protocol 1

The law relating to blight notices is set out in Part VI, Chapter II of the Town and Country Planning Act 1990. Landowners can only benefit from the blight notice procedure if they have a 'qualifying interest' as defined by s. 149 of that Act. To qualify the interest must either be that of an owner-occupier, where the annual value of the property does not exceed an amount prescribed by statutory instrument (currently £18,000), or a resident owner-occupier (s. 149(3)). In essence this includes all owner-occupied residential property as well as small business premises which are owner-occupied and fall within the prescribed valuation restriction. The blight notice provisions also apply where the interest is in an agricultural unit, or part thereof, and is owner-occupied (s. 149(2)). The procedure enables the holder of the qualifying interest, whose land is affected by public works (e.g., a threat of compulsory purchase for a proposed development), to require the local authority to purchase his or her interest prematurely before the acquiring authority would otherwise choose to do so. This can clearly be

---

[39] Ibid., at para. 197.

advantageous to the landowner who may otherwise be left with land which is extremely difficult to sell at its market value for some years due to the fact that there is a threat of a compulsory purchase order hanging over it. It is arguable that where a landowner does not have a qualifying interest, either because the premises are business premises which are too valuable to qualify or because the owner is an investment owner and thus the property is not owner-occupied, the landowner may be in a position to claim a breach of Convention rights under the HRA 1998. In those instances where the blight notice procedure is not available, the acquiring local authority has a discretion as to when to acquire the land and may wait up to three years from the date that the compulsory purchase order becomes operative (s. 4 of the Compulsory Purchase Act 1965). In addition, there may be a further delay of up to three years before the expiration of the notice to treat. Given the limited availability of blight notices and the consequent risk of a delay of up to six years for those landowners without a qualifying interest, there is scope for a potential challenge to the blight notice procedure under the HRA 1998.

A landowner who is denied the opportunity to serve a blight notice may be in a position to allege a violation of Article 1, Protocol 1. The interference with the land, in the form of the CPO, is similar to the expropriation permits in *Sporrong and Lönnroth v Sweden* and the public interest declarations in *Matos e Silva, Lda and others v Portugal* (see Appendix 3). In these cases there was an interference with the owners' peaceful enjoyment of their possessions within the ambit of the first rule. The fact that, under the current restrictions to the blight notice procedure, it is possible for a landowner to suffer a delay of up to six years without receiving any compensation during that period, will be a relevant factor in assessing proportionality and may be sufficient to upset the fair balance to be struck between the demands of the general interest of the community and the protection of the individual's fundamental rights.

There is also scope for a challenge under Article 14 in conjunction with Article 1, Protocol 1 due to discrimination on the grounds of wealth. An owner-occupier of small business premises, whose interest falls within the prescribed valuation restrictions, has the benefit of being able to serve a blight notice. However, this advantage is denied to an owner-occupier whose interest exceeds the permitted annual value. Unless the state is able to justify this differential treatment of persons placed in an analogous situation, it may be found to constitute discrimination in contravention of Article 14. With this in mind, Redman suggests that: 'enabling investors, as well as owner-occupiers, to serve a blight notice and abolishing the rateable value limit for owners of commercial property would go a considerable way to reducing the chances of English law being held incompatible with Convention rights'.[40]

---

[40] Redman (n. 36 above) at p. 321.

8.10   PLANNING LAW

8.10.1   Article 6(1) and planning procedures

In *Bryan* v *UK* (see Appendix 3), the European Court was satisfied that the enforcement notice appeal procedures in English law, which include a right of appeal to the Secretary of State (involving an inquiry by an inspector) and a statutory right of appeal to the High Court on a point of law, are sufficient to comply with Article 6(1). The area of contention concerns the appeal hearing before the inspector which in itself was found not to comply with Article 6(1). The reason for the non-compliance is the existence of a process known as 'recovery' which allows the Secretary of State to issue a direction at any time to revoke the power of an appointed inspector to decide an appeal thereby leaving the Secretary of State to decide the appeal (paragraph 3(1) of the Sixth Schedule to the Town and Country Planning Act 1990). Although rarely used, the presence of the recovery process led the European Court to conclude (at para. 38) that:

> In the context of planning appeals the very existence of this power available to the Executive, whose own policies may be in issue, is enough to deprive the inspector of the requisite appearance of independence, notwithstanding the limited exercise of the power in practice ... and irrespective of whether its existence was or could have been at issue in the present case.

In the light of the criticism in *Bryan* by the European Court, Crow has argued that it may be preferable for the right of recovery to be removed altogether.[41] In proposing this he does not suggest that cases involving, for example, a substantial deviation from the development plan should be decided by an inspector rather than a minister. He accedes that decisions which affect the whole community ought to be taken by an elected Government representative who is politically accountable. However, to remove the power of recovery does not prevent such cases from reaching ministers. He notes (at p. 369) that:

> there are two ways in which such decisions reach ministers; as 'call-ins' under section 77 before applications are determined, and as recovered appeals. There is an element of illogicality here, because if the same criteria were applied to both (which they manifestly are not), such cases would never reach appeal. The Northern Ireland example, in which there are statutory criteria for the local equivalent of 'call-in' and no power for the recovery of appeals, has much to commend it.

Crow, therefore, suggests that the availability of the 'call-in' procedure at an early stage in the determination of planning permission makes the recovery process at

---

[41] Crow, S., 'Lessons from Bryan' [1996] JPL 359.

the appeal stage unnecessary and readily dispensable as a means of ensuring compliance with Article 6(1).

This, however, raises the question of whether the 'call-in' procedure is Convention compliant. The Scottish case of *County Properties Limited* v *Scottish Ministers* 2000 SLT 965 suggests that it is not, but the more recent decision of the House of Lords in *R* v *Secretary of State for the Environment, Transport and the Regions, ex parte Holding and Barnes plc* (the *Alconbury* case) (9 May 2001) provides a very different answer. *County Properties Limited* v *Scottish Ministers* resulted in a successful challenge to the planning procedure in Scotland under the Scotland Act 1998 (the Scottish equivalent to the Human Rights Act 1998). County Properties Ltd (the petitioner), the owner of listed buildings situated in the Glasgow Central Conservation Area, applied for planning permission and listed building consent for the demolition of its buildings and the erection of a new building. In the initial application for planning permission the new building was to be a building of a similar appearance to the existing buildings, but in the later application a five-storey modern office building was proposed. The planning permission was granted by the local planning authority but the Scottish Ministers (the respondents) decided to 'call-in' the application for listed building consent. A reporter was appointed to hold a public inquiry and to report on the application. The petitioner alleged that there was a breach of Article 6(1) on the grounds that neither the respondents nor the reporter constituted an independent and impartial tribunal within the meaning of Article 6(1). The petitioner maintained that the decision to call-in the application was made as a result of an objection raised by Historic Scotland. Since Historic Scotland was an executive agency of the respondents they could not be seen to be impartial in any decision on the listed building consent. In addition, the petitioner complained that the reporter could not be seen to be impartial because he was employed by the respondents. It was also relevant that the reporter was employed on a part-time basis only and therefore lacked certain safeguards in respect of his employment. The respondents admitted the apparent absence of impartiality but, applying *Bryan* v *UK*, maintained that the petitioner's right of appeal to the Court of Session by way of judicial review satisfied the requirements of Article 6(1). Therefore the Court of Session had to determine whether, on the facts, the petitioner's limited right of appeal to it was sufficient to satisfy the requirements of Article 6(1). Lord Macfadyen observed (at para. 26) that:

> It is the petitioners' Convention right to have their civil rights determined by an independent and impartial tribunal. In my view the respondents' decision to call in the application for their decision has brought about a situation in which the determination of the petitioners' civil rights will be made by the respondents, who are admittedly not independent and impartial, and against whose decision there is only a limited right of appeal to this court. The limitations on the right of appeal are such that it may well be

impossible for this court, although indisputably an independent and impartial tribunal, to bring those qualities to bear on the real issues in the case.

On the facts, the central issue for determination by the tribunal was essentially one of planning judgment involving a choice between replacing the listed buildings with a building of similar appearance or with a modern one. This issue was not one which could have been reviewed by the Court of Session on appeal due to its limited scope of review. Therefore if the respondents' decision went against the petitioner on the basis of planning judgment, the determination of the petitioner's civil rights would not have been made by, nor capable of review by, a tribunal satisfying the requirements of Article 6(1). Lord Macfadyen concluded that 'in the circumstances of this case determination of the petitioners' application for listed building consent by the respondents after an inquiry conducted by the reporter would not satisfy the requirements of Article 6(1)' (at para. 27). The Scottish Ministers have lodged an appeal with the Inner Court of Session. Reliant upon the House of Lords' decision in the *Alconbury* case, it seems likely that the appeal will be allowed and the decision of the Court of Session reversed. The Lord Advocate intervened in the argument before the House of Lords in support of the application to reverse the decision of the Divisional Court (see below).

The House of Lords in *R* v *Secretary of State for the Environment, Transport and the Regions, ex parte Holding and Barnes plc* delivered its judgment on 9 May 2001, reversing the earlier decision of the Divisional Court (13 December 2000). The Divisional Court had held that certain decision-making processes of the Secretary of State for the Environment, Transport and the Regions were incompatible with Article 6(1) and accordingly made a declaration of incompatibility under s. 4, HRA 1998. Four unrelated cases were heard together as each raised the same question concerning the compatibility with Article 6(1) of certain procedures by which the Secretary of State makes decisions under the Town and Country Planning Act (TCPA) 1990, the Transport and Works Act (TWA) 1992, the Highways Act 1980 and the Acquisition of Land Act 1981. Two of the cases involved a 'call-in' under s. 77 of the TCPA 1990, while the third case concerned the exercise by the Secretary of State of his power, under ss. 78 and 79 of the TCPA 1990, to 'recover' an appeal against a refusal by the local planning authority to grant planning permission. The third case also involved a proposed order under s. 1, TWA 1992 in respect of the construction and operation of a railway. The fourth case involved an inquiry by an inspector concerning highway orders and related compulsory purchase orders in connection with a motorway improvement scheme where the promoter of the scheme was the Secretary of State himself.

It was conceded that the Secretary of State did not constitute an impartial tribunal since in each case his own policy was in issue. However, it is well established by the Strasbourg case law that, even where a decision maker is not an independent and impartial tribunal, there is, nevertheless, no breach of Article

6(1) where the decision is subject to subsequent control by a judicial body that has 'full jurisdiction' (see 7.7.4). Therefore, the question for determination was whether the limited jurisdiction of judicial review (and the statutory powers of review akin to judicial review) constituted 'full jurisdiction' on the facts. The Divisional Court was satisfied that judicial review is sufficient to constitute full jurisdiction where it concerns a review of a decision of a planning inspector, but not where it is of a decision of the Secretary of State. The difference being that the procedure by which the inspector reaches a decision is quasi-judicial in character and contains safeguards required by Article 6(1), while the Secretary of State is free to make his own decisions after consideration of confidential internal legal and policy matters. The Divisional Court stated that: 'What is objectionable in terms of Article 6 is that he should be the judge in his own cause where his policy is in play. In other words he cannot be both policy maker and decision taker'. In these circumstances the decision-making process lacked sufficient safeguards to justify the High Court's restricted power of review and consequently breached Article 6(1).

The House of Lords reversed the decision of the Divisional Court and concluded that there was no violation of Article 6(1). In answering the question of whether judicial review constituted 'full jurisdiction', the House of Lords acknowledged that the meaning of 'full jurisdiction' depends upon 'the subject matter of the decision appealed against, the manner in which the decision was arrived at, and the content of the dispute' (*Bryan* v *UK* (1995) 21 EHRR 342 at para. 45). Lord Hoffman distinguished between two different types of planning decision. Firstly, decisions on policy and expediency, such as a decision to grant or refuse planning permission and, secondly, decisions on findings of fact, for example, a decision as to whether or not a breach of planning control has occurred. In the case of the latter type of decision, the limited scope of judicial review can only be remedied by the existence of certain 'safeguards' in the decision-making process itself (see *Bryan* v *UK*, para. 46). For example, where a planning inspector is involved in the evaluation of facts, the inspector is under a duty to exercise independent judgment and to uphold principles of openness, fairness and impartiality. However, Lord Hoffman stated that where the inspector's decision is based on policy or expediency, these 'safeguards' are irrelevant. The inspector is not impartial in applying the Secretary of State's policy and in this respect there is no difference between the position of the inspector and that of the Secretary of State. In relation to policy decisions Lord Hoffman observed (at para. 117) that: 'The reason why judicial review is sufficient ... to satisfy Article 6 has nothing to do with the "safeguards" but depends upon the *Zumtobel* principle of respect for the decision of an administrative authority on questions of expediency'. In *Zumtobel* v *Austria* (1993) 17 EHRR 116 the European Court had decided that the absence of any review, by an independent and impartial tribunal, of the merits of a policy decision made by an administrative authority did not violate Article 6(1) (see 7.7.4). Having analysed the decisions in four European cases on the English planning system (*ISKCON* v *UK* (App. No. 20490/92), *Bryan* v *UK*, *Varey* v *UK* (App. No. 26662/95) and *Chapman* v *UK* (App. No. 27238/95)), Lord Hoffman concluded (at para. 122) that: 'for decisions on questions of policy or expediency such as arise in these appeals, whether made by an inspector or the Secretary of State, there has never been a single voice in the Commission or the European Court to suggest that our provisions for judicial review are inadequate to satisfy Article 6'. Lord Hoffman noted that the Divisional Court's misunderstanding of the law was due to the fact that it had not distinguished between policy decisions and decisions based upon findings of fact. It had incorrectly assumed that the 'safeguards' enumerated in *Bryan* v *UK* applied in all cases including those decisions concerned with policy and expediency.

Lord Clyde emphasised the significance of *Chapman* v *UK* (18 January 2001) in which the European Court stated (at para. 124) that: 'in the specialised area of town planning law full review of the facts may not be required by Article 6 of the Convention'. In that case the opportunity for the applicant to challenge the inspector's decision to dismiss her appeal against the enforcement notices on the basis that the decision was perverse, irrational, had no basis on the evidence or had been made with reference to irrelevant factors or without regard to relevant factors was found to afford adequate judicial control of the administrative decision in issue to constitute full jurisdiction for the purposes of Article 6(1). The Strasbourg institutions have recognised that it is a frequent feature throughout the contracting states that in specialised areas of the law such as judicial control of administrative decisions, review by a court does not extend to a review of the merits of a decision and to interpret Article 6(1) in such a way as to provide a right to a full appeal on the merits of administrative decisions would 'lead to a result which was inconsistent with the existing and long-standing legal position in most of the contracting states' (*Kaplan* v *UK* (1980) 4 EHRR 64 at para. 161).

The House of Lords laid considerable emphasis on the nature of planning decisions and the fact that many decisions involve public interest considerations embracing social and economic interests. Lord Clyde expressed concern (at para. 144) that to remove major policy decisions from a minister, who is answerable to Parliament and ultimately the electorate, to an independent body, who is answerable to no one, would 'be a somewhat startling proposition and it would be surprising if the Convention which is rooted in the ideas of democracy and the rule of law should lead to such a result'.

8.10.2   The right of a third party objector to a fair trial under Article 6(1)

Under the existing planning appeal procedure a third party, aggrieved by the grant of planning permission, has no right of appeal to the Secretary of State on the merits of the decision, but is limited to a right of appeal to the High Court on a point of law. Given that one stage in the procedure approved in *Bryan* v *UK* as complying with Article 6(1) is missing, the question of compliance once again needs to be addressed.

Clearly the first question for consideration is whether Article 6(1) is in fact relevant to a third party's right of appeal against the grant of planning permission. In *Ortenberg v Austria* (1994) 19 EHRR 524 the European Court decided that where the grant of planning permission adversely affects the value of land owned by a third party, that person has the right to a fair hearing under Article 6(1). The applicant objected to land use and development plans which designated an area of land, adjoining the applicant's property, as building land. The district council subsequently authorised the construction of terraced houses on the land. The applicant alleged that she had not had access to a court with full jurisdiction or a fair and public hearing and consequently there had been an infringement of Article 6(1). The Government contended that Article 6(1) was inapplicable because the right of a neighbour to object to the grant of planning permission is a public law right and in any event the grant of planning permission concerned the relationship between the public authority and the individual applying for permission and did not concern the owner of the adjacent land. The European Court rejected this contention pointing out (at para. 28) that: 'Article 6(1) applies where the subject-matter of an action is 'pecuniary' in nature and is founded on an alleged infringement of rights which are likewise pecuniary'. The applicant, believing that the works on the adjoining land would reduce the market value of her land, wished to avoid an infringement of her pecuniary rights and therefore Article 6(1) was applicable. However the European Court decided that there was no infringement of Article 6(1), on the facts, because sufficient procedural safeguards were already in place in the form of the Austrian Administrative Court which had carefully scrutinised the applicant's complaints.

Since Article 6(1) does apply to third party objectors the question of compliance needs to be examined. In *Bryan v UK*, it was the combination of the procedures before the inspector, the Secretary of State and the High Court which together ensured compliance with Article 6(1). It could be argued that the absence of this combination of procedures, by the removal of a right of appeal to the Secretary of State on the merits of the decision, denies a third party objector the protection afforded under Article 6(1). However, it is hard to envisage that this argument will find favour with the courts. Corner remarks that:

> in applying Article 6 in the area of administrative decision-making on the basis of policy, the European Court and the Commission have usually been reluctant to require more than an appeal on what are essentially judicial review principles. To demand a right of appeal on the merits to an independent tribunal, or even one with some, but not total, independence such as an Inspector, would appear to be usurping the power of government to make and apply policy.[42]

---

[42] Corner (n. 35 above) at p. 308.

He does, however, concede that the HRA 1998 may make it easier for third parties, aggrieved by the grant of a planning permission, to put pressure on the Secretary of State to 'call in' an application that is considered to be controversial.

8.10.3   The right of a third party to compensation

In a situation where a grant of planning permission adversely affects the value of adjoining land but the interference does not actually constitute a nuisance, the question arises whether the adjoining landowner has a right to compensation under Convention rights. There is currently no such right to compensation under English law. For example, if planning permission were granted allowing a developer to construct a large, unsightly amusement park opposite a country home situated in a quiet countryside location, the owner of the country home may have valid grounds for arguing that the grant of planning permission and subsequent development will depreciate the value of his land. The owner could not bring proceedings in nuisance in respect of a loss of view because it does not constitute an actionable private nuisance. However, could he claim that in the absence of any compensation there has been a violation of Article 1, Protocol 1 or Article 8? As discussed at 8.8.3.1, the case of *S* v *France* raises the possibility that severe visual intrusion, for which the property owner has received no compensation, may give rise to a breach of the Convention rights. Corner tentatively suggests (at p. 309) that: 'The case raises the intriguing possibility that where permission is granted for development which reduces the value of a neighbour's property, even though it does not cause nuisance, there may be a breach of Article 8 and First Protocol, Article 1, unless compensation is paid'.

8.10.4   The effective nullification of planning permission without compensation

A local planning authority has power to revoke or modify planning permission which it has already granted to an applicant (s. 97 of the Town and Country Planning Act 1990). Where planning permission is revoked or modified, the Act provides for the payment of compensation and this is likely to be compatible with Convention rights. However there are instances, falling outside the ambit of s. 97, where planning permission is effectively nullified by the act of a public authority but for which no compensation is payable. This may raise the question of the compliance of the public authority's action with Convention rights. For example, in *R* v *Cardiff County Council, ex parte Sears Group Properties Limited* [1998] 3 PLR 55, planning permission was granted subject to the highway authority entering into a s. 278 agreement (s. 278 of the Highways Act 1980) in respect of the highway arrangements. There was a lapse of a number of years during which time, according to the highway authority, the traffic conditions at the roundabout affected by the proposed development had substantially deteriorated and as a result the highway authority decided to defer signing the s. 278 agreement until an updated traffic impact analysis had been submitted. The developers sought judicial review of the highway authority's decision since it effectively frustrated the grant of planning permission to them. The court upheld the decision of the highway authority on the basis that there had been a change of circumstances, after the planning permission had been granted, which justified the highway authority's resolution to review whether to enter into the s. 278 agreement. However, the court conceded that there is a strong presumption that where a public authority has made a formal decision which affects private rights, that decision will be binding on other public authorities directly involved, unless the presumption has been rebutted by a significant change in circumstances which undermines the basis of the original decision (see *R* v *Warwickshire County Council, ex parte Powergen* [1998] JPL 131).

Therefore in some cases where there has been a significant change in circumstances, it may be possible for a highway authority to frustrate a grant of planning permission by refusing to enter into a s. 278 agreement. If this occurs, it will amount to an interference by a public authority with a person's property rights without the payment of compensation. It is arguable that such action could be challenged under the HRA 1998 as infringing Article 1, Protocol 1. However, a victim, intending to challenge the act of a highway authority as incompatible with his or her Convention rights, should bear in mind the decision in *Pine Valley Developments Ltd and others* v *Ireland* (see Appendix 3). The applicants purchased land relying upon an existing grant of outline planning permission for industrial development. The outline planning permission was subsequently held by the Irish Supreme Court to be a nullity due to the fact that it was *ultra vires* the relevant legislation. Legislation was passed to validate retrospectively those planning permissions affected by the Irish Supreme Court's ruling; however, it did not apply to the applicants. The applicants submitted that they were victims of a violation of Article 1, Protocol 1, but the European Court rejected their allegation. The European Court found the annulment of the planning permission to be a control of use, within the scope of the third rule, which was justifiable on the facts. It pursued a legitimate aim and it satisfied the principle of proportionality. The fact that the applicants did not receive any compensation for the annulment of their planning permission did not upset the fair balance to be struck between the general interest of the community and the applicants' individual property rights, because of the inherent risk factor involved in speculative development. The European Court observed that: 'The applicants were engaged on a commercial venture which, by its very nature, involved an element of risk'. Compensation was not, therefore, necessary even though the planning permission had been annulled. A similar line of reasoning could be adopted by the English courts if a person alleged a violation of Convention rights reliant upon an act of a public authority which effectively frustrated the grant of planning permission without the payment of any compensation.

8.10.5   The exercise of administrative discretion in planning decisions

Corner suggests that 'the area of administrative discretion is likely to be the most important area for the impact of the Convention in Planning Law'.[43] The reason for this, he argues, is the fact that there is a potential tension between, on the one hand, current planning policy, which makes decisions in accordance with the public interest, and, on the other, the emphasis that Convention rights place on individual rights and freedoms. The case of *Westminster City Council* v *Great Portland Estates plc* [1985] AC 662 exemplifies the existing approach to the exercise of administrative discretion in planning decisions. In that case the council's industrial policy, set out in its district plan, provided for the protection of specific industrial activities. Great Portland Estates plc sought a declaration to quash those parts of the plan protecting the specified activities on the grounds that, in formulating the plan, the council had had regard to an irrelevant factor, namely the interests of individual occupiers. The House of Lords stated that the test of what is a material consideration in the preparation of local plans is, as in the grant or refusal of planning permission, whether it serves a planning purpose which relates to the character of the use of the land. Lord Scarman (at p. 670) emphasised the fact that the interests of private individuals are only relevant in exceptional circumstances:

> Personal circumstances of an occupier, personal hardship, the difficulties of businesses which are of value to the character of a community are not to be ignored in the administration of planning control. It would be inhuman pedantry to exclude from the control of our environment the human factor. The human factor is always present, of course, indirectly as the background to the consideration of the character of land use. It can, however, and sometimes should, be given direct effect as an exceptional or special circumstance. But such circumstances, when they arise, fall to be considered not as a general rule but as exceptions to a general rule to be met in special cases. If a planning authority is to give effect to them, a specific case has to be made and the planning authority must give reasons for accepting it.

It is likely that the impact of the HRA 1998 may be to induce a change in approach from this current approach, where the private interests of individuals are only relevant to planning decisions in exceptional circumstances, to a system in which local planning authorities will need to show that the relevant Convention rights have been taken into account in the exercise of their administrative discretion in planning decisions.

---

[43] Ibid., at p. 312.

Appendix One

Human Rights Act 1998

CHAPTER 42

ARRANGEMENT OF SECTIONS

Derogations and reservations

Judges of the European Court of Human Rights

Parliamentary procedure

Supplemental

HUMAN RIGHTS ACT 1998

1998 CHAPTER 42

An Act to give further effect to rights and freedoms guaranteed under the European Convention on Human Rights; to make provision with respect to holders of certain judicial offices who become judges of the European Court of Human Rights; and for connected purposes. [9th November 1998]

BE IT ENACTED by the Queen's most Excellent Majesty, by and with the advice and consent of the Lords Spiritual and Temporal, and Commons, in this present Parliament assembled, and by the authority of the same, as follows:—

Introduction

1. The Convention Rights

(1) In this Act 'the Convention rights' means the rights and fundamental freedoms set out in—

   (a)   Articles 2 to 12 and 14 of the Convention,

   (b)   Articles 1 to 3 of the First Protocol, and

   (c)   Articles 1 and 2 of the Sixth Protocol,

as read with Articles 16 to 18 of the Convention.

(2) Those Articles are to have effect for the purposes of this Act subject to any designated derogation or reservation (as to which see sections 14 and 15).

(3) The Articles are set out in Schedule 1.

(4) The Secretary of State may by order make such amendments to this Act as he considers appropriate to reflect the effect, in relation to the United Kingdom, of a protocol.

(5) In subsection (4) 'protocol' means a protocol to the Convention—

   (a)   which the United Kingdom has ratified; or

   (b)   which the United Kingdom has signed with a view to ratification.

(6) No amendment may be made by an order under subsection (4) so as to come into force before the protocol concerned is in force in relation to the United Kingdom.

2. Interpretation of Convention rights

(1) A court or tribunal determining a question which has arisen in connection with a Convention right must take into account any—

   (a)   judgment, decision, declaration or advisory opinion of the European Court of Human Rights,

   (b)   opinion of the Commission given in a report adopted under Article 31 of the Convention,

   (c)   decision of the Commission in connection with Article 26 or 27(2) of the Convention, or

(d)   decision of the Committee of Ministers taken under Article 46 of the Convention,

whenever made or given, so far as, in the opinion of the court or tribunal, it is relevant to the proceedings in which that question has arisen.

(2)   Evidence of any judgment, decision, declaration or opinion of which account may have to be taken under this section is to be given in proceedings before any court or tribunal in such manner as may be provided by rules.

(3)   In this section 'rules' means rules of court or, in the case of proceedings before a tribunal, rules made for the purposes of this section—

(a)   by the Lord Chancellor or the Secretary of State, in relation to any proceedings outside Scotland;

(b)   by the Secretary of State, in relation to proceedings in Scotland; or

(c)   by a Northern Ireland department, in relation to proceedings before a tribunal in Northern Ireland—

(i)   which deals with transferred matters; and

(ii)   for which no rules made under paragraph (a) are in force.

Legislation

3.   Interpretation of legislation

(1)   So far as it is possible to do so, primary legislation and subordinate legislation must be read and given effect in a way which is compatible with the Convention rights.

(2)   This section—

(a)   applies to primary legislation and subordinate legislation whenever enacted;

(b)   does not affect the validity, continuing operation or enforcement of any incompatible primary legislation; and

(c)   does not affect the validity, continuing operation or enforcement of any incompatible subordinate legislation if (disregarding any possibility of revocation) primary legislation prevents removal of the incompatibility.

4.   Declaration of incompatibility

(1)   Subsection (2) applies in any proceedings in which a court determines whether a provision of primary legislation is compatible with a Convention right.

(2)   If the court is satisfied that the provision is incompatible with a Convention right, it may make a declaration of that incompatibility.

(3)   Subsection (4) applies in any proceedings in which a court determines whether a provision of subordinate legislation, made in the exercise of a power conferred by primary legislation, is compatible with a Convention right.

(4)   If the court is satisfied—

(a)   that the provision is incompatible with a Convention right, and

(b)   that (disregarding any possibility of revocation) the primary legislation concerned prevents removal of the incompatibility, it may make a declaration of that incompatibility.

(5) In this section 'court' means—

(a) the House of Lords;

(b) the Judicial Committee of the Privy Council;

(c) the Courts-Martial Appeal Court;

(d) in Scotland, the High Court of Justiciary sitting otherwise than as a trial court or the Court of Session;

(e) in England and Wales or Northern Ireland, the High Court or the Court of Appeal.

(6) A declaration under this section ('a declaration of incompatibility')—

(a) does not affect the validity, continuing operation or enforcement of the provision in respect of which it is given; and

(b) is not binding on the parties to the proceedings in which it is made.

5. Right of Crown to intervene

(1) Where a court is considering whether to make a declaration of incompatibility, the Crown is entitled to notice in accordance with rules of court.

(2) In any case to which subsection (1) applies—

(a) a Minister of the Crown (or a person nominated by him),

(b) a member of the Scottish Executive,

(c) a Northern Ireland Minister,

(d) a Northern Ireland department,

is entitled, on giving notice in accordance with rules of court, to be joined as a party to the proceedings.

(3) Notice under subsection (2) may be given at any time during the proceedings.

(4) A person who has been made a party to criminal proceedings (other than in Scotland) as the result of a notice under subsection (2) may, with leave, appeal to the House of Lords against any declaration of incompatibility made in the proceedings.

(5) In subsection (4)—

'criminal proceedings' includes all proceedings before the Courts-Martial Appeal Court; and

'leave' means leave granted by the court making the declaration of incompatibility or by the House of Lords.

Public authorities

6. Acts of public authorities

(1) It is unlawful for a public authority to act in a way which is incompatible with a Convention right.

(2) Subsection (1) does not apply to an act if—

(a) as the result of one or more provisions of primary legislation, the authority could not have acted differently; or

(b)   in the case of one or more provisions of, or made under, primary legislation which cannot be read or given effect in a way which is compatible with the Convention rights, the authority was acting so as to give effect to or enforce those provisions.

(3)   In this section 'public authority' includes—

(a)   a court or tribunal, and

(b)   any person certain of whose functions are functions of a public nature, but does not include either House of Parliament or a person exercising functions in connection with proceedings in Parliament.

(4)   In subsection (3) 'Parliament' does not include the House of Lords in its judicial capacity.

(5)   In relation to a particular act, a person is not a public authority by virtue only of subsection (3)(b) if the nature of the act is private.

(6)   'An act' includes a failure to act but does not include a failure to—

(a)   introduce in, or lay before, Parliament a proposal for legislation; or

(b)   make any primary legislation or remedial order.

7.   Proceedings

(1)   A person who claims that a public authority has acted (or proposes to act) in a way which is made unlawful by section 6(1) may—

(a)   bring proceedings against the authority under this Act in the appropriate court or tribunal, or

(b)   rely on the Convention right or rights concerned in any legal proceedings,

but only if he is (or would be) a victim of the unlawful act.

(2)   In subsection (1)(a) 'appropriate court or tribunal' means such court or tribunal as may be determined in accordance with rules; and proceedings against an authority include a counterclaim or similar proceeding.

(3)   If the proceedings are brought on an application for judicial review, the applicant is to be taken to have a sufficient interest in relation to the unlawful act only if he is, or would be, a victim of that act.

(4)   If the proceedings are made by way of a petition for judicial review in Scotland, the applicant shall be taken to have title and interest to sue in relation to the unlawful act only if he is, or would be, a victim of that act.

(5)   Proceedings under subsection (1)(a) must be brought before the end of—

(a)   the period of one year beginning with the date on which the act complained of took place; or

(b)   such longer period as the court or tribunal considers equitable having regard to all the circumstances,

but that is subject to any rule imposing a stricter time limit in relation to the procedure in question.

(6)   In subsection (1)(b) 'legal proceedings' includes—

(a)   proceedings brought by or at the instigation of a public authority; and

(b)   an appeal against the decision of a court or tribunal.

(7)   For the purposes of this section, a person is a victim of an unlawful act only if he would be a victim for the purposes of Article 34 of the Convention if proceedings were brought in the European Court of Human Rights in respect of that act.

(8)   Nothing in this Act creates a criminal offence.

(9)   In this section 'rules' means—

(a)   in relation to proceedings before a court or tribunal outside Scotland, rules made by the Lord Chancellor or the Secretary of State for the purposes of this section or rules of court,

(b)   in relation to proceedings before a court or tribunal in Scotland, rules made by the Secretary of State for those purposes,

(c)   in relation to proceedings before a tribunal in Northern Ireland—

(i)   which deals with transferred matters; and

(ii)   for which no rules made under paragraph (a) are in force,

rules made by a Northern Ireland department for those purposes,

and includes provision made by order under section 1 of the Courts and Legal Services Act 1990.

(10)   In making rules, regard must be had to section 9.

(11)   The Minister who has power to make rules in relation to a particular tribunal may, to the extent he considers it necessary to ensure that the tribunal can provide an appropriate remedy in relation to an act (or proposed act) of a public authority which is (or would be) unlawful as a result of section 6(1), by order add to—

(a)   the relief or remedies which the tribunal may grant; or

(b)   the grounds on which it may grant any of them.

(12)   An order made under subsection (11) may contain such incidental, supplemental, consequential or transitional provision as the Minister making it considers appropriate.

(13)   'The Minister' includes the Northern Ireland department concerned.

8.   Judicial remedies

(1)   In relation to any act (or proposed act) of a public authority which the court finds is (or would be) unlawful, it may grant such relief or remedy, or make such order, within its powers as it considers just and appropriate.

(2)   But damages may be awarded only by a court which has power to award damages, or to order the payment of compensation, in civil proceedings.

(3)   No award of damages is to be made unless, taking account of all the circumstances of the case, including—

(a)   any other relief or remedy granted, or order made, in relation to the act in question (by that or any other court), and

(b)   the consequences of any decision (of that or any other court) in respect of that act,

the court is satisfied that the award is necessary to afford just satisfaction to the person in whose favour it is made.

(4)   In determining—

(a)   whether to award damages, or

(b)   the amount of an award,

the court must take into account the principles applied by the European Court of Human Rights in relation to the award of compensation under Article 41 of the Convention.

(5)   A public authority against which damages are awarded is to be treated—

(a)   in Scotland, for the purposes of section 3 of the Law Reform (Miscellaneous Provisions) (Scotland) Act 1940 as if the award were made in an action of damages in which the authority has been found liable in respect of loss or damage to the person to whom the award is made;

(b)   for the purposes of the Civil Liability (Contribution) Act 1978 as liable in respect of damage suffered by the person to whom the award is made.

(6)   In this section—

'court' includes a tribunal;

'damages' means damages for an unlawful act of a public authority; and

'unlawful' means unlawful under section 6(1).

9.   Judicial acts

(1)   Proceedings under section 7(1)(a) in respect of a judicial act may be brought only—

(a)   by exercising a right of appeal;

(b)   on an application (in Scotland a petition) for judicial review; or

(c)   in such other forum as may be prescribed by rules.

(2)   That does not affect any rule of law which prevents a court from being the subject of judicial review.

(3)   In proceedings under this Act in respect of a judicial act done in good faith, damages may not be awarded otherwise than to compensate a person to the extent required by Article 5(5) of the Convention.

(4)   An award of damages permitted by subsection (3) is to be made against the Crown; but no award may be made unless the appropriate person, if not a party to the proceedings, is joined.

(5)   In this section—

'appropriate person' means the Minister responsible for the court concerned, or a person or government department nominated by him;

'court' includes a tribunal;

'judge' includes a member of a tribunal, a justice of the peace and a clerk or other officer entitled to exercise the jurisdiction of a court;

'judicial act' means a judicial act of a court and includes an act done on the instructions, or on behalf, of a judge; and

'rules' has the same meaning as in section 7(9).

Remedial action

10. Power to take remedial action

(1) This section applies if—

(a) a provision of legislation has been declared under section 4 to be incompatible with a Convention right and, if an appeal lies—

(i) all persons who may appeal have stated in writing that they do not intend to do so;

(ii) the time for bringing an appeal has expired and no appeal has been brought within that time; or

(iii) an appeal brought within that time has been determined or abandoned; or

(b) it appears to a Minister of the Crown or Her Majesty in Council that, having regard to a finding of the European Court of Human Rights made after the coming into force of this section in proceedings against the United Kingdom, a provision of legislation is incompatible with an obligation of the United Kingdom arising from the Convention.

(2) If a Minister of the Crown considers that there are compelling reasons for proceeding under this section, he may by order make such amendments to the legislation as he considers necessary to remove the incompatibility.

(3) If, in the case of subordinate legislation, a Minister of the Crown considers—

(a) that it is necessary to amend the primary legislation under which the subordinate legislation in question was made, in order to enable the incompatibility to be removed, and

(b) that there are compelling reasons for proceeding under this section, he may by order make such amendments to the primary legislation as he considers necessary.

(4) This section also applies where the provision in question is in subordinate legislation and has been quashed, or declared invalid, by reason of incompatibility with a Convention right and the Minister proposes to proceed under paragraph 2(b) of Schedule 2.

(5) If the legislation is an Order in Council, the power conferred by subsection (2) or (3) is exercisable by Her Majesty in Council.

(6) In this section 'legislation' does not include a Measure of the Church Assembly or of the General Synod of the Church of England.

(7) Schedule 2 makes further provision about remedial orders.

Other rights and proceedings

11. Safeguard for existing human rights

A person's reliance on a Convention right does not restrict—

(a)   any other right or freedom conferred on him by or under any law having effect in any part of the United Kingdom; or

(b)   his right to make any claim or bring any proceedings which he could make or bring apart from sections 7 to 9.

12. Freedom of expression

(1)   This section applies if a court is considering whether to grant any relief which, if granted, might affect the exercise of the Convention right to freedom of expression.

(2)   If the person against whom the application for relief is made ('the respondent') is neither present nor represented, no such relief is to be granted unless the court is satisfied—

(a)   that the applicant has taken all practicable steps to notify the respondent; or

(b)   that there are compelling reasons why the respondent should not be notified.

(3)   No such relief is to be granted so as to restrain publication before trial unless the court is satisfied that the applicant is likely to establish that publication should not be allowed.

(4)   The court must have particular regard to the importance of the Convention right to freedom of expression and, where the proceedings relate to material which the respondent claims, or which appears to the court, to be journalistic, literary or artistic material (or to conduct connected with such material), to—

(a)   the extent to which—

(i)   the material has, or is about to, become available to the public; or

(ii)   it is, or would be, in the public interest for the material to be published;

(b)   any relevant privacy code.

(5)   In this section—

'court' includes a tribunal; and

'relief' includes any remedy or order (other than in criminal proceedings).

13. Freedom of thought, conscience and religion

(1)   If a court's determination of any question arising under this Act might affect the exercise by a religious organisation (itself or its members collectively) of the Convention right to freedom of thought, conscience and religion, it must have particular regard to the importance of that right.

(2)   In this section 'court' includes a tribunal.

Derogations and reservations

14. Derogations

(1)   In this Act 'designated derogation' means—

(a)   the United Kingdom's derogation from Article 5(3) of the Convention; and

(b)   any derogation by the United Kingdom from an Article of the Convention, or of any protocol to the Convention, which is designated for the purposes of this Act in an order made by the Secretary of State.

(2)   The derogation referred to in subsection (1)(a) is set out in Part I of Schedule 3.

(3)   If a designated derogation is amended or replaced it ceases to be a designated derogation.

(4)   But subsection (3) does not prevent the Secretary of State from exercising his power under subsection (1)(b) to make a fresh designation order in respect of the Article concerned.

(5)   The Secretary of State must by order make such amendments to Schedule 3 as he considers appropriate to reflect—

(a)   any designation order; or

(b)   the effect of subsection (3).

(6)   A designation order may be made in anticipation of the making by the United Kingdom of a proposed derogation.

15. Reservations

(1)   In this Act 'designated reservation' means—

(a)   the United Kingdom's reservation to Article 2 of the First Protocol to the Convention; and

(b)   any other reservation by the United Kingdom to an Article of the Convention, or of any protocol to the Convention, which is designated for the purposes of this Act in an order made by the Secretary of State.

(2)   The text of the reservation referred to in subsection (1)(a) is set out in Part 11 of Schedule 3.

(3)   If a designated reservation is withdrawn wholly or in part it ceases to be a designated reservation.

(4)   But subsection (3) does not prevent the Secretary of State from exercising his power under subsection (1)(b) to make a fresh designation order in respect of the Article concerned.

(5)   The Secretary of State must by order make such amendments to this Act as he considers appropriate to reflect—

(a)   any designation order; or

(b)   the effect of subsection (3).

16. Period for which designated derogations have effect

(1)   If it has not already been withdrawn by the United Kingdom, a designated derogation ceases to have effect for the purposes of this Act—

(a)   in the case of the derogation referred to in section 14(1)(a), at the end of the period of five years beginning with the date on which section 1(2) came into force;

(b)   in the case of any other derogation, at the end of the period of five years beginning with the date on which the order designating it was made.

(2)   At any time before the period—

(a)   fixed by subsection (1)(a) or (b), or

(b)   extended by an order under this subsection,

comes to an end, the Secretary of State may by order extend it by a further period of five years.

(3)   An order under section 14(1)(b) ceases to have effect at the end of the period for consideration, unless a resolution has been passed by each House approving the order.

(4)   Subsection (3) does not affect—

(a)   anything done in reliance on the order; or

(b)   the power to make a fresh order under section 14(1)(b).

(5)   In subsection (3) 'period for consideration' means the period of forty days beginning with the day on which the order was made.

(6)   In calculating the period for consideration, no account is to be taken of any time during which—

(a)   Parliament is dissolved or prorogued; or

(b)   both Houses are adjourned for more than four days.

(7)   If a designated derogation is withdrawn by the United Kingdom, the Secretary of State must by order make such amendments to this Act as he considers are required to reflect that withdrawal.

17. Periodic review of designated reservations

(1)   The appropriate Minister must review the designated reservation referred to in section 15(1)(a)—

(a)   before the end of the period of five years beginning with the date on which section 1(2) came into force; and

(b)   if that designation is still in force, before the end of the period of five years beginning with the date on which the last report relating to it was laid under subsection (3).

(2)   The appropriate Minister must review each of the other designated reservations (if any)—

(a)   before the end of the period of five years beginning with the date on which the order designating the reservation first came into force; and

(b)   if the designation is still in force, before the end of the period of five years beginning with the date on which the last report relating to it was laid under subsection (3).

(3)   The Minister conducting a review under this section must prepare a report on the result of the review and lay a copy of it before each House of Parliament.

Judges of the European Court of Human Rights

18.   Appointment to European Court of Human Rights

(1)   In this section 'judicial office' means the office of—

(a)   Lord Justice of Appeal, Justice of the High Court or Circuit judge, in England and Wales;

(b)   judge of the Court of Session or sheriff, in Scotland;

(c)   Lord Justice of Appeal, judge of the High Court or county court judge, in Northern Ireland.

(2)   The holder of a judicial office may become a judge of the European Court of Human Rights ('the Court') without being required to relinquish his office.

(3)   But he is not required to perform the duties of his judicial office while he is a judge of the Court.

(4)   In respect of any period during which he is a judge of the Court—

(a)   a Lord Justice of Appeal or Justice of the High Court is not to count as a judge of the relevant court for the purposes of section 2(1) or 4(1) of the Supreme Court Act 1981 (maximum number of judges) nor as a judge of the Supreme Court for the purposes of section 12(1) to (6) of that Act (salaries etc.);

(b)   a judge of the Court of Session is not to count as a judge of that court for the purposes of section 1(1) of the Court of Session Act 1988 (maximum number of judges) or of section 9(1)(c) of the Administration of Justice Act 1973 ('the 1973 Act') (salaries etc.);

(c)   a Lord Justice of Appeal or judge of the High Court in Northern Ireland is not to count as a judge of the relevant court for the purposes of section 2(1) or 3(1) of the Judicature (Northern Ireland) Act 1978 (maximum number of judges) nor as a judge of the Supreme Court of Northern Ireland for the purposes of section 9(1)(d) of the 1973 Act (salaries etc.);

(d)   a Circuit judge is not to count as such for the purposes of section 18 of the Courts Act 1971 (salaries etc.);

(e)   a sheriff is not to count as such for the purposes of section 14 of the Sheriff Courts (Scotland) Act 1907 (salaries etc.);

(f)   a county court judge of Northern Ireland is not to count as such for the purposes of section 106 of the County Courts Act (Northern Ireland) 1959 (salaries etc.).

(5)   If a sheriff principal is appointed a judge of the Court, section 11(1) of the Sheriff Courts (Scotland) Act 1971 (temporary appointment of sheriff principal) applies, while he holds that appointment, as if his office is vacant.

(6)   Schedule 4 makes provision about judicial pensions in relation to the holder of a judicial office who serves as a judge of the Court.

(7)   The Lord Chancellor or the Secretary of State may by order make such transitional provision (including, in particular, provision for a temporary increase in the maximum number of judges) as he considers appropriate in relation to any holder of a judicial office who has completed his service as a judge of the Court.

Parliamentary procedure

19.   Statements of compatibility

(1)   A Minister of the Crown in charge of a Bill in either House of Parliament must, before Second Reading of the Bill—

(a)   make a statement to the effect that in his view the provisions of the Bill are compatible with the Convention rights ('a statement of compatibility'); or

(b)   make a statement to the effect that although he is unable to make a statement of compatibility the government nevertheless wishes the House to proceed with the Bill.

(2)   The statement must be in writing and be published in such manner as the Minister making it considers appropriate.

Supplemental

20.   Orders etc. under this Act

(1)   Any power of a Minister of the Crown to make an order under this Act is exercisable by statutory instrument.

(2)   The power of the Lord Chancellor or the Secretary of State to make rules (other than rules of court) under section 2(3) or 7(9) is exercisable by statutory instrument.

(3)   Any statutory instrument made under section 14, 15 or 16(7) must be laid before Parliament.

(4)   No order may be made by the Lord Chancellor or the Secretary of State under section 1(4), 7(11) or 16(2) unless a draft of the order has been laid before, and approved by, each House of Parliament.

(5)   Any statutory instrument made under section 18(7) or Schedule 4, or to which subsection (2) applies, shall be subject to annulment in pursuance of a resolution of either House of Parliament.

(6)   The power of a Northern Ireland department to make—

(a)   rules under section 2(3)(c) or 7(9)(c), or

(b)   an order under section 7(11),

is exercisable by statutory rule for the purposes of the Statutory Rules (Northern Ireland) Order 1979.

(7) Any rules made under section 2(3)(c) or 7(9)(c) shall be subject to negative resolution; and section 41(6) of the Interpretation Act (Northern Ireland) 1954 (meaning of 'subject to negative resolution') shall apply as if the power to make the rules were conferred by an Act of the Northern Ireland Assembly.

(8) No order may be made by a Northern Ireland department under section 7(11) unless a draft of the order has been laid before, and approved by, the Northern Ireland Assembly.

21. Interpretation etc.

(1) In this Act—

'amend' includes repeal and apply (with or without modifications);

'the appropriate Minister' means the Minister of the Crown having charge of the appropriate authorised government department (within the meaning of the Crown Proceedings Act 1947);

'the Commission' means the European Commission of Human Rights;

'the Convention' means the Convention for the Protection of Human Rights and Fundamental Freedoms, agreed by the Council of Europe at Rome on 4th November 1950 as it has effect for the time being in relation to the United Kingdom;

'declaration of incompatibility' means a declaration under section 4;

'Minister of the Crown' has the same meaning as in the Ministers of the Crown Act 1975;

'Northern Ireland Minister' includes the First Minister and the deputy First Minister in Northern Ireland;

'primary legislation' means any—

    (a) public general Act;

    (b) local and personal Act;

    (c) private Act;

    (d) Measure of the Church Assembly;

    (e) Measure of the General Synod of the Church of England;

    (f) Order in Council—

        (i) made in exercise of Her Majesty's Royal Prerogative;

        (ii) made under section 38(1)(a) of the Northern Ireland Constitution Act 1973 or the corresponding provision of the Northern Ireland Act 1998; or

        (iii) amending an Act of a kind mentioned in paragraph (a), (b) or (c);

and includes an order or other instrument made under primary legislation (otherwise than by the National Assembly for Wales, a member of the Scottish Executive, a Northern Ireland Minister or a Northern Ireland department) to the extent to which it operates to bring one or more provisions of that legislation into force or amends any primary legislation;

'the First Protocol' means the protocol to the Convention agreed at Paris on 20th March 1952;

'the Sixth Protocol' means the protocol to the Convention agreed at Strasbourg on 28th April 1983;

'the Eleventh Protocol' means the protocol to the Convention (restructuring the control machinery established by the Convention) agreed at Strasbourg on 11th May 1994;

'remedial order' means an order under section 10;

'subordinate legislation' means any—

(a)   Order in Council other than one—

(i)   made in exercise of Her Majesty's Royal Prerogative;

(ii)   made under section 38(1)(a) of the Northern Ireland Constitution Act 1973 or the corresponding provision of the Northern Ireland Act 1998; or

(iii)   amending an Act of a kind mentioned in the definition of primary legislation;

(b)   Act of the Scottish Parliament;

(c)   Act of the Parliament of Northern Ireland;

(d)   Measure of the Assembly established under section 1 of the Northern Ireland Assembly Act 1973;

(e)   Act of the Northern Ireland Assembly;

(f)   order, rules, regulations, scheme, warrant, byelaw or other instrument made under primary legislation (except to the extent to which it operates to bring one or more provisions of that legislation into force or amends any primary legislation);

(g)   order, rules, regulations, scheme, warrant, byelaw or other instrument made under legislation mentioned in paragraph (b), (c), (d) or (e) or made under an Order in Council applying only to Northern Ireland;

(h)   order, rules, regulations, scheme, warrant, byelaw or other instrument made by a member of the Scottish Executive, a Northern Ireland Minister or a Northern Ireland department in exercise of prerogative or other executive functions of Her Majesty which are exercisable by such a person on behalf of Her Majesty;

'transferred matters' has the same meaning as in the Northern Ireland Act 1998; and

'tribunal' means any tribunal in which legal proceedings may be brought.

(2)   The references in paragraphs (b) and (c) of section 2(1) to Articles are to Articles of the Convention as they had effect immediately before the coming into force of the Eleventh Protocol.

(3)   The reference in paragraph (d) of section 2(1) to Article 46 includes a reference to Articles 32 and 54 of the Convention as they had effect immediately before the coming into force of the Eleventh Protocol.

(4)   The references in section 2(1) to a report or decision of the Commission or a decision of the Committee of Ministers include references to a report or

decision made as provided by paragraphs 3, 4 and 6 of Article 5 of the Eleventh Protocol (transitional provisions).

(5) Any liability under the Army Act 1955, the Air Force Act 1955 or the Naval Discipline Act 1957 to suffer death for an offence is replaced by a liability to imprisonment for life or any less punishment authorised by those Acts; and those Acts shall accordingly have effect with the necessary modifications.

22. Short title, commencement, application and extent

(1) This Act may be cited as the Human Rights Act 1998.

(2) Sections 18, 20 and 21(5) and this section come into force on the passing of this Act.

(3) The other provisions of this Act come into force on such day as the Secretary of State may by order appoint; and different days may be appointed for different purposes.

(4) Paragraph (b) of subsection (1) of section 7 applies to proceedings brought by or at the instigation of a public authority whenever the act in question took place; but otherwise that subsection does not apply to an act taking place before the coming into force of that section.

(5) This Act binds the Crown.

(6) This Act extends to Northern Ireland.

(7) Section 21(5), so far as it relates to any provision contained in the Army Act 1955, the Air Force Act 1955 or the Naval Discipline Act 1957, extends to any place to which that provision extends.

SCHEDULES

Section 1(3)

SCHEDULE 1
THE ARTICLES

PART I
THE CONVENTION

RIGHTS AND FREEDOMS

Article 2
Right to life

1. Everyone's right to life shall be protected by law. No one shall be deprived of his life intentionally save in the execution of a sentence of a court following his conviction of a crime for which this penalty is provided by law.

2. Deprivation of life shall not be regarded as inflicted in contravention of this Article when it results from the use of force which is no more than absolutely necessary:

(a) in defence of any person from unlawful violence;

(b) in order to effect a lawful arrest or to prevent the escape of a person lawfully detained;

(c) in action lawfully taken for the purpose of quelling a riot or insurrection.

Article 3
Prohibition of torture

No one shall be subjected to torture or to inhuman or degrading treatment or punishment.

Article 4
Prohibition of slavery and forced labour

1. No one shall be held in slavery or servitude.

2. No one shall be required to perform forced or compulsory labour.

3. For the purpose of this Article the term 'forced or compulsory labour' shall not include:

(a) any work required to be done in the ordinary course of detention imposed according to the provisions of Article 5 of this Convention or during conditional release from such detention;

(b) any service of a military character or, in case of conscientious objectors in countries where they are recognised, service exacted instead of compulsory military service;

(c) any service exacted in case of an emergency or calamity threatening the life or well-being of the community;

(d) any work or service which forms part of normal civic obligations.

Article 5
Right to liberty and security

1. Everyone has the right to liberty and security of person. No one shall be deprived of his liberty save in the following cases and in accordance with a procedure prescribed by law:

(a) the lawful detention of a person after conviction by a competent court;

(b) the lawful arrest or detention of a person for non-compliance with the lawful order of a court or in order to secure the fulfilment of any obligation prescribed by law;

(c) the lawful arrest or detention of a person effected for the purpose of bringing him before the competent legal authority on reasonable suspicion of having committed an offence or when it is reasonably considered necessary to prevent his committing an offence or fleeing after having done so;

(d) the detention of a minor by lawful order for the purpose of educational supervision or his lawful detention for the purpose of bringing him before the competent legal authority;

(e)   the lawful detention of persons for the prevention of the spreading of infectious diseases, of persons of unsound mind, alcoholics or drug addicts or vagrants;

(f)   the lawful arrest or detention of a person to prevent his effecting an unauthorised entry into the country or of a person against whom action is being taken with a view to deportation or extradition.

2.   Everyone who is arrested shall be informed promptly, in a language which he understands, of the reasons for his arrest and of any charge against him.

3.   Everyone arrested or detained in accordance with the provisions of paragraph 1(c) of this Article shall be brought promptly before a judge or other officer authorised by law to exercise judicial power and shall be entitled to trial within a reasonable time or to release pending trial. Release may be conditioned by guarantees to appear for trial.

4.   Everyone who is deprived of his liberty by arrest or detention shall be entitled to take proceedings by which the lawfulness of his detention shall be decided speedily by a court and his release ordered if the detention is not lawful.

5.   Everyone who has been the victim of arrest or detention in contravention of the provisions of this Article shall have an enforceable right to compensation.

Article 6
Right to a fair trial

1.   In the determination of his civil rights and obligations or of any criminal charge against him, everyone is entitled to a fair and public hearing within a reasonable time by an independent and impartial tribunal established by law. Judgment shall be pronounced publicly but the press and public may be excluded from all or part of the trial in the interest of morals, public order or national security in a democratic society, where the interests of juveniles or the protection of the private life of the parties so require, or to the extent strictly necessary in the opinion of the court in special circumstances where publicity would prejudice the interests of justice.

2.   Everyone charged with a criminal offence shall be presumed innocent until proved guilty according to law.

3.   Everyone charged with a criminal offence has the following minimum rights:

(a)   to be informed promptly, in a language which he understands and in detail, of the nature and cause of the accusation against him;

(b)   to have adequate time and facilities for the preparation of his defence;

(c)   to defend himself in person or through legal assistance of his own choosing or, if he has not sufficient means to pay for legal assistance, to be given it free when the interests of justice so require;

(d)   to examine or have examined witnesses against him and to obtain the attendance and examination of witnesses on his behalf under the same conditions as witnesses against him;

(e)   to have the free assistance of an interpreter if he cannot understand or speak the language used in court.

Article 7
No punishment without law

1.   No one shall be held guilty of any criminal offence on account of any act or omission which did not constitute a criminal offence under national or international law at the time when it was committed. Nor shall a heavier penalty be imposed than the one that was applicable at the time the criminal offence was committed.

2.   This Article shall not prejudice the trial and punishment of any person for any act or omission which, at the time when it was committed, was criminal according to the general principles of law recognised by civilised nations.

Article 8
Right to respect for private and family life

1.   Everyone has the right to respect for his private and family life, his home and his correspondence.

2.   There shall be no interference by a public authority with the exercise of this right except such as is in accordance with the law and is necessary in a democratic society in the interests of national security, public safety or the economic well being of the country, for the prevention of disorder or crime, for the protection of health or morals, or for the protection of the rights and freedoms of others.

Article 9
Freedom of thought, conscience and religion

1.   Everyone has the right to freedom of thought, conscience and religion; this right includes freedom to change his religion or belief and freedom, either alone or in community with others and in public or private, to manifest his religion or belief, in worship, teaching, practice and observance.

2.   Freedom to manifest one's religion or beliefs shall be subject only to such limitations as are prescribed by law and are necessary in a democratic society in the interests of public safety, for the protection of public order, health or morals, or for the protection of the rights and freedoms of others.

Article 10
Freedom of expression

1.   Everyone has the right to freedom of expression. This right shall include freedom to hold opinions and to receive and impart information and ideas without interference by public authority and regardless of frontiers. This Article shall not prevent States from requiring the licensing of broadcasting, television or cinema enterprises.

2. The exercise of these freedoms, since it carries with it duties and responsibilities, may be subject to such formalities, conditions, restrictions or penalties as are prescribed by law and are necessary in a democratic society, in the interests of national security, territorial integrity or public safety, for the prevention of disorder or crime, for the protection of health or morals, for the protection of the reputation or rights of others, for preventing the disclosure of information received in confidence, or for maintaining the authority and impartiality of the judiciary.

Article 11
Freedom of assembly and association

1. Everyone has the right to freedom of peaceful assembly and to freedom of association with others, including the right to form and to join trade unions for the protection of his interests.

2. No restrictions shall be placed on the exercise of these rights other than such as are prescribed by law and are necessary in a democratic society in the interests of national security or public safety, for the prevention of disorder or crime, for the protection of health or morals or for the protection of the rights and freedoms of others. This Article shall not prevent the imposition of lawful restrictions on the exercise of these rights by members of the armed forces, of the police or of the administration of the State.

Article 12
Right to marry

Men and women of marriageable age have the right to marry and to found a family, according to the national laws governing the exercise of this right.

Article 14
Prohibition of discrimination

The enjoyment of the rights and freedoms set forth in this Convention shall be secured without discrimination on any ground such as sex, race, colour, language, religion, political or other opinion, national or social origin, association with a national minority, property, birth or other status.

Article 16
Restrictions on political activity of aliens

Nothing in Articles 10, 11 and 14 shall be regarded as preventing the High Contracting Parties from imposing restrictions on the political activity of aliens.

Article 17
Prohibition of abuse of rights

Nothing in this Convention may be interpreted as implying for any State, group or person any right to engage in any activity or perform any act aimed at the destruction of any of the rights and freedoms set forth herein or at their limitation to a greater extent than is provided for in the Convention.

Article 18
Limitation on use of restrictions on rights

The restrictions permitted under this Convention to the said rights and freedoms shall not be applied for any purpose other than those for which they have been prescribed.

PART II
THE FIRST PROTOCOL

Article 1
Protection of property

Every natural or legal person is entitled to the peaceful enjoyment of his possessions. No one shall be deprived of his possessions except in the public interest and subject to the conditions provided for by law and by the general principles of international law.

The preceding provisions shall not, however, in any way impair the right of a State to enforce such laws as it deems necessary to control the use of property in accordance with the general interest or to secure the payment of taxes or other contributions or penalties.

Article 2
Right to education

No person shall be denied the right to education. In the exercise of any functions which it assumes in relation to education and to teaching, the State shall respect the right of parents to ensure such education and teaching in conformity with their own religious and philosophical convictions.

Article 3
Right to free elections

The High Contracting Parties undertake to hold free elections at reasonable intervals by secret ballot, under conditions which will ensure the free expression of the opinion of the people in the choice of the legislature.

PART III
THE SIXTH PROTOCOL

Article 1
Abolition of the death penalty

The death penalty shall be abolished. No one shall be condemned to such penalty or executed.

Article 2
Death penalty in time of war

A State may make provision in its law for the death penalty in respect of acts committed in time of war or of imminent threat of war; such penalty shall be applied only in the instances laid down in the law and in accordance with its provisions. The State shall communicate to the Secretary General of the Council of Europe the relevant provisions of that law.

SCHEDULE 2
REMEDIAL ORDERS

Orders

1.—(1)   A remedial order may—

(a)   contain such incidental, supplemental, consequential or transitional provision as the person making it considers appropriate;

(b)   be made so as to have effect from a date earlier than that on which it is made;

(c)   make provision for the delegation of specific functions;

(d)   make different provision for different cases.

(2)   The power conferred by sub-paragraph (1)(a) includes—

(a)   power to amend primary legislation (including primary legislation other than that which contains the incompatible provision); and

(b)   power to amend or revoke subordinate legislation (including subordinate legislation other than that which contains the incompatible provision).

(3)   A remedial order may be made so as to have the same extent as the legislation which it affects.

(4)   No person is to be guilty of an offence solely as a result of the retrospective effect of a remedial order.

Procedure

2.   No remedial order may be made unless—

(a)   a draft of the order has been approved by a resolution of each House of Parliament made after the end of the period of 60 days beginning with the day on which the draft was laid; or

(b)   it is declared in the order that it appears to the person making it that, because of the urgency of the matter, it is necessary to make the order without a draft being so approved.

Orders laid in draft

3.—(1)   No draft may be laid under paragraph 2(a) unless—

(a)   the person proposing to make the order has laid before Parliament a document which contains a draft of the proposed order and the required information; and

(b)   the period of 60 days, beginning with the day on which the document required by this sub-paragraph was laid, has ended.

(2)   If representations have been made during that period, the draft laid under paragraph 2(a) must be accompanied by a statement containing—

(a)   a summary of the representations; and

(b)   if, as a result of the representations, the proposed order has been changed, details of the changes.

Urgent cases

4.—(1)   If a remedial order ('the original order') is made without being approved in draft, the person making it must lay it before Parliament, accompanied by the required information, after it is made.

(2)   If representations have been made during the period of 60 days beginning with the day on which the original order was made, the person making it must (after the end of that period) lay before Parliament a statement containing—

(a)   a summary of the representations; and

(b)   if, as a result of the representations, he considers it appropriate to make changes to the original order, details of the changes.

(3)   If sub-paragraph (2)(b) applies, the person making the statement must—

(a)   make a further remedial order replacing the original order; and

(b)   lay the replacement order before Parliament.

(4)   If, at the end of the period of 120 days beginning with the day on which the original order was made, a resolution has not been passed by each House approving the original or replacement order, the order ceases to have effect (but without that affecting anything previously done under either order or the power to make a fresh remedial order).

Definitions

5.   In this Schedule—

'representations' means representations about a remedial order (or proposed remedial order) made to the person making (or proposing to make) it and includes any relevant Parliamentary report or resolution; and

'required information' means—

(a)   an explanation of the incompatibility which the order (or proposed order) seeks to remove, including particulars of the relevant declaration, finding or order; and

(b)   a statement of the reasons for proceeding under section 10 and for making an order in those terms.

Calculating periods

6.   In calculating any period for the purposes of this Schedule, no account is to be taken of any time during which—

(a)   Parliament is dissolved or prorogued; or

(b)   both Houses are adjourned for more than four days.

SCHEDULE 3
DEROGATION AND RESERVATION

PART I
DEROGATION

The 1988 notification

The United Kingdom Permanent Representative to the Council of Europe presents his compliments to the Secretary General of the Council, and has the honour to convey the following information in order to ensure compliance with the obligations of Her Majesty's Government in the United Kingdom under Article 15(3) of the Convention for the Protection of Human Rights and Fundamental Freedoms signed at Rome on 4 November 1950.

There have been in the United Kingdom in recent years campaigns of organised terrorism connected with the affairs of Northern Ireland which have manifested themselves in activities which have included repeated murder, attempted murder, maiming, intimidation and violent civil disturbance and in bombing and fire raising which have resulted in death, injury and widespread destruction of property. As a result, a public emergency within the meaning of Article 15(1) of the Convention exists in the United Kingdom.

The Government found it necessary in 1974 to introduce and since then, in cases concerning persons reasonably suspected of involvement in terrorism connected with the affairs of Northern Ireland, or of certain offences under the legislation, who have been detained for 48 hours, to exercise powers enabling further detention without charge, for periods of up to five days, on the authority of the Secretary of State. These powers are at present to be found in Section 12 of the Prevention of Terrorism (Temporary Provisions) Act 1984, Article 9 of the Prevention of Terrorism (Supplemental Temporary Provisions) Order 1984 and Article 10 of the Prevention of Terrorism (Supplemental Temporary Provisions) (Northern Ireland) Order 1984.

Section 12 of the Prevention of Terrorism (Temporary Provisions) Act 1984 provides for a person whom a constable has arrested on reasonable grounds of suspecting him to be guilty of an offence under Section 1, 9 or 10 of the Act, or to be or to have been involved in terrorism connected with the affairs of Northern Ireland, to be detained in right of the arrest for up to 48 hours and thereafter, where the Secretary of State extends the detention period, for up to a further five days. Section 12 substantially re-enacted Section 12 of the Prevention of Terrorism (Temporary Provisions) Act 1976 which, in turn, substantially re-enacted Section 7 of the Prevention of Terrorism (Temporary Provisions) Act 1974.

Article 10 of the Prevention of Terrorism (Supplemental Temporary Provisions) (Northern Ireland) Order 1984 (SI 1984/417) and Article 9 of the Prevention of Terrorism (Supplemental Temporary Provisions) Order 1984 (SI 1984/418) were both made under Sections 13 and 14 of and Schedule 3 to the 1984 Act and substantially re-enacted powers of detention in Orders made under the 1974 and 1976 Acts. A person who is being examined under Article 4 of either Order on his arrival in, or on seeking to leave, Northern Ireland or Great Britain for the purpose of determining whether he is or has been involved in terrorism connected with the affairs of Northern Ireland, or whether there are grounds for suspecting that he has committed an offence under Section 9 of the 1984 Act, may be detained under Article 9 or 10, as appropriate, pending the conclusion of his examination. The period of this examination may exceed 12 hours if an examining officer has reasonable grounds for suspecting him to be or to have been involved in acts of terrorism connected with the affairs of Northern Ireland.

Where such a person is detained under the said Article 9 or 10 he may be detained for up to 48 hours on the authority of an examining officer and thereafter, where the Secretary of State extends the detention period, for up to a further five days.

In its judgment of 29 November 1988 in the Case of *Brogan and Others*, the European Court of Human Rights held that there had been a violation of Article 5(3) in respect of each of the applicants, all of whom had been detained under Section 12 of the 1984 Act. The Court held that even the shortest of the four periods of detention concerned, namely four days and six hours, fell outside the constraints as to time permitted by the first part of Article 5(3). In addition, the Court held that there had been a violation of Article 5(5) in the case of each applicant.

Following this judgment, the Secretary of State for the Home Department informed Parliament on 6 December 1988 that, against the background of the terrorist campaign, and the over-riding need to bring terrorists to justice, the Government did not believe that the maximum period of detention should be reduced. He informed Parliament that the Government were examining the matter with a view to responding to the judgment. On 22 December 1988, the Secretary of State further informed Parliament that it remained the Government's wish, if it could be achieved, to find a judicial process under which extended detention might be reviewed and where appropriate authorised by a judge or other judicial officer. But a further period of reflection and consultation was necessary before the Government could bring forward a firm and final view.

Since the judgment of 29 November 1988 as well as previously, the Government have found it necessary to continue to exercise, in relation to terrorism connected with the affairs of Northern Ireland, the powers described above enabling further detention without charge for periods of up to 5 days, on the authority of the Secretary of State, to the extent strictly required by the exigencies of the situation to enable necessary enquiries and investigations properly to be completed in order to decide whether criminal proceedings should be instituted. To the extent that the exercise of these powers may be inconsistent with the obligations imposed by the Convention the Government has availed itself of the right of derogation conferred by Article 15(1) of the Convention and will continue to do so until further notice.

Dated 23 December 1988.

The 1989 notification

The United Kingdom Permanent Representative to the Council of Europe presents his compliments to the Secretary General of the Council, and has the honour to convey the following information.

In his communication to the Secretary General of 23 December 1988, reference was made to the introduction and exercise of certain powers under section 12 of the Prevention of Terrorism (Temporary Provisions) Act 1984, Article 9 of the Prevention of Terrorism (Supplemental Temporary Provisions) Order 1984 and Article 10 of the Prevention of Terrorism (Supplemental Temporary Provisions) (Northern Ireland) Order 1984.

These provisions have been replaced by section 14 of and paragraph 6 of Schedule 5 to the Prevention of Terrorism (Temporary Provisions) Act 1989, which make comparable provision. They came into force on 22 March 1989. A copy of these provisions is enclosed.

The United Kingdom Permanent Representative avails himself of this opportunity to renew to the Secretary General the assurance of his highest consideration.

23 March 1989.

PART II
RESERVATION

At the time of signing the present (First) Protocol, I declare that, in view of certain provisions of the Education Acts in the United Kingdom, the principle affirmed in the second sentence of Article 2 is accepted by the United Kingdom only so far as it is compatible with the provision of efficient instruction and training, and the avoidance of unreasonable public expenditure.

Dated 20 March 1952. Made by the United Kingdom Permanent Representative to the Council of Europe.

SCHEDULE 4
JUDICIAL PENSIONS

Duty to make orders about pensions

1.—(1)   The appropriate Minister must by order make provision with respect to pensions payable to or in respect of any holder of a judicial office who serves as an ECHR judge.

(2)   A pensions order must include such provision as the Minister making it considers is necessary to secure that—

(a)   an ECHR judge who was, immediately before his appointment as an ECHR judge, a member of a judicial pension scheme is entitled to remain as a member of that scheme;

(b)   the terms on which he remains a member of the scheme are those which would have been applicable had he not been appointed as an ECHR judge; and

(c)   entitlement to benefits payable in accordance with the scheme continues to be determined as if, while serving as an ECHR judge, his salary was that which would (but for section 18(4)) have been payable to him in respect of his continuing service as the holder of his judicial office.

Contributions

2.   A pensions order may, in particular, make provision—

(a)   for any contributions which are payable by a person who remains a member of a scheme as a result of the order, and which would otherwise be payable by deduction from his salary, to be made otherwise than by deduction from his salary as an ECHR judge; and

(b)   for such contributions to be collected in such manner as may be determined by the administrators of the scheme.

Amendments of other enactments

3.   A pensions order may amend any provision of, or made under, a pensions Act in such manner and to such extent as the Minister making the order considers necessary or expedient to ensure the proper administration of any scheme to which it relates.

Definitions

4.   In this Schedule—

'appropriate Minister' means—

(a)   in relation to any judicial office whose jurisdiction is exercisable exclusively in relation to Scotland, the Secretary of State; and

(b)   otherwise, the Lord Chancellor;

'ECHR judge' means the holder of a judicial office who is serving as a judge of the Court;

'judicial pension scheme' means a scheme established by and in accordance with a pensions Act;

'pensions Act means—

(a)   the County Courts Act (Northern Ireland) 1959;

(b)   the Sheriffs' Pensions (Scotland) Act 1961;

(c)   the Judicial Pensions Act 1981; or

(d)   the Judicial Pensions and Retirement Act 1993; and

'pensions order' means an order made under paragraph 1.

Appendix Two

European Convention on Human Rights

CONVENTION FOR THE PROTECTION OF HUMAN RIGHTS AND
FUNDAMENTAL FREEDOMS AS AMENDED BY PROTOCOL NO. 11
(Date of entry into force 1 November 1998)

The governments signatory hereto, being members of the Council of Europe,

Considering the Universal Declaration of Human Rights proclaimed by the General Assembly of the United Nations on 10th December 1948;

Considering that this Declaration aims at securing the universal and effective recognition and observance of the Rights therein declared;

Considering that the aim of the Council of Europe is the achievement of greater unity between its members and that one of the methods by which that aim is to be pursued is the maintenance and further realisation of human rights and fundamental freedoms;

Reaffirming their profound belief in those fundamental freedoms which are the foundation of justice and peace in the world and are best maintained on the one hand by an effective political democracy and on the other by a common understanding and observance of the human rights upon which they depend;

Being resolved, as the governments of European countries which are like-minded and have a common heritage of political traditions, ideals, freedom and the rule of law, to take the first steps for the collective enforcement of certain of the rights stated in the Universal Declaration,

Have agreed as follows:

Article 1
Obligation to respect human rights

The High Contracting Parties shall secure to everyone within their jurisdiction the rights and freedoms defined in Section I of this Convention.

Section I — Rights and freedoms

Article 2
Right to life

1 Everyone's right to life shall be protected by law. No one shall be deprived of his life intentionally save in the execution of a sentence of a court following his conviction of a crime for which this penalty is provided by law.

2 Deprivation of life shall not be regarded as inflicted in contravention of this article when it results from the use of force which is no more than absolutely necessary:

a in defence of any person from unlawful violence;

b in order to effect a lawful arrest or to prevent the escape of a person lawfully detained;

c in action lawfully taken for the purpose of quelling a riot or insurrection.

Article 3
Prohibition of torture

No one shall be subjected to torture or to inhuman or degrading treatment or punishment.

Article 4
Prohibition of slavery and forced labour

1 No one shall be held in slavery or servitude.

2 No one shall be required to perform forced or compulsory labour.

3 For the purpose of this article the term 'forced or compulsory labour' shall not include:

a any work required to be done in the ordinary course of detention imposed according to the provisions of Article 5 of this Convention or during conditional release from such detention;

b any service of a military character or, in case of conscientious objectors in countries where they are recognised, service exacted instead of compulsory military service;

c any service exacted in case of an emergency or calamity threatening the life or well-being of the community;

d any work or service which forms part of normal civic obligations.

Article 5
Right to liberty and security

1 Everyone has the right to liberty and security of person. No one shall be deprived of his liberty save in the following cases and in accordance with a procedure prescribed by law:

a the lawful detention of a person after conviction by a competent court;

b   the lawful arrest or detention of a person for non-compliance with the lawful order of a court or in order to secure the fulfilment of any obligation prescribed by law;

c   the lawful arrest or detention of a person effected for the purpose of bringing him before the competent legal authority on reasonable suspicion of having committed an offence or when it is reasonably considered necessary to prevent his committing an offence or fleeing after having done so;

d   the detention of a minor by lawful order for the purpose of educational supervision or his lawful detention for the purpose of bringing him before the competent legal authority;

e   the lawful detention of persons for the prevention of the spreading of infectious diseases, of persons of unsound mind, alcoholics or drug addicts or vagrants;

f   the lawful arrest or detention of a person to prevent his effecting an unauthorised entry into the country or of a person against whom action is being taken with a view to deportation or extradition.

2   Everyone who is arrested shall be informed promptly, in a language which he understands, of the reasons for his arrest and of any charge against him.

3   Everyone arrested or detained in accordance with the provisions of paragraph 1.c of this article shall be brought promptly before a judge or other officer authorised by law to exercise judicial power and shall be entitled to trial within a reasonable time or to release pending trial. Release may be conditioned by guarantees to appear for trial.

4   Everyone who is deprived of his liberty by arrest or detention shall be entitled to take proceedings by which the lawfulness of his detention shall be decided speedily by a court and his release ordered if the detention is not lawful.

5   Everyone who has been the victim of arrest or detention in contravention of the provisions of this article shall have an enforceable right to compensation.

Article 6
Right to a fair trial

1   In the determination of his civil rights and obligations or of any criminal charge against him, everyone is entitled to a fair and public hearing within a reasonable time by an independent and impartial tribunal established by law. Judgment shall be pronounced publicly but the press and public may be excluded from all or part of the trial in the interests of morals, public order or national security in a democratic society, where the interests of juveniles or the protection of the private life of the parties so require, or to the extent strictly necessary in the opinion of the court in special circumstances where publicity would prejudice the interests of justice.

2   Everyone charged with a criminal offence shall be presumed innocent until proved guilty according to law.

3   Everyone charged with a criminal offence has the following minimum rights:

a   to be informed promptly, in a language which he understands and in detail, of the nature and cause of the accusation against him;

b   to have adequate time and facilities for the preparation of his defence;

c   to defend himself in person or through legal assistance of his own choosing or, if he has not sufficient means to pay for legal assistance, to be given it free when the interests of justice so require;

d   to examine or have examined witnesses against him and to obtain the attendance and examination of witnesses on his behalf under the same conditions as witnesses against him;

e   to have the free assistance of an interpreter if he cannot understand or speak the language used in court.

Article 7
No punishment without law

1   No one shall be held guilty of any criminal offence on account of any act or omission which did not constitute a criminal offence under national or international law at the time when it was committed. Nor shall a heavier penalty be imposed than the one that was applicable at the time the criminal offence was committed.

2   This article shall not prejudice the trial and punishment of any person for any act or omission which, at the time when it was committed, was criminal according to the general principles of law recognised by civilised nations.

Article 8
Right to respect for private and family life

1   Everyone has the right to respect for his private and family life, his home and his correspondence.

2   There shall be no interference by a public authority with the exercise of this right except such as is in accordance with the law and is necessary in a democratic society in the interests of national security, public safety or the economic well-being of the country, for the prevention of disorder or crime, for the protection of health or morals, or for the protection of the rights and freedoms of others.

Article 9
Freedom of thought, conscience and religion

1   Everyone has the right to freedom of thought, conscience and religion; this right includes freedom to change his religion or belief and freedom, either alone or in community with others and in public or private, to manifest his religion or belief, in worship, teaching, practice and observance.

2   Freedom to manifest one's religion or beliefs shall be subject only to such limitations as are prescribed by law and are necessary in a democratic society in the interests of public safety, for the protection of public order, health or morals, or for the protection of the rights and freedoms of others.

Article 10
Freedom of expression

1   Everyone has the right to freedom of expression. This right shall include freedom to hold opinions and to receive and impart information and ideas without interference by public authority and regardless of frontiers. This article shall not prevent States from requiring the licensing of broadcasting, television or cinema enterprises.

2   The exercise of these freedoms, since it carries with it duties and responsibilities, may be subject to such formalities, conditions, restrictions or penalties as are prescribed by law and are necessary in a democratic society, in the interests of national security, territorial integrity or public safety, for the prevention of disorder or crime, for the protection of health or morals, for the protection of the reputation or rights of others, for preventing the disclosure of information received in confidence, or for maintaining the authority and impartiality of the judiciary.

Article 11
Freedom of assembly and association

1   Everyone has the right to freedom of peaceful assembly and to freedom of association with others, including the right to form and to join trade unions for the protection of his interests.

2   No restrictions shall be placed on the exercise of these rights other than such as are prescribed by law and are necessary in a democratic society in the interests of national security or public safety, for the prevention of disorder or crime, for the protection of health or morals or for the protection of the rights and freedoms of others. This article shall not prevent the imposition of lawful restrictions on the exercise of these rights by members of the armed forces, of the police or of the administration of the State.

Article 12
Right to marry

Men and women of marriageable age have the right to marry and to found a family, according to the national laws governing the exercise of this right.

Article 13
Right to an effective remedy

Everyone whose rights and freedoms as set forth in this Convention are violated shall have an effective remedy before a national authority notwithstanding that the violation has been committed by persons acting in an official capacity.

Article 14
Prohibition of discrimination

The enjoyment of the rights and freedoms set forth in this Convention shall be secured without discrimination on any ground such as sex, race, colour, language, religion, political or other opinion, national or social origin, association with a national minority, property, birth or other status.

Article 15
Derogation in time of emergency

1   In time of war or other public emergency threatening the life of the nation any High Contracting Party may take measures derogating from its obligations under this Convention to the extent strictly required by the exigencies of the situation, provided that such measures are not inconsistent with its other obligations under international law.

2   No derogation from Article 2, except in respect of deaths resulting from lawful acts of war, or from Articles 3, 4 (paragraph 1) and 7 shall be made under this provision.

3   Any High Contracting Party availing itself of this right of derogation shall keep the Secretary General of the Council of Europe fully informed of the measures which it has taken and the reasons therefor. It shall also inform the Secretary General of the Council of Europe when such measures have ceased to operate and the provisions of the Convention are again being fully executed.

Article 16
Restrictions on political activity of aliens

Nothing in Articles 10, 11 and 14 shall be regarded as preventing the High Contracting Parties from imposing restrictions on the political activity of aliens.

Article 17
Prohibition of abuse of rights

Nothing in this Convention may be interpreted as implying for any State, group or person any right to engage in any activity or perform any act aimed at the destruction of any of the rights and freedoms set forth herein or at their limitation to a greater extent than is provided for in the Convention.

Article 18
Limitation on use of restrictions on rights

The restrictions permitted under this Convention to the said rights and freedoms shall not be applied for any purpose other than those for which they have been prescribed.

Section II — European Court of Human Rights

Article 19
Establishment of the Court

To ensure the observance of the engagements undertaken by the High Contracting Parties in the Convention and the Protocols thereto, there shall be set up a European Court of Human Rights, hereinafter referred to as 'the Court'. It shall function on a permanent basis.

Article 20
Number of judges

The Court shall consist of a number of judges equal to that of the High Contracting Parties.

Article 21
Criteria for office

1   The judges shall be of high moral character and must either possess the qualifications required for appointment to high judicial office or be jurisconsults of recognised competence.

2   The judges shall sit on the Court in their individual capacity.

3   During their term of office the judges shall not engage in any activity which is incompatible with their independence, impartiality or with the demands of a full-time office; all questions arising from the application of this paragraph shall be decided by the Court.

Article 22
Election of judges

1   The judges shall be elected by the Parliamentary Assembly with respect to each High Contracting Party by a majority of votes cast from a list of three candidates nominated by the High Contracting Party.

2   The same procedure shall be followed to complete the Court in the event of the accession of new High Contracting Parties and in filling casual vacancies.

Article 23
Terms of office

1   The judges shall be elected for a period of six years. They may be re-elected. However, the terms of office of one-half of the judges elected at the first election shall expire at the end of three years.

2   The judges whose terms of office are to expire at the end of the initial period of three years shall be chosen by lot by the Secretary General of the Council of Europe immediately after their election.

3   In order to ensure that, as far as possible, the terms of office of one-half of the judges are renewed every three years, the Parliamentary Assembly may decide, before proceeding to any subsequent election, that the term or terms of office of one or more judges to be elected shall be for a period other than six years but not more than nine and not less than three years.

4   In cases where more than one term of office is involved and where the Parliamentary Assembly applies the preceding paragraph, the allocation of the terms of office shall be effected by a drawing of lots by the Secretary General of the Council of Europe immediately after the election.

5   A judge elected to replace a judge whose term of office has not expired shall hold office for the remainder of his predecessor's term.

6   The terms of office of judges shall expire when they reach the age of 70.

7   The judges shall hold office until replaced. They shall, however, continue to deal with such cases as they already have under consideration.

Article 24
Dismissal

No judge may be dismissed from his office unless the other judges decide by a majority of two-thirds that he has ceased to fulfil the required conditions.

Article 25
Registry and legal secretaries

The Court shall have a registry, the functions and organisation of which shall be laid down in the rules of the Court. The Court shall be assisted by legal secretaries.

Article 26
Plenary Court

The plenary Court shall
    a   elect its President and one or two Vice-Presidents for a period of three years; they may be re-elected;
    b   set up Chambers, constituted for a fixed period of time;
    c   elect the Presidents of the Chambers of the Court; they may be re-elected;
    d   adopt the rules of the Court, and
    e   elect the Registrar and one or more Deputy Registrars.

Article 27
Committees, Chambers and Grand Chamber

1   To consider cases brought before it, the Court shall sit in committees of three judges, in Chambers of seven judges and in a Grand Chamber of seventeen judges. The Court's Chambers shall set up committees for a fixed period of time.

2   There shall sit as an *ex officio* member of the Chamber and the Grand Chamber the judge elected in respect of the State Party concerned or, if there is

none or if he is unable to sit, a person of its choice who shall sit in the capacity of judge.

3   The Grand Chamber shall also include the President of the Court, the Vice-Presidents, the Presidents of the Chambers and other judges chosen in accordance with the rules of the Court. When a case is referred to the Grand Chamber under Article 43, no judge from the Chamber which rendered the judgment shall sit in the Grand Chamber, with the exception of the President of the Chamber and the judge who sat in respect of the State Party concerned.

Article 28
Declarations of inadmissibility by committees

A committee may, by a unanimous vote, declare inadmissible or strike out of its list of cases an application submitted under Article 34 where such a decision can be taken without further examination. The decision shall be final.

Article 29
Decisions by Chambers on admissibility and merits

1   If no decision is taken under Article 28, a Chamber shall decide on the admissibility and merits of individual applications submitted under Article 34.

2   A Chamber shall decide on the admissibility and merits of inter-State applications submitted under Article 33.

3   The decision on admissibility shall be taken separately unless the Court, in exceptional cases, decides otherwise.

Article 30
Relinquishment of jurisdiction to the Grand Chamber

Where a case pending before a Chamber raises a serious question affecting the interpretation of the Convention or the protocols thereto, or where the resolution of a question before the Chamber might have a result inconsistent with a judgment previously delivered by the Court, the Chamber may, at any time before it has rendered its judgment, relinquish jurisdiction in favour of the Grand Chamber, unless one of the parties to the case objects.

Article 31
Powers of the Grand Chamber

The Grand Chamber shall

a   determine applications submitted either under Article 33 or Article 34 when a Chamber has relinquished jurisdiction under Article 30 or when the case has been referred to it under Article 43; and

b   consider requests for advisory opinions submitted under Article 47.

Article 32
Jurisdiction of the Court

1   The jurisdiction of the Court shall extend to all matters concerning the interpretation and application of the Convention and the protocols thereto which are referred to it as provided in Articles 33, 34 and 47.

2   In the event of dispute as to whether the Court has jurisdiction, the Court shall decide.

Article 33
Inter-State cases

Any High Contracting Party may refer to the Court any alleged breach of the provisions of the Convention and the protocols thereto by another High Contracting Party

Article 34
Individual applications

The Court may receive applications from any person, non-governmental organisation or group of individuals claiming to be the victim of a violation by one of the High Contracting Parties of the rights set forth in the Convention or the protocols thereto. The High Contracting Parties undertake not to hinder in any way the effective exercise of this right.

Article 35
Admissibility criteria

1   The Court may only deal with the matter after all domestic remedies have been exhausted, according to the generally recognised rules of international law, and within a period of six months from the date on which the final decision was taken.

2   The Court shall not deal with any application submitted under Article 34 that

    a   is anonymous; or

    b   is substantially the same as a matter that has already been examined by the Court or has already been submitted to another procedure of international investigation or settlement and contains no relevant new information.

3   The Court shall declare inadmissible any individual application submitted under Article 34 which it considers incompatible with the provisions of the Convention or the protocols thereto, manifestly ill-founded, or an abuse of the right of application.

4   The Court shall reject any application which it considers inadmissible under this Article. It may do so at any stage of the proceedings.

Article 36
Third party intervention

1   In all cases before a Chamber of the Grand Chamber, a High Contracting Party one of whose nationals is an applicant shall have the right to submit written comments and to take part in hearings.

2   The President of the Court may, in the interest of the proper administration of justice, invite any High Contracting Party which is not a party to the proceedings or any person concerned who is not the applicant to submit written comments or take part in hearings.

Article 37
Striking out applications

1   The Court may at any stage of the proceedings decide to strike an application out of its list of cases where the circumstances lead to the conclusion that

a   the applicant does not intend to pursue his application; or

b   the matter has been resolved; or

c   for any other reason established by the Court, it is no longer justified to continue the examination of the application.

However, the Court shall continue the examination of the application if respect for human rights as defined in the Convention and the protocols thereto so requires.

2   The Court may decide to restore an application to its list of cases if it considers that the circumstances justify such a course.

Article 38
Examination of the case and friendly settlement proceedings

1   If the Court declares the application admissible, it shall

a   pursue the examination of the case, together with the representatives of the parties, and if need be, undertake an investigation, for the effective conduct of which the States concerned shall furnish all necessary facilities;

b   place itself at the disposal of the parties concerned with a view to securing a friendly settlement of the matter on the basis of respect for human rights as defined in the Convention and the protocols thereto.

2   Proceedings conducted under paragraph 1.b shall be confidential.

Article 39
Finding of a friendly settlement

If a friendly settlement is effected, the Court shall strike the case out of its list by means of a decision which shall be confined to a brief statement of the facts and of the solution reached.

Article 40
Public hearings and access to documents

1   Hearings shall be in public unless the Court in exceptional circumstances decides otherwise.

2   Documents deposited with the Registrar shall be accessible to the public unless the President of the Court decides otherwise.

Article 41
Just satisfaction

If the Court finds that there has been a violation of the Convention or the protocols thereto, and if the internal law of the High Contracting Party concerned allows only partial reparation to be made, the Court shall, if necessary afford just satisfaction to the injured party.

Article 42
Judgments of Chambers

Judgments of Chambers shall become final in accordance with the provisions of Article 44, paragraph 2.

Article 43
Referral to the Grand Chamber

1   Within a period of three months from the date of the judgment of the Chamber, any party to the case may, in exceptional cases, request that the case be referred to the Grand Chamber.

2   A panel of five judges of the Grand Chamber shall accept the request if the case raises a serious question affecting the interpretation or application of the Convention or the protocols thereto, or a serious issue of general importance.

3   If the panel accepts the request, the Grand Chamber shall decide the case by means of a judgment.

Article 44
Final judgments

1   The judgment of the Grand Chamber shall be final.

2   The judgment of a Chamber shall become final

   a   when the parties declare that they will not request that the case be referred to the Grand Chamber; or

   b   three months after the date of the judgment, if reference of the case to the Grand Chamber has not been requested; or

   c   when the panel of the Grand Chamber rejects the request to refer under Article 43.

3   The final judgment shall be published.

Article 45
Reasons for judgments and decisions

1   Reasons shall be given for judgments as well as for decisions declaring applications admissible or inadmissible.

2   If a judgment does not represent, in whole or in part, the unanimous opinion of the judges, any judge shall be entitled to deliver a separate opinion.

Article 46
Binding force and execution of judgments

1   The High Contracting Parties undertake to abide by the final judgment of the Court in any case to which they are parties.

2   The final judgment of the Court shall be transmitted to the Committee of Ministers, which shall supervise its execution.

Article 47
Advisory opinions

1   The Court may, at the request of the Committee of Ministers, give advisory opinions on legal questions concerning the interpretation of the Convention and the protocols thereto.

2   Such opinions shall not deal with any question relating to the content or scope of the rights or freedoms defined in Section I of the Convention and the protocols thereto, or with any other question which the Court or the Committee of Ministers might have to consider in consequence of any such proceedings as could be instituted in accordance with the Convention.

3   Decisions of the Committee of Ministers to request an advisory opinion of the Court shall require a majority vote of the representatives entitled to sit on the Committee.

Article 48
Advisory jurisdiction of the Court

The Court shall decide whether a request for an advisory opinion submitted by the Committee of Ministers is within its competence as defined in Article 47.

Article 49
Reasons for advisory opinions

1   Reasons shall be given for advisory opinions of the Court.

2   If the advisory opinion does not represent, in whole or in part, the unanimous opinion of the judges, any judge shall be entitled to deliver a separate opinion.

3   Advisory opinions of the Court shall be communicated to the Committee of Ministers.

Article 50
Expenditure on the Court

The expenditure on the Court shall be borne by the Council of Europe.

Article 51
Privileges and immunities of judges

The judges shall be entitled, during the exercise of their functions, to the privileges and immunities provided for in Article 40 of the Statute of the Council of Europe and in the agreements made thereunder.

Section III — Miscellaneous provisions

Article 52
Inquiries by the Secretary General

On receipt of a request from the Secretary General of the Council of Europe any High Contracting Party shall furnish an explanation of the manner in which its internal law ensures the effective implementation of any of the provisions of the Convention.

Article 53
Safeguard for existing human rights

Nothing in this Convention shall be construed as limiting or derogating from any of the human rights and fundamental freedoms which may be ensured under the laws of any High Contracting Party or under any other agreement to which it is a Party.

Article 54
Powers of the Committee of Ministers

Nothing in this Convention shall prejudice the powers conferred on the Committee of Ministers by the Statute of the Council of Europe.

Article 55
Exclusion of other means of dispute settlement

The High Contracting Parties agree that, except by special agreement, they will not avail themselves of treaties, conventions or declarations in force between them for the purpose of submitting, by way of petition, a dispute arising out of the interpretation or application of this Convention to a means of settlement other than those provided for in this Convention.

Article 56
Territorial application

1   Any State may at the time of its ratification or at any time thereafter declare by notification addressed to the Secretary General of the Council of Europe that

the present Convention shall, subject to paragraph 4 of this Article, extend to or any of the territories for whose international relations it is responsible.

2 The Convention shall extend to the territory or territories named in the notification as from the thirtieth day after the receipt of this notification by the Secretary General of the Council of Europe.

3 The provisions of this Convention shall be applied in such territories with due regard, however, to local requirements.

4 Any State which has made a declaration in accordance with paragraph 1 of this article may at any time thereafter declare on behalf of one or more of the territories to which the declaration relates that it accepts the competence of the Court to receive applications from individuals, non-governmental organisations or groups of individuals as provided by Article 34 of the Convention.

Article 57
Reservations

1 Any State may, when signing this Convention or when depositing its instrument of ratification, make a reservation in respect of any particular provision of the Convention to the extent that any law then in force in its territory is not in conformity with the provision. Reservations of a general character shall not be permitted under this article.

2 Any reservation made under this article shall contain a brief statement of the law concerned.

Article 58
Denunciation

1 A High Contracting Party may denounce the present Convention only after the expiry of five years from the date on which it became a party to it and after six months' notice contained in a notification addressed to the Secretary General of the Council of Europe, who shall inform the other High Contracting Parties.

2 Such a denunciation shall not have the effect of releasing the High Contracting Party concerned from its obligations under this Convention in respect of any act which, being capable of constituting a violation of such obligations, may have been performed by it before the date at which the denunciation became effective.

3 Any High Contracting Party which shall cease to be a member of the Council of Europe shall cease to be a Party to this Convention under the same conditions.

4 The Convention may be denounced in accordance with the provisions of the preceding paragraphs in respect of any territory to which it has been declared to extend under the terms of Article 56.

Article 59
Signature and ratification

tion shall be open to the signature of the members of the
It shall be ratified. Ratifications shall be deposited with the
f the Council of Europe.

..... present Convention shall come into force after the deposit of ten
instruments of ratification.

3   As regards any signatory ratifying subsequently, the Convention shall come
into force at the date of the deposit of its instrument of ratification.

4   The Secretary General of the Council of Europe shall notify all the
members of the Council of Europe of the entry into force of the Convention, the
names of the High Contracting Parties who have ratified it, and the deposit of all
instruments of ratification which may be effected subsequently.

Done at Rome this 4th day of November 1950, in English and French, both texts
being equally authentic, in a single copy which shall remain deposited in the
archives of the Council of Europe.

The Secretary General shall transmit certified copies to each of the signatories.

PROTOCOL [NO. 1] TO THE CONVENTION FOR THE PROTECTION OF HUMAN RIGHTS AND FUNDAMENTAL FREEDOMS, AS AMENDED BY PROTOCOL NO. 11

The governments signatory hereto, being members of the Council of Europe,

Being resolved to take steps to ensure the collective enforcement of certain
rights and freedoms other than those already included in Section I of the
Convention for the Protection of Human Rights and Fundamental Freedoms
signed at Rome on 4 November 1950 (hereinafter referred to as 'the Convention'),

Have agreed as follows:

Article 1
Protection of property

Every natural or legal person is entitled to the peaceful enjoyment of his
possessions. No one shall be deprived of his possessions except in the public
interest and subject to the conditions provided for by law and by the general
principles of international law.

The preceding provisions shall not, however, in any way impair the right of a
State to enforce such laws as it deems necessary to control the use of property in
accordance with the general interest or to secure the payment of taxes or other
contributions or penalties.

Article 2
Right to education

No person shall be denied the right to education. In the exercise of any functions which it assumes in relation to education and to teaching, the State shall respect the right of parents to ensure such education and teaching in conformity with their own religious and philosophical convictions.

Article 3
Right to free elections

The High Contracting Parties undertake to hold free elections at reasonable intervals by secret ballot, under conditions which will ensure the free expression of the opinion of the people in the choice of the legislature.

Article 4
Territorial application

Any High Contracting Party may at the time of signature or ratification or at any time thereafter communicate to the Secretary General of the Council of Europe a declaration stating the extent to which it undertakes that the provisions of the present Protocol shall apply to such of the territories for the international relations of which it is responsible as are named therein.

Any High Contracting Party which has communicated a declaration in virtue of the preceding paragraph may from time to time communicate a further declaration modifying the terms of any former declaration or terminating the application of the provisions of this Protocol in respect of any territory.

A declaration made in accordance with this article shall be deemed to have been made in accordance with paragraph 1 of Article 56 of the Convention.

Article 5
Relationship to the Convention

As between the High Contracting Parties the provisions of Articles 1, 2, 3 and 4 of this Protocol shall be regarded as additional articles to the Convention and all the provisions of the Convention shall apply accordingly.

Article 6
Signature and ratification

This Protocol shall be open for signature by the members of the Council of Europe, who are the signatories of the Convention; it shall be ratified at the same time as or after the ratification of the Convention. It shall enter into force after the deposit of ten instruments of ratification. As regards any signatory ratifying subsequently, the Protocol shall enter into force at the date of the deposit of its instrument of ratification.

The instruments of ratification shall be deposited with the Secretary General of the Council of Europe, who will notify all members of the names of those who have ratified.

Done at Paris on the 20th day of March 1952, in English and French, both texts being equally authentic, in a single copy which shall remain deposited in the archives of the Council of Europe. The Secretary General shall transmit certified copies to each of the signatory governments.

PROTOCOL NO. 4 TO THE CONVENTION FOR THE PROTECTION OF HUMAN RIGHTS AND FUNDAMENTAL FREEDOMS, SECURING CERTAIN RIGHTS AND FREEDOMS OTHER THAN THOSE ALREADY INCLUDED IN THE CONVENTION AND IN THE FIRST PROTOCOL THERETO, AS AMENDED BY PROTOCOL NO. 11

The governments signatory hereto, being members of the Council of Europe,

Being resolved to take steps to ensure the collective enforcement of certain rights and freedoms other than those already included in Section 1 of the Convention for the Protection of Human Rights and Fundamental Freedoms signed at Rome on 4th November 1950 (hereinafter referred to as the 'Convention') and in Articles 1 to 3 of the First Protocol to the Convention, signed at Paris on 20th March 1952,

Have agreed as follows:

Article 1
Prohibition of imprisonment for debt

No one shall be deprived of his liberty merely on the ground of inability to fulfil a contractual obligation.

Article 2
Freedom of movement

1   Everyone lawfully within the territory of a State shall, within that territory, have the right to liberty of movement and freedom to choose his residence.

2   Everyone shall be free to leave any country, including his own.

3   No restrictions shall be placed on the exercise of these rights other than such as are in accordance with law and are necessary in a democratic society in the interests of national security or public safety, for the maintenance of *ordre public*, for the prevention of crime, for the protection of health or morals, or for the protection of the rights and freedoms of others.

4   The rights set forth in paragraph 1 may also be subject, in particular areas, to restrictions imposed in accordance with law and justified by the public interest in a democratic society.

Article 3
Prohibition of expulsion of nationals

1   No one shall be expelled, by means either of an individual or of a collective measure, from the territory of the State of which he is a national.

2   No one shall be deprived of the right to enter the territory of the state of which he is a national.

Article 4
Prohibition of collective expulsion of aliens

Collective expulsion of aliens is prohibited.

Article 5
Territorial application

1   Any High Contracting Party may, at the time of signature or ratification of this Protocol, or at any time thereafter, communicate to the Secretary General of the Council of Europe a declaration stating the extent to which it undertakes that the provisions of this Protocol shall apply to such of the territories for the international relations of which it is responsible as are named therein.

2   Any High Contracting Party which has communicated a declaration in virtue of the preceding paragraph may, from time to time, communicate a further declaration modifying the terms of any former declaration or terminating the application of the provisions of this Protocol in respect of any territory.

3   A declaration made in accordance with this article shall be deemed to have been made in accordance with paragraph 1 of Article 56 of the Convention.

4   The territory of any State to which this Protocol applies by virtue of ratification or acceptance by that State, and each territory to which this Protocol is applied by virtue of a declaration by that State under this article, shall be treated as separate territories for the purpose of the references in Articles 2 and 3 to the territory of a State.

5   Any State which has made a declaration in accordance with paragraph 1 or 2 of this Article may at any time thereafter declare on behalf of one or more of the territories to which the declaration relates that it accepts the competence of the Court to receive applications from individuals, non-governmental organisations or groups of individuals as provided in Article 34 of the Convention in respect of all or any of Articles 1 to 4 of this Protocol.

Article 6
Relationship to the Convention

As between the High Contracting Parties the provisions of Articles 1 to 5 of this Protocol shall be regarded as additional Articles to the Convention, and all the provisions of the Convention shall apply accordingly.

Article 7
Signature and ratification

1 This Protocol shall be open for signature by the members of the Council of Europe who are the signatories of the Convention; it shall be ratified at the same time as or after the ratification of the Convention. It shall enter into force after the deposit of five instruments of ratification. As regards any signatory ratifying subsequently, the Protocol shall enter into force at the date of the deposit of its instrument of ratification.

2 The instruments of ratification shall be deposited with the Secretary General of the Council of Europe, who will notify all members of the names of those who have ratified.

In witness whereof the undersigned, being duly authorised thereto, have signed this Protocol.

Done at Strasbourg, this 16th day of September 1963, in English and in French, both texts being equally authoritative, in a single copy which shall remain deposited in the archives of the Council of Europe. The Secretary General shall transmit certified copies to each of the signatory states.

PROTOCOL NO. 6 TO THE CONVENTION FOR THE PROTECTION OF HUMAN RIGHTS AND FUNDAMENTAL FREEDOMS CONCERNING THE ABOLITION OF THE DEATH PENALTY, AS AMENDED BY PROTOCOL NO. 11

The member States of the Council of Europe, signatory to this Protocol to the Convention for the Protection of Human Rights and Fundamental Freedoms, signed at Rome on 4 November 1950 (hereinafter referred to as 'the Convention'),

Considering that the evolution that has occurred in several member States of the Council of Europe expresses a general tendency in favour of abolition of the death penalty;

Have agreed as follows:

Article 1
Abolition of the death penalty

The death penalty shall be abolished. No-one shall be condemned to such penalty or executed.

Article 2
Death penalty in time of war

A State may make provision in its law for the death penalty in respect of acts committed in time of war or of imminent threat of war; such penalty shall be applied only in the instances laid down in the law and in accordance with its provisions. The State shall communicate to the Secretary General of the Council of Europe the relevant provisions of that law.

Article 3
Prohibition of derogations

No derogation from the provisions of this Protocol shall be made under Article 15 of the Convention.

Article 4
Prohibition of reservations

No reservation may be made under Article 57 of the Convention in respect of the provisions of this Protocol.

Article 5
Territorial application

1   Any State may at the time of signature or when depositing its instrument of ratification, acceptance or approval, specify the territory or territories to which this Protocol shall apply.

2   Any State may at any later date, by a declaration addressed to the Secretary General of the Council of Europe, extend the application of this Protocol to any other territory specified in the declaration. In respect of such territory the Protocol shall enter into force on the first day of the month following the date of receipt of such declaration by the Secretary General.

3   Any declaration made under the two preceding paragraphs may, in respect of any territory specified in such declaration, be withdrawn by a notification addressed to the Secretary General. The withdrawal shall become effective on the first day of the month following the date of receipt of such notification by the Secretary General.

Article 6
Relationship to the Convention

As between the States Parties the provisions of Articles 1 to 5 of this Protocol shall be regarded as additional articles to the Convention and all the provisions of the Convention shall apply accordingly.

Article 7
Signature and ratification

The Protocol shall be open for signature by the member States of the Council of Europe, signatories to the Convention. It shall be subject to ratification, acceptance or approval. A member State of the Council of Europe may not ratify, accept or approve this Protocol unless it has, simultaneously or previously, ratified the Convention. Instruments of ratification, acceptance or approval shall be deposited with the Secretary General of the Council of Europe.

Article 8
Entry into force

1   This Protocol shall enter into force on the first day of the month following the date on which five member States of the Council of Europe have expressed their consent to be bound by the Protocol in accordance with the provisions of Article 7.

2   In respect of any member State which subsequently expresses its consent to be bound by it, the Protocol shall enter into force on the first day of the month following the date of the deposit of the instrument of ratification, acceptance or approval.

Article 9
Depositary functions

The Secretary General of the Council of Europe shall notify the member States of the Council of:

a   any signature;

b   the deposit of any instrument of ratification, acceptance or approval;

c   any date of entry into force of this Protocol in accordance with Articles 5 and 8;

d   any other act, notification or communication relating to this Protocol.

In witness whereof the undersigned, being duly authorised thereto, have signed this Protocol.

Done at Strasbourg, this 28th day of April 1983, in English and in French, both texts being equally authentic, in a single copy which shall be deposited in the archives of the Council of Europe. The Secretary General of the Council of Europe shall transmit certified copies to each member State of the Council of Europe.

PROTOCOL NO. 7 TO THE CONVENTION FOR THE PROTECTION OF HUMAN RIGHTS AND FUNDAMENTAL FREEDOMS, AS AMENDED BY PROTOCOL NO. 11

The member States of the Council of Europe signatory hereto,

Being resolved to take further steps to ensure the collective enforcement of certain rights and freedoms by means of the Convention for the Protection of Human Rights and Fundamental Freedoms signed at Rome on 4 November 1950 (hereinafter referred to as 'the Convention'),

Have agreed as follows

Article 1
Procedural safeguards relating to expulsion of aliens

1   An alien lawfully resident in the territory of a State shall not be expelled therefrom except in pursuance of a decision reached in accordance with law and shall be allowed:

a   to submit reasons against his expulsion,

b   to have his case reviewed, and

c   to be represented for these purposes before the competent authority or a person or persons designated by that authority.

2   An alien may be expelled before the exercise of his rights under paragraph 1.a, b and c of this Article, when such expulsion is necessary in the interests of public order or is grounded on reasons of national security.

Article 2
Right of appeal in criminal matters

1   Everyone convicted of a criminal offence by a tribunal shall have the right to have his conviction or sentence reviewed by a higher tribunal. The exercise of this right, including the grounds on which it may be exercised, shall be governed by law.

2   This right may be subject to exceptions in regard to offences of a minor character, as prescribed by law, or in cases in which the person concerned was tried in the first instance by the highest tribunal or was convicted following an appeal against acquittal.

Article 3
Compensation for wrongful conviction

When a person has by a final decision been convicted of a criminal offence and when subsequently his conviction has been reversed, or he has been pardoned, on the ground that a new or newly discovered fact shows conclusively that there has been a miscarriage of justice, the person who has suffered punishment as a result of such conviction shall be compensated according to the law or the practice of the State concerned, unless it is proved that the non-disclosure of the unknown fact in time is wholly or partly attributable to him.

Article 4
Right not to be tried or punished twice

1   No one shall be liable to be tried or punished again in criminal proceedings under the jurisdiction of the same State for an offence for which he has already been finally acquitted or convicted in accordance with the law and penal procedure of that State.

2   The provisions of the preceding paragraph shall not prevent the reopening of the case in accordance with the law and penal procedure of the State concerned, if there is evidence of new or newly discovered facts, or if there has been a fundamental defect in the previous proceedings, which could affect the outcome of the case.

3   No derogation from this Article shall be made under Article 15 of the Convention.

Article 5
Equality between spouses

Spouses shall enjoy equality of rights and responsibilities of a private law character between them, and in their relations with their children, as to marriage, during marriage and in the event of its dissolution. This Article shall not prevent States from taking such measures as are necessary in the interests of the children.

Article 6
Territorial application

1   Any State may at the time of signature or when depositing its instrument of ratification, acceptance or approval, specify the territory or territories to which the Protocol shall apply and state the extent to which it undertakes that the provisions of this Protocol shall apply to such territory or territories.

2   Any State may at any later date, by a declaration addressed to the Secretary General of the Council of Europe, extend the application of this Protocol to any other territory specified in the declaration. In respect of such territory the Protocol shall enter into force on the first day of the month following the expiration of a period of two months after the date of receipt by the Secretary General of such declaration.

3   Any declaration made under the two preceding paragraphs may, in respect of any territory specified in such declaration, be withdrawn or modified by a notification addressed to the Secretary General. The withdrawal or modification shall become effective on the first day of the month following the expiration of a period of two months after the date of receipt of such notification by the Secretary General.

4   A declaration made in accordance with this Article shall be deemed to have been made in accordance with paragraph 1 of Article 56 of the Convention.

5   The territory of any State to which this Protocol applies by virtue of ratification, acceptance or approval by that State, and each territory to which this Protocol is applied by virtue of a declaration by that State under this Article, may be treated as separate territories for the purpose of the reference in Article 1 to the territory of a State.

6   Any State which has made a declaration in accordance with paragraph 1 or 2 of this Article may at any time thereafter declare on behalf of one or more of the

territories to which the declaration relates that it accepts the competence of the Court to receive applications from individuals, non-governmental organisations or groups of individuals as provided in Article 34 of the Convention in respect of Articles 1 to 5 of this Protocol.

Article 7
Relationship to the Convention

As between the States Parties, the provisions of Article 1 to 6 of this Protocol shall be regarded as additional Articles to the Convention, and all the provisions of the Convention shall apply accordingly.

Article 8
Signature and ratification

This Protocol shall be open for signature by member States of the Council of Europe which have signed the Convention. It is subject to ratification, acceptance or approval. A member State of the Council of Europe may not ratify, accept or approve this Protocol without previously or simultaneously ratifying the Convention. Instruments of ratification, acceptance or approval shall be deposited with the Secretary General of the Council of Europe.

Article 9
Entry into force

1   This Protocol shall enter into force on the first day of the month following the expiration of a period of two months after the date on which seven member States of the Council of Europe have expressed their consent to be bound by the Protocol in accordance with the provisions of Article 8.

2   In respect of any member State which subsequently expresses its consent to be bound by it, the Protocol shall enter into force on the first day of the month following the expiration of a period of two months after the date of the deposit of the instrument of ratification, acceptance or approval.

Article 10
Depositary functions

The Secretary General of the Council of Europe shall notify all the member States of the Council of Europe of:

a   any signature;
b   the deposit of any instrument of ratification, acceptance or approval;
c   any date of entry into force of this Protocol in accordance with Articles 6 and 9;
d   any other act, notification or declaration relating to this Protocol.

In witness whereof the undersigned, being duly authorised thereto, have signed this Protocol.

Done at Strasbourg, this 22nd day of November 1984, in English and French, both texts being equally authentic, in a single copy which shall be deposited in the archives of the Council of Europe. The Secretary General of the Council of Europe shall transmit certified copies to each member State of the Council of Europe.

PROTOCOL NO. 12 TO THE CONVENTION FOR THE PROTECTION OF HUMAN RIGHTS AND FUNDAMENTAL FREEDOMS

The member states of the Council of Europe signatory hereto,

Having regard to the fundamental principle according to which all persons are equal before the law and are entitled to the equal protection of the law;

Being resolved to take further steps to promote the equality of all persons through the collective enforcement of a general prohibition of discrimination by means of the Convention for the Protection of Human Rights and Fundamental Freedoms signed at Rome on 4 November 1950 (hereinafter referred to as 'the Convention');

Reaffirming that the principle of non-discrimination does not prevent States Parties from taking measures in order to promote full and effective equality, provided that there is an objective and reasonable justification for those measures,

Have agreed as follows:

Article 1
General prohibition of discrimination

1   The enjoyment of any right set forth by law shall be secured without discrimination on any ground such as sex, race, colour, language, religion, political or other opinion, national or social origin, association with a national minority, property, birth or other status.

2   No one shall be discriminated against by any public authority on any ground such as those mentioned in paragraph 1.

Article 2
Territorial application

1   Any state may, at the time of signature or when depositing its instrument of ratification, acceptance or approval, specify the territory or territories to which this Protocol shall apply.

2   Any state may at any later date, by a declaration addressed to the Secretary General of the Council of Europe, extend the application of this Protocol to any other territory specified in the declaration, in respect of such territory the Protocol shall enter into force on the first day of the month following the expiration of a period of three months after the date of receipt by the Secretary General of such declaration.

3   Any declaration made under the two preceding paragraphs may, in respect of any territory specified in such declaration, be withdrawn or modified by a notification addressed to the Secretary General. The withdrawal or modification shall become effective on the first day of the month following the expiration of a period of three months after the date of receipt of such notification by the Secretary General.

4   A declaration made in accordance with this article shall be deemed to have been made in accordance with paragraph 1 of Article 56 of the Convention.

5   Any state which has made a declaration in accordance with paragraph 1 or 2 of this article may at any time thereafter declare on behalf of one or more of the territories to which the declaration relates that it accepts the competence of the Court to receive applications from individuals, non-governmental organisations or groups of individuals as provided by Article 34 of the Convention in respect of Article 1 of this Protocol.

Article 3
Relationship to the Convention

As between the States Parties, the provisions of Articles 1 and 2 of this Protocol shall be regarded as additional articles to the Convention, and all the provisions of the Convention shall apply accordingly.

Article 4
Signature and ratification

This Protocol shall be open for signature by member states of the Council of Europe which have signed the Convention. It is subject to ratification, acceptance or approval. A member state of the Council of Europe may not ratify, accept or approve this Protocol without previously or simultaneously ratifying the Convention. Instruments of ratification, acceptance or approval shall be deposited with the Secretary General of the Council of Europe.

Article 5
Entry into force

1   This Protocol shall enter into force on the first day of the month following the expiration of a period of three months after the date on which ten member states of the Council of Europe have expressed their consent to be bound by the Protocol in accordance with the provisions of Article 4.

2   In respect of any member state which subsequently expresses its consent to be bound by it, the Protocol shall enter into force on the first day of the month following the expiration of a period of three months after the date of the deposit of the instrument of ratification, acceptance or approval.

Article 6
Depositary functions

The Secretary General of the Council of Europe shall notify all the member states of the Council of Europe of:

a any signature;

b the deposit of any instrument of ratification, acceptance or approval;

c any date of entry into force of this Protocol in accordance with Articles 2 and 5;

d any other act, notification or communication relating to this Protocol.

In witness whereof the undersigned, being duly authorised thereto, have signed this Protocol.

Done at ...., this .... day of .... 2000, in English and French, both texts being equally authentic, in a single copy which shall be deposited in the archives of the Council of Europe. The Secretary General of the Council of Europe shall transmit certified copies to each member state of the Council of Europe.

Appendix Three

Case Summaries

1. *Handyside* v *UK* (1976) 1 EHRR 737
2. *Marckx* v *Belgium* (1979) 2 EHRR 330
3. *Sporrong and Lönnroth* v *Sweden* (1982) 5 EHRR 35
4. *James* v *UK* (1986) 8 EHRR 123
5. *Lithgow* v *UK* (1986) 8 EHRR 329
6. *Howard* v *UK* (1987) 9 EHRR 91
7. *S* v *UK* (App. No. 11716/85)
8. *App. No. 11949/86* v *UK* (1988) 10 EHRR 123
9. *AGOSI* v *UK* (1987) 9 EHRR 1
10. *Gillow* v *UK* (1989) 11 EHRR 335
11. *Tre Traktörer Aktiebolag* v *Sweden* (1989) 13 EHRR 309
12. *Powell and Rayner* v *UK* (1990) 12 EHRR 355
13. *Pine Valley Developments Ltd and others* v *Ireland* (1991) 14 EHRR 319
14. *Papamichalopoulos* v *Greece* (1993) 16 EHRR 440
15. *Hentrich* v *France* (1994) 18 EHRR 440
16. *Holy Monasteries* v *Greece* (1994) 20 EHRR 1
17. *Lopez Ostra* v *Spain* (1994) 20 EHRR 277
18. *Air Canada* v *UK* (1995) 20 EHRR 150
19. *Gasus Dosier- und Fordertechnik GmbH* v *Netherlands* (1995) 20 EHRR 403
20. *Bryan* v *UK* (1996) 21 EHRR 342
21. *Buckley* v *UK* (1996) 23 EHRR 101
22. *Loizidou* v *Turkey* (1996) 23 EHRR 513
23. *Matos e Silva, Lda and others* v *Portugal* (1996) 24 EHRR 573
24. *National and Provincial Building Society and others* v *UK* (1997) 25 EHRR 127

These case summaries relate to those decisions of the European Court of Human Rights (the European Court) and the European Commission of Human Rights (the European Commission) that are especially relevant to property law. The summaries concentrate on those Articles of the European Convention on Human Rights (the Convention) that are particularly relevant to property law, i.e., Article 1, Protocol 1 and Articles 6(1), 8 and 14. Some of the cases include challenges under other Articles, for example, *Handyside* v *UK* concerned freedom of expression under Article 10. However, the summaries exclude any consideration of the other Convention Articles.

HANDYSIDE v *UK* (1976) 1 EHRR 737

Facts

The applicant was an English publisher and was convicted under the Obscene Publications Acts of 1959 and 1964 of possessing obscene books for publication. The book entitled 'The Little Red Schoolbook' was intended to be distributed in schools to be read by children and adolescents. However, copies of the book were seized by police and, following the applicant's conviction, the books were forfeited and destroyed. The applicant alleged that his rights under the Convention had been infringed.

Decision

Most of the European Court's judgment examined whether there had been a breach of Article 10 which protects a person's right to freedom of expression; however, the European Court also considered whether there had been an infringement of Article 1, Protocol 1. The European Court held that there had been no violation of Article 10 nor Article 1, Protocol 1.

Analysis

Article 1, Protocol 1

The European Court identified two separate instances of interference. First, the books were seized by the police and secondly the books were forfeited and destroyed. In respect of the initial seizure the European Court noted that the seizure was only temporary and if the criminal proceedings against the applicant had resulted in an acquittal, the books would have been returned to him. This did not, as submitted by the applicant, constitute a deprivation under the second rule. Referring to the inapplicability of the second rule on the facts, the European Court noted (at para. 62) that:

> Admittedly the expression 'deprived of his possessions', in the English text, could lead one to think otherwise but the structure of Article 1 shows that that sentence, which originated moreover in a Belgian amendment drafted in French, applies only to someone who is 'deprived of ownership'.

This case, therefore, provides authority for the principle that a temporary deprivation of possessions does not infringe the second rule of Article 1, Protocol 1. Instead the European Court concluded that the initial seizure fell within the ambit of the third rule as a control of use of the property.

In assessing whether this interference was justifiable under the third rule the European Court observed (at para. 62) that:

> the seizure did relate to 'the use of property' and thus falls within the ambit of the second paragraph. Unlike Article 10(2) of the Convention, this paragraph sets the Contracting States up as sole judges of the 'necessity' for an interference. Consequently, the European Court must restrict itself to supervising the lawfulness and the purpose of the restriction in question.

The European Court was satisfied that the seizure was lawful and therefore the only question was whether it pursued a legitimate aim. The aim of the seizure was the protection of morals and the European Court accepted that this aim was within the 'general interest' and thereby constituted a legitimate aim for the purposes of Article 1, Protocol 1.

In respect of the second interference with the possessions, the European Court acknowledged that the forfeiture and destruction of the books, which clearly deprived the applicant of his ownership, was a deprivation of possessions within the ambit of the second rule. However, the European Court stated (at para. 63) that:

> However these measures were authorised by the second paragraph of Article 1 of Protocol 1, interpreted in the light of the principle of law, common to the Contracting States, whereunder items whose use has been lawfully adjudged illicit and dangerous to the general interest are forfeited with a view to destruction.

Consequently there was no breach of Article 1, Protocol 1.

MARCKX v *BELGIUM* (1979) 2 EHRR 330

Facts

Under illegitimacy laws in Belgium there was a requirement that maternal affiliation could be established only by a formal act of recognition. There were also limits on the mother's capacity to bequeath property and the illegitimate child's capacity to inherit it. The applicants, a mother and her illegitimate infant daughter, complained that these aspects of the illegitimacy laws infringed Article 8 taken alone and in conjunction with Article 14 and Article 1, Protocol 1 in conjunction with Article 14.

Decision

The European Court found that there was a violation of Article 8 taken alone and in conjunction with Article 14 as well as a breach of Article 1, Protocol 1 taken in conjunction with Article 14.

Analysis

(1)   The maternal affiliation laws

Article 8

The meaning of 'respect' for family life   The European Court had to clarify the meaning and purport of the words 'respect for ... private and family life'. This was something which it had scarcely had occasion to consider previously (see *Belgian Linguistic Case* (1968) and *Klass* v *Germany* (1978) 2 EHRR 214).

In the *Belgian Linguistic Case* the European Court had stated the object of Article 8 to be that of essentially protecting the individual against arbitrary interference by the public authorities. However, the European Court recognised (at para. 31) that: 'Nevertheless, it does not merely compel the State to abstain from such interference: in addition to this primarily negative undertaking, there may be positive obligations inherent in an effective 'respect' for family life'. On this basis the state had a positive obligation to ensure the existence, in domestic law, of legal safeguards to render possible the applicant child's integration into its family.

An interference with family life   The European Court referred to the position under Belgian law by which an unmarried mother had to choose either to recognise her child formally and thereby prejudice the child since her capacity to give or bequeath her property to the child would be restricted, or to renounce establishing a family tie in order to retain the chance to make gifts and bequests freely to the child. The European Court concluded (at para. 36) that 'the dilemma which exists at present is not consonant with "respect" for family life; it thwarts and impedes the normal development of such life' and therefore amounts to a violation of Article 8.

Article 14 in conjunction with Article 8
The state argued a number of grounds for justifying the requirement that a mother must take action to recognise her illegitimate child formally. Whilst the European Court accepted that some unmarried mothers did not want to take care of their child, this fact did not justify making legal recognition of maternity conditional on a voluntary recognition procedure or a court declaration. Similarly, the European Court accepted that laws to support and encourage the traditional family pursued a legitimate aim, but it rejected that such measures should prejudice the illegitimate family. The European Court observed (at para 40) that: 'the members of the "illegitimate" family enjoy the guarantees of Article 8 on an equal footing with the members of the traditional family'.

The European Court stated (at para. 41) that:

It is true that, at the time when the Convention of 4 November 1950 was drafted, it was regarded as permissible and normal in many European countries to draw a distinction in this area between the 'illegitimate' and the 'legitimate' family. However, the European Court recalls that this Convention must be interpreted in the light of present-day conditions. In the instant case, the European Court cannot but be struck by the fact that the domestic law of the great majority of the member States of the Council of Europe has evolved and is continuing to evolve, in company with the relevant international instruments, towards full juridical recognition of the maxim *mater semper certa est*.

Taking all these factors into account, the European Court concluded that the distinction between the maternal affiliation of legitimate and illegitimate children lacked any objective and reasonable justification and was in violation of Article 14 in conjunction with Article 8.

(2)   The inheritance laws

Article 14 in conjunction with Article 8
The majority of the European Commission concluded that the inheritance rights of a child on intestacy are not within the scope of Article 8. However the European Court disputed this. It observed (at para. 52) that: 'Matters of intestate succession — and of disposition — between near relatives prove to be intimately connected with family life'. However, the European Court acknowledged that Article 8 does not require that a child be entitled to some share in their parents' estate or the estates of other near relatives. Consequently, the restrictions which the Belgian law placed on inheritance rights on intestacy were not in themselves in conflict with Article 8 taken alone. But the distinction which the law made between legitimate and illegitimate children did raise an issue under Articles 14 and 8 when they were taken in conjunction. The European Court decided that the need for the applicant to adopt her child in order to eliminate this differential treatment was discriminatory because the state was unable to provide any objective and reasonable justification for it. Consequently there was a violation of Article 14.

Article 14 in conjunction with Article 1, Protocol 1
The European Court described the object of Article 1, Protocol 1 as guaranteeing the right of property. It stated (at para. 63) that:

> By recognising that everyone has the right to the peaceful enjoyment of his possessions, Article 1 is in substance guaranteeing the right of property. This is the clear impression left by the words 'possessions' and 'use of property' (in French: *biens, propriété, usage des biens*); the *travaux préparatoires*, for their part, confirm this unequivocally: the drafters continually spoke of 'right of property' or 'right to property' to describe the subject-matter of the successive drafts which were the forerunners of the present Article 1.

The European Court noted (at para. 63) that 'the right to dispose of one's property constitutes a traditional and fundamental aspect of the right of property'. Therefore the right of the applicant mother to give or bequeath her property freely to her illegitimate child concerns a property right within the scope of Article 1. However the third rule of Article 1, Protocol 1 permits the contracting states to introduce legislation to control the use of property in the area of dispositions *inter vivos* or by will, provided that the requirements of the third rule as to 'the general interest' and necessity are met. Consequently, it was accepted that the limitation was not in itself in conflict with Article 1, Protocol 1 taken alone. It was nevertheless found to be in breach of Article 14 in conjunction with Article 1, Protocol 1 due to the fact that the disputed limitation applied only to unmarried and not to married mothers. The European Court stated (at para. 65) that:

> In view of Article 14 of the Convention, the European Court fails to see on what 'general interest', or on what objective and reasonable justification, a State could rely to limit an unmarried mother's right to make gifts or legacies in favour of her child when at the same time a married woman is not subject to any similar restriction.

SPORRONG AND LÖNNROTH v SWEDEN (1982) 5 EHRR 35

Facts

The applicants owned land in an area of the City of Stockholm that fell within the perimeters of a proposed redevelopment site. As a result of this redevelopment both properties were subject to expropriation permits issued by the Government on an application by the local authority and to a prohibition on any construction imposed by the local administration board. The properties were never expropriated and the prohibition notices eventually lapsed. The applicants did not dispute the lawfulness of the expropriation permits and prohibitions on construction, but maintained that the length of the period that they were in force (23 and 8 years for the permits and 25 and 12 years for the prohibitions), and the fact that they never received any compensation, amounted to an infringement of their right to the peaceful enjoyment of their possessions contrary to Article 1, Protocol 1. In addition, the applicants alleged that their complaints concerning the expropriation permits could not be heard by the Swedish courts and this amounted to a breach of Article 6(1).

Decision

The European Court held that there had been a violation of Article 1, Protocol 1 and of Article 6(1).

Analysis

Article 1, Protocol 1

An interference with the applicants' right of property   The European Court had
to determine whether the measures were sufficient to constitute an interference
with property. It noted (at para. 60) that: 'Although the expropriation permits left
intact in law the owners' right to use and dispose of their possessions, they
nevertheless in practice significantly reduced the possibility of its exercise'. The
applicants' right to property was both precarious and defeasible given that the
City of Stockholm could lawfully expropriate whenever it wished to. On these
grounds the European Court held that the expropriation permits interfered with
the applicants' right of property. The prohibitions on construction clearly
restricted the applicants' use of their possessions and constituted an interference.

The applicable rule   The European Court first gave (at para. 61) its now familiar
analysis of Article 1, Protocol 1 as comprising three rules:

> That Article comprises three distinct rules. The first rule, which is of a general nature,
> enounces the principle of peaceful enjoyment of property; it is set out in the first
> sentence of the first paragraph. The second rule covers deprivation of possessions and
> subjects it to certain conditions; it appears in the second sentence of the same paragraph.
> The third rule recognises that the States are entitled, amongst other things, to control the
> use of property in accordance with the general interest, by enforcing such laws as they
> deem necessary for the purpose; it is contained in the second paragraph.

The European Court considered each rule separately to determine whether or not
there had been a violation of Article 1.

(a)   The second rule   There was no legal expropriation and therefore the
ownership of the properties remained with the applicants. However, because the
Convention is intended to guarantee rights that are 'practical and effective', the
European Court said that it would look to the realities of the situation to determine
whether or not there had been a *de facto* expropriation as was argued by the
applicants. The European Court observed that the applicants were entitled to use,
sell, donate or mortgage their properties. Although it was more difficult to sell the
properties due to the imposed limitations, there was evidence that several sales
had been effected in the area. On this basis the European Court concluded that
there had not been a *de facto* deprivation and consequently there was no room for
applying the second rule.

(b) *The third rule* The prohibitions on construction clearly amounted to a control of use, however, the expropriation permits were not intended to control the use of the property and did not come within the ambit of the third rule.

(c) *The first rule* The European Court found the expropriation permits to constitute an interference within the first rule.

Proportionality In order to determine whether there had been a violation of Article 1, Protocol 1, the European Court had to determine (at para. 69):

> whether a fair balance was struck between the demands of the general interest of the community and the requirements of the protection of the individual's fundamental rights. The search for this balance is inherent in the whole of the Convention and is also reflected in the structure of Article 1.

It observed (also at para. 69) that:

> In an area as complex and difficult as that of the development of large cities, the Contracting States should enjoy a wide margin of appreciation in order to implement their town-planning policy. Nevertheless, the Court cannot fail to exercise its power of review and must determine whether the requisite balance was maintained in a manner consonant with the applicants' right to the 'peaceful enjoyment of [their] possessions', within the meaning of the first sentence of Article 1.

The European Court found that the expropriation permits, whose consequences were aggravated by the prohibitions on construction, upset the fair balance between the demands of the general interest and the protection of the applicants' right of property. The applicants were found to bear an 'individual and excessive burden which could have been rendered legitimate only if they had had the possibility of seeking a reduction of the time-limits or of claiming compensation' (at para. 73). Both of these possibilities were denied to the applicants and therefore the permits were held to violate Article 1, Protocol 1.

Article 6(1)
The applicants' right of property was accepted as a 'civil right' within the ambit of Article 6(1). The applicants had established the existence of a 'dispute' on the ground that there was an arguable grievance that the Government had not complied with Swedish law because of the exceptionally long time periods of the permits. Having satisfied itself that Article 6(1) was applicable on the facts, the European Court then had to assess the question of compliance with Article 6(1). One aspect of a 'right to a court' is the right of access to a court, being the right to commence proceedings before a competent court or tribunal. The European

Court examined whether Swedish law gave the applicants the opportunity to challenge the lawfulness of the decisions of the authorities to issue and extend the long-term expropriation permits. It noted that although the Government's decision to issue the permits was open to judicial review by the Supreme Administrative Court, this is an extraordinary remedy that is rarely used because it is only exercisable on limited grounds. It does not enable that court to assess the merits of the case nor undertake a full review of the measures affecting a civil right. There was consequently a violation of Article 6(1).

JAMES v *UK* (1986) 8 EHRR 123

Facts

The applicants were trustees acting under the will of the second Duke of Westminster. The Westminster family owned land in Belgravia and developed an estate comprising approximately 2,000 houses. The applicants submitted that there was a violation of their rights under Article 1, Protocol 1 based on the fact that they had been deprived of their ownership of a number of the properties on the estate. This deprivation of property was a direct result of leasehold enfranchisement under the Leasehold Reform Act (LRA) 1967 which conferred on certain tenants the right to compulsorily purchase the freehold reversion from the landlord on certain terms and conditions. These rights of acquisition are limited to residential properties where the tenant occupies under a long lease (over 21 years) at a low rent. The system of long leases typically involves the tenant acquiring the lease by the payment of a capital sum and thereafter paying the landlord a small or nominal ground rent. Therefore the landlord's interest in the property lies in the rent payable throughout the term of the lease and in the prospect of the reversion at the expiration of the contractual term. Since the lease is a wasting asset, the tenant's interest in the property will diminish over time in direct proportion to the landlord's increasing interest. At the end of the term the tenant's interest terminates and the property reverts back to the landlord who enjoys the benefit of any repairs and improvements without the need to pay the tenant any compensation. To alleviate this injustice the Government introduced the leasehold enfranchisement scheme. The conditions that the tenants had to satisfy under the LRA 1967, in order to qualify for enfranchisement, were as follows:

(a)   the tenancy must be a long lease (21 years or more); and
(b)   the rateable value of the house must not exceed £750 (or £1,500 in Greater London); and
(c)   it must be a low rent. This means that the annual rent must be less than two-thirds of the rateable value; and

(d) the tenant must have occupied the house as his or her only or main residence and must have done so for at least three years prior to giving notice to enfranchise.

The purchase price payable to the landlord was calculated using two bases of valuation: the 1967 basis of valuation and the 1974 basis of valuation. Generally the 1967 basis applies to less valuable properties (those with a rateable value of £500 or, if in Greater London, £1,000), while the 1974 basis applies to more valuable properties (those with a rateable value of between £500 and £750, or if in Greater London, between £1,000 and £1,500). The essence of the 1967 basis of valuation is that the tenant only pays for the land but not for the buildings. (This reflects the policy of the Government's White Paper[1] which stated that: 'The price of enfranchisement must be calculated in accordance with the principle that in equity the bricks and mortar belong to the qualified leaseholder and the land to the landlord'.) This calculation is achieved by reliance upon a fiction that the tenant has obtained a 50-year extension of the lease and the house is sold on the open market to an independent purchaser subject to the 50-year lease. The 1974 basis of valuation is more favourable to the landlord and is calculated on the assumption that at the end of the tenancy the tenant acquires a statutory tenancy under the Landlord and Tenant Act 1954 and pays a 'fair rent' and the land is sold on the open market subject to this. Thus the landlord can expect to receive a market value for the land and buildings subject to the statutory tenancy.

In the present case, between 1979 and 1983, 80 long leasehold tenants on the Belgravia estate owned by the Westminster family exercised their rights to acquire the freehold. In 28 transactions the purchase price was calculated on the 1967 basis of valuation and the 1974 basis was used in the remaining 52 cases. The applicants noted that in some cases the tenants sold the freehold within a year of acquiring it and made large profits on the sale. The applicants cited one case where the tenant had moved into occupation of the property in 1966 having paid a low price for an end-of-term lease (£9,000) with no prospect of enfranchisement. This individual, taking advantage of the rights subsequently given by the LRA 1967, acquired the freehold at 28 per cent of its value (as assessed by the applicants) and was then able to sell it within a year for a profit of 636 per cent (£116,000).

According to the applicants' calculations, by having to sell their freeholds on the statutory terms, as opposed to the market value, they sustained a loss amounting to £1,479,407 for properties using the 1967 basis of valuation and £1,050,496 where the 1974 basis was used. The applicants submitted that there had been a violation of their rights under Article 1, Protocol 1 taken alone and in conjunction with Article 14 as well as a breach of Article 6(1).

---

[1] The Government's White Paper, 'Leasehold Reform in England and Wales', 1966, Cmnd 2916.

Decision

The European Court held that there had been no violation of the Convention.

Analysis

Article 1, Protocol 1

The applicable rule   The applicants contended that the European Court should examine each act of enfranchisement to determine whether or not it complied with Article 1, Protocol 1. The European Court rejected this approach. It stated that the question to be determined was whether the contested legislation itself, in empowering tenants to acquire the freehold, was compatible with the Convention. To this purpose the individual cases of enfranchisement would be relevant but only as illustrations of the impact of the legislation in practice.

The European Court referred to the 'three distinct rules' (see *Sporrong and Lönnroth* v *Sweden*) and observed (at para 37) that:

> before inquiring whether the first general rule has been complied with, it must determine whether the last two are applicable. The three rules are not, however, 'distinct' in the sense of being unconnected. The second and third rules are concerned with particular instances of interference with the right to peaceful enjoyment of property and should therefore be construed in the light of the general principle enunciated in the first rule.

The European Court was satisfied that the second rule applied because the applicants had been deprived of their possessions. The question was whether that deprivation was justifiable as being 'in the public interest and subject to the conditions provided for by law and by the general principles of international law'.

In the public interest   The European Court had to consider whether the deprivation could be regarded as being 'in the public interest' given that the general community enjoyed no direct benefit from the property which had been transferred between private individuals. The European Court accepted that if the deprivation had been for no other reason than to confer a benefit on a private party then it could not be regarded as being 'in the public interest'. However it stated (at para. 45) that: 'a taking of property effected in pursuance of legitimate social, economic or other policies may be 'in the public interest', even if the community at large has no direct use or enjoyment of the property taken'. It was the fact that the deprivation was made in pursuance of a policy to enhance social justice within the community that enabled a transfer from one private party to another to be regarded as being 'in the public interest' for the purposes of Article 1, Protocol 1.

The applicants further suggested that the use of different phrases, 'public interest' in the second rule dealing with deprivation and 'general interest' in the third rule concerning the control of property, indicates an intention to refer to different concepts. Accordingly the applicants argued that the state is granted more latitude to control the use of property than it has to deprive an owner of it. However, the European Court did not decide this issue on the ground that any such distinction, if it did exist, was irrelevant to the facts at hand.

The margin of appreciation   The European Court explained the justification for the margin of appreciation in the following terms (at para. 46):

> Because of their direct knowledge of their society and its needs, the national authorities are in principle better placed than the international judge to appreciate what is 'in the public interest' ... it is thus for the national authorities to make the initial assessment both of the existence of a problem of public concern warranting measures of deprivation of property and of the remedial action to be taken.

The European Court acknowledged that due to the policy decisions surrounding the leasehold enfranchisement legislation the state would be given a very wide margin of appreciation. It stated (also at para. 46) that:

> The decision to enact laws expropriating property will commonly involve consideration of political, economic and social issues on which opinions within a democratic society may reasonably differ widely. The Court, finding it natural that the margin of appreciation available to the legislature in implementing social and economic policies should be a wide one, will respect the legislature's judgment as to what is 'in the public interest' unless that judgment be manifestly without reasonable foundation. In other words, although the Court cannot substitute its own assessment for that of the national authorities, it is bound to review the contested measures under Article 1 of Protocol 1 and, in so doing, to make an inquiry into the facts with reference to which the national authorities acted.

Therefore whilst recognising its own supervisory role, the European Court took into account the fact that, in this particular area of law, the state has a very wide margin of discretion in the observance of its obligations under the Convention.

A legitimate aim   Having reference to the state's margin of appreciation the European Court observed (at para. 47) that:

> The margin of appreciation is wide enough to cover legislation aimed at securing greater social justice in the sphere of people's homes, even where such legislation interferes with existing contractual relations between private parties and confers no direct benefit on the State or the community at large.

Therefore the LRA 1967 was found to pursue a legitimate aim by seeking to eliminate social injustice in the housing sector. As to whether or not there was in fact any social injustice that needed rectifying by the contested legislation was a question of debate for which there was room for legitimate conflicts of opinion. The applicants contended that long leaseholders did not suffer from any unfairness and so the offending legislation was not required to eliminate social injustice. However, the Government felt that the leaseholders had a 'moral entitlement' to ownership of their house, which was inadequately protected by the previous legislation. In ascertaining the existence of a legitimate aim in the public interest, the European Court identified its role as follows: it had to satisfy itself that the belief of the UK Parliament, in the existence of the social injustice, was not manifestly unreasonable. Such a test clearly gives the state considerable latitude in identifying a problem of public concern to justify its action.

Proportionality   The principle of proportionality requires that there be 'a reasonable relationship of proportionality between the means employed and the aim sought to be realised' (at para. 50). The European Court endorsed the 'fair balance' test enunciated in *Sporrong and Lönnroth* v *Sweden*, which expressed the principle of proportionality in terms of a fair balance test. This refers to the need to strike a fair balance 'between the demands of the general interest of the community and the requirements of the protection of the individual's fundamental rights'. This fair balance does not exist where a person has had to bear 'an individual and excessive burden'.

The applicants maintained that security of tenure provided adequate protection for long leaseholders and that to deprive freeholders of their property was excessive. They argued that expropriation under Article 1, Protocol 1 should only be permitted where there is no alternative, less drastic remedy available. The European Court rejected this argument stating (at para. 51) that: 'This amounts to reading a test of strict necessity into the Article, an interpretation which the Court does not find warranted. The availability of alternative solutions does not in itself render the leasehold reform legislation unjustified'. The European Court stated that, provided the legislation was reasonable and suitable for achieving its aim, the European Court would not assess whether it was the best solution for the problem it sought to remedy. Since Parliament considered the leaseholder to have a 'moral entitlement' to the property, the perceived social injustice went to the very issue of ownership and was not merely a security of tenure concern. In these circumstances the European Court concluded that leasehold enfranchisement was not an inappropriate means of meeting the public concern.

Proportionality and compensation   Article 1, Protocol 1 is silent on the issue of compensation. However the European Court accepted that the availability and amount of compensation is a material consideration in assessing whether the LRA

1967 satisfied the fair balance test and in particular whether it imposed a disproportionate burden on the applicants. The European Court noted (at para. 54) that:

> The taking of property without payment of an amount reasonably related to its value would normally constitute a disproportionate interference which could not be considered justifiable under Article 1 (P1–1). Article 1 (P1–1) does not, however, guarantee a right to full compensation in all circumstances. Legitimate objectives of 'public interest', such as pursued in measures of economic reform or measures designed to achieve greater social justice, may call for less than reimbursement of the full market value.

The state enjoys a wide margin of appreciation in providing means for compensation to property owners and the European Court's power of review is limited to ascertaining whether the choice of compensation terms falls outside the state's wide margin of appreciation in this domain.

The applicants argued that the 1967 basis of valuation did not provide a full market value for the property. In this respect the European Court noted two relevant factors. First, Parliament's view at the time was that the tenant already owned the buildings and therefore should only be required to pay for that part of the property which he or she had not already paid for, i.e. the land itself. The second factor was that Parliament, in passing the legislation, sought to prevent landlords enjoying an unjust enrichment on the reversion of the property. On this basis the European Court felt (at para. 56) that:

> it had not been established, having regard to the respondent State's wide margin of appreciation, that the 1967 basis of valuation is not such as to afford a fair balance between the interests of the private parties concerned and thereby between the general interest of society and the landlord's right of property.

The general principles of international law   The applicants argued that the international law requirement of prompt, adequate and effective compensation for the expropriation of property belonging to foreigners also applied to nationals under Article 1, Protocol 1. The European Court rejected this stating that the general principles of international law remain within their normal sphere of applicability meaning that they only apply to acts of a state in relation to non-nationals (for a more in-depth explanation of the European Court's reasoning see *Lithgow v UK*).

The conditions provided for by law   The European Court reasserted its consistent approach to the term 'law' in this context. The term does 'not merely refer back to domestic law but also [relates] to the quality of the law, requiring it to be compatible with the rule of law' (at para. 67). Therefore the fundamental principles of law, common to all of the contracting states, become relevant. On the facts the European Court found no grounds for finding that the enfranchisement of the applicants' properties was arbitrary and not provided for by law.

The relationship between the first and second rule   In the alternative the applicants asserted a violation of their right to the peaceful enjoyment of their possessions as guaranteed under the first rule. Since the deprivation of property is the most radical kind of interference with the peaceful enjoyment of property, the applicants submitted that even if there was no violation under the second rule, there could nevertheless be a violation within the wider scope of the first rule. The European Court rejected this submission stating (at para. 71) that:

> the second sentence supplements and qualifies the general principle enunciated in the first sentence. This being so, it is inconceivable that application of that general principle to the present case should lead to any conclusion different from that already arrived at by the Court in application of the second sentence.

Article 14 in conjunction with Article 1, Protocol 1
The applicants submitted that the leasehold reform legislation was discriminatory on the ground of 'property' because it only applied to the restricted class of property occupied by long leaseholders and it disadvantageously treated those landlords who owned property of a lower value. The European Court observed (at para. 75) that:

> For the purposes of Article 14, a difference of treatment is discriminatory if it has no objective and reasonable justification, that is, if it does not pursue a legitimate aim or if there is not a reasonable relationship of proportionality between the means employed and the aim sought to be realised ... As in relation to the means for giving effect to the right of property, the Contracting States enjoy a certain margin of appreciation in assessing whether and to what extent differences in otherwise similar situations permit a different treatment in law.

The European Court found legitimate reasons to justify the differential treatment. As to the applicants' first head of complaint, the European Court held that it was inevitable that, since the legislation was designed to remedy a perceived imbalance in the relations between landlords and long leasehold tenants, it would affect landlords falling within that restricted class of property owners rather than all other property owners.

In respect of the second head of complaint, the European Court found that the provisions, which entailed the progressively disadvantageous treatment for landlords the lower the value of their property, could also be justified. The introduction of rateable value limits and the use of two compensation schemes reflected Parliament's intention to exclude a small percentage of wealthy tenants from the benefits of enfranchisement and to provide more favourable terms of purchase for the vast majority of tenants who were in need of economic protection. Therefore, having regard to the margin of appreciation, the European Court declared that the state had not transgressed the principle of proportionality and consequently there was no breach of Article 14 taken in conjunction with Article 1, Protocol 1.

Article 6(1)

The applicants complained that landlords had no means of challenging the tenant's right to acquire the freehold compulsorily once the criteria laid down by the legislation had been satisfied. The applicants submitted that because no question of the individual merits of an acquisition, or of the tenant's hardship, were susceptible to review by a court or tribunal, the legislation was in violation of Article 6(1). However, the European Court found that in so far as the applicants alleged any non-compliance with the leasehold reform legislation they had unimpeded access to a tribunal competent to determine the issue. Consequently there was no breach of Article 6(1).

LITHGOW v *UK* (1986) 8 EHRR 329

Facts

The case concerned the nationalisation of certain industries in accordance with the provisions of the Aircraft and Shipbuilding Industries Act 1977. Thirty-one companies relating to aerospace, shipbuilding, marine engineering and shipbuilding training were listed for nationalisation. The applicants, whose interests were subject to nationalisation, did not contest the principle of nationalisation itself but maintained that the level of compensation which they received was grossly inadequate and discriminatory.

The legislation had had a turbulent time passing through Parliament and several times the Bill lapsed due to lack of Parliamentary time. The debates in Parliament concentrated on the alleged unfairness of the compensation terms. Due to disagreements between the two Houses, the Bill was finally introduced into the House of Lords under a special procedure whereby it could pass into law without the assent of that House. It finally received the Royal Assent and came into force on 17 March 1977. One of the applicants' complaints was that under the legislation the compensation was assessed by reference to the value of shares on nationalisation rather than the value of the underlying assets. Due to the alleged inadequate compensation terms the applicants maintained that there had been a violation of Article 1, Protocol 1 taken alone and in conjunction with Article 14.

Decision

The European Court held that there had been no breach of Article 1, Protocol 1 taken alone or in conjunction with Article 14.

Analysis

Article 1, Protocol 1

The applicable rule   All parties accepted that the applicants had clearly been deprived of their possessions within the ambit of the second rule.

In the public interest   The applicants contended that taking property for a fraction of its value was unfair compensation which could not be regarded as being 'in the public interest'. The European Court, in rejecting this contention, stated (at para. 109) that: 'The obligation to pay compensation derives from an implicit condition in Article 1 of Protocol 1 read as a whole rather than from the 'public interest' requirement itself'. The European Court noted that the 'public interest' requirement relates to the state's justifications and reasons for depriving the applicants of their property. There must be a legitimate aim for the deprivation. The applicants did not contest the reasons for the nationalisation and therefore the deprivation was in the public interest.

Subject to the conditions provided for by law   The applicants argued that, as the compensation was arbitrary and bore no reasonable relationship to the value of the property, the taking could not be regarded as being 'subject to the conditions provided for by law'. The European Court confirmed (at para. 110) that the test provided for by this wording 'requires in the first place the existence of and compliance with adequately accessible and sufficiently precise domestic legal provisions'. The applicants did not dispute the existence of such domestic legal provisions.

The general principles of international law   The European Court rejected the applicants' contention that the reference to 'the general principles of international law' meant that the international law requirement of prompt, adequate and effective compensation for the deprivation of property of foreigners also applied to nationals. The European Court endorsed the reasoning applied in *James v UK* for limiting the general principles of international law to non-nationals. These reasons are summarised as follows:

(a)   the principles of international law were specifically developed for the benefit of non-nationals;

(b)   the words of the treaty should be given their ordinary meaning and should not extend the scope of the words 'general principles of international law' beyond their normal sphere of applicability;

(c)   Article 1 states that any deprivation of property must be 'in the public interest'. If the general principles of international law applied to nationals, the express provision for the taking to be 'in the public interest' would be clearly superfluous because this requirement has always been included amongst the general principles of international law;

(d)   differentiation in treatment on the ground of nationality does not constitute discrimination in breach of Article 14 if there is an objective and reasonable justification for the differentiation. Where property is taken for the purpose of social reform or economic restructuring of the country there may be good reasons for distinguishing between nationals and non-nationals in respect of the compensation to be given. For example, non-nationals play no role in the election of the Government that effects the taking. In addition, it is natural for nationals to bear a greater burden in the public interest than non-nationals;

(e)   the European Court had recourse to the *travaux préparatoires* as a supplementary means of interpretation and this provided clear statements supporting the view that the reference to the general principles of international law did not extend to nationals.

The European Court recognised (at para. 115) that the wording served at least two purposes:

> Firstly, it enables non-nationals to resort directly to the machinery of the Convention to enforce their rights on the basis of the relevant principles of international law, whereas otherwise they would have to seek recourse to diplomatic channels or to other available means of dispute settlement to do so. Secondly, the reference ensures that the position of non-nationals is safeguarded, in that it excludes any possible argument that the entry into force of Protocol No. 1 (P1) has led to a diminution of their rights.

Proportionality and compensation   Since Article 1, Protocol 1 is silent on the issue of compensation, the European Court had to consider whether the availability of compensation constitutes a material consideration when assessing proportionality under the second rule. To this end the European Court observed (at para. 120) that:

> the taking of property in the public interest without payment of compensation is treated as justifiable only in exceptional circumstances not relevant for the present purposes. As far as Article 1 (P1–1) is concerned, the protection of the right of property it affords would be largely illusory and ineffective in the absence of any equivalent principle.

Thus the European Court acknowledged that the payment of compensation is a material factor in assessing whether a fair balance has been struck between the various interests at stake.

In respect of the amount of compensation, the European Court further observed (at para. 121) that: 'the taking of property without payment of an amount reasonably related to its value would normally constitute a disproportionate interference which could not be considered justifiable under Article 1'. Therefore the compensation provisions are clearly relevant to the assessment of whether a fair balance has been struck between the demands of the general interest of the community and the requirements of the protection of the individual's fundamental rights and, in particular, whether a disproportionate burden has been imposed on the applicants. In most cases an owner of property who does not receive payment of a sum reasonably related to the value of the property taken will be seen to suffer a disproportionate burden. However, the European Court stated (also at para. 121) that:

> Article 1 (P1–1) does not, however, guarantee a right to full compensation in all circumstances, since legitimate objectives of 'public interest', such as pursued in measures of economic reform or measures designed to achieve greater social justice, may call for less than reimbursement of the full market value.

Nationalisation legislation, by its very nature, involves the consideration of a large number of competing interests which the national authorities are better placed than an international judge to consider. On this basis the European Court acknowledged that its power of review is very limited in relation to programmes of nationalisation. It stated (at para. 122) that:

> A decision to enact nationalisation legislation will commonly involve consideration of various issues on which opinions within a democratic society may reasonably differ widely. Because of their direct knowledge of their society and its needs and resources, the national authorities are in principle better placed than the international judge to appreciate what measures are appropriate in this area and consequently the margin of appreciation available to them should be a wide one. It would, in the Court's view, be artificial in this respect to divorce the decision as to the compensation terms from the actual decision to nationalise, since the factors influencing the latter will of necessity also influence the former. Accordingly, the Court's power of review in the present case is limited to ascertaining whether the decisions regarding compensation fell outside the United Kingdom's wide margin of appreciation; it will respect the legislature's judgment in this connection unless that judgment was manifestly without reasonable foundation.

The European Court considered each of the reasons put forward by the applicants for their claim that the compensation formula was unfair and resulted in a disproportionate burden being imposed upon them. For each reason the European Court found sufficiently cogent reasons for the adoption of the particular provision. The European Court concluded that the decision to adopt the particular compensation formula was one which the state was reasonably entitled to make in the exercise of its wide margin of appreciation. Therefore the European Court concluded that there had been no violation of Article 1, Protocol 1.

Article 14 in conjunction with Article 1, Protocol 1
The European Court summarised the law governing Article 14 in the following terms (at para. 177):

> Article 14 does not forbid every difference in treatment in the exercise of the rights and freedoms recognised by the Convention (see the *'Belgian Linguistic'* judgment of 23 July 1968, Series A no. 6, p. 34, para. 10). It safeguards persons (including legal persons) who are 'placed in analogous situations' against discriminatory differences of treatment; and, for the purposes of Article 14, a difference of treatment is discriminatory if it 'has no objective and reasonable justification', that is, if it does not pursue a 'legitimate aim' or if there is not a 'reasonable relationship of proportionality between the means employed and the aim sought to be realised' (see, amongst many authorities, the *Rasmussen* judgment of 28 November 1984, Series A no. 87, p. 13, para. 35, and p. 14, para. 38). Furthermore, the Contracting States enjoy a certain margin of appreciation in assessing whether and to what extent differences in otherwise similar situations justify a different treatment in law; the scope of this margin will vary according to the circumstances, the subject-matter and its background (ibid., p. 15, para. 40).

For each instance of differential treatment put forward by the applicants as discriminatory, the European Court found that reasonable and objective justifications existed. Consequently there was found to be no breach of Article 14 in conjunction with Article 1, Protocol 1.

HOWARD v *UK* (1987) 9 EHRR 91

Facts

The applicants, two brothers, were the owners and occupiers of Rose Cottage and the surrounding land where they had lived for over 50 years. The local authority issued a compulsory purchase order in respect of the applicants' land pursuant to s. 112(1) of the Town and Country Planning Act 1971 (as amended by the Local Government Planning Act 1980). The local authority proposed to demolish Rose Cottage, which was unsightly having a high corrugated iron fence and heaps of scrap, in order to make the land available for the construction of new houses as part of a scheme to redevelop the area which was a run-down inner city area in need of improvement. The Secretary of State, following the recommendations of the inspector, confirmed the compulsory purchase order. The applicants alleged that their rights under Article 8 and Article 1, Protocol 1 had been violated.

Decision

The European Commission found that the complaints under Article 8 and Article 1, Protocol 1 were manifestly ill-founded and therefore inadmissible.

Analysis

Article 8

The European Commission found that there was an interference with the applicants' right to respect for their home under Article 8(1) by virtue of the compulsory purchase order (CPO). However the European Commission was satisfied that the interference was justifiable under Article 8(2). The CPO pursued a legitimate aim and was in accordance with the law having been made under statutory provisions that were readily accessible and foreseeable. In concluding that a fair balance had been struck between the applicants' interests and the interests of the community as a whole the European Commission took account of the following factors.

(a) The applicants' land was low lying and level land that was ideal for the proposed sheltered accommodation for the elderly and if the applicants' land were excluded from the redevelopment scheme, sheltered housing would be impracticable.

(b) The applicants were offered alternative residential accommodation in the immediate vicinity of Rose Cottage.

(c) The applicants were entitled to full compensation for the value of their land together with disturbance and removal expenses.

The European Commission therefore concluded that the interference was justified as 'necessary in a democratic society' for the protection of the rights and freedoms of others who would benefit from the proposed redevelopment. Consequently there was no breach of Article 8.

Article 1, Protocol 1

The European Commission considered the interaction of Article 8 with Article 1, Protocol 1 and recognised that: 'where, as here, administrative actions impinge on two separate but partially overlapping provisions of the Convention, the application of the relevant provisions must be reconciled'. It further observed that: 'the measure of necessity referred to in the second sentence of [Article 1,

Protocol 1] closely resembles that which applies to the justification for an interference with the rights guaranteed by Art. 8(1)'. In particular, where there is a deprivation of property by the state it has to be ascertained whether a fair balance has been struck between the rights of the owners and the rights of the community. A significant factor to be weighed in the balance is the availability of compensation reflecting the value of the property expropriated. The European Commission concluded that:

> In view of the carefully balanced appraisal of the applicants' rights against the advantages to the community of proceeding with the development which are set out in the inspector's report, and the availability of compensation for the value of the property expropriated from the applicants, the Commission finds that the compulsory purchase of their property, which was clearly in the public interest for the purposes of the development plan, was in accordance with the requirements of [Article 1, Protocol 1].

Therefore there had been a carefully balanced appraisal of the applicants' right of property against the advantages to the community, an important factor being the availability of compensation, and consequently there was no breach of Article 1, Protocol 1.

S v *UK* (App. No. 11716/85)

Facts

The applicant lived with Mrs R in a lesbian relationship. Mrs R was a secure tenant of her council house and when she died, the applicant claimed to be qualified to succeed Mrs R under a secured tenancy. Section 30 of the Housing Act 1980 provides that the rights of succession can be enjoyed by the tenant's spouse or by a member of the tenant's family. A definition of family member is given in s. 50(3) and includes a couple who 'live together as husband and wife'. The county court granted the local authority a possession order and the applicant was evicted from the flat. On appeal the Court of Appeal held that the term 'living together as husband and wife' did not include homosexual relationships and therefore the applicant could not succeed to the tenancy. The applicant alleged a violation of Article 1, Protocol 1 and Article 8 taken alone and in conjunction with Article 14.

Decision

The European Commission found all of the applicant's claims to be manifestly ill-founded and inadmissible.

Analysis

Article 8
The European Commission had to determine whether the eviction of the applicant by the local authority interfered with her right to respect for her home. This raised the question of whether the council house could be regarded as her 'home' within the ambit of Article 8. The European Commission noted that the applicant was occupying the house:

> without any legal title whatsoever. Contractual relations were established between the local authority and the deceased partner and that contractual agreement may or may not have permitted long-term visitors. The fact remains, however, that on the death of the partner, under the ordinary law, the applicant was no longer entitled to remain in the house, and the local authority was entitled to possession so that the house could no longer be regarded as 'home' for the applicant within the meaning of Article 8.

Therefore the European Commission's first line of reasoning was that the house did not constitute her home for the purposes of Article 8. In the alternative the European Commission considered the position if her lack of proprietary interest did not prevent the house from being her 'home' within the meaning of Article 8 (this in fact is the current position as a result of the decision in *Khatun and 180 others* v *UK* (1998) 26 EHRR CD 212). The European Commission stated that:

> even if the applicant's right to respect for her home, as guaranteed by Article 8, could be regarded as having been interfered with by order of the county court for possession against her, the Commission considers that such interference was clearly in accordance with the law and was also necessary for the protection of the contractual rights of the landlord to have the property back at the end of the tenancy.

The interference was justifiable under Article 8(2) and consequently there was found to be no violation of Article 8.

Article 14 in conjunction with Article 8
The European Commission recalled that:

> a difference in treatment in the enjoyment of the rights and freedoms set forth in the Convention is not to be regarded as discrimination for the purposes of Article 14 if that difference has an objective and reasonable justification provided that the means employed are reasonably proportional to the aim sought to be realised.

To this end the European Commission noted that the aim of the Housing Act 1980, in protecting the family, was a legitimate aim and similar to the protection guaranteed to family life under Article 8. The question for decision was whether it was justifiable to exclude homosexual relationships from the protection afforded to families. Since existing Strasbourg case law had already established the principle that homosexual partners do not fall within the meaning of family under Article 8, the European Commission concluded that the differential treatment of homosexual partners' rights of succession compared to heterosexual partners' rights could be objectively and reasonably justified.

Article 1, Protocol 1

The European Commission noted that there was no contractual nexus between the applicant and the local authority. The fact that the applicant had been living in the house for some time without any legal title could not constitute a 'possession' for the purposes of Article 1, Protocol 1. Therefore her eviction by the local authority did not interfere with her possessions.

App. No. 11949/86 v *UK* (1988) 10 EHRR 123

Facts

The applicant purchased a long lease of a flat in 1975 for £6,000. At the time of the European Court judgment she valued the flat at £30,000. Under the terms of the lease she was liable to make a service charge payment, by way of additional rent, to the landlord in respect of her proportion of the insurance and any repair and maintenance costs. There was a disagreement between the landlord and tenant as to the amount of service charge payable and as a result of this the tenant withheld payment of the charge. The landlord commenced possession proceedings in the county court and the court granted an order requiring the tenant to pay the outstanding sum, amounting to little more than £300, by a certain date or to give up possession of the flat. She did not pay the sum by the specified date and the landlord evicted her. She sought relief from forfeiture first in the county court and then in the High Court. Due to a loophole in the legislation existing at the time neither court had jurisdiction, on the facts, to grant the tenant relief although both courts indicated that the tenant would have been granted relief had it had the jurisdiction to do so (see *Di Palma* v *Victoria Square Property* [1984] 2 All ER 92). The applicant claimed to be a victim of a violation of Article 1, Protocol 1 and Articles 6 and 8 taken alone and in conjunction with Article 14.

Decision

The European Commission decided that all of the applicant's complaints were inadmissible.

Analysis

Article 1, Protocol 1

The European Commission had to examine whether the facts gave rise to sufficient state responsibility for the deprivation of the applicant's property to invoke the Convention. The landlord's exercise of his remedy of forfeiture was a direct result of the presence of a forfeiture clause in the lease. The terms of the lease regulated the private law contractual arrangements between the applicant as tenant and the landlord. The forfeiture of the lease, and hence the consequent deprivation of property, was occasioned by the contractual provisions of the lease. The existence of the forfeiture clause was neither directly prescribed nor amended by any legislation. Taking these factors into account the European Commission concluded that:

> In view of the exclusively private law relationship between the parties to the lease the Commission considers that the respondent Government cannot be responsible by the mere fact that the landlord by its agents, who were private individuals, brought the applicant's lease to an end in accordance with the terms of that lease, which set out the agreement between the applicant and the company.

The fact that the landlord had issued possession proceedings in the county court and obtained an order enabling him to forfeit the lease was not sufficient to bring in the requisite element of state responsibility. The European Commission stated that:

> This fact alone is not however sufficient to engage state responsibility in respect of the applicant's rights to property, since the public authority in the shape of the County Court merely provided a forum for the determination of the civil right in dispute between the parties.

Article 8

The applicant contended that the eviction from her home constituted an unjustified interference with the right to respect for her home under Article 8. The state had not itself interfered with the applicant's home and therefore the applicant's allegation rested upon the premise that the state was under a positive duty to take measures to prevent an interference with the applicant's home. The European Commission doubted that Article 8 required the state to take any such positive action, but in any event, it concluded that any interference with the applicant's right to respect for her home consequent upon the forfeiture of her lease, was in conformity with Article 8(2) as a measure which was in accordance with the law and necessary in a democratic society for the protection of the rights of others. Therefore the interference could be justified and was not in violation of Article 8.

Article 6(1)

Under the law at that time the county court had no jurisdiction to grant relief once the possession order had been executed. The High Court did have jurisdiction to grant relief after execution of the possession order but only where the initial possession proceedings for the non-payment of rent had been instituted in the High Court and not, as in this case, in the county court. As a result of this case the UK legislature recognised the injustice that ensued and enacted s. 55 of the Administration of Justice Act 1985 to rectify the mischief by enabling the county court to grant relief from forfeiture on a similar basis to that available in the High Court. However, the legislative amendments did not assist the applicant and she claimed that she had been denied access to a court due to the fact that neither court had jurisdiction to grant her relief from forfeiture. The European Commission accepted that 'the dispute between the applicant and her landlord as to her obligations under the lease, and the question whether or not it should be ordered forfeit, involved the determination of her civil rights and obligations'. Therefore, Article 6(1) was applicable on the facts and guaranteed her the right to a fair and public hearing by an independent and impartial tribunal. However, the European Commission noted that the applicant had had such a hearing before the county court in the initial possession proceedings. Thus the essence of the applicant's complaint was the lack of a superior review jurisdiction. In this respect the European Commission observed that: 'Art. 6(1) of the Convention cannot be interpreted so as to require the existence of a further jurisdiction to review or expand upon the jurisdiction provided by an inferior court, where that first court is capable of determining all questions of fact and law'. Consequently there was no violation of Article 6(1).

Article 14

The applicant submitted that she had been discriminated against on the grounds that neither the county court nor the High Court had jurisdiction to grant her relief from forfeiture because the possession proceedings against her had been instituted in the county court. She argued that a tenant against whom possession had been granted in the High Court could apply for relief from forfeiture in that court. The applicant contended that this distinction, which benefits more wealthy tenants who can afford to occupy the expensive properties, is arbitrary and unjustifiable.

At a general level the European Commission considered the reasons for differences in treatment between litigants in the county court and those in the High Court. It observed that the difference in the proceedings of the two courts reflects the limited and unlimited jurisdiction of the county court and High Court respectively. In addition, it took account of the fact that the proceedings in the county court are designed to be less complex in order to reduce costs. Therefore the offending legislation, which reflected these aims by ensuring the finality of the decision in the county court, was found to pursue a legitimate aim. The European

Commission concluded that the measures complained of were not so disproportionate to that aim as to give rise to a violation of Article 14.

AGOSI v *UK* (1986) 9 EHRR 1

Facts

The applicant company sold and delivered to X and Y 1,500 Krugerrands (gold
coins). The import of gold coins into the UK is illegal and X and Y were arrested
and convicted of attempting to smuggle the coins into the UK. The gold coins
were seized by customs and subsequently declared forfeit. The applicant company
maintained that it still owned the coins because the contract of sale had contained
a clause whereby the seller retained title of the coins until full payment of the
purchase price had been discharged. Since X and Y's cheque tendering payment
had been dishonoured, title to the coins remained with the applicant. The
applicant contended that the forfeiture of the coins constituted a breach of Article
1, Protocol 1 since it was the legal owner of the coins and was innocent of any
wrongdoing.

Decision

The European Court held that there was no violation of Article 1, Protocol 1.

Analysis

Article 1, Protocol 1

The applicable rule   The European Court first considered whether there had been
a deprivation under the second rule or a control of use under the third rule. It noted
that the prohibition on importing gold coins into the UK was a control of use of
property and that the forfeiture of the gold coins was a measure taken to enforce
that prohibition. It stated (at para. 51) that: 'The forfeiture of the coins did, of
course, involve a deprivation of property, but in the circumstances the deprivation
formed a constituent element of the procedure for the control of the use in the
United Kingdom of gold coins'. Thus it concluded that the applicable rule was the
third rule.

Was the interference justifiable?   As the prohibition on the importation of gold
coins was within the general interest, the European Court concentrated on the
requirement for proportionality. It noted (at para. 52) that:

In determining whether a fair balance exists, the Court recognises that the state enjoys a wide margin of appreciation with regard both to choosing the means of enforcement [of the prohibition on importing gold coins] and to ascertaining whether the consequences of enforcement are justified in the general interest for the purpose of achieving the object of the law in question.

The European Commission took the view that if the owner is innocent of any wrongdoing, it should be entitled to recover the forfeited goods. The European Court did not share this view. However it recognised (at para. 54) that, in striking a fair balance, 'the behaviour of the owner of the property, including the degree of fault or care which he has displayed, is one element of the entirety of circumstances which should be taken into account'.

The European Court observed (at para. 55) that although there are no procedural requirements explicit within the wording of the third rule, nevertheless, the European Court must:

> consider whether the applicable procedures in the present case were such as to enable, amongst other things, reasonable account to be taken of the degree of fault or care of the applicant company ... and also whether the procedures in question afforded the applicant company a reasonable opportunity of putting its case to the responsible authorities. In ascertaining whether these conditions were satisfied a comprehensive view must be taken of the applicable procedures.

This statement demonstrates the importance of the due process factor in assessing proportionality in this case. The customs and excise commissioners had chosen not to exercise their discretion to restore the gold coins to the applicants. This was a purely administrative procedure involving them in exercising their statutory discretion. The commissioners were bound by English law to be guided by relevant considerations and the European Court accepted that the owner's alleged innocence and diligence were relevant considerations. However, the availability of judicial review of the commissioners' decision was held to be an adequate means of protecting the innocent owner and of complying with the procedural requirements of the third rule in Article 1, Protocol 1. The European Court was satisfied that the measures were proportionate to the aim to be achieved.

GILLOW v *UK* (1989) 11 EHRR 335

Facts

The applicants, who were husband and wife, were both born in England and enjoyed British citizenship. They moved to Guernsey in 1956, bought a plot of land and built a house called 'Whiteknights'. Due to work commitments they left Guernsey to work abroad and 'Whiteknights' was let to tenants. Under the legislation in force at that time the applicants had resident qualifications which enabled them to occupy 'Whiteknights' without a licence. However, in 1970 legislation was introduced which imposed a residency requirement in order to be able to occupy controlled housing without a licence. The effect of the 1970 legislation was that the applicants were no longer entitled to occupy 'White-knights' without a licence. They returned to Guernsey to apply for a licence to occupy 'Whiteknights' as their retirement home, or for a period sufficient to put the property into repair for the purposes of sale or letting. The licences were refused in the light of the adverse housing situation in Guernsey at that time. Mr Gillow was subsequently prosecuted for the unlawful occupation of his house and was fined.

Decision

The European Court agreed with the European Commission in finding that there had been a breach of Article 8 and that there was no breach of Article 6 nor of Article 14. However, whilst the European Commission had concluded that Article 1, Protocol 1 had been violated, the European Court held the Article to be inapplicable on the facts.

Analysis

Article 8

Was 'Whiteknights' the applicants' home? It was not disputed that the applicants had lived in 'Whiteknights' as their home until 1960 when they left Guernsey to work abroad. The question was whether or not the property remained their home, within the meaning of Article 8, after they had left. The applicants maintained that they had always intended to return to 'Whiteknights' and retained their ownership for that purpose. The fact that they had left their furniture in the property was further evidence of their intention to return which they did in fact do in 1979 when they moved back to Guernsey. The European Commission observed (at para. 114) that:

> ownership of a property is not in itself sufficient to establish it as one's home, where one has never in fact lived in the property. However, where continued ownership follows occupation of a property as one's home, such ownership is evidence of a strong continuing link with the property.

The European Commission held that 'Whiteknights' was the applicants' home. It was satisfied that during the period of their absence from Guernsey the applicants possessed a continuing intention to return to the property. A key evidential factor of this continuing intention to return was the actual return of the applicants to the property in 1979. The fact that they owned another property in Hertfordshire, which had been occupied by Mrs Gillow's mother since they purchased it in 1965, did not exclude 'Whiteknights' from being considered as their home. Ownership of a property, even for a considerable length of time, is not in itself sufficient to make it a person's home nor does it exclude the fact that another property may in fact constitute that person's home. The European Court endorsed this approach stating (at para. 46) that: 'Although the applicants had been absent from Guernsey for almost nineteen years, they had in the circumstances retained sufficient continuing links with Whiteknights for it to be considered their home, for the purposes of Article 8'.

Was there an interference with their right to respect for their home? The European Court stated (at para. 47) that, in its opinion:

> the fact that, on pain of prosecution, they were obliged to obtain a licence to live in their own house on their return to Guernsey in 1979, the refusal of the licences applied for, the institution of criminal proceedings against them for unlawful occupation of the property and, in Mr Gillow's case, his conviction and the imposition of a fine constituted interferences with the exercise of the applicants' right to respect for their home.

Was the interference in accordance with the law? The applicants complained that the relevant legislation gave the housing authority such wide discretionary powers that it made its decisions unforeseeable and unpredictable. However, the European Court was satisfied that the interference was in accordance with the law. It stated (at para. 51) that:

> A law which confers a discretion is not in itself inconsistent with the requirement of foreseeability, provided that the scope of the discretion and the manner of its exercise are indicated with sufficient clarity, having regard to the legitimate aim of the measure in question, to give the individual adequate protection against arbitrary interference. In the present case, the Court finds that the scope of the discretion, coupled with the provision for judicial control of its exercise, is sufficient to satisfy the requirements of the Convention inherent in the expression in accordance with the law.

Did it pursue a legitimate aim? The European Commission found that the licensing system pursued the legitimate aim of the economic well-being of the country. It noted (at para. 130) that:

the aim of this legislation has been to ensure that housing availability is not determined by market forces alone, and to maintain a balance between the requirements of the existing population, horticultural, and other economic interests, the interests of those wishing to come to live in Guernsey, and the interests of the tourist industry and of holidaymakers, who play an important part in the Guernsey economy.

The European Court agreed with this approach stating (at para. 54) that it was legitimate for the authorities 'to try to maintain the population within limits that permit the balanced economic development of the island'.

Was the interference necessary in a democratic society?

(a)   A pressing social need   The European Commission explained (at para. 132) that: 'As the Convention organs have repeatedly recognised, to satisfy the requirement of necessity referred to in Art. 8(2) of the Convention, it must be established that the measure in question was not merely desirable or convenient, but responded to a real requirement'. This real requirement is often referred to as a 'pressing social need'.

The reasons given to the applicants for the refusal of a residence licence relied principally upon the adverse housing situation existing in Guernsey as perceived by the Government. The European Court deferred to the Government's assessment of the situation, stating that: 'the Guernsey legislature is better placed than the international judge to assess the effects of any relaxation of the housing controls'. It took account of the fact that the legislation gave the housing authority sufficiently wide discretionary powers to grant residence licences in individual cases to avoid disproportionality, and concluded that there was no breach of Article 8 in respect of the terms of the contested legislation. However, in the application of the legislation, the European Court had to consider whether the manner in which the housing authority exercised its discretion in the applicants' case constituted a breach of Article 8 and to this end it had to assess the principle of proportionality.

(b)   Proportionality   The European Commission observed (at para. 141) that 'In view of the protection given by Art. 8, the prohibition of the enjoyment of a property built and owned by an individual as his home can only be justified in the most exceptional circumstances'. It noted the fact that the applicants had initially built 'Whiteknights' and had let the house during their 18 years of absence from the island. In this respect they had significantly contributed to the housing stock of Guernsey. It concluded (at para. 141) that: 'Whilst the respondent Government have established the existence of some population pressure in Guernsey, they have not shown that it was so acute as to justify refusing the applicants the opportunity of returning to occupy their own property which was vacant and ready

for occupation as their home'. The European Court agreed with the European Commission's analysis of the situation. Therefore the interference with the applicants' right to respect for their home was not necessary in a democratic society because it was disproportionate to the aim to be achieved. Consequently there had been a violation of Article 8.

Article 1, Protocol 1
The European Court, having being informed that the UK had not extended the application of Protocol 1 to the Island of Guernsey, had no option but to conclude that it had no jurisdiction to entertain the applicants' complaints under Article 1, Protocol 1. The Government had omitted to raise this crucial piece of information before the European Commission which therefore proceeded to examine the application of Article 1, Protocol 1. Although its decision that the complaint under Article 1 was admissible has since lost relevance in the light of the new information before the European Court, the admissibility decision is nevertheless a valuable illustration of the application of Article 1, Protocol 1 and is worth consideration.

The applicable rule The European Commission referred to the 'three distinct rules' from *Sporrong and Lönnroth* v *Sweden* and observed (at para. 145) that:

> the three rules referred to by the Court are not entirely separate or watertight. The first 'general' rule contains a general guarantee of the right of property. This general guarantee is then qualified or limited by the second and third rules. The second and third rules must be interpreted in their context and in the light of the general guarantee contained in the first sentence.

The European Commission decided that the interference involved a control of use within the scope of the third rule because the applicants still retained ownership of the house and could rent or sell it.

In accordance with the law The European Commission observed (at para. 152) that: 'the requirements of [Article 1, Protocol 1] permit the domestic legislature greater latitude in the choice of legislation which is appropriate for the control of the use of property than under Art. 8 of the Convention'. As the European Commission had already satisfied itself that the legislation was sufficiently foreseeable and certain to satisfy the requirement of law under Article 8, it must also be considered sufficiently certain to satisfy Article 1, Protocol 1.

In the general interest The European Commission had already found that the contested legislation pursued a legitimate aim within the ambit of Article 8(2).

Therefore, given that the aim of the legislation was legitimate for one of the specific purposes of Article 8(2), it followed that it must be equally legitimate for the more general requirement of being in the 'general interest' under Article 1, Protocol 1.

Proportionality   The European Commission recognised the variable degree of scrutiny which it exercises in reviewing proportionality and in establishing the existence of a legitimate aim. It observed (at para. 147) that: 'in assessing the necessity of a measure under [Article 1, Protocol 1] the Commission retains a limited review of the legitimacy of the aim of the legislation and a fuller review of the proportionality of the actual interference with the applicant's rights'. The European Commission also made reference to the different measure of proportionality dependent upon which of the three rules is applicable. Whilst a deprivation of property involves the loss of ownership, full ownership is retained by the owner where the state only interferes with the control of use of the property. Therefore the measure of proportionality clearly differs in the application of these two rules because a deprivation of property is inherently more serious than a control of its use.

The European Commission recognised (again at para. 147) that: 'The principal criterion for establishing whether a fair balance has now been struck in the control of use of personal property is therefore the use for which that property was intended by the individual owner'. 'Whiteknights' was built and equipped for residential use. The licensing requirement imposed by the legislation therefore deprived the applicants of the sole, direct use that they could personally enjoy in the property. The European Commission further emphasised (at para. 154) the greater leniency in the necessity test under the third rule and the importance of the intended use of the property as a factor to be weighed in the fair balance test:

> Whereas the Commission has recognised a close parallel between the test of necessity in respect of deprivations of property and interferences with the right to respect for one's home under Art. 8 (e.g., *App. No. 9261/81* v *UK*), the test applicable in respect of measures for the control of property is less stringent and must depend principally upon the severity of the restrictions imposed. Hence the measures applied to control the property's use must be considered in the light of the way in which the property could still be used and the purpose for which it was originally intended.

The applicants were refused a licence entitling them to live in the property and were also refused a temporary licence enabling them to occupy 'Whiteknights' temporarily in order to carry out the substantial repairs needed after 18 years of letting the property. The property was in no state to be sold or let until the repairs had been carried out. These were clearly very severe restrictions on the applicants' use of their property. The European Commission considered the reasons given to the applicants for the refusal of their licence, principally the adverse housing situation in Guernsey, and concluded that the applicants had suffered a disproportionate burden and consequently there was an infringement of Article 1, Protocol 1.

Article 6(1)

The applicants contested the fairness of the appeal lodged with the Royal Court of Guernsey against the decision of the housing authority to refuse to grant them licences to occupy their house. Article 6(1) was clearly applicable since the proceedings concerned the applicants' right to occupy their own home, which is a 'civil right' within the meaning of Article 6(1). The applicants submitted that their access to the court was unfairly impeded. Reliance was placed on a number of factors all of which were rejected by the European Court. For example, the applicants complained of the fact that they had either to lodge the appeal from a hotel or from outside Guernsey, or face prosecution. The European Court, however, remained unconvinced by this argument stating (at para. 69) that: 'the applicants have failed to show how their effective right of access to court has been interfered with by the refusal to allow them to occupy their house without facing prosecution'.

Article 14 in conjunction with Article 8

The applicants relied upon two discriminatory measures which allegedly violated Article 14 in conjunction with Article 8. First, they contended that the existence of a category of open market houses constituted a discrimination in favour of wealthy persons who are able to purchase and occupy open market houses without the need to apply for a residential licence. Secondly, the applicants maintained that the housing legislation discriminated in favour of Britons born in Guernsey as against Britons born elsewhere. As to the applicants' first head of complaint, the European Court accepted that the use of the rateable value limits reflected the Government's intention to exclude a small percentage of expensive houses from the control of the housing authority and the licensing system. It was felt that the wealthy persons seeking to buy these expensive houses were not in need of protection. However, it was legitimate for the state to protect the poorer sections of the community by ensuring adequate housing for those with strong connections with Guernsey but without the resources. The European Court concluded (at para. 66) that:

> In view of the legitimate objectives being pursued in the general interest and having regard to the state's margin of appreciation, that policy of different treatment cannot be considered as unreasonable or as imposing a disproportionate burden on owners of more modest houses like the applicants, taking into account the possibilities open to them under the licensing system.

In relation to the second head of complaint, the European Court found that the preferential treatment for persons with strong attachments to Guernsey pursued a legitimate aim and was justified on the facts. Consequently there had been no violation of Article 14 in conjunction with Article 8.

TRE TRAKTÖRER AKTIEBOLAG v *SWEDEN* (1989) 13 EHRR 309

Facts

In 1980 the applicant, Tre Traktörer Aktiebolag, a limited company with a sole shareholder, took over the management of a restaurant. It obtained a licence to serve beer, wine and other alcoholic beverages. The licence was subsequently revoked by an administrative authority on the grounds that the applicant had failed to demonstrate sufficient competence in bookkeeping and internal control following the discovery of irregularities in the applicant's bookkeeping which, according to the applicant, were due to thefts of alcoholic beverages. The restaurant subsequently closed as a result of the withdrawal of the licence. The applicant complained of a violation of Article 1, Protocol 1 and Article 6(1).

Decision

The European Court held that there had been a violation of Article 6(1), but not of Article 1, Protocol 1.

Analysis

Article 1, Protocol 1

The meaning of possessions   The state argued that a licence to serve alcoholic beverages could not be considered to be a possession. However, the European Court took the view that the economic interests connected with the running of the restaurant were 'possessions'. The maintenance of the licence was one of the principal requirements for the carrying on of the applicant's business as a restaurant and its revocation had an adverse effect on the goodwill and value of the business. Therefore the withdrawal of the licence constituted an interference with the applicant's peaceful enjoyment of its possessions.

The applicable rule   The European Court examined the complaint under the third rule rather than the second. Although the revocation of the licence meant that the applicant could not operate a restaurant business, it still kept some economic interests in the property represented by the leasing of the premises and the property assets contained within it. Therefore there had not been a deprivation of property under the second rule.

In the general interest The European Court accepted that by subjecting the sale of alcohol to a system of licences, the legislature was taking steps to implement the long-standing Swedish policy of restricting the consumption and abuse of alcohol. This was a legitimate aim in accordance with the general interest.

Proportionality The European Court next considered whether there was a reasonable relationship of proportionality between the means employed and the aim sought to be realised. It was recognised that the revocation of the licence was a severe measure in the circumstances and had serious financial repercussions on the applicant. The administrative body could have adopted other less severe measures. However, the heavy burden placed upon the applicant had to be weighed against the general interest of the community in restricting the consumption and abuse of alcohol. Bearing in mind the state's wide margin of appreciation, the European Court concluded (at para. 62) that: 'the respondent state did not fail to strike a 'fair balance' between the economic interests of the applicant company and the general interest of Swedish society'.

Article 6
The applicant alleged that there had been a violation of Article 6(1) due to the fact that there was no opportunity for the revocation of its licence to be reviewed by a court. The European Court stated (at para. 36) that:

> Article 6(1) extends only to disputes (*contestations*) over 'civil rights and obligations' which can be said, at least on arguable grounds, to be recognised under domestic law. The two questions to be answered by the Court are thus: whether there was a dispute over a 'right' and whether this 'right' was of a 'civil' nature.

Applicability of Article 6(1) In assessing the existence of a 'dispute' the European Court applied (at para. 37) the following principles from its previous case law:

> the dispute must be genuine and of a serious nature; it may relate not only to the actual existence of a right but also to its scope and the manner of its existence and, finally, the result of the proceedings concerning the dispute at issue must be directly decisive for such a right.

The Government contended that there was no right to retain such a licence and the licence could not in itself confer any such right. The European Court did not share this view. It accepted that the licence conferred a 'right' on the applicant in the form of an authorisation to sell alcoholic beverages subject to the conditions in the licence. The European Court noted that the administrative body could have taken other less severe measures than revocation. It accepted that the applicant had arguable grounds for maintaining that under Swedish law it was entitled to continue to retain the licence unless it contravened the conditions set out in the licence or any of the statutory grounds for revocation applied. Therefore there was a dispute recognised under the domestic law. The European Court next had to consider whether the right at issue was a 'civil right'. The Government emphasised the public law features of the licensing system for the distribution of alcoholic beverages and argued that the licence could not be considered to confer a civil right. However, the European Court noted that the private individuals and companies entrusted to serve alcohol carry on private commercial activities running restaurants and bars. These commercial activities have the object of earning profits and are based on a contractual relationship between the licence-holder and the customers. On this basis the European Court considered that the rights conferred on the applicant by virtue of the licence were of a civil character and that the public law aspects of the licensing system were not sufficient to outweigh this.

Compliance with Article 6(1)   Article 6(1) gives the applicant the right to have any dispute over its civil rights, i.e. the revocation of its liquor licence, to be brought before a court or tribunal. This right was denied to the applicant and therefore the European Court held that there had been a breach of Article 6(1).

POWELL AND RAYNER v *UK* (1990) 12 EHRR 355

Facts

The applicants complained of excessive noise pollution due to aircraft arriving and departing from Heathrow Airport. The airport was opened in 1946 and has drastically expanded over the years. Mr Rayner's home, where he has lived since 1961, falls within a 60 NNI (Noise and Number Index) which is regarded as an area of high noise-annoyance for residents. The NNI is used in the UK to assess the disturbance from aircraft noise to communities near the airport. Mr Powell's home falls within a much lower noise-annoyance rating. Under the Land Compensation Act 1973, compensation for any loss in the value of houses as a result of noise from an airport is available but only in respect of airports built after 1969 and not in respect of an intensification of an existing airport. Therefore the applicants were not entitled to any compensation under that legislation. Nor could the applicants commence an action in private nuisance due to the effect of s. 76(1) of the Civil Aviation Act 1982. The applicants invoked Article 1, Protocol 1 and Articles 6, 8 and 13 of the Convention.

Decision

The European Commission found the application under Article 1, Protocol 1 and Articles 6 and 8 inadmissible. The application in respect of Article 13 was found to be admissible and this was referred to the European Court. Article 13 gives a right to a national remedy for anyone whose rights under the Convention are infringed. Mr Rayner argued that there was no remedy in the national courts for the breach of his rights under Article 8. Therefore the European Court had first to consider whether or not the applicant had an arguable case that his rights under Article 8 had been breached, even though the European Commission had found his application under Article 8 inadmissible. The European Court found that there was no breach of Article 8 on the facts and consequently Article 13 was not applicable.

Analysis

Article 8

In its admissibility decision, the European Commission had found a 'clear interference' with the rights of Mr Rayner which 'involved the Government's positive obligations under Article 8'. The European Commission recognised that: 'Considerable noise nuisance can undoubtedly affect the physical well-being of a person and thus interfere with his private life. It may also deprive a person of the possibility of enjoying the amenities of his home'. However, on the facts, the European Commission concluded that the interference was justified in a democratic society in the interests of the economic well-being of the country.

The European Court concurred with the view of the European Commission that Article 8:

> cannot be interpreted so as to apply only with regard to direct measures taken by the authorities against the privacy and/or home of an individual. It may also cover indirect intrusions which are unavoidable consequences of measures not at all directed against private individuals. In this context it has to be noted that a State has not only to respect but also to protect the rights guaranteed by Art. 8(1).

In examining the state's responsibility for the noise, the European Court noted (at para. 41) that:

> Whether the present case be analysed in terms of a positive duty on the State to take reasonable and appropriate measures to secure the applicants' rights under paragraph 1 of Article 8 or in terms of an 'interference by a public authority' to be justified in accordance with paragraph 2, the applicable principles are broadly similar. In both contexts regard must be had to the fair balance that has to be struck between the competing interests of the individual and of the community as a whole; and in both

contexts the State enjoys a certain margin of appreciation in determining the steps to be taken to ensure compliance with the Convention.

Furthermore, even in relation to the positive obligations flowing from Article 8(1), 'in striking [the required] balance the aims mentioned in the second paragraph may be of a certain relevance' (also at para. 41).

The applicants conceded that the operation of Heathrow Airport, occupying an important position in relation to international trade, communications and the economy of the UK, pursued a legitimate aim. It was noted that: 'Heathrow Airport contributes around £200 million to UK's balance of payments, provides direct employment for some 48,600 persons, in addition to the substantial number of workers employed locally in servicing the industry, and pays over £16 million in local rates and rents'.

In assessing proportionality, the European Court took into account the various measures introduced by the relevant state authorities to control, abate and compensate for aircraft noise. These measures were in accordance with established international standards. The European Court recognised that the state policy had been to deal with the problem of aircraft noise by specific regulatory measures rather than by nuisance claims in the courts. In reference to this recognition the European Court stated (at para. 44) that:

> It is not for the Commission or the Court to substitute for the assessment of the national authorities another assessment of what might be the best policy in this difficult social and technical sphere. This is an area where the Contracting States are to be recognised as enjoying a wide margin of appreciation.

The European Court concluded that the state could not be said to have exceeded its margin of appreciation. As there was no arguable claim of a violation of Article 8 there could be no entitlement for a remedy under Article 13.

Article 6(1)

In its admissibility decision the European Commission had rejected the applicants' claim under Article 6(1) on the ground that the applicants had no 'civil right' under English law to compensation for nuisance caused by aircraft noise (except where the noise was caused by aircraft flying in breach of aviation regulations). This was due to the effect of s. 76(1) of the Civil Aviation Act 1982 which provides that:

> No action shall lie in respect of ... nuisance, by reason only of the flight of an aircraft over any property at a height above the ground which, having regard to wind weather and all the circumstances of the case is reasonable, or the ordinary incidents of such flight, so long as the provisions of any Air Navigation Order ... have been duly complied with ....

The European Court agreed with this decision. It noted (at para. 36) that:

> As the Commission pointed out in its admissibility decisions, the effect of s. 76(1) is to exclude liability in nuisance with regard to the flight of aircraft in certain circumstances, with the result that the applicants cannot claim to have a substantive right under English law to obtain relief for exposure to aircraft noise in those circumstances. To this extent there is no 'civil right' recognised under domestic law to attract the application of Article 6(1).

Accordingly Article 6(1) was not applicable.

PINE VALLEY DEVELOPMENTS LTD AND OTHERS v *IRELAND* (1991) 14 EHRR 319

Facts

The first applicant (Pine Valley) purchased land in 1978 relying on an existing grant of outline planning permission for industrial development. The planning permission was then refused by the planning authority on the ground that the land was part of a site earmarked as a green belt. However, in May 1981 this decision was overturned by the domestic courts following an appeal by Pine Valley. In July 1981, Pine Valley sold the land to the second applicant (Healy Holdings). Healy Holdings was solely owned by the third applicant (Mr Healy).

In February 1982 the outline planning permission was held by the Irish Supreme Court to be a nullity due to the fact that it was *ultra vires* the relevant legislation. In response to this decision, the Local Government (Planning and Development) Act (LGPDA) 1982 was enacted and the effect of s. 6 was to validate retrospectively all those planning permissions which had been declared a nullity by virtue of the decision of the Irish Supreme Court. However, the applicants maintained that their outline planning permission had not been validated by s. 6 as was contended by the Government. As a result, the applicants argued that the decision of the Supreme Court nullifying their outline planning permission, together with the inapplicability of the LGPDA 1982, violated their rights under Article 1, Protocol 1 taken alone and in conjunction with Article 14. The Government maintained that the complaint was inadmissible because the applicants were not victims within the meaning of the Convention.

Decision

The European Court held that there was no violation of Article 1, Protocol 1 taken alone. However, there was a breach of Article 14 in conjunction with Article 1, Protocol 1.

Analysis

Victim status

The Government challenged the admissibility of the application on the ground that there was no 'victim'. To support this submission the Government observed that the first applicant, Pine Valley, had sold the land to Healy Holdings in July 1981, prior to the relevant decision of the Irish Supreme Court in February 1982, and was later struck off the register of companies and thereby ceased to exist. The second applicant, Healy Holdings, was in receivership and its receiver was not a party to the proceedings before the Strasbourg institutions. Finally, the third applicant, Mr Healy, had been adjudged bankrupt in July 1990. On this basis the Government claimed that none of the applicants enjoyed sufficient victim status to enable them to bring proceedings under the Convention. In reply to this submission the European Court observed (at para. 42) that:

> Pine Valley and Healy Holdings were no more than vehicles through which Mr Healy proposed to implement the development for which outline planning permission had been granted. On this ground alone it was artificial to draw a distinction between the three applicants as regards their entitlement to claim to be 'victims' of a violation.

However, the European Court proceeded to examine each applicant in turn and held each one to constitute a victim. Pine Valley had been the owner of the land at the time of the application for planning permission and had initiated the court proceedings which had resulted in overturning the initial refusal to grant planning permission. The fact that it sold the land and its subsequent dissolution were not relevant to the question of admissibility as a victim. In respect of Healy Holdings and Mr Healy the European Court held that their subsequent insolvency did not extinguish their right to constitute a 'victim' under the Convention.

Article 1, Protocol 1

An interference with the peaceful enjoyment of possessions The first question for the European Court was whether the applicants ever enjoyed a right to develop the land which could have been the subject of interference by the state. This basically required the European Court to determine whether the outline planning permission constituted a possession under Article 1, Protocol 1. In reaching a decision the European Court observed (at para. 51) that:

> When Pine Valley purchased the site, it did so in reliance on the permission which had been duly recorded in a public register kept for the purpose and which it was perfectly entitled to assume was valid. That permission amounted to a favourable decision as to the principle of the proposed development, which could not be re-opened by the

planning authority. In these circumstances it would be unduly formalistic to hold that the Irish Supreme Court's decision did not constitute an interference. Until it was rendered, the applicants had at least a legitimate expectation of being able to carry out their proposed development and this has to be regarded, for the purposes of Article 1 of Protocol No. 1, as a component part of the property in question.

The European Court accepted that the applicants did not enjoy the benefit of retrospective validation by s. 6, LGPDA 1982. Therefore the decision of the Irish Supreme Court, that the outline planning permission was a nullity *ab initio*, amounted to an interference with the peaceful enjoyment of the possessions of Healy Holdings and Mr Healy. However, there was no interference with the property of Pine Valley because it had sold the land prior to the decision of the Irish Supreme Court so that any loss was borne by the other two applicants.

The applicable rule   Having established the existence of a state interference with property the European Court sought to ascertain which of the three rules in Article 1, Protocol 1 applied. The applicants contended that there had been a deprivation of their possessions within the scope of the second rule. However, the European Court held that there was no formal expropriation nor a *de facto* deprivation. It noted that Healy Holdings had retained ownership of the land and although it could not be used for industrial development, it could be used for alternative means such as agricultural purposes. The European Court observed (at para. 56) that: 'Although the value of the site was substantially reduced, it was not rendered worthless, as is evidenced by the fact that it was subsequently sold in the open market'. On this basis the European Court held that the interference came within the ambit of the third rule and was a control of use of the property.

In accordance with the law and in the general interest   The interference was in conformity with planning legislation designed to protect the environment. The protection of the environment was, in the European Court's view, clearly a legitimate aim in accordance with the general interest.

Proportionality   According to the applicants the interference was not proportionate to the aim pursued because the outline planning permission was not retrospectively validated by the LGPDA 1982 nor did the applicants receive any compensation in respect of the interference. The European Court noted that the decision of the Irish Supreme Court, nullifying the outline planning permission, was designed to ensure that the relevant Government Minister correctly applied the planning legislation, not just in the applicants' case but in all similar cases. Therefore the European Court stated (at para. 59) that: 'The decision of the Supreme Court, the result of which was to prevent building in an area zoned for the future development of agriculture so as to preserve a green belt, must be regarded as a proper way — if not the only way — of achieving that aim'. Consequently, the decision of the Irish Supreme Court was held to be proportionate to the aim to be achieved.

In considering whether the applicants should have been compensated, the European Court observed (at para. 59) that: 'The applicants were engaged on a commercial venture which, by its very nature, involved an element of risk and they were aware not only of the zoning plan but also of the opposition of the local authority . . . to any departure from it'. With this in mind the European Court did not consider the absence of compensation to upset the fair balance to be struck between the general interest and the applicants' rights. Consequently, since the state action could not be regarded as a disproportionate measure there was no violation of Article 1, Protocol 1.

Article 14 in conjunction with Article 1, Protocol 1

In response to the Irish Supreme Court's decision, legislation was enacted giving compensation to all the holders of planning permission affected by the ruling. However, it did not apply to the applicants and on this basis they maintained that they were victims of discrimination contrary to Article 14. The Government failed to advance any justification for this differential treatment and therefore the European Court found it to constitute a breach of Article 14 in conjunction with Article 1, Protocol 1.

PAPAMICHALOPOULOS v *GREECE* (1993) 16 EHRR 440

Facts

The applicants were all Greek nationals. During the time of a dictatorship in Greece, land owned by the applicants was effectively transferred to the Navy Fund who occupied the land for use as a naval base and holiday resort for officers. Following the restoration of democracy in Greece, the authorities recognised the applicants' title to the disputed land but ordered that other land of equal value be given to the applicants in its place. However, the land chosen by the authorities for this exchange could not be used for that purpose. At the time of the European Court's judgment no compensation had been awarded to the applicants in respect of their loss.

Decision

The European Court held that there had been an infringement of Article 1, Protocol 1.

Analysis

Article 1, Protocol 1

The applicable rule   The European Court considered whether or not there had been a deprivation within the scope of the second rule. It stated that the occupation of the applicants' land by the Navy Fund represented a clear interference with the applicants' peaceful enjoyment of their possessions. However, the applicants' land had never been formally expropriated because the legislation had not transferred legal ownership to the Navy Fund. Nevertheless, the European Court sought to ascertain whether the situation amounted to a *de facto* expropriation on the grounds that the Convention is intended to safeguard rights that are 'practical and effective'. The Navy Fund, having taken possession of the land, constructed a naval base and a holiday resort for officers on it. From that date the applicants were unable to use, sell, mortgage, bequeath or make a gift of their property. They were even refused access to the land. All attempts to exchange the land for other land of equal value had been unsuccessful and the applicants had not received any compensation for their loss. Taking these factors into account the European Court decided (at para. 45) that:

> the loss of all ability to dispose of the land in issue, taken together with the failure of the attempts made so far to remedy the situation complained of, entailed sufficiently serious consequences for the applicants *de facto* to have been expropriated in a manner incompatible with their rights to the peaceful enjoyment of their possessions.

Proportionality   The occupation of the land as a naval base formed part of the national defence policy which is clearly a legitimate aim within the public interest and an area in which the states enjoy a wide margin of appreciation. However, the occupation of the applicants' land had lasted over 25 years and this imposed an excessively heavy burden on them, which only the payment of compensation could have rendered compatible with Article 1, Protocol 1. The absence of any compensation, and the fact that the national proceedings to deal with the applicants' case had been unsatisfactory and protracted, meant that the proper balance between the protection of the right of property and the demands of the general interest had been destroyed. Consequently there was a violation of Article 1, Protocol 1.

HENTRICH v *FRANCE* (1994) 18 EHRR 440

Facts

The applicant purchased a plot of land and shortly after this the Revenue exercised a right of pre-emption over the land, thereby transferring ownership of the land to the state. The reason for this expropriation was stated to be the fact that the purchase price paid by the applicant had been too low with a consequent loss to the state of the appropriate transfer duty paid on the sale of the land. The applicant alleged that there had been an infringement of Article 1, Protocol 1. In addition, she maintained that Article 6(1) had been violated because the national proceedings did not afford her an adequate opportunity to present her case to the national courts.

Decision

The Court held that there had been a violation of Article 1, Protocol 1 and Article 6(1).

Analysis

Article 1, Protocol 1
Neither party disputed that the pre-emption amounted to a deprivation of property. Therefore the European Court started its examination of the case by considering whether or not the measure pursued a legitimate aim in the public interest. It reiterated that the notion of 'public interest' is necessarily extensive and affords states a wide margin of appreciation to organise their fiscal policies. On this basis the European Court was satisfied that the prevention of tax evasion was in the public interest.

Next the European Court had to consider whether the deprivation was 'subject to the conditions provided for by law'. In considering the lawfulness of the interference by the state the European Court observed (at para. 42) that: 'In the instant case the pre-emption operated arbitrarily and selectively and was scarcely foreseeable, and it was not attended by the basic procedural safeguards'. In particular the European Court noted that the relevant legislation, as applied to the applicant, did not satisfy the requirements of precision and foreseeability implied by the concept of law within the meaning of the Convention.

Even though the European Court had ruled on the unlawfulness of the deprivation, it nevertheless went on to consider the issue of proportionality. The due process factor was particularly relevant in this case. The European Court stated that in assessing proportionality it would examine the degree of protection from arbitrariness afforded to the applicant. It made the following observations:

(a)   the Revenue could exercise the right of pre-emption against a purchaser acting in good faith for the sole purpose of deterring others from tax evasion;

(b)   the tax systems of the other contracting states do not have an equivalent measure;

(c) the right of pre-emption is not applied systemically to all cases where property is sold at an undervalue but is in fact only exercised on rare occasions which are scarcely foreseeable;

(d) the state has other suitable methods for discouraging tax evasion with less severe consequences for the purchaser.

Having regard to the above factors the European Court decided (at para. 49) that the applicant bore an individual and excessive burden which, 'could have been rendered legitimate only if she had had the possibility — which was refused her — of effectively challenging the measure taken against her'. Thus the fair balance was upset and the measure was disproportionate.

It is interesting to note in this case that the payment of full compensation was not sufficient to prevent a violation of Article 1, Protocol 1. The European Court observed (at para. 48) that: 'Merely reimbursing the price paid — increased by 10 per cent — and the costs and fair expenses of the contract cannot suffice to compensate for the loss of a property acquired without any fraudulent intent'.

Article 6(1)

The applicant maintained that she had not been given a 'fair hearing'. She had not been able to challenge effectively the Revenue's assessment of the situation by adducing evidence that she had acted in good faith and that the proper price had been paid. Therefore she complained that the principle of equality of arms had been contravened. The European Court noted (at para. 56) that:

> one of the requirements of a 'fair trial' is 'equality of arms', which implies that each party must be afforded a reasonable opportunity to present his case under conditions that do not place him at a substantial disadvantage vis-à-vis his opponent. In the instant case, the proceedings on the merits did not afford the applicant such an opportunity.

Therefore there was a breach of Article 6(1) in this respect.

In addition, the European Court found a further breach of Article 6(1) in relation to the unreasonable length of time of the proceedings in the national courts. The appeal proceedings had taken four years due to the backlog of judicial business. The European Court held that this was not a justifiable excuse for the delay. Similarly, the two-year time period for the proceedings in the Court of Cassation due to that court's wish to hear four cases raising similar issues at the same time was not justifiable. Therefore the European Court concluded that the lapse of time was not reasonable having regard to what was at stake for the applicant.

HOLY MONASTERIES v GREECE (1994) 20 EHRR 1

Facts

The applicant monasteries challenged an Act which effectively provided for the transfer of a large part of the monastic estate to the Greek state. The applicants alleged that this constituted an infringement of Article 1, Protocol 1 and Articles 6 and 14.

Decision

The European Court held that there had been a breach of Article 1, Protocol 1 and Article 6(1). There was held to be no breach of Article 14.

Analysis

Article 1, Protocol 1

The applicable rule   The European Court stated that it would not review the legislation in the abstract but would examine the effect of the Act upon the monasteries' property rights. The offending Act created a presumption of state ownership over the applicable land which could only be rebutted by the monasteries adducing specified types of evidence, e.g., a duly registered title deed. A large part of the monasteries' land had been acquired by adverse possession and this was a particularly relevant factor to the European Court because it meant that the required evidence of title would be lacking in most cases. On this basis the European Court concluded that the effect of the Act on the monasteries' property was not merely procedural by shifting the burden of proof, but was a substantive provision which effectively transferred ownership of the property to the state. The fact that, at the time of the European Court's judgment, the state had not yet served any administrative eviction orders on the monasteries, did not prevent the offending Act from constituting an interference with the monasteries' right to the peaceful enjoyment of their possessions. The European Court held that there was a deprivation of property within the ambit of the second rule.

In the public interest   The European Court accepted that the state's reasons for the Act, being to end illegal sales, encroachments, abandonments and uncontrolled development of land, were legitimate objectives in the public interest.

Proportionality   The European Court sought to ascertain whether there was a reasonable relationship of proportionality between the means employed and the aim sought to be achieved. A particularly relevant factor was the absence of any compensation. The European Court observed (at para. 71) that:

> Compensation terms under the relevant legislation are material to the assessment whether the contested measure respects the requisite fair balance and, notably, whether it does not impose a disproportionate burden on the applicants. In this connection, the taking of property without payment of an amount reasonably related to its value will normally constitute a disproportionate interference and a total lack of compensation can be considered justifiable under Article 1 only in exceptional circumstances.

It is interesting to note that the European Commission considered that exceptional circumstances did exist in this case which justified the absence of compensation. The European Commission relied upon a number of matters, including the way in which the land was acquired and used, the monasteries' dependence on the Greek Church and the Church's dependence on the state, to constitute exceptional circumstances. However, the European Court did not agree with this view. It held that the absence of any compensation imposed a considerable burden on the applicant monasteries and therefore the Act did not preserve a fair balance between the various interests in question. As a result there was a breach of Article 1, Protocol 1.

Article 6(1)

The offending legislation deprived the monasteries of locus standi before the Greek courts in relation to disputes concerning their property. The Greek Church was given exclusive authority to litigate before the national courts on these matters. The European Commission considered that this system was justified because the Greek Church had taken over the management of the property and therefore had an interest in defending it in any legal proceedings. However, the European Court disputed this view and, referring to the monasteries' new position, noted (at para. 83) that:

> By depriving them of any further possibility of bringing before the appropriate courts any complaint they might make against the Greek State, third parties or the Greek Church itself in relation to their rights of property, or even of intervening in such proceedings, [the legislation] impairs the very essence of their 'right to a court'.

The European Court therefore found that the legislation was in breach of Article 6(1).

Article 14 in conjunction with Article 6(1) and Article 1, Protocol 1

The applicants claimed to be victims of discrimination because only those monasteries belonging to the Greek Church were affected by the offending legislative provisions. However, the European Court found that the differential treatment did not lack all objective and reasonable justification bearing in mind the close links between the Greek Church and the applicant monasteries as distinct from other monasteries. Consequently there was found to be no discrimination.

LOPEZ OSTRA v *SPAIN* (1994) 20 EHRR 277

Facts

The applicant lived near a town with a heavy concentration of leather industries. A tannery waste treatment plant was built by a limited company, using a state subsidy, on municipal land only 12 metres away from the applicant's home. The waste treatment plant began to operate without a licence from the municipal authorities in breach of state regulations. Owing to a malfunction, the plant released gas fumes and smells into the atmosphere which immediately caused health problems and nuisance to local residents including the applicant.

Decision

The European Court found that there had been a breach of Article 8.

Analysis

Article 8

Environmental pollution   The initial question for consideration was whether environmental pollution could give rise to an interference with the rights protected by Article 8. To this end the European Court noted (at para. 51) that: 'severe environmental pollution may affect individuals' well-being and prevent them from enjoying their homes in such a way as to affect their private and family life adversely, without, however, seriously endangering their health'.

The European Commission had also reached a similar conclusion. After considering all the expert reports it had found that the level of the severity of the nuisance, particularly in adversely affecting the health of the applicant and her family, made it impossible for the applicant 'to enjoy the amenities of her home in a normal way, preventing her from leading a normal family and private life, so that it infringes her right to respect for her private and family life within the meaning of Article 8(1)'.

State responsibility   The Spanish authorities were not directly responsible for the fumes and smells because the waste treatment plant was built and owned by a private company; however, the plant was built on municipal land and the state subsidised the construction. In its decision on admissibility, the European Commission had noted that regardless of the level of responsibility, direct or indirect, imputable to the state authorities, 'the Convention contains Articles which not only protect the individual against the state but also oblige the state to protect the rights of the individual even against the actions of third parties'. The European Commission relied on the positive obligations under Article 8(1) to find that the Government had omitted to take the necessary measures to ensure the practical and effective protection of the rights guaranteed under Article 8(1).

The European Court noted that there were two ways to analyse the question of state responsibility for the interference complained of. The question could either be analysed in terms of the state's positive obligation to take reasonable measures to secure the applicant's right to respect for her private life, family life and home (under Article 8(1)); or it could be examined in terms of 'an interference by a public authority' (under Article 8(2)). The European Court observed that whichever of the two approaches was adopted, the applicable principles are broadly similar. It noted (at para. 51) that:

> In both contexts regard must be had to the fair balance that has to be struck between the competing interests of the individual and of the community as a whole, and in any case the state enjoys a certain margin of appreciation. Furthermore even in relation to the positive obligations flowing from the first paragraph of Article 8, in striking the required balance the aims mentioned in the second paragraph may be of a certain relevance.

Proportionality   The European Court stated that its task was to 'establish whether the national authorities took the measures necessary for protecting the applicant's right to respect for her home'. To this end the European Court found that the state authorities had not only failed to take the necessary steps but had contributed to prolonging the interference by appealing against a domestic court decision to close the plant temporarily. The European Court noted that the applicant and her family had endured the nuisance for three years and the municipality had only taken steps to move them from their home after the daughter's paediatrician recommended that she be moved away for health reasons.

The European Court found that the state had not succeeded in striking a fair balance between the interests of the town's economic well-being (that of having a waste treatment plant to solve the serious pollution problem caused by the concentration of tanneries) and the applicant's enjoyment of her right to respect for her home and family life. Accordingly there was a violation of Article 8.

AIR CANADA v *UK* (1995) 20 EHRR 150

Facts

There were a number of incidents over a three-year period that gave rise to concern about the adequacy of Air Canada's security procedures at Heathrow Airport. This culminated in the commissioners of customs and excise writing to all of the airline operators warning them about the possible penalties for the finding of illegal imports aboard their aircraft. The letter specifically stated that the commissioners: 'will consider exercising their powers under the law, including the seizure and forfeiture of aircraft or the imposition of monetary penalties in lieu of such forfeiture'. Customs officers subsequently found a consignment of cannabis resin on board an Air Canada airliner and seized the aircraft as liable to forfeiture. The applicant was required to pay the sum of £50,000 for its return. The applicant alleged that this amounted to a breach of Article 1, Protocol 1 and Article 6(1).

Decision

The European Court found that there was no violation of Article 1, Protocol 1 nor of Article 6(1).

Analysis

Article 1, Protocol 1

The applicable rule   The applicant contended that it had been deprived of its possessions (a temporary deprivation of the aircraft and a permanent deprivation of £50,000) within the ambit of the second rule. However, the European Court decided that the interference amounted to a control of use under the third rule. The seizure of the airliner was only a temporary restriction on its use as Air Canada had paid the sum required for its release. Thus the seizure of the aircraft had not involved a transfer of ownership of the aircraft. The scheme of the legislation involved a control of use of property thereby preventing the aircraft from being used as a means of transporting illegal drugs. The forfeiture of the aircraft was a measure taken in furtherance of that policy and as such it amounted to a control of use and not a deprivation of property.

Compliance with the third rule   The European Court was satisfied that the state action pursued the legitimate aim of combating international drug trafficking which was clearly within the general interest. The European Court then turned its attention to the principle of proportionality. The applicant alleged that there was not a reasonable relationship of proportionality between the means employed and the aim pursued. It put forward two reasons to substantiate this allegation, first, the forfeiture of the property did not depend on showing any fault on the part of the owner and secondly, the seizure powers of customs and excise officials were exercised without any hearing before a judicial body. The European Court responded by noting (at para. 41) that:

> While the width of the powers of forfeiture conferred on the commissioners ... is striking, the seizure of the applicant's aircraft and its release subject to payment were undoubtedly exceptional measures which were resorted to in order to bring about an improvement in the company's security procedures.

It referred to the fact that the discovery of the cannabis resin was only the latest incident in a long series of alleged security lapses that had been brought to the applicant's attention by the customs and excise officers.

The European Court found that the availability of judicial review was a sufficient and effective remedy to safeguard the applicant in respect of the commissioners' exercise of their statutory discretion. It stated (at para. 46) that:

> The Court recalls that on a previous occasion it reached the conclusion that the scope of judicial review under English law is sufficient to satisfy the requirements of the second paragraph of Article 1 of Protocol No. 1. In particular, it is open to the domestic courts to hold that the exercise of discretion by the Commissioners was unlawful on the grounds that it was tainted with illegality, irrationality or procedural impropriety.

The European Court was satisfied that a fair balance had been achieved bearing in mind the state's margin of appreciation. Taking into account the large quantity of cannabis discovered, its street value, and the value of the aircraft seized, the European Court did not consider that the requirement to pay £50,000 was disproportionate to the aim of preventing the importation of prohibited drugs into the UK. Consequently, there was no breach of Article 1, Protocol 1.

Article 6(1)
It was not disputed that Article 6(1) was applicable because the case concerned a dispute relating to the applicant's civil rights. The matter for determination by the European Court was the question of compliance with Article 6(1).

Compliance with Article 6(1) In relation to the seizure of the aircraft the commissioners had to take condemnation proceedings in the High Court. The European Court noted (at para. 61) that: 'Such proceedings were in fact brought and, with the agreement of the parties, were limited to the determination of specified questions of law. In such circumstances, the requirement of access to a court inherent in Article 6(1) was satisfied'.

In addition, it was open to the applicant to commence judicial review proceedings to challenge the decision to require the payment of £50,000 for the return of the aircraft. However, on the facts, the applicants had not instituted judicial review proceedings and therefore the European Court did not consider it appropriate to examine in the abstract the scope of judicial review to determine whether it is capable of satisfying Article 6(1).

GASUS DOSIER- UND FORDERTECHNIK GmbH v *NETHERLANDS* (1995) 20 EHRR 403

Facts

The applicant German company (G) sold a concrete-mixer to a Dutch company (A) subject to a retention of title clause and, therefore, the title to the property would not pass to A until it had paid the full purchase price. Shortly after installation the mixer was seized by the Tax Bailiff to cover A's tax debts. At the time of the seizure the full price had not been paid. The mixer was subsequently sold to another company. G retained its claim against A for the recovery of the purchase price but due to A's subsequent bankruptcy, G's claim was rendered worthless. G alleged that the seizure of the mixer constituted a deprivation of its property under the second rule and that there had been a violation of Article 1, Protocol 1.

Decision

The European Court held that there was no breach of Article 1, Protocol 1.

Analysis

Article 1, Protocol 1

The meaning of possessions   The Government argued that retention of title was more in the nature of a security *in rem* than of 'true' ownership. The European Court reiterated the well established principle that 'possessions' under Article 1, Protocol 1 has an autonomous meaning which is not limited to ownership of physical goods. It stated (at para. 53) that:

> In the present context it is therefore immaterial whether Gasus's right to the concrete-mixer is to be considered as a right of ownership or as a security right in rem. In any event, the seizure and sale of the concrete-mixer constituted an 'interference' with the applicant company's right 'to the peaceful enjoyment' of a 'possession' within the meaning of Article 1 of Protocol 1.

The applicable rule   The interference with G's property arose as a direct result of the tax authority's exercise of its powers of enforcement in respect of unpaid tax debts. The Dutch legislation permitted the seizure of all movable goods on the debtor's premises irrespective of who actually owned those goods. Therefore the European Court chose to apply the third rule and deal with G's complaint under the head of 'securing the payment of taxes' instead of considering it as a deprivation under the second rule.

Compliance with the third rule   The purpose of the power given to the tax authorities, to seize goods present on the debtor's premises regardless of who actually owns the goods, is to facilitate the enforcement of tax debts. The European Court was satisfied that this constituted a legitimate aim in the general interest.

The European Court examined whether there was a reasonable relationship of proportionality between the means employed and the aim pursued. It observed (at para. 60) that in passing laws that regulate the formalities of taxation (including the enforcement of tax debts):

> the legislature must be allowed a wide margin of appreciation, especially with regard to the question whether — and if so, to what extent — the tax authorities should be put in a better position to enforce tax debts than ordinary creditors are in to enforce commercial debts. The Court will respect the legislature's assessment in such matters unless it is devoid of reasonable foundation.

The European Court noted that the tax authorities did not have the same means at their disposal as commercial creditors for protecting themselves against the debtor's financial demise. Therefore the granting of additional enforcement powers to the tax authorities could be seen as reasonable because it attempted to counteract this imbalance.

In addition, it was considered to be immaterial that G bore no responsibility for A's tax debt. G was engaged in a commercial venture which, by its very nature, involved an element of risk and G could have eliminated that risk by stipulating full payment of the price in advance and thereby refusing to extend credit to A.

Having regard to all of these factors the European Court concluded that the requirement of proportionality had been satisfied and consequently there was no violation of Article 1, Protocol 1.

BRYAN v *UK* (1995) 21 EHRR 342

Facts

The applicant was served with an enforcement notice requiring him to demolish two brick buildings on farm land which he had purchased two years earlier. The notice stated that the buildings had been erected without the necessary planning permission. The applicant appealed to the Secretary of State for the Environment. One of the grounds of appeal he relied upon was that the matters alleged in the enforcement notice did not constitute a breach of planning control. The essence of the applicant's argument was that the buildings were designed for the purposes of agriculture and were therefore permitted development under the General Development Order. An inspector was appointed to conduct an inquiry and reach a decision on the appeal. The inspector was a civil servant and a member of staff at the Department of Environment and had been appointed by the Secretary of State. The inspector rejected the applicant's appeal. In determining that there had been a breach of planning control, the inspector proceeded on a finding of fact that the buildings, as originally constructed, were houses, not barns. The applicant appealed to the High Court. The aspect of the appeal alleging that there was no breach of planning law was abandoned apparently because the applicant accepted that it did not involve a point of law but rested on a finding of fact. The High Court, finding no error of law in the inspector's decision, dismissed the judicial review application. The applicant contended that the judicial review by the High Court failed to comply with the requirements of Article 6(1).

Decision

The European Court held that there was no violation of Article 6(1).

Analysis

Article 6(1)

Applicability of Article 6(1) The Government did not contest that the planning proceedings at issue involved a determination of the applicant's 'civil rights'. The European Court agreed that Article 6(1) was applicable to the facts.

Compliance with Article 6(1) The applicant submitted that the inspector, appointed by the Secretary of State to carry out a review of the disputed enforcement notice, did not satisfy the criterion of independence as required by Article 6(1). The European Court agreed with this submission (at para. 38) stating that:

> It is true that the inspector was required to decide the applicant's planning appeal in a quasi-judicial, independent and impartial, as well as fair, manner. However, as pointed out by the Commission in its report, the Secretary of State can at any time, even during the course of proceedings which are in progress, issue a direction to revoke the power of an inspector to decide an appeal. In the context of planning appeals the very existence

of this power available to the Executive, whose own policies may be in issue, is enough to deprive the inspector of the requisite appearance of independence, notwithstanding the limited exercise of the power in practice as described by the Government and irrespective of whether its exercise was or could have been at issue in the present case. For this reason alone, the review by the inspector does not of itself satisfy the requirements of Article 6 of the Convention, despite the existence of various safeguards customarily associated with an 'independent and impartial tribunal'.

This finding was not, however, sufficient to amount to an infringement of Article 6(1) because as the European Court explained (at para. 40) by reference to its judgment in *Albert and Le Compte* v *Belgium* (1983) 5 EHRR 533:

> even where an adjudicatory body determining disputes over 'civil rights and ob-ligations' does not comply with Article 6(1) in some respect, no violation of the Convention can be found if the proceedings before that body are 'subject to subsequent control by a judicial body that has full jurisdiction and does provide the guarantees of Article 6(1)'.

Therefore, provided that the High Court, in exercising its judicial review role, satisfied the requirements of Article 6(1), the planning appeal procedure as a whole could be found to comply with Article 6(1).

The European Court examined the scope of the High Court's jurisdiction and concluded that it was sufficient to comply with Article 6(1) even though the appeal to the High Court was on a 'points of law' basis only and did not permit the court to substitute its own decision on the merits for that of the inspector. The European Court took into account the various grounds on which the High Court could have quashed the decision of the inspector, for example if the inspector had had regard to irrelevant factors or had failed to consider all of the relevant factors. Furthermore the European Court stated (at para. 45) that:

> in assessing the sufficiency of the review available to Mr Bryan on appeal to the High Court, it is necessary to have regard to matters such as the subject matter of the decision appealed against, the manner in which that decision was arrived at, and the content of the dispute, including the desired and actual grounds of appeal.

In this respect the European Court noted that, since the applicant had abandoned the ground of appeal which had been reliant upon a finding of fact, the High Court had jurisdiction to entertain all the remaining grounds of appeal by the applicant and that 'his submissions were adequately dealt with point by point'.

The European Court remarked that even if the applicant had not abandoned the ground of appeal that was reliant on a finding of fact, the appeal procedure would still comply with Article 6(1). The High Court, although not able to substitute its own findings of fact for those of the inspector, nevertheless had the power to ensure that the inspector's findings of fact are not perverse or irrational. The European Court stated (at para. 47) that:

> Such an approach by an appeal tribunal on questions of fact can reasonably be expected in specialised areas of law such as the one at issue, particularly where the facts have already been established in the course of a quasi-judicial procedure governed by many of the safeguards required by Article 6(1). It is also frequently a feature in the systems of judicial control of administrative decisions found throughout the Council of Europe Member States. Indeed, in the instant case, the subject matter of the contested decision by the inspector was a typical example of the exercise of discretionary judgement in the regulation of citizens' conduct in the sphere of town and country planning.

Taking all these factors into account, the European Court concluded that, on the facts, the scope of the review by the High Court was sufficient to comply with Article 6(1).

BUCKLEY v *UK* (1996) 23 EHRR 101

Facts

The applicant, a gypsy, lived in caravans parked on land which she owned. Her three children lived with her there. She applied for retrospective planning permission to permit her to park her caravans on her land. Her application was refused by the Local Planning Authority (LPA), which subsequently issued an enforcement notice requiring her to remove the caravans within a month. She was invited to apply for a pitch on an official site for gypsies nearby, but she declined because she felt that it was unsuitable for a single woman with children. She was later prosecuted for failing to comply with the enforcement notice. She complained of a violation of Article 8 taken alone and in conjunction with Article 14.

Decision

The European Court held that there was no violation of Article 8 nor of Article 14 in conjunction with Article 8.

Analysis

Article 8

The meaning of 'home'   The Government contended that only a home that had been legally established could attract the protection of Article 8. The European Court rejected this, noting that there is nothing in the wording of Article 8 to suggest that the concept of 'home' is limited to residences that have been lawfully established. The European Court stated that even though the applicant lived in the caravans in violation of national planning laws she still had a right to respect for her home. By reference to the decision in *Gillow* v *UK*, the European Court stated that the following factors were relevant in establishing that the land constituted her 'home' within the meaning of Article 8:

(a) the applicant had purchased the land for the purpose of establishing her residence there; and

(b) she had lived there almost continuously since buying the land; and

(c) she had not established another residence elsewhere.

An interference by a public authority   The European Court accepted that the acts of the LPA in refusing her application for planning permission, serving an enforcement notice on her and prosecuting her for failing to comply with the terms of the enforcement notice, constituted an interference by a public authority.

In accordance with the law   There was no dispute that the LPA was acting in accordance with the provisions of the Town and Country Planning Act 1990. The legislation was accessible and foreseeable and consequently the actions of the LPA were in accordance with the law.

A legitimate aim   It was not contested that the LPA had acted in furtherance of a legitimate aim. Its actions were aimed at furthering highway safety, preservation of the environment and public health which came within the following specific aims listed in Article 8(2): public safety, the economic well-being of the country, the protection of health and the protection of the rights of others.

Necessary in a democratic society   As a starting point the European Court recognised (at para. 74) that:

> It is for the national authorities to make the initial assessment of the 'necessity' for an interference, as regards both the legislative framework and the particular measure of implementation. Although a margin of appreciation is thereby left to the national authorities, their decision remains subject to review by the Court for conformity with the requirements of the Convention.

It was recognised that in the sphere of town and country planning, the states are generally allowed a wide margin of appreciation. The European Court acknowledged (at para. 75) that:

By reason of their direct and continuous contact with the vital forces of their countries, the national authorities are in principle better placed than an international court to evaluate local needs and conditions. In so far as the exercise of discretion involving a multitude of local factors is inherent in the choice and implementation of planning policies, the national authorities in principle enjoy a wide margin of appreciation.

Town and country planning schemes inevitably involve the exercise of discretionary powers by the public authorities acting in the interests of the whole community. There may be scope for differences of judgment in the use of this discretion, but the European Court stressed that it will not substitute its own view of what would be the best policy in the planning sphere.

A particularly relevant factor in determining whether the state had exceeded its margin of appreciation was the availability to the applicant of procedural safeguards. The European Court stated (at para. 76) that: 'It is settled case law that, whilst Article 8 contains no explicit procedural requirements, the decision-making process leading to measures of interference must be fair and such as to afford due respect to the interests safeguarded to the individual by Article 8'. In the present case the applicant had a right of appeal to the Secretary of State. The appeal procedure involved an assessment by a qualified independent expert, the inspector, to whom the applicant was entitled to make representations. In addition, judicial review by the High Court was available. Therefore the European Court was satisfied that procedural safeguards existed that protected the applicant's interests under Article 8.

The European Court was satisfied that the public authorities had given due regard to the interests of the applicant. They had taken her special needs as a gypsy, following a traditional lifestyle, into account and had had regard to the shortage of gypsy caravan sites in the area. However, they had concluded that the general interest of the public in conforming to the planning policy, which was to promote open countryside and to prevent all but essential development, outweighed the applicant's needs. The European Court also had regard to the fact that she had declined an invitation to apply for a pitch on an official caravan site because she felt that it was unsuitable for a single woman with children. It observed (at para. 81) that: 'Article 8 does not necessarily go so far as to allow individuals' preferences as to their place of residence to override the general interest'.

Taking into account all of the above considerations, the European Court concluded (at para. 84) that:

> proper regard was had to the applicant's predicament both under the terms of the regulatory framework, which contained adequate procedural safeguards protecting her interest under Article 8, and by the responsible planning authorities when exercising their discretion in relation to the particular circumstances of her case. The latter

authorities arrived at the contested decision after weighing in the balance the various competing interests at issue.

Consequently, there was no violation of Article 8.

Article 14 in conjunction with Article 8
The applicant claimed to be the victim of discrimination on the ground of her gypsy status. However, it was noted that she had not been penalised nor subjected to any detrimental treatment for following a traditional gypsy lifestyle. Accordingly there was no violation of Article 14 in conjunction with Article 8.

LOIZIDOU v *TURKEY* (1996) 23 EHRR 513

Facts

The applicant, a Greek Cypriot, owned land in northern Cyprus, where she had grown up and where her family had lived for generations. She had not lived there since 1972 having moved away when she got married. However, in 1974 construction work began of a number of flats on the land. She intended to live in one of the flats but, due to the Turkish occupation of Northern Cyprus in 1974, the construction works had not been completed. The Turkish forces occupying Northern Cyprus prevented her from returning to her land. She alleged that this constituted a breach of Article 1, Protocol 1 and Article 8.

Decision

The European Court held that there had been a violation of Article 1, Protocol 1 but not of Article 8.

Analysis

Article 1, Protocol 1

State responsibility   The European Court stressed that the concept of 'jurisdiction' under Article 1, Protocol 1 is not restricted to the national territory of the contracting state. State responsibility can arise where the acts of state authorities have effects outside their own territory. Thus the European Court stated (at para. 52) that:

> In conformity with the relevant principles of international law governing state responsibility, the responsibility of a Contracting Party could also arise when as a consequence of military action — whether lawful or unlawful — it exercises effective

control of an area outside its national territory. The obligation to secure, in such an area, the rights and freedoms set out in the Convention, derives from the fact of such control whether it be exercised directly, through its armed forces, or through a subordinate local administration.

Consequently, there was sufficient state responsibility for the applicant to invoke the Convention against Turkey.

The applicable rule   The European Court did not accept the European Commission's characterisation of the applicant's complaint as being limited to the right to freedom of movement. The European Court accepted that by denying her access to her property over a 16-year period, Turkey had interfered with her right to the peaceful enjoyment of her possessions, thereby invoking Article 1, Protocol 1.

The European Court considered which of the three rules was applicable on the facts. It noted that the applicant retained legal ownership of the land, but was refused access to it and effectively lost all control over its use. In the exceptional circumstances of the case, the interference could not be regarded as either a deprivation under the second rule nor as a control of use within the ambit of the third rule. However, the European Court was satisfied that the interference clearly fell within the scope of the first rule.

The European Court noted (at para. 64) that the Turkish Government had failed to explain how the need to rehouse displaced Turkish Cypriot refugees following the Turkish occupation of Northern Cyprus in 1974, 'could justify the complete negation of the applicant's property rights in the form of a total and continuous denial of access and a purported expropriation without compensation. Consequently, the measures were disproportionate and imposed an excessive burden upon the applicant.

Article 8

The applicant alleged an unjustified interference with the right to respect for her home in breach of Article 8. However, the European Court held that the land in question did not constitute the applicant's home. It stated (at para. 66) that:

> In its opinion it would strain the meaning of the notion of 'home' in Article 8 to extend it to comprise property on which it is planned to build a house for residential purposes. Nor can that term be interpreted to cover an area of a State where one has grown up and where the family has its roots but where one no longer lives.

Accordingly Article 8 was not applicable on the facts.

MATOS E SILVA, LDA AND OTHERS v *PORTUGAL* (1996) 24 EHRR 573

Facts

The applicant, Matos e Silva, a private limited company, owned land which it used for cultivating, extracting salts and breeding fish. Part of this land was undisputedly owned by the applicant, having been purchased over a number of years. The remaining part of the land had been worked under a concession granted under a royal decree of 21 July 1884 which permitted the land to be expropriated without any payment of compensation. There was a dispute between the applicant and the state as to whether or not Matos e Silva owned this part of the land or merely held it under the concession.

The Portuguese Government decided to create a nature reserve for animals on the Algarve coast which included part of the land owned by the applicant. In pursuance of this scheme a number of public-interest declarations were made as a preliminary to expropriating the relevant land and other restrictions were put in place including a ban on building. The applicant commenced five sets of proceedings in the national courts challenging the declarations. The proceedings were still pending at the time of the European Court's judgment.

Decision

The European Court held that there was a violation of Article 6(1) on account of the length of the proceedings in the national courts and that Article 1, Protocol 1 had been infringed. The European Court did not consider it necessary to consider whether there had been a breach of Article 14 in conjunction with Article 1, Protocol 1.

Analysis

Article 1, Protocol 1

The meaning of possessions The state submitted that because the applicant's alleged ownership of the land was debatable under domestic law, the applicant could not claim an infringement of a property right that had not been established. The European Court acknowledged that it was not its role to determine whether or not the right to property existed in domestic law; however, it reiterated that: 'the notion of 'possessions' in Article 1 of Protocol 1 has an autonomous meaning' and it was satisfied (at para. 75) that: 'the applicants' unchallenged rights over the disputed land for almost a century and the revenue they derive from working it may qualify as 'possessions' for the purposes of Article 1'.

The applicable rule The applicant submitted that the combined effects of the five measures had resulted in a *de facto* expropriation of its possessions. The European Court disputed this, observing that all reasonable manner of exploiting the land had not disappeared evidenced by the fact that the applicant did in fact continue to work its land. Therefore the European Court concluded that the second rule was not applicable. Whilst the European Commission, having reached the same conclusion, applied the first and third rule, the European Court only applied the first rule.

Proportionality The European Court was satisfied that the various measures, being for the purpose of protecting the environment, pursued a public interest. As to proportionality, the European Court considered that the length of the proceedings, resulting in a period of more than 13 years during which the applicant neither knew what would become of its possessions nor whether any compensation would be paid, upset the balance to be struck between the protection of property and the requirements of the general interest. This resulted in a violation of Article 1, Protocol 1.

Article 6
The five sets of proceedings were commenced on 18 April 1983, 15 November 1983, 9 July 1984, 8 February 1988 and 13 March 1991 respectively. All of them were still pending when the European Court gave its judgment on 16 September 1996. The state conceded that the length of the proceedings exceeded what could legitimately be expected. The European Court found that there was a breach of Article 6(1) due to the unreasonable length of the proceedings.

NATIONAL AND PROVINCIAL BUILDING SOCIETY AND OTHERS v UK (1997) 25 EHRR 127

Facts

The case concerned changes to the system for taxation on interest paid to investors of building societies. Transitional regulations, adopted to cover a gap period, were subsequently successfully challenged in the House of Lords by the Woolwich Building Society and declared to be invalid. The Inland Revenue was required to return to the Woolwich the sum of £57,000,000 with interest. Following the House of Lords' decision, the applicant building societies, having been refused any repayment by the Inland Revenue, commenced proceedings in 1991 for the restitution of the monies paid under the invalid regulations. Meanwhile the Government announced the introduction of legislation to remedy the technical defects in the regulations. Section 53 of the Finance Act 1991 came into force and it provided that the invalid transitional regulations were retrospectively validated, except that the provision did not apply to building societies that had commenced proceedings prior to a specified date. Only the Woolwich satisfied this condition. The applicants were thereby prevented from insisting on the repayment of sums similar to that paid to the Woolwich. They alleged violations of Article 1, Protocol 1 taken alone and in conjunction with Article 14 as well as a breach of Article 6(1).

Decision

The European Court held that there had been no violations of Article 1, Protocol 1 taken alone and in conjunction with Article 14 nor of Article 6(1).

Analysis

Article 1, Protocol 1

The meaning of possessions The applicants contended that their legal claims to restitution of the sums paid to the Inland Revenue constituted 'possessions' within the meaning of Article 1, Protocol 1. The Government disputed this and argued that Article 1, Protocol 1 was inapplicable because the applicants could not validly claim to have 'possessions'. The European Court stated (at para. 70) that:

> While expressing no concluded view as to whether any of the claims asserted by the applicant societies could properly be considered to constitute possessions, the Court, like the Commission, is prepared to proceed on the working assumption that in light of the Woolwich ruling the applicant societies did have possessions in the form of vested rights to restitution which they sought to exercise in direct and indirect ways in the various legal proceedings instituted in 1991 and 1992.

The European Court therefore chose to treat Article 1, Protocol 1 as applicable and proceeded to ascertain whether the interference with the applicants' possessions could be justified.

Compliance with the third rule The European Court examined the applicants' complaint under the third rule as a control of use to secure the payment of taxes rather than under the second rule as a deprivation of the rights to restitution of the monies paid to the Inland Revenue under the invalid regulations. Having decided on the applicability of the third rule, the European Court acknowledged (at para. 80) that the state, 'when framing and implementing policies in the area of taxation, enjoys a wide margin of appreciation and the Court will respect the legislature's assessment in such matters unless it is devoid of reasonable foundation'. It concluded that the actions taken by the state did not upset the fair balance which must be struck between the protection of the applicants' rights to restitution and the public interest in securing the payment of taxes.

Article 14 in conjunction with Article 1, Protocol 1
The European Court adopted two approaches to finding that there was no infringement of Article 14. First, it considered that since the Woolwich had accepted the risks of litigation and borne the associated legal costs, the applicants were not in an analogous or relevantly similar position to the Woolwich. Alternatively, the European Court stated that even if the applicants were in a similar position to the Woolwich, a reasonable and objective justification for the differential treatment existed. The European Court recognised that the English Parliament, in enacting the disputed legislation, would not have wanted to have interfered with the House of Lords' decision in favour of the Woolwich.

Article 6(1)
The applicants alleged that the effect of the Finance Act 1991 was to extinguish their private law claims for restitution and thereby deprive them of access to a court for a determination of their civil rights contrary to Article 6(1).

The applicability of Article 6(1)   The applicants maintained that the subject matter of the restitution proceedings was pecuniary in nature and was therefore decisive for their private rights. The Government disputed the applicability of Article 6(1) arguing that the matter concerned tax legislation which, being fiscal in nature, is outside the scope of Article 6. The European Court concluded (at para. 97) that the restitution proceedings

> were private law actions and were decisive for the determination of private law rights to quantifiable sums of money. This conclusion is not affected by the fact that the rights asserted in those proceedings had their background in tax legislation and the obligation of the applicant societies to account for tax under that legislation.

Compliance with Article 6(1)   The European Court started its deliberations by summarising the approach it takes to ascertaining a state's compliance with Article 6(1). It stated (at para. 105) that:

> Article 6(1) of the Convention embodies the 'right to a court', of which the right of access, that is, the right to institute proceedings before a court in civil matters, constitutes one aspect. However, this right is not absolute, but may be subject to limitations; these are permitted by implication since the right of access by its very nature calls for regulation by the State. In this respect the Contracting States enjoy a certain margin of appreciation, although the final decision as to the observance of the Convention's requirements rests with the Court. It must be satisfied that the limitations

applied do not restrict or reduce the access left to the individual in such a way or to such an extent that the very essence of the right is impaired. Furthermore, a limitation will not be compatible with Article 6(1) if it does not pursue a legitimate aim and if there is not a reasonable relationship of proportionality between the means employed and the aim sought to be achieved.

The European Court noted that there were clear public interest considerations to justify the retrospective effect of the legislation even though its effect was to deprive the applicants of any chance of winning their restitution proceedings against the Inland Revenue. The European Court took account of the fact that the applicants must have anticipated that, as a result of the Woolwich ruling, the Treasury would not allow a substantial sum of revenue to be lost on account of a technicality and that retrospective legislation would follow. The European Court observed (at para. 112) that:

> the applicant societies in their efforts to frustrate the intention of Parliament were at all times aware of the probability that Parliament would equally attempt to frustrate those efforts having regard to the decisive stance taken when enacting … section 53 of the 1991 Act.

In these circumstances the European Court concluded that the applicants could not justifiably complain that they had been denied a right of access to a court.

GUERRA AND OTHERS v *ITALY* (1998) 26 EHRR 357

Facts

The 40 applicants lived in a town 1 km away from a chemical factory. The factory, which produced fertilisers and caprolactam, was classified in 1988 as 'high risk' pursuant to criteria set out in a Presidential Decree. In the course of its production cycle the factory released large quantities of inflammable gas and other toxic substances, including arsenic trioxide. Due to the geographical location of the factory, emissions into the atmosphere were often channelled towards the town where the applicants lived. The applicants complained that the state had failed to provide information to local residents about the risks of pollution and what to do in the event of an accident at the factory. This, they claimed, was a violation of Article 8.

Decision

The European Court held that there had been a breach of Article 8.

Analysis

Article 8

Environmental pollution   The European Court endorsed its decision in *Lopez Ostra* v *Spain* by reiterating (at para. 60) that, 'severe environmental pollution may affect individuals' well being and prevent them from enjoying their homes in such a way as to affect their private and family life adversely'. Therefore it accepted that severe pollution from a chemical factory could cause an interference with a person's rights under Article 8.

The state's positive obligations under Article 8   The European Court had to decide whether or not the state could be held responsible for the pollution from the chemical factory. The state had not acted directly to cause the pollution, but nevertheless, the European Court was able to direct responsibility towards the state on the basis of its failure to act in accordance with the positive obligations imposed upon it by Article 8(1). The European Court reasoned (at para. 58) that:

> Italy cannot be said to have 'interfered' with the applicants' private or family life; they complained not of an act by the State but of its failure to act. However, although the object of Article 8 is essentially that of protecting the individual against arbitrary interference by the public authorities, it does not merely compel the State to abstain from such interference: in addition to this primarily negative undertaking, there may be positive obligations inherent in effective respect for private or family life.

Therefore the state had a positive obligation under Article 8 and in this respect the European Court identified its task in the following terms (at para. 58): 'In the present case it need only be ascertained whether the national authorities took the necessary steps to ensure effective protection of the applicants' right to respect for their private and family life as guaranteed by Article 8'.

To this end the European Court concluded that the state did not fulfil its obligation to secure the applicants' rights because it persistently failed to provide them with essential information necessary for them to assess the risks involved in continuing to live at the town and on how to proceed in the event of an accident at the factory. This failure, which was the result of maladminstration, was sufficient to constitute a breach of Article 8.

KHATUN AND 180 OTHERS v *UK* (1998) 26 EHRR CD 212

Facts

This case reached the European Commission as a result of the House of Lords' decision in *Hunter* v *Canary Wharf* [1997] 2 All ER 426. It concerned severe dust contamination of residential properties emanating from the construction of the Limehouse link road in the London Docklands. In order to undertake a programme of regeneration the Secretary of State designated the London Docklands as an enterprise zone which, under the relevant legislation, meant that the area was deemed to be granted planning permission for any development. The usual procedures in the grant of planning permission that safeguard the interests of local residents e.g., a public inquiry, were very limited. Under the enterprise zone scheme the Limehouse link road was constructed, linking the Docklands to Central London. The construction of the road lasted from November 1989 to May 1993 and caused considerable dust contamination to the homes of local residents. Many of the applicants had no proprietary interest in their homes, being the spouse or relative of the owner or being only a lodger. The House of Lords' decision meant that those applicants with no proprietary interest in their home could not bring an action in private nuisance. Those applicants who did have a proprietary right in their home could bring an action in nuisance, but on the basis of the test for calculating compensation, the House of Lords concluded that the predicted value of the collective claim by the applicants was so low that it was futile to pursue an action in private nuisance. The applicants alleged that their right to respect for their private life and home had been violated as a result of the dust contamination. In addition, they claimed a breach of Article 14 in conjunction with Article 8 on the basis of the discriminatory effect of the test for calculating compensation. This test calculated compensation for dust nuisance as the difference in value between the property as affected by the dust and the property when not so affected. This test discriminated against the applicants because the majority of them lived in low cost housing and therefore the dust contamination had little effect on the market value of their property but nevertheless caused them considerable personal discomfort.

Decision

The European Commission found that the application under Article 8 taken alone and in conjunction with Article 14 was manifestly ill-founded and inadmissible.

Analysis

Article 8

A proprietary interest The first matter for consideration was whether or not it was necessary for the applicants to have a proprietary interest in their home in order to enjoy the protection afforded to the home under Article 8. The European Commission made a clear statement on this issue in the following terms:

The Commission notes that in the domestic proceedings, a distinction was made between those applicants with a proprietary interest in the land and those without such an interest. For the purposes of Article 8 of the Convention, there is no such distinction. 'Home' is an autonomous concept which does not depend on classification under domestic law. Whether or not a particular habitation constitutes a 'home' which attracts the protection of Article 8(1) of the Convention will depend on the factual circumstances, namely the existence of sufficient and continuous links (see *Gillow* v *UK*). Even where occupation of the property is illegal, this will not necessarily prevent that occupation from being that person's 'home' within the meaning of Article 8 of the Convention (see *Buckley* v *UK*). The Commission considers that Article 8(1) applies to all the applicants in the present case whether they are the owners of the property or merely occupiers living on the property, for example the children of the owner of the property.

Compliance with Article 8 The European Commission accepted that dust contamination could constitute an interference under Article 8. It relied upon the European Court's decision in *Lopez Ostra* v *Spain* where it was held that severe environmental pollution can affect an individual's private life and prevent him or her from enjoying his or her home, even in cases where there is no injury to health. Further reliance was placed on *Lopez Ostra* v *Spain* to ascertain the correct approach to be taken. The European Commission noted that it is irrelevant whether the case is analysed in terms of the state's positive obligations under Article 8(1) or as an interference by a public authority under Article 8(2). In each case the state must establish that the measures were taken in pursuance of a legitimate aim and that a fair balance had been struck between the competing interests of the individual and of the community.

The offending legislation, authorising the designation of enterprise zones, was accessible and foreseeable and was consequently 'in accordance with the law'. Its purpose, being the regeneration of derelict urban areas, pursued the legitimate aim of the economic well-being of the country. Therefore the European Commission was satisfied that the interference was in accordance with the law and pursued a legitimate aim under Article 8(2). The question remained whether it was 'necessary in a democratic society'. In assessing the fair balance test the European Commission noted that the construction of the Limehouse link road was essential to the development of the area. Against this important public interest it weighed the considerable degree of inconvenience caused to the applicants from the dust produced during the construction of the road. The European Commission noted that, 'the inconvenience, whilst undoubtedly unpleasant, has not been claimed to have given rise to health problems for any of the applicants. Further, it was limited in time to the period of the works, some three-and-a-half years'. Taking these factors into account, and bearing in mind the importance of the public interest, the European Commission concluded that a fair balance had been achieved and that there was no breach of Article 8.

Article 14 in conjunction with Article 8

Article 14 affords protection against the discriminatory treatment of persons in similar situations. The European Commission observed that:

> For a claim of violation of this Article to succeed, it has therefore to be established, *inter alia*, that the situation of the alleged victim can be considered similar to that of persons who have been better treated (see *Fredin* v *Sweden* (1991) 13 EHRR 784, para. 60). The applicants must show that they are persons in the same category as another, that they have been treated differently, that such treatment was not objectively and reasonably justified, and the treatment was carried out by the Contracting State against which the complaint is being made. There are no other persons in 'relevantly' similar situations to the applicants. There is no evidence that there are persons in the same category as the applicants who have been treated more favourably.

The absence of any persons in the same category as the applicants but who were enjoying preferential treatment meant that the application under Article 14 failed.

McLEOD v *UK* (1999) 27 EHRR 493

Facts

The divorce of the applicant and her husband resulted in substantial, acrimonious court proceedings concerning the former matrimonial home and its contents. The court ordered that the home be transferred to the applicant on the payment of a lump sum and that the furniture be divided between the parties in accordance with a specified list. The applicant failed to deliver the furniture to her ex-husband in accordance with the court order and a further court order was made backed by a penal notice. She eventually delivered furniture to her ex-husband, but it was not the items that were on the list. Following further court proceedings, an order was made committing her to prison but it was suspended for seven days to allow her to deliver the property. Immediately after this hearing the ex-husband, through his counsel, offered to collect the property and suggested a particular time and date. The ex-husband went to the former matrimonial home on this date, believing that the applicant had agreed to this. His solicitors had arranged for two police officers to be present while the property was being removed. When they arrived at the house, the applicant's mother told them that the applicant was not at home. The furniture was nevertheless removed from the house. The applicant alleged that this constituted a violation of her rights under Article 8.

Decision

The European Court concluded that there was a breach of Article 8.

Analysis

Article 8

In accordance with the law   The applicant maintained that the common law power of the police to enter private property without a warrant on the grounds of preventing an anticipated breach of the peace was not 'in accordance with the law'. The European Court reiterated the well-established meaning of 'in accordance with the law' in terms of the need for the measures to be accessible and foreseeable. In respect of foreseeability, the European Court stressed (at para. 41) the need for the measure to be formulated with sufficient precision to enable a person concerned:

> to foresee, to a degree that is reasonable in the circumstances, the consequences which a given action may entail. However, those consequences need not be foreseeable with absolute certainty, since such certainty might give rise to excessive rigidity, and the law must be able to keep pace with changing circumstances.

The European Court was satisfied that the common law concept of a breach of the peace had been sufficiently established by the national courts and that the police power of entry without warrant to prevent a breach of the peace was, as determined by the national courts, still applicable in cases of domestic disturbance. The European Court therefore concluded that this police power of entry was defined with sufficient precision to satisfy the foreseeability criterion.

A legitimate aim   The police power to enter into and remain on private premises without permission, to prevent the occurrence of a breach of the peace, was in pursuit of a legitimate aim within Article 8(2), namely the prevention of disorder or crime.

Necessary in a democratic society   The European Court accepted that when the ex-husband's solicitor requested the police presence at the house during the removal of the goods, the situation was such that a breach of the peace might have been anticipated and therefore the police were right to respond to the solicitor's request for assistance. However, the following factors led the European Court to conclude that the means employed by the police, on their arrival at the house, were disproportionate to the aim that they pursued.

(a)   The police did not take steps to verify that the ex-husband was entitled to enter the property to remove the furniture. If the police had seen the order they would have realised that it was the applicant's responsibility to deliver the property and that she still had three days left in which to do so.

(b) The police should not have assumed that the parties had agreed for the ex-husband to come and collect the furniture. The applicant was absent from the home and her mother had no knowledge of any such agreement.

(c) Having being informed of the applicant's absence by her elderly mother, the police should not have entered the house as there was no longer any risk that a breach of the peace might occur.

Taking these facts into account the European Court concluded that there had been a breach of Article 8. This case demonstrates that even though the law itself may be in compliance with the Convention, a breach of the Convention may nevertheless ensue if, in operational terms, the law is disproportionate to the aim to be achieved.

IATRIDIS v *GREECE* (2000) 30 EHRR 97

Facts

The case arose from a complex set of facts which started with a land ownership dispute between the state and a certain person known as KN for the purposes of the case. KN had built an open-air cinema on part of his land. He commenced proceedings against the state to establish title to his land after part of it was designated by royal decree to be reafforested and another part was transferred by the state to a housing co-operative. On the death of KN, his heirs continued the proceedings. In 1978 KN's heirs leased the open-air cinema to the applicant, who completely restored it. In 1988 the State Lands Authority assigned the cinema to the town council and the applicant was ordered to vacate the premises within five days. He did not vacate and eventually, in 1989, he was evicted by town council officials who forced an entry into the cinema while the applicant was absent from the property. In that same year an Athens court quashed the eviction order due to the fact that proceedings were pending in the land ownership dispute between KN's heirs and the state concerning the land on which the cinema had been built. The applicant made various attempts to have the cinema returned to him, but at the date of the European Court's judgment in March 1999, the cinema was still being operated by the town council and the applicant had not set up a cinema elsewhere. The applicant complained that his right to the peaceful enjoyment of his possessions under Article 1, Protocol 1 had been violated.

Decision

The European Court held that there was a violation of Article 1, Protocol 1. It found it unnecessary to rule on the complaints made under Article 6(1) and Article 8.

Analysis

Article 1, Protocol 1

The meaning of possessions   The state maintained that since it owned the land on which the cinema was situated, the lease between KN's heirs and the applicant was invalid and therefore the lease had never given the applicant a sufficiently established property right that could be enforced against the state. It further submitted that the eviction order merely deprived him of the right to use the land in issue, but it did not prevent him from carrying on his business elsewhere and consequently his business suffered no harm from the eviction. In response, the European Court reiterated the well-established principle that the concept of 'possessions' has an autonomous meaning which is not limited to the ownership of physical goods. The European Court stated that it was not for it to determine whether the land in question did in fact belong to the state or to KN's heirs or whether the lease was invalid or not. Instead it stated (at para. 54) that it would:

> confine itself to observing that, before the applicant was evicted, he had operated the cinema for 11 years under a formally valid lease without any interference by the authorities, as a result of which he had built up a clientele that constituted an asset.

On this basis the European Court concluded that the applicant's rights were sufficient to constitute a possession for the purposes of Article 1, Protocol 1.

The applicable rule   The European Court was satisfied that the eviction of the applicant from the cinema and the authorities' continued refusal to comply with the domestic court's decision quashing the eviction order, amounted to an interference with his property rights. In determining the applicable rule, the European Court observed (at para. 55) that:

> Since he holds only a lease of his business premises, this interference neither amounts to an expropriation nor is an instance of controlling the use of property but comes under the first sentence of the first paragraph of Article 1.

On this basis it concluded that the interference fell within the ambit of the first rule.

The lawfulness of the interference   The European Court observed (at para. 58) that: 'the first and most important requirement of Article 1, Protocol 1 is that any interference by a public authority with the peaceful enjoyment of possessions should be lawful'. Whilst the second and third rule make express reference to the requirement for the interference to be lawful, there is no such reference to this in the first rule. Nevertheless the European Court stated (at para. 58) that:

> the rule of law, one of the fundamental principles of a democratic society, is inherent in all the Articles of the Convention and entails a duty on the part of the State or other public authority to comply with judicial orders or decisions against it.

The European Court noted that once the Athens Court had quashed the eviction order the town council became an unlawful occupier of the cinema and should have returned it to the applicant. It concluded (at para. 62) that: 'the interference in question is manifestly in breach of Greek law and accordingly incompatible with the applicant's right to the peaceful enjoyment of his possessions'.

Selected Bibliography

ON THE EUROPEAN CONVENTION ON HUMAN RIGHTS

Anderson, D., 'Compensation for Interference with Property' [1999] EHRLR 543.
Harris, D. J., O'Boyle, M., and Warbrick, C., *Law of the European Convention on Human Rights*, London: Butterworths, 1995.
Matscher, F. and Petztold, H. (eds), *Protecting Human Rights: The European Dimension*, Koln: Carl Heymanns Verlag KG, 1988.
Peukert, W., 'Protection of Ownership under Article 1 of the First Protocol to the European Convention on Human Rights' (1981) 2 HRLJ 37.
Sermet, L., *The European Convention on Human Rights and property rights*, Council of Europe Press, human rights files No. 11, 1992.

ON THE HUMAN RIGHTS ACT 1998

Clayton, R. and Tomlinson, H., *The Law of Human Rights*, Oxford: Oxford University Press, 2000.
Starmer, K., *European Human Rights Law*, London: Legal Action Group, 1999.
Wadham, J. and Mountfield, H., *Blackstone's Guide to the Human Rights Act 1998*, London: Blackstone Press, 1999.

ON THE IMPACT OF THE HUMAN RIGHTS ACT 1998 ON PROPERTY LAW

Alder, J., 'Housing Law and the Human Rights Act 1998' (1999) 2 JHL 67.
Allen, T., 'The Human Rights Act (UK) and Property Law' in McLean, J. (ed), *Property and the Constitution*, Oxford: Hart Publishing, 1999.

Bruce, A., 'Barring Peaceable Re-entry' (2000) NLJ Practitioner, 31 March, p. 462.

Corner, T., 'Planning, Environment, and the European Convention on Human Rights' [1998] JPL 301.

Crow, S., 'Lessons from *Bryan*' [1996] JPL 359.

Hart, D., 'The Impact of the European Convention on Human Rights on Planning and Environmental Law' [2000] JPL 117.

Howell, J., 'Land and Human Rights' [1999] Conv 285.

Jones, T., 'Property Rights, Planning and the European Convention' [1996] EHRLR 233.

Karas, J. and Maurici, J., 'The human rights factor' (1999) EG, 1 May, 126.

Purdue, M., 'Planning and the Human Rights Act 1998' [2000] JPL 1090.

Redman, M., 'Compulsory Purchase, Compensation and Human Rights' [1999] JPL 315.

Smyth, M., 'The United Kingdom's Incorporation of the European Convention and Its Implications for Business' [1998] EHRLR 273.

ON COMPARATIVE LAW

Allen, T., *The Right to Property in Commonwealth Constitutions*, Cambridge: Cambridge University Press, 2000.

Roberts, N., 'The Law Lords and Human Rights: The Experience of the Privy Council in Interpreting Bills of Rights' [2000] EHRLR 147.

Willmore, C., 'Of missiles and mice: property rights in the USA' in Cooke, E. (ed), *Modern Studies in Property Law, Volume 1: Property 2000*, Oxford: Hart Publishing, 2001.

Index